"ARMIES OF THE NAPOLEONIC WARS RESEARCH SERIES"

NAPOLEON'S *GRANDE ARMÉE* OF 1813

NAPOLEON'S
GRANDE ARMÉE
OF
1813

by

SCOTT BOWDEN

THE EMPEROR'S PRESS
Chicago, Illinois
"Simply the Finest!"

Original Edition; Published in 1990

Printed and Bound in the United States of America

ISBN 0-9626655-1-7

Published by: The Emperor's Press
                  5744 West Irving Park Road
                  Chicago, IL. 60634 U.S.A.
                  Toll Free, if calling in USA: 1-800-59EAGLE
                  Calling from outside USA: 312-777-8664
                  "Simply the Finest!"

TABLE OF CONTENTS

Books by Scott Bowden

Napoleon's Grande Armée of 1813

Armies on the Danube 1809

Armies at Waterloo

Armies at Gettysburg

Armies at First Manassas

Empire

Stars*n*Bars

Redcoat

Coeur de Lion

J.E.B.!

Minuteman

For information on Scott Bowden's books and other titles of related interest, write:

The Emperor's Press
5744 West Irving Park Road
Chicago, IL. 60634   U.S.A.
Toll Free, if calling in USA: 1-800-59EAGLE
Calling from outside USA: 312-777-8664

PREFACE

With the single exception of the Hundred Days, the 1813 struggle for Germany is perhaps the most frequently studied campaign in Napoleonic history. Virtually every central European country contributed troops to this decisive war. Yet, 177 years after the epic confrontation between the armies of France and her enemies, not a single English language study of Napoleon's *Grande Armée* of 1813 has been attempted.

On the one hand, this is curious, while on the other, not at all surprising. It is curious in the respect that any real understanding of the 1813 campaign must come from a thorough knowledge of the war's central character—Napoleon's *Grande Armée* of 1813. What happened within this army directly impacted every phase of the 1813 war. Without that understanding and knowledge, one can only guess as to why events unfolded in the manner they did.

On the other hand, it is not surprising that an English language treatment of this epic army has never before been forthcoming. The main reason for this is that any original research on Napoleon's army must start and end at the main depository of French military history, the French army archives (Archives du Service Historique) at the Château de Vincennes, Paris.

The contents of 87 different cartons at Vincennes, totalling many thousands of pieces of correspondence and troops returns, were utilized in compiling the manuscript material for this work. In pouring through these, the author frequently referred back to the 'roadmap' left by Camille Rousset (*La Grande Armée de 1813*, Paris, 1871) and expanded to other reports as well as to the "situations" (parade states) of the army, so that the complete story could be told about the 1813 French Imperial army.

Thus, the principal purpose of this volume is to bring together the most information practical on the raising and formation of Napoleon's war machine, its level of training, its combat effectiveness, and the opinions of its strengths and weaknesses made by the people closest to the army—the officers and ministers themselves. Also, this volume includes extensive, detailed parade states of the army throughout 1813 which, to the author's knowledge, have never before been in print to the depth and detail presented herein.

Naturally, it is impossible to do all the above without some sort of campaign and battlefield narrative. However, the descriptions of the battles and the campaign strategy has been purposely written in a succinct manner which relates to the subject matter of this book. To try and combine a comprehensive history of the 1813 campaign for Germany, along with a detailed study of the Emperor's army, within the page confines of one project, would do an injustice to both subjects. Therefore, one should keep in mind that this volume is not intended to be a narrative of the campaign, but rather a detailed history of Napoleon's *Grande Armée* of 1813.

This work could have never been undertaken or completed without the kind assistance of many. In France, my sincere thanks to the General, and to the staff of the Service Historique, Vincennes, as well as to those who assisted at Musée de l'Armée and Bibliothèque Nationale. I appreciate the patience and courtesy extended me by the Frenchmen of these distinguished institutions.

In the United States, my heartfelt thanks go to many good friends, including: Jim Getz, Kip Trexel, and Bill Ward whose observations and recommendations on the manuscript improved it significantly; Robert J. Holland and Charles Tarbox, who were never too busy to answer a question whenever I called; Nathalie Alliez and Pascal Chollet, for their assistance with the translations of the more difficult passages in the official documents; to George Nafziger, for his kind help regarding the 25 April parade states; to my publisher, Todd Fisher, for his grace and ease in working with me on this project; and to Jane Waddel, for her production assistance.

It is my sincere hope that you enjoy *Napoleon's Grande Armée of 1813*.

Scott Bowden
Arlington, Texas

NAPOLEON'S *GRANDE ARMÉE* OF 1813

CHAPTER I
"Survivors of 1812"

January 8, 1813 was an important date in the history of Napoleonic France. For the first time that eventful year, parade states were taken for a corps of the once proud *Grande Armée* which had participated in the utterly disastrous Russian campaign of 1812. Outside the village of Thorn, on the Vistula River, amist the snowy and picturesque backdrop of an otherwise peaceful Polish winter, Marshal Louis Davout, commander of the I Corps, reviewed his weakened and frostbitten survivors of the Russian debâcle. Later that day, the Prince of Eckmühl[1] sent to the Major General,[2] Marshal Louis Alexandre Berthier,[3] his findings. "Monseigneur, I have the honor of addressing to Your Most Serene Highness a report by number of the rank of officers, non-commissioned officers, and soldiers of the I Corps. It is the nominal roll which each regiment addressed to the review inspector. I do not think that many will be rejoining us, and, if the entire I Corps receives a total of 500 more men, I will indeed be surprised... I think, Monseigner, that in order to carry out the Emperor's intention to send the cadres back to France, we should retain in each regiment the soldiers capable of active service which would form one or two companies [per regiment], and send the rest to the regimental depots."[4]

Along with the Imperial Guard, Davout's I Corps formed the backbone of Napoleon's 1812 *Grande Armée*. Of the 36 French line and light infantry regiments which had marched and fought from the Nieman River to Moscow and back, 16—almost half— were in I Corps.[5] Of these 16 veteran formations, all but a single regiment had 5 field battalions numbered 1st through 4th and 6th (the 5th battalion acting as the regimental depot formation), while the 33rd Light Infantry Regiment fielded only 4 battalions numbered 1st through 4th.[6] On June 15, 1812, just days prior to crossing the Nieman— which signalled the start of the Russian campaign—the parade states of the 79 French infantry battalions comprising Davout's corps numbered 55,865 officers and other ranks present and under arms.[7] On that same day, the total number of effectives in these battalions, which included those who were sick, detached, or for some reason were not with the colors that day, amounted to 64,708.[8] Excluded from these numbers are the returns from the companies of regimental artillery that were attached to each of the French line and light infantry regiments during this campaign.[9] When Marshal Davout inspected his corps on January 8, 1813, the total strength of *all* units in I Corps—infantry, cavalry, artillery, and support personnel— was only 3,019.[10] After deducting those in hospitals or detached from their unit, the pitiful remnants numbered a mere 674 officers and 1,607 other ranks, for a total of 2,281 combatants still present and under arms.[11]

Such was the numerical state of the legendary I Corps, the best disciplined, best officered, and best cared for of all of Napoleon's line troops.[12] Also, these men were under the command of the Emperor's premier lieutenant, who was unmatched by any other marshal in his abilities as a meticulous organizer, ruthlessly efficient administrator, and strict disciplinarian.[13] The result of these efforts and diligent care was that the men of I Corps were, through discipline and leadership, the best soldiers in the *Grande Armée* excepting a few select regiments, such as the Old and Middle Guard.[14] Despite all these factors, the I Corps suffered an utterly staggering casualty ratio of over 95% during the 1812 campaign.

When Davout's report reached Imperial headquarters, Napoleon's outward reaction was one of incredulousness. The Emperor had left the army at Smorgoni on December 5, 1812,[15] thinking that he still had an army intact and in decent fighting shape. Three weeks later, on December 30th, he broadly calculated the *Grande Armée's* infantry losses at about half their June effective strength![16] This incredible overestimation is especially surprising because the majority of French infantry battalions had already lost 50% or more of their June effectives before the bloodbath at Borodino on September 7, 1812.[17] Nevertheless, still thinking that his infantry losses were no where near what they actual were, Napoleon ordered that the cadres of two battalions per French line and light infantry regiment be sent back to France to train new recruits.[18] The remainder of the units in the field were to act as corps of observation. This thinking is clearly evidenced by Napoleon's letter of January 27, 1813, to his step-son, Prince Eugène de Beauharnais, Viceroy of Italy,[19] then nominal commander of the *Grande Armée*.[20] In this communique, the Emperor wrote: "The First [Corps] which will be in Stettin, is very strong and will be able to keep an eye on Pomerania."[21] For Napoleon to write this type of fiction to Eugène weeks after reading Davout's first report shows that the Emperor evidently did not want to believe the Prince of Eckmühl's January 8 parade states report. However, other action taken by Napoleon on the same day which Davout's report was received—discussed in the following chapter— clearly indicates that the Emperor was deeply concerned about what remained of his army and how it could be rebuilt.

However, with Davout's report in hand, Napoleon had nevertheless received the initial evidence that all was not as he wished. Napoleon had to act on this information in some way. The Emperor's military response was to order Eugène to review and compile accurate parade states for the entire *Grande Armée*. In another letter to Eugène dated January 27, 1813, Napoleon wrote: "My son, I do not yet have any clear ideas on how the army is to be organized... For that, I am waiting for new information."[22]

That new information was, of course, the inspection of the entire army conducted by Eugène beginning on January 26 and completed on February 1, 1813.[23] These reviews removed all doubt as to the numerical state of the army. From his headquarters in Posen, the Viceroy penned the sorrowful report back to his master in Paris. Only 1,608 French infantry of I Corps, 1,910 of II Corps, 1,007 of III Corps, and 1,911 of IV Corps—only 6,436 *fantassins* present and under arms[24]—were all that remained of the 36 regiments, of the 156 battalions, of the 107,097 wholly French line and light infantry which had once proudly stood in ranks on the eve of the Russian campaign.[25] Instead of an average company strength of 115 officers and other ranks present and under arms, there were, on February 1, 1813, less than 7 survivors still present per company!

As devistating as these losses were among the line and light infantry, the wastage in the French line cavalry regiments was worse. By February 1, 1813, entire regiments had completely ceased to exist[26] while many others had only a handful—mainly officers— answering roll.[27] If one distinguishes between the severity of the losses by type of cavalry, the cuirassier regiments seem to have suffered the most. For example, the 5th Cuirassiers—which General Auguste de Caulaincourt had led in the famous charge that helped capture the Raevsky Reboubt at the Battle of Borodino[28]—were in better shape than most other cuirassier regiments. They had 40 officers and 918 other ranks present for duty on June 15, 1812;[29] only 11 officers and 8 other ranks of this regiment were still present and under arms on February 1, 1813![30] Other cuirassier regiments had no one present to answer roll when Eugène made his inspection.[31] Similar horror stories were repeated over

The Retreat from Russia, 1812. *Painting by von L. Kratfé*

The Debris of the *Grande Armée* at Königsberg.
Composition by Philippoteaux.

and over with the review of the cavalry, prompting General François Bourcier to comment to General Clarke, Minister of War: "They might as well have excluded the cavalry from the inspection. The survivors of 1812 are too few to bother counting."[32]

There was, however, one notable exception to this carnage. Colonel Marcellin Marbot's 23rd Chasseurs à Cheval, probably the finest French light cavalry regiment outside the Imperial Guard, were still in remarkably good shape. Out of the 31 officers and 885 other ranks present and under arms on June 1, 1812, Marbot brought out of Russia some 693 combatants.[33] This represented the best survival record of any unit in the entire French army which participated in the Russian campaign, and serves as a tribute to the tireless and talented colonel who commanded this superb regiment.[34]

The situation in the Imperial Guard was scarcely better than with most French line troops, and in some instances even worse. All that remained of the infantry of the 1st and 2nd Guard Infantry Divisions which had campaigned in Russia were 126 Middle Guard Fusilier Chasseurs, 118 Middle Guard Fusilier Grenadiers, along with 208 scarecrows of the Hessian Leibgarde and Leib regiments,[35] and 95 officers and men of the 1st Young Guard Voltigeurs and 1st Tirailleurs.[36] These surviving elements of the 1st and 2nd Guard Infantry Divisions had been reinforced in December when two regiments, the 2nd Voltigeurs and the 2nd Tirailleurs, arrived from Spain.[37] On February 1, 1813, the 2nd Voltigeurs had 916 combatants present for duty in their two battalions while the two battalions of the 2nd Tirailleurs fielded 884 effectives present and under arms.[38] However, most of the Young Guard regiments which had gone into Russia were completely destroyed. The 6th Young Guard Voltigeurs, who marched across the Nieman with 34 officers and 1,535 other ranks,[39] had been reduced to only 12 officers and 8 men present and under arms by December 26, 1812.[40] Finally, the regiment had no one left by February 1, 1813.[41] The other Young Guard regiments completely perished as well. By February 1, 1813, there were no officers or men answering roll for the 4th Voltigeurs, 4th Tirailleurs, 5th Voltigeurs, 5th Tirailleurs, 6th Tirailleurs, or the Flanker Grenadiers![42] Where were the survivors of these units? No one knew. To the blank rolls of these Young Guard regiments, Eugène matter-of-factly added: "Most of the Young Guard has ceased to exist."[43]

The 3rd Guard Infantry Division—the Old Guard—fared slightly better than the Middle Guard. The 1st and 2nd Regiments of Old Guard Grenadiers, totalling 4 battalions, had a combined strength of 83 officers and 2,808 other ranks present and under arms on July 1, 1812.[44] On February 1, 1813, these incomparable veterans had been reduced to only 408 combatants still with the colors.[45] On July 1, 1812, the 1st and 2nd Regiments of Old Guard Chasseurs fielded 94 officers and 3,076 other ranks in their 4 battalions.[46] Only 415 of these distinguished soldiers—many of who were frostbitten— were remaining in ranks on February 1, 1813.[47] The 3rd (Dutch) Grenadiers had a disastrous campaign in Russia. Of the 34 officers and 1,462 other ranks that crossed the Nieman in the regiment's 2 battalions, there were only 11 survivors.[48]

The other formations of the Imperial Guard were likewise devistated by the Russian ordeal. The engineers, sappers, and other, numerous support units of the Guard which had numbered over 3,000 combatants on July 1, 1812,[49] were reduced to a mere 26 effectives on February 1, 1813.[50] On that same date, the *Marins* of the Guard mustered only 4 officers and 17 *matelots* still with the colors.[51] The once awesome and magnificent artillery of the Imperial Guard was, on January 26, 1813, reduced to only 265 gunners and train personnel serving 9 pieces of ordnance.[52]

The cavalry of the Imperial Guard was also gutted from the 1812 experience. Of the 5,996 officers and troopers in the six main cavalry regiments of "The Gilded Phalanx"[53] to enter Russia[54], only 125 Polish lancers, 31 Dutch ("Red") lancers, 260 Chasseurs à

Cheval, 120 Empress Dragoons, and 127 Grenadiers à Cheval were all that remained to be counted in Posen by Prince Eugène.[55] The few survivors of the Gendarmes d'élite had already returned to Paris by January 26.[56]

Napoléon Ier

Comparison of Strengths of the French Line and Light Infantry in the *Grande Armée*

I CORPS Marshal Davout	# of bns	*15 June 1812* Present & Under Arms	Total Effectives	*1 February 1813* Present & Under Arms
1st Division—				
13th Light Infantry	(5)	3,445	4,211	87
17th Line	(5)	3,425	3,932	89
30th Line	(5)	3,721	4,273	110
2nd Division—				
15th Light Infantry	(5)	3,848	4,310	111
33rd Line	(5)	3,685	4,171	102
48th Line	(5)	3,463	4,196	98
3rd Division—				
7th Light Infantry	(5)	3,664	4,097	103
12th Line	(5)	3,627	4,053	102
21st Line	(5)	3,546	4,258	92
4th Division—				
33rd Light Infantry	(4)	2,209	2,612	77
85th Line	(5)	3,753	4,004	104
108th Line	(5)	3,447	4,185	83
5th Division—				
25th Line	(5)	3,390	4,118	84
57th Line	(5)	3,390	4,060	165
61st Line	(5)	3,567	4,009	96
111th Line	(5)	3,685	4,219	105
I Corps French Infantry Totals	(79)	55,865	64,708	1,608

II CORPS Marshal Oudinot	# of bns	*1 June 1812* Present & Under Arms		*1 February 1813* Present & Under Arms
6th Division—				
26th Light Infantry	(4)	2,945		328
56th Line	(4)	2,703		308
19th Line	(4)	2,810		319

8th Division—			
11th Light Infantry	(4)	3,103	398
2nd Line	(5)	3,131	280
37th Line	(4)	<u>2,509</u>	<u>277</u>
II Corps French Infantry Totals	(25)	17,201	1,910

III CORPS		*25 May 1812*	*1 February 1813*
Marshal Ney	# of	Present &	Present &
	<u>bns</u>	<u>Under Arms</u>	<u>Under Arms</u>
10th Division—			
24th Light Infantry	(4)	3,114	199
46th Line	(4)	2,856	165
72nd Line	(4)	2,700	151
11th Division—			
4th Line	(4)	2,259	102
18th Line	(4)	2,659	159
93rd Line	(4)	<u>2,786</u>	<u>231</u>
III Corps French Infantry Totals	(24)	16,374	1,007

IV CORPS		*15 June 1812*	*1 February 1813*
Prince Eugène	# of	Present &	Present &
	<u>bns</u>	<u>Under Arms</u>	<u>Under Arms</u>
13th Division—			
8th Light Infantry	(2)	1,404	154
84th Line	(4)	2,567	322
92nd Line	(4)	2,625	317
106th Line	(4)	2,733	265
14th Division—			
18th Light Infantry	(2)	1,403	145
9th Line	(4)	2,350	237
35th Line	(4)	2,242	219
53rd Line	(4)	<u>2,333</u>	<u>252</u>
IV Corps French Infantry Totals	(28)	17,657	1,911
Army Totals	(156)	107,097	6,436

The above totals exclude the personnel in the regimental artillery companies.

Comparison of French Imperial Guard Cavalry Strengths

SIX MAIN REGIMENTS OF THE GUARD	*1 July 1812* Present & Under Arms		*1 February 1813* Present &Under Arms
	Officers	Other Ranks	All Ranks
Chasseurs à Cheval	70	1,107	
Mamelukes	8	67	260
Empress Dragoons	64	1,015	120
Grenadiers à Cheval	70	1,096	127
1st (Polish) Lancers	69	887	125
2nd (Red, or Dutch) Lancers	57	1,095	31
Gendarmes d'élite	<u>28</u>	<u>363</u>	survivors in Paris
Totals	366	5,630	663

     The heavy losses from the Russian campaign were also felt in the ranks of general officers throught the army. Combat casualties claimed the lives of dozens of Napoleon's generals, including the irreplaceable Gudin and Montbrun.[57] Also, the rigors of the 1812 ordeal were so strenuous that numerous generals were worn down into exhaustion. General Raymond-Gaspard Saint-Sulpice, the noted heavy cavalry commander, was so completely spent that he had to be returned to France.[58] General Emmanuel Grouchy, the talented commanding officer of the former III Reserve Cavalry corps[59] and, during the Battle of the Berezina, the leader of the "sacred squadron"[60], also had to return to France in February, 1813, to recover from physical exhaustion. He was later reassigned for duty with the Army of Italy.[61] General Delaborde, commander of the 1st Guard Infantry Division, likewise had to return home to convalesce for three months before being able to rejoin the army.[62]

     Other generals worn out from the Russian invasion were not as fortunate. General Jean Lariboisière, commander of the army artillery, died of exhaustion on December 21, 1812.[63] Several days later, on December 31, 1812, exhaustion also claimed the life of General Jean-Baptiste Eblé, commander of the army's bridging train. Had it not been for Eblé, there might not have been any survivors from Napoleon's main army group. Elbé would forever be remembered as the officer responsible for saving the bridge train and miracuously constructing the bridges across the Berezina over which the remnants of the *Grande Armée* escaped from Russia.[64] Including killed, captured, and died from exhaustion, the 1812 campaign cost Napoleon the services of 48 generals and more than 3,000 other officers.[65]

     While the losses among the officers were crippling, the most horrendous casualties among Napoleon's 1812 army were suffered not by men but by horses. The loss of horseflesh incurred by the *Grande Armée* during the Russian campaign was enormous. Most animals which went into Russia never returned. It is estimated that over 175,000 trained horses perished in 1812,[66] representing an irreplaceable loss from which Napoleon would never recover. After Russia, the armies of Napoleonic France would be shy of horses for every subsequent campaign.[67]

As the horseflesh of the *Grande Armée* perished, so did most of its guns, limbers, caissons, and other mobile equipment. Of the more than 1,300 artillery pieces which were taken into Russia, over 900 were lost.[68] Not surprisingly, most of the ordnance which survived belonged to the flanking corps which did not experience many of the horrors visited upon the main body of the army.

Before the distressing numbers of Eugène's inspection were placed before Napoleon, there is ample evidence to show that the Emperor had already begun to suspect that the wreakage of the 1812 army might be more than what he had wanted to believe, and certainly more devistating than what he wanted others to know. The best example of this is clearly illustrated by the written instructions given by Napoleon to a council held at Fontainbleau on January 24, 1813. After ordering a report comparing the military forces of the Empire in January, 1812, and in January, 1813, the Emperor expressly added: "For the latter [date], you may dispense with including the *Grande Armée*; I will take care of it."[69]

If Napoleon was beginning to anticipate bad news, it indeed arrived just over a week later. When Eugène's empirical report on the strength of the army was received, it became clear that the casualties suffered in Russia precluded sending cadres back to France because there were barely enough survivors to form single company per regiment! Finally, the light dawned and all illusions ceased. The army was no more. The great captain then realized that he would have to pour his infatigable energy, iron will, great imagination, and incomparable organizational genius into the molding of an entire new command. Reorganization was not possible because the very framework of the former army had been totally destroyed. Indeed, all that remained of the Emperor's 1812 forces was the prestige of a glorious name which Napoleon would use to create his new *Grande Armée* of 1813.

Prince Eugène de Beauharnais. *Musée de l'Armée.*

CHAPTER II
"All Resources Will Be Used"

With Russia and Prussia preparing for the "Befreiungskrieg"—the war to liberate Germany from French domination[1]—Napoleon's decision to stay and fight in central Europe required him to build his new army posthaste. Consequentally, the Emperor turned to every possible resource at his disposal that could immediately produce manpower. The formation of the *Grande Armée* of 1813, and the multiple reorganizations from February, 1813, to the end of the Leipzig campaign late that same year, is an intricate, detailed story. This chapter will discuss the resources which Napoleon had available to create his new command.

There were ten major manpower pools which the Emperor could draw upon. These ten main resources may be broadly categorized into two groups. The first group consisted of the men already in uniform at the beginning of 1813, serving in various capacities somewhere within the Empire. The second group comprised those individuals who were brought into the service of France during 1813 for the new *Grande Armée*. Every separate manpower pool within each group brought a unique aspect to the army.

The first group which Napoleon could call upon—those men already in uniform— consisted of five manpower pools. These were: 1) the infantry companies at ports being used as ships' guards; 2) the cohorts; 3) the departmental and city militias and municipal guards; 4) the naval artillery corps; and 5) the veterans in the Army of Spain.[2]

Among the first of Napoleon's concerns was securing the garrison towns on the Oder River so that these cities could act as a screen behind which the mobile army could be formed. In order to accomplish this, Napoleon sent an order to recall a large number of infantry companies from depot battalions which had years before been loaned to the navy to guard ships penned up in the naval ports of the Empire.[3] More importantly, these infantrymen were needed to help reconstitute the army's depleted cadres. In November, 1812, the strength of these garrison companies was over 7,300 officers and men.[4] By the end of January, 1813, these men had been ordered to Germany, but only the ships' garrisons from Escant and Texel (Frisian group island in the Netherlands) had arrived and were stationed at Spandau and at Custrin (Kostrzyn). Other ships' garrisons from Toulon, Rochefort, Brest, and Cherbourg were expected to arrive on the Oder in March, 1813.[5]

Having made provision to secure the frontier fortifications, Napoleon turned his undivided attention to the raising of the new army. Of the men already in uniform, the second major resource that Napoleon had at his call was the cohorts. The cohorts were created in March, 1812,[6] when Napoleon, about to embark on a new war in far eastern Europe, decided to leave behind him an armed reserve composed entirely of mature Frenchmen capable of defending the homeland. In a technical sense, the cohorts were members of the National Guard. To Napoleon, however, these men were neither members of the National Guard, nor were they troops of the line, even though their uniforms were identical to the latter.[7] Nevertheless, in an emergency, the Emperor thought that these men could be rapidly incorporated into the army. So in order to completely distinguish this intermediary force from the troops of the National Guard and those of the regular army, Napoleon named these units the "cohorts."[8] This title seemed fitting enough for the

Emperor, who had already borrowed many ideas from ancient Imperial Rome.[9] Indeed, the symbolic name was chosen to fit in with the military legacy of the Napoleonic Empire.

Napoleon wanted the cohorts to serve only within the limits of the Empire[10] and to be composed entirely of mature men. To accomplish the latter, a *sénatus-consulte*[11] on March 13, 1812,[12] set forth three proclamations (bans) regulating who would be obligated to serve in the cohorts. The first ban called on men ages 20 to 26 years old from the classes of 1807 through 1812 who had not yet been drawn on for active duty. Like most drafts, the French conscript classes before 1813 were able to fully furnish their contingents while not disturbing tens of thousands of young men who simply continued with their civilian lives and occupations. During that time, it was legal for a man to get out of his military obligation if he or his family could afford to buy a "replacement". Typically, the "replacements" were youths from poorer families who needed the money that those not wishing to serve in the army could afford to pay.[13] Therefore, the first ban processed into the cohorts many men who had not seen service when their class furnished its contingent. The second ban was designed to draft able-bodied men ages 26 to 40, while the third ban required a smaller number of healthy men ages 40 to 60 to report for duty. In this decree, there were to be a total of 100 cohorts, of which 12 were to be formed from the second and third bans. However, the very next day, Napoleon changed his mind about calling to the colors the older men mentioned in the second and third bans. In an Imperial decree of March 14, 1812, the Emperor set the number of cohorts at 88, all of which were to be composed of men of the first ban.[14]

In order to most efficiently organize the cohorts, they were formed and numbered by geographical department. Often times, contingents from neighboring departments were combined to form a single cohort.[15] Regardless of departmental makeup, every cohort consisted of 6 equal companies of fusiliers of 140 combatants per company, plus 1 depot company of 100 officers and men.[16] Finally, attached to each cohort was a company of foot artillery numbering 100 effectives.[17] Therefore, at least on paper, the strength of each cohort was to be 1,040 combatants of which 940 were infantrymen and 100 were artillerists. The officers and non-commissioned officers of the cohorts were selected from fully retired veterans, or from veterans on compulsory retirement, or from National Guard units.[18] In the latter case, if any officers or non-commissioned officers came out of the National Guard into the cohorts, they only could do so if they already had seen service in the regular army.[19] As previously mentioned, the uniforms of the cohorts were identical to that of the fusiliers of the line, while the artillerists of the cohorts had the same uniform as the foot artillery of the line.[20]

The supplementary levy on the Classes of 1807 through 1812 which raised the cohorts was accomplished within a few weeks after decree. By the time the *Grande Armée* crossed the Nieman River into Russia in June, 1812, the officers and men of the cohorts were training at their depots.[21] Once in the training centers, the officers drilled the men in company and battalion evolutions while the artillerists received their training separately at the army's regular artillery schools.[22]

At full strength, the 88 cohorts should have totalled 91,520 officers and other ranks. However, as is often the case with military units, full paper strength was never realized. During 1812, the total strength of all the cohorts peaked at just over 78,000.[23] The shortage prompted Napoleon to impose an additional levy on the Class of 1813—the *sénatus-consulte* of September 22, 1812[24]—whereby 17,000 more conscripts from that class were ordered to report to the cohorts. By January 15, 1813, of the 17,000 youths of 1813 earmarked for duty with the cohorts, only 6,959 had already reached the depots.[25] The remainder of the additional levy straggled into their assigned training centers during the remainder of January, February, and March.[26]

It was also during the first month of 1813 when it became obvious to Napoleon that the cohorts were going to have to be taken into the regular army. This choice was an easy one for the Emperor, as the cohorts had already sent numerous pleas to their master, asking permission to take the field.[27] Napoleon, looking for ways to help prop up morale at home and in the army following the Russian disaster, promptly had the appeals from the cohorts published in the *Moniteur*. Not long afterwards, on January 11, 1813, a *sénatus-consulte* pronounced that: "The...cohorts of the first ban...will become part of the army."[28] Almost immediately, couriers were swiftly carrying the word to each of the 88 cohorts to be on the march within 24 hours to selected cities within each department, there to be united with other cohorts to form regiments of the line. Once part of the army, each cohort became a battalion consisting as before of 6 fusilier companies, each of 140 effectives. Battalions were grouped by fours to form 22 new regiments of the line, numbered 135th through 156th.[29] The 4 depot companies of the cohorts which formed each regiment became, in turn, the depot battalion for the regiment. Therefore, each regiment formed from the cohorts had a theoretical strength of 3,760 combatants, representing 3,360 infantry in 4 battalions of 840 combatants each, plus 1 depot battalion of 400 officers and men. Thus, the paper strength of all 22 of these regiments was 82,720 infantrymen in 88 field, or war, battalions and 22 depot battalions.[30]

Once the cohorts officially became troops of the line, they lost their artillery personnel. This really was of little concern since the artillerists of the old cohorts had always trained just as any other artillery unit, and had never been attached—except on paper—to their parent infantry unit.[31] Thus, the artillery branch gained approximately 8,000 already well drilled officers and gunners—enough to form 88 new companies of artillery.[32] In keeping with the desire to have direct artillery support for his infantry, Napoleon decided that 22 of these companies would serve directly with these new regiments, acting as regimental artillery, with a single company of guns attached to each infantry regiment formed from the old cohorts.[33] The remaining 66 companies of artillery personnel were quickly organized into 3 new regiments of foot artillery, 2 regiments each consisting of 22 companies[34], a third regiment with 18 companies[35], with the remaining 4 companies going into the Imperial Guard to form the 1st through 4th companies of the Young Guard foot artillery.[36] Therefore, the cohorts supplied the army with enough artillerists to serve approximately 572 pieces of ordnance.[37]

Having encorporated the cohorts into the army, Napoleon sought to add all other active personnel serving in various city and departmental militias and guards. The men which comprised these local forces were usually retired veterans.[38] The best of these units—the Municipal Guard of Paris—boasted two full battalions totalling 1,050 effectives.[39] Ordered to Erfurt, they, along with various elements of the 69th, 76th, and 79th Regiments of the Line, combined to form the 1st and 2nd battalions of the new 134th Regiment of the Line.[40] Likewise, throughout France, virtually every city or department maintained a guard or militia similar to the Municipal Guard of Paris. The Emperor ordered the Prefects of the various departments to summon the city or departmental guard companies to Mayence, there to be incorporated into the army. Some 116 of these companies, most of them very small contingents, soon arrived at Mayence where they were organized into the 37th Regiment of Light Infantry.[41] By March 1, 1813, this regiment consisting of 4 field battalions totalling 3,307 officers and other ranks, plus a depot battalion of 750 effectives, making for a total of 4,057 combatants.[42] However, the regimen of army life was not easy for many of the older men of the former municipal guards. The oldest and weakest were soon unable to remain in ranks, despite that fact that

---

LINE REGIMENTS FORMED FROM THE COHORTS

Line Regiment Number	Cohort Numbers which Comprised the Regiment	Department from which the Cohort Came
135	1	Seine
	8	Aisne
	9	Eure-et-Loir; Loiret
	11	Seine-et-Marne
136	12	Seine-et-Oise
	13	Ardennes; Marne
	14	Marne; Meuse
	67	Indre-et-Loire; Loir-et-Cher
137	2	Rome; Trasimène
	84	Apennins; Taro
	85	Gènes; Montenotte
	86	Arno; Ombrone; Méditerranée
138	44	Calvados
	45	Manche
	46	Orne
	64	Cher; Nièvre
139	16	Meurthe
	17	Vosges
	65	Allier; Creuse
	66	Indre; Haute-Vienne
140	40	Finistère
	41	Côtes-du-Nord
	42	Ille-et-Vilaine
	43	Morbihan
141	37	Charente-Inférieure; Vendée
	38	Loire-Inférieure
	39	Deux-Sèvres; Vienne
	61	Charente; Dordogne
142	5	Gironde
	36	Landes; Basses-Pyrénées
	62	Corrèze; Dordogne
	63	Lot-et-Garonne; Lot
143	28	Hérault
	29	Aveyron
	30	Ardèche; Lozère
	31	Gard; Tarn

144......................	32	Haute-Garonne
	33	Ariége; Hautes-Pyrénées
	34	Gers; Tarn-et-Garonne
	35	Aude; Pyrénées-Orientales
145......................	6	Bouches-du-Rhône
	23	Isère
	24	Hautes-Alpes; Drôme
	25	Léman; Mont-Blanc
146......................	3	Zuyderzée
	76 ....Meuse-Inférieure; Lippe; Bouches-du-Rhin
	77	Roër
	88 ....Bouches-de-la-Meuse; Issel-Supérieur
147......................	15	Forêts; Moselle
	71	Dyle; Bouches-de-l'Escaut
	78	Ourte; Sambre-et-Meuse
	87	Ems-Oriental; Ems-Occidental; Bouches-de-l'Issel; Frise
148......................	72	Escaut
	73	Escaut; Jemmapes
	74	Jemmapes
	75	Deux-Nèthes
149......................	47	Seine-Inférieure
	48	Eure
	49	Somme
	79	Mont-Tonnerre
150......................	68	Maine-et-Loire
	69	Mayenne
	80	Rhin-et-Moselle
	81	Sarre
151......................	7	Bouches-de-l'Elbe; Bouches-du-Weser; Ems-Supérieur
	50	Nord
	51	Nord
	52	Lys
152......................	18	Bas-Rhin
	19	Haut-Rhin
	53	Pas-de-Calais
	54	Pas-de-Calais
153......................	55	Côte-d'Or
	56	Aube; Haute-Marne
	57	Saône-et-Loire
	58	yonne
154......................	4	Rhône; Loire
	20	Ain; Doubs
	21	Jura
	22	Haute-Saône

155	10	Oise
	59	Cantal; Haute-Loire
	60	Puy-de-Dôme
	70	Sarthe
156	26	Basses-Alpes; Alpes-Maritimes; Baucluse
	27	Var
	82	Doire; Pô; Sesia
	83	Marengo; Stura

they had not started any real campaigning. By April 15, 1813, the regiment was already reduced to 2,851 effectives, including the depot personnel.[43] Having already experienced a shrinkage of 30%, Marshal Marmont ordered the regiment be reorganized into 3 field, or war, battalions and that the area hospitals return all its men possible to the colors.[44] On April 25—the eve of the spring campaign—the 37th Light Infantry numbered 44 officers and 2,707 other ranks present and under arms.[45]

Another source of existing military manpower which the Emperor took into the army was the naval artillery corps, or the *régiments d'artillerie de la marine*, which were abbreviated in the army returns as "de marine".[46] Over the years, the designation of these regiments has been shortened to *marins*, and Anglicized to simply "marines". These were not marines in the same sense of British or American marines, but rather naval gunners which were part of the French navy. As such, the *marins* had no knowledge of infantry tactics or maneuvers prior to entering the army in 1813.[47] This body of veteran cannoniers, numbering 4 regiments which at first were comprised of 12 total battalions[48], averaged 23 years of age.[49]

For many years, these regiments had been closed up in the numerous ports of the Empire. Their status dramatically changed on January 23, 1813, when Napoleon ordered them to report for duty with the new *Grande Armée*. "I have just issued a decree," the Emperor announced to Clarke that same day, "by which I place at the disposition of your ministry the 12 naval battalions, and since there are many former soldiers [in their ranks], I have decided to double the battalions and, instead of 12 to form out of them 24. Those battalions, 840 men strong, will form at full strength 20,000 men. Now, today there are only 16,000; therefore, I will need 4,000 more men; of these 4,000 men, I want 2,000 supplied from the ['levy of the four classes'] conscription of 100,000 men, and 2,000 from the conscription of 1814."[50] When it became clear that there would not be enough marines to field 24 battalions, the Emperor reduced the number of to 20.[51]

Before the naval gunners joined the army they reformed their scattered detachments into regimental formations. The 1st regiment gathered at Brest, the 2nd at Toulon, the 3rd at Cherbourg, and the 4th at Anvers.[52] As the regiments formed in these cities, they organized themselves for war. Each regiment had a headquarters and staff headed by 1 colonel and 3 majors. Each battalion had as its commander, 1 chef de bataillon, assisted by 1 adjudant-major and 2 adjudants sous-officiers. Every battalion of marines consisted of 6 equal companies of men, each composed of 1 captain, 1 lieutenant, 1 sous-lieutenant, and 137 other ranks, resulting in a paper strength of 844 combatants per battalion.[53] Thus organized, the marines marched off to war. They arrived in Mayence and reported to Marshal Marmont, commander of the 2nd Observation Corps of the Rhine.[54] However, instead of receiving the 16,000 men promised, Marmont counted far fewer marines. The reason for this was that the navy balked at giving up all of its gunners, successfully arguing

Infantryman of the French Naval Artillery Corps (Regiments de Marine) 1813-1814, in campaign dress. *Painting by Gaston Roullet.*

with Clarke that some personnel had to be retained in order for the port batteries to be manned.[55] Clarke agreed[56], but evidently forgot to tell Napoleon. Also diminishing the number of these men sent to Mayence was the fact that the best gunners within each of the naval artillery regiments had already been transferred into the artillery branch thereby insuring continued use of their training.[57] Of these, some 571 naval gunners went into the artillery of the Imperial Guard.[58]

When Marmont did not receive all the marines expected, he complained to the Emperor, who answered him unknowingly: "You were supposed to have 20 battalions of 16,000 men; it seems that, for the moment they only come to 10,000 men, since it will take a lot of time for the detachments en route to arrive at their regiments."[59] Napoleon then quizzed Clarke about the shortage, who confessed as to the compromise made with the navy.[60] Napoleon agreed with the decision. Thereafter, the Emperor knew that the number of veteran marines earmarked for the army would be less than what was originally anticipated. However, in order to have enough men in the battalions of these troops, the Emperor had already decided to augment their ranks with conscripts. "All resources will be used to make the army ready for war," the Emperor told Clarke on April 1, "I am especially anxious to bring the battalions from the naval regiments up to strength."[61] Monitoring closely the strengths of the marines, Napoleon wrote to Marmont on April 7th: "The battalions from the naval regiments are too weak; you will leave in Mayence 6 battalions as cadres for these regiments, so that you will bring the [14] battalions you keep up to 600 men each."[62]

Another parade states report from Marmont's corps dated April 15, 1813, shows the 20 battalions of marines—of which 14 were war battalions—with a total effective force of 12,080, representing an average strength of 604 officers and men per battalion.[63] Invaribaly, the war battalions were stronger than those remaining behind as depot formations.[64] This is illustrated by the parade states of the corps taken 10 days later. The 14 war battalions of marines had 9,670 officers and other ranks present and under arms on April 25, 1813,[65] for an average strength of 691 effectives per war battalion. Another 2,974 effectives were present and under arms with the 6 depot units[66]—an average of less than 500 persons standing in ranks per depot battalion. When all the men of these regiments were counted, including those who were in hospitals, detached, or for some reason not on parade, the total strength of all 20 battalions of the naval artillery corps amounted to 16,895 officers and other ranks.[67] Further, of the total number of 12,644 marines in the war and depot battalions which were present and under arms on April 25, just over 3,000 of these men were young conscripts.[68] Therefore, with the incorporation of the naval artillery corps, the Emperor was successful in adding more than 16,000 bayonets into the infantry of the army, of which approximately 12,000 were mature men,[69] as well as further augmenting the artillery branch with approximately 1,000 already trained specialists.

The last major resource pool of soldiers already in uniform which the Emperor could call on was the Army of Spain. Since this army was composed of long-time veterans,[70] the Emperor wanted to immediately draw upon it to accomplish 3 important objectives, which were: 1) refill the ranks of the Old and Middle Guard infantry; 2) rebuild the cavalry; and 3) provide the new army in Germany with existing battalions of line and light infantry. To accomplish the first goal, Napoleon ordered that the 250 combat hardened battalions of line and light infantry serving in the Iberian peninsula each nominate 12 of their best veterans.[71] Of these 12 soldiers from every battalion, half those nominated had to be distinguished veterans with at least 8 years of service. These soldiers went into the infantry of the Old Guard.[72] The remaining 6 hand-picked veterans from each battalion had to have at least 4 years' service; these men reported for duty with the Middle Guard Fusilier and Chasseur regiments.[73] Thus, the Army of Spain gave up 3,000 of its best, most experienced infantrymen in order to help rebuild the Old and Middle Guard infantry. Also in Spain were the intact regiments of the Young Guard 3rd Voltigeurs and 3rd Tirailleurs, along with elements of the Young Guard 1st Voltigeurs and 1st Tirailleurs.[74] These formations would form the nucleus around which the new Young Guard was built. To accomplish the second objective, Napoleon ordered the depot squadrons of the cavalry regiments in Spain to report for duty along the Rhine, there to be formed with other elements into new regiments. Also, the 30 cavalry regiments serving in Spain were to each nominate 20 of their best, most deserving veteran troopers for service in the Guard cavalry. Later, another call up of 200 veteran horsemen from the Army of Spain would help reconstitute the Gendarmes d'élite.[75] Finally, to provide the new army with existing battalions, Napoleon ordered various 3rd, 4th, and depot battalions of the Army of Spain to quit the Peninsula and make by forced march to the staging areas in Germany.[76] The result of all these measures was that the Army of Spain immediately provided 20,000 proven veterans for Napoleon's new *Grande Armée*.[77]

The Inspection—Napoleon reviewing the Grenadiers à Pied of the Old Guard. *Lithograph by Raffet.*

The second group to which Napoleon had access for fleshing out the new army were the young men of France who had yet to see military service. These youths were subsequently conscripted into the army by a flurry of levies which can be defined as five separate manpower pools. These were: 1) the conscription Class of 1813, including what remained of the Class of 1812; 2) the draft known as the "levy of the four classes"; 3) the Class of 1814; 4) the supplementary levy of the Classes 1807 through 1812; and 5) the "volunteers" who, in part, formed the cavalry regiments known as the Guards of Honor along with the Young Guard squadrons of the senior regiments of the Imperial Guard cavalry.

The first of these manpower pools was the conscription Class of 1813, including the remnants of the conscription class of the preceeding year. When Napoleon studied the strength returns of the army in early February, 1813, he saw that the 120,000 youths of the Class of 1812 had been virtually consumed during the Russian campaign. Indeed, the parade states of February, 1, 1813, show almost no one of the Class of 1812 remaining in the depots.[78] The reason for this was that the divisions of the IX Corps and XI Corps of the 1812 army had been formed from the conscripts of 1812, and were all but destroyed in the hard fighting late that year and early in 1813.[79]

That the Russian campaign totally consumed the conscription Class of 1812 is also born out in correspondence between Napoleon and his Minister of War beginning in October, 1812. During that month, the Emperor ordered Clarke to hold a series of rigorous reviews in all regimental depots and to immediately send to the front any malingerers. The object of these reviews was simple enough—to forward to the army in Russia all those of the Class of 1812 (and anyone else) who did not belong in the hospitals.[80] Clarke promptly carried out the order and found a grand total of 1,822 young men who were in condition to rejoin their comrades on campaign.[81] These were all that remained of the 1812 conscription.[82] Once these men joined the army, the Class of 1812 officially completed its contribution to France.[83]

Therefore, in creating the new *Grande Armée* of 1813, Napoleon's first major manpower source among those who had not yet seen military service was the conscription class of that year. The call up of these youths actually began while Napoleon was in the depths of Russia. With the consumption of the Class of 1812 evident, Napoleon issued a *sénatus-consulte* raising 120,000 men of the Class of 1813, modified from Moscow on September 22, 1812, by calling for an additional levy of 17,000 to go into the cohorts.[84] As a result, the class of 1813 yielded 137,000 young men between the ages of 19 and 20.[85] Of this number, 105,000 were assigned to the regiments of line and light infantry, 17,000 earmarked for the cohorts, and the remaining 15,000 were directed either into the Young Guard (who had first pick of all members of the class), the cavalry, or the artillery train.[86] By the end of October, 1812, the formalities of this class' conscription had been finalized and by the end of December, 1812, most of the youths had arrived at regimental depots.[87] Returns show that on January 15, 1813, all but 20,000 men of the Class of 1813 had reported for duty[88], and by March 1, 1813, almost all of the men comprising the conscription of 1813 were in uniform.[89]

Even with the Class of 1813 and what remained of the Class of 1812 called to the colors, and even prior to seeing the results of Prince Eugène's famous report of February 1, Napoleon knew that he did not have enough soldiers for the upcoming campaign. He therefore decided on January 9, 1813,[90] to issue another call up of men from the Classes of 1809 through 1812. This meant that those men who had not been drafted during their class year were once again eligible for conscription. This draft, known as the "levy of the four classes"[91] was immediately implemented and yielded another 100,000 men[92] who were between 20 and 24 years of age.[93]

Also, when the Emperor called up the "levy of the four classes", he requested in the same *sénatus-consulte* of January 11, a call to arms for 150,000 young men ages 18 and 19 years old of the Class of 1814.[94] This levy, calling upon the adolescents of France one full year before they normally would have been eligible for military service clearly illustrates Napoleon's desparate need for numbers of troops. Interestingly enough, the Emperor's sudden call up of the "levy of the four classes" and Class of 1814 correspond exactly to the day on which he received Davout's January 8 parade states of the I Corps.[95] Even if Napoleon did not want to believe Davout, he nevertheless allowed for his own miscalculation by immediately ordering to the colors the manpower necessary to rebuild the army. Napoleon further instructed that the Class of 1814 not be ordered to report until February so that the Class of 1813 could have time to pass through the training centers. "It is necessary," explained the Emperor to Clarke on January 16, "that the conscripts of 1814 be bothered and moved only when the others [the 'levy of the four classes' and the Class of 1813] will leave. It would be inconvenient to arm so many conscripts at one time."[96]

Even with 100,000 men from the "levy of the four classes" and 150,000 young men from the Class of 1814 reporting as ordered, Napoleon still did not think he had enough men available for the upcoming struggle. Therefore, the Emperor issued another *sénatus-consulte* on April 3, 1813, authorizing yet another supplementary levy. This decree called for the men of the Classes of 1807 through 1812 to yield another 80,000 soldiers for the army of which 24,000 were to report for duty with the Young Guard. In this same *sénatus-consulte*, the Emperor called for another 90,000 youngsters to supplement the Class of 1814, as well as called for an additional levy of 10,000 mounted men to be drafted into the army for the Guards of Honor, the Young Guard cavalry squadrons, and other cavalry regiments.[97]

The last group mentioned in this *sénatus-consulte* differed somewhat from the first group of men who formed the initial framework of the Guards of Honor. The first group were, in a strict sense, volunteers that arrived at the army in January.[98] Raised and organized in the departments and cities throughout France, these cavalrymen were mounted and equipped at their own expense.[99] "I have accepted," the Emperor wrote Berthier on January 9, "the offers made to me of the 6 squadrons of life guardsmen, 200 men in each squadron. They will be formed from volunteers from the departments, all having an allowance of 10,000 francs from their families."[100]

These volunteers first numbered about 15,000 men and 20,000 horses[101], but so many deserted so fast that their unit title was changed from Life Guards to Guards of Honor.[102] Part of the reason why many of these men ages 20 to 26 quit the army so soon was that they were typically from noble or wealthy, middle class families who had escaped the former levies due to being able to purchase replacements. When the call for new volunteers went out in late 1812, the Prefects of the departments organized these mounted regiments and then "volunteered" them for service with the army.[103] Despite the desertion of many of these men, those who remained in ranks showed promise[104] and so desperate was the need for cavalry, the Emperor called for another 10,000 men to be sent to the army as Guards of Honor, Young Guard squadrons, and other cavalry. This was accomplished by the department Prefects appointing more men as previously described. However, the men of this supplemental draft who were destined for the Guards of Honor were hardly enthusiastic about the prospects of military life. This is perhaps best illustrated by the fact that the rest of the army dubiously referred to the men of these regiments as "hostages".[105]

To summarize, the major manpower pools which Napoleon used in creating the *Grande Armée* of 1813 were as follows:

A. Soldiers Already in Uniform at the Beginning of 1813
1. 20,000 veterans from the Army of Spain, of which 3,000 were distinguished soldiers selected for service in the infantry of the Old and Middle Guard. Average age of the Peninsular veterans was 28 years old;
2. 7,300 men of various companies of infantry depot battalions serving as ships' garrisons in naval ports throught the Empire. The ages of these men were between 20 to 23 years old;
3. 78,000 men of the old cohorts, all with 9 to 10 months of training. Of this total, approximately 70,000 were infantry and 8,000 were artillerists. Ages of these men were between 20 to 26 years old;
4. 5,000 retired soldiers comprising city and departmental militias and guard units; and
5. 12,000 veterans from the naval artillery corps, of which 571 transferred with their gunnery skills into the artillery branch of the army and the remaining 11,400 were converted into infantry. The average age of the *marins* was 23 years old.

B. Men Conscripted for Military Service
1. 137,000 of the Class of 1813, ages 19 or 20 years old;
2. 100,000 of the "levy of the four classes" of 1809-1812, ages 20 to 24 years old;
3. 80,000 of the supplementary levy of the Classes 1807-1812, ages 20 to 26 years old;
4. 25,000 "volunteers" for service with the cavalry, including the regiments known as Guards of Honor and the Young Guard squadrons of the Imperial Guard. Ages of these men were between 20 to 26 years of age.
5. 240,000 of the Class of 1814, ages 18 or 19 years old.

Excluding the 7,300 men of the ships' garrisons who were initially sent to the Oder River garrisons, Napoleon's total manpower resources available to create the new *Grande Armée* amounted to 697,000 men, of which approximately 465,000, or two-thirds, were just teenagers. Therefore, it was primarily with the conscripted youth of France that the Emperor began the monumental task of organizing and forging his new instrument of war. The creation of the *Grande Armée* of 1813 was a Herculean effort which only Napoleon the ruler could undertake, and which only Napoleon the organizer could successfully accomplish.

Henry–Jacques–G. Clarke, Duke of Feltre

Born in Landrecies on 17 October 1765, Clarke became a cadet at the École militaire in Paris in September of 1781. He saw extensive service in the cavalry during the early part of the revolution and was promoted Général de division on 7 September 1795. His career then took a turn towards administrative activities; and on 9 August 1807, he was appointed Minister of War, a position which he held until 3 April 1814. Clarke was an able administrator and utterly devoted to Napoleon. *Musée de l'Armée.*

Marshal Kellermann, Duke of Valmy

Marshal Kellermann was born in Strasbourg on 28 May 1735. He saw service during the Seven Years War in the dragoons and rose to the rank of lieutenant general under the *Ancien Regime.* He will forever be remembered as the man who saved France at the Battle of Valmy, 20 September 1792. An active army commander until the last years of the Revolution, Kellermann was an extremely able administrator and was employed as such by Napoleon. In 1813, Kellermann was 78 years old. *Musée de l'Armée.*

The Emperor and his staff reviewing the cavalry.

CHAPTER III
"Being Created From Thin Air"

With hundreds of thousands of young men soon to be under the tricolor, Napoleon had to devise a new organization into which the tidalwave of conscripts and other personnel could be directed. Before the results of Prince Eugène's February 1 inspection reached Paris, the Emperor labored under a general misconception regarding the damage suffered by his army in the 1812 campaign.[1] Probably the most glaring of these was Napoleon's belief that the depot battalions of the 28 French line and light infantry regiments of the I, II, and III Corps could easily fill out the 1st battalion of their parent regiment. The 2nd battalions of each regiment of these corps were then to stop in Erfurt and there await the conscripts of 1813 as they were sent out from their training centers. These 2nd battalions, along with the Oder River garrisons, would form the "advance guard" of the army.[2]

While this was taking place, the 3rd, 4th, and 6th battalions of these regiments were to be withdrawn to the west so that they could form three corps of observation, consisting of single corps on the Elbe River and two on the Rhine River. Meanwhile, the 8 French line and light infantry regiments of IV Corps would reconstitute their 2nd battalions in Augsburg from the new conscripts while the remaining battalions of the IV Corps marched back to Italy. There they would be organized into another corps of observation. The reserve cavalry corps would rebuild along the Rhine while the Imperial Guard reconstituted its corps from its depots in France. From these interior positions, the new army would be organized and strengthened with the arrival of the cohorts, the naval artillery corps, the conscripts of the various levies, and the veterans from Spain.[3] This, then, was Napoleon's initial plan based on his assumptions of the condition of the army.

However, once Prince Eugène's February 1 report was received, and the seriousness of the situation clearly known, Napoleon recognized that his most immediate and pressing problem in rebuilding the army was the virtual absence of available cadres. These nuclei of officers and non-commissioned officers around which military units were built and expanded were, in every practical sense, non-existent. Since there remained a mere average of only 7 combatants for every French line and light company, Napoleon authorized Prince Eugène to consolidate the survivors of I, II, III Corps—the IV Corps having already departed for Italy. This was accomplished in Erfurt by forming one, and in some rare instances, two companies from each of the 28 French line and light infantry regiments of the first three corps of the former army. To the south, at Augsburg, the French line and light infantry survivors of IV Corps formed their new companies.[4]

Indeed, there were not many of these men, as clearly evidenced by Napoleon's February 11, 1813, letter to Clarke. " The Viceroy informs me that he doesn't think the cadres of the 5 battalions which each regiment of the *Grande Armée* had to send, either to Erfurt or to Augsburg, can furnish [enough manpower for] more than the formation of the 2nd battalions, officers as well as non-coms."[5] Consequentally, Prince Eugène was ordered to reorganize in Erfurt as quickly as possible the so-called "advance guard" of the army, comprised of the 2nd battalions of the previously-mentioned 28 French line and light infantry regiments of the old I, II, and III Corps.[6]

To assist his step-son in the urgent task of rebuilding these 28 battalions, Napoleon dispatched General Pierre Doucet, the long time military governor of Paris.[7] Doucet arrived in Erfurt in late January and immediately set about his business. Inspecting the cadres around which the new 2nd battalions were to be formed, Doucet reported the appalling state of affairs. Of the regiments of the former I Corps, the 2nd battalion cadre in the best shape was the famous 57th Regiment of the Line.[8] The cadre for "The Terrible"[9] had only 8 officers and 5 non-commissioned officers to head its new 2nd battalion.[10] The regiment in the worst shape—the 33rd Light Infantry—had no one in its 2nd battalion cadre![11] Further, Doucet reported that a sampling of 8 regiments from the old I Corps from the period of February 4 through 6, 1813, revealed only 42 officers and 27 non-coms and corporals[12] in ranks to lead the men of the new 2nd battalions.[13]

Once appraised of this dismal situation, Napoleon acted swiftly. He authorized General Doucet to resolve the critical shortage of both officers and non-commissioned officers by redirecting enough cadres from other battalions so that the Erfurt 2nd battalions would have their full compliment of officers and non-commissioned officers.[14] Attempts were made to accomplish this quickly, and by the last week of February, some cadres of the 28 battalions at Erfurt were at full strength.[15] However, there was still a dearth of officers and non-coms. This was loudly proclaimed in a report by General Jean-Toussaint Arrighi de Casanova, the Duke of Padoua and Napoleon's nephew, who was also dispatched to Erfurt to monitor the organization of the 2nd battalions. Arrighi's report of February 23 through 25 noted that many battalions lacked both officers and non-commissioned officers. For example, 4 battalions which Arrighi inspected lacked 20 officers—more than a 25% shortage—and, even more important, lacked 257 non-commissioned officers and corporals.[16] Thus, these 4 battalions had a whopping shortage in the ranks of non-coms and corporals of more than 75% of their establishment.[17] Another battalion—the 2nd/85th Line—had only 4 sergeants[18] instead of the 30 called for by regulations.[19]

Arrighi de Casanova, Duke of Padoua

Napoleon's nephew was born on Corsica on 8 March 1778. After an education in France, he was a staff officer in Napoleon's Army of Italy in 1797. Arrighi served in virtually every campaign of the Napoleonic wars, rising to the rank of Général de division on 25 May 1809. He excelled as a cavalry officer; and as commander of the III Reserve Cavalry Corps in 1813, Arrighi distinguished himself at Dennewitz on 6 September as well as at numerous battles in 1814. He was later Governor of Corsica. *Musée de l'Armée.*

The shortages in Erfurt was just one indicator of the virtual non-existence of officers and non-commissioned officers available for the creation of the cadres for all the corps of observation. Since no significant numbers of officers and non-coms remained to form the cadres of the line cavalry and line and light infantry, the new formations would literally have to be created from scratch. Napoleon waisted little time in summoning all available resources to form cadres for the new line formations.

All over France, Holland, Italy, Germany, and Illyria were isolated battalions of both war and depot status. Invariably, these formations were far below their numerical establishment as other battalions of these regiments usually drew strength from the detached, inactive battalions. Included in this group were many 3rd and 4th battalions, as well as depot battalions (numerically designated as 5th battalions) of regiments serving in Spain. Napoleon ordered most of these isolated battalions to report for duty to both observation corps of the Rhine, and the observation corps of Italy.[20] Upon arrival, the corps commanders noted, with some astonishment, that most of these battalions were formed around very incomplete cadres, while others had almost no officers or non-commissioned officers whatsoever![21] Thus, it was clear that these battalions would be of little help in forming the cadres for the new army.

The already desparate need to find officers and non-commissioned officers intensified. It was imperative that the leadership for the young conscripts be procured immediately or there could be no army at all. Therefore, the Emperor looked once again to his Army of Spain to provide the sorely needed key personnel for the new *Grande Armée*.

In Spain, there were hundreds of extra officers, especially in the army supply train and artillery, who were confined to their depots due to a lack of horseflesh needed to transport the equipment. The Emperor authorized the Ministry of War to order these men back to France for reassignment.[22] Further, the Emperor ordered that the depot personnel of the 80 French line and light infantry regiments of the Army of Spain be stripped from their parent units and marched to the observation corps forming in Germany and in Italy.

This was a frantic, unprecedented move, but one which was necessary nonetheless since the decision to fight for Germany had already been made. By ordering this transfer, Napoleon eviscerated the last reserve of an army that needed every resource possible if it was expected to be able to achieve a stalemate against a formidable foe led by England's greatest general.[23] Nevertheless, the cadres brought from Spain were a much needed and prized source of officers and non-coms which the newly forming regiments enviously fought over.[24]

Unlike the troops of the line, the cadres and depots of the Imperial Guard still existed[25], most of them being located in and around Paris.[26] Immediately, the regiments of the Guard began reforming. The Old Guard grenadier and chasseur regimental depots immediately produced officers and non-coms for the reforming of the 1st battalions of the 1st and 2nd Regiments.[27] The Middle Guard Fusilier regiments reformed at Panthémont with their depots providing most of the officers and non-commissioned officers.[28] Likewise, the depot of the Flanker Grenadiers was intact and was moved to the Saint-Denis barracks where its 1st battalion was reconstituted.[29] The Guard cavalry regiments were more difficult to reform as there were fewer officers and non-coms of the Guard regiments remaining in their depots at Gotha and Fulda.[30] However, at the latter depot there were over 1,000 dismounted veteran cavalrymen and officers of the line aimlessly loitering about, awaiting orders. General Frédéric-Henri Walther, long-time leader of Guard cavalry, took matters into his own hands by using many of these men to form new squadrons of the Old Guard cavalry mounted on horses donated by the Rhine princes.[31]

During the same time that Napoleon was hurriedly seeking cadres as a basis of the new regiments of the army, the conscripts of the various levies began to flood into the training centers. It was at these depots that the conscripts were uniformed, equipped, armed, and supposedly trained for four weeks.[32] During the time at the training center, every new infantry recruit was to fire several blank cartridges and two 'live' rounds at a target. This was, however, "a useless regulation."[33] Due to the prodigous influx of personnel into the training centers, the commanders of the depots were hard pressed to do more than just provide uniforms, equipment, firearms, and pass the men out of the depots as soon as possible. Sometimes even this was difficult because there were acute shortages of everything, especially money to purchase and provide these goods.[34] This is evidenced by the March 27, 1813, letter of the general commanding the 16th Military Division (an administrative organization rather than an operational formation) to the Minister of War. In this communique, the former apologized for having sent incomplete formations to the army because uniforms and arms were lacking. This commander even comments that if he were to field, clothe, equip, and arm all the conscripts in the depots at Boulogne, he would have to undress and disarm every person assigned for duty at those training centers![35]

Another problem which arose in the early months of 1813 was that the arming of so many new recruits in such a short period of time resulted in a lack of muskets. "This situation is absolutely alarming," Napoleon wrote Clarke on March 10. "Not only is there not a moment to lose in giving the arms manufacturers the activity necessary so that the production of the last months (of the year) be 150,000 muskets, it is necessary to accelerate this production by extraordinary means. What are 150,000 muskets? Almost nothing. 300,000 would be needed in order to arm the 1815 conscripts which I will call up probably on January 1, 1814, and to have 150,000 left in the arsenal."[36] Three days later, still worried about the shortage of firearms, the Emperor again wrote to his Minister of War: "Perhaps a part of the 1814 conscripts could be armed with foreign muskets, but of the same caliber, except to have in reserve in Mayence, Wesel, and Strasbourg, which are the points of our frontiers from which our troops depart entering Germany, the number needed of French manufactured pieces to arm the French troops who would be leaving."[37] From another note in a book of situations on the military divisions produced by the Ministry of War, this exact same thing had already been done for some of the old cohorts.[38]

Another inhibiting factor in training the masses of conscripts was the fact that the officers and non-coms of the training centers were responsible for the conduct of the recruits until they joined their regiment. As a result, many depot personnel were constantly on the road, escorting the newly conscripted men to the training center, and from there, to their regiment.[39] This, plus the hurried nature of pushing as many youths through the depots as fast as possible, forced a great deal of improvization with the training of the conscripts. From the moment the instructors from the depot met a detachment destined for their base, they drilled the men, even while in route. The instructors continued the drill at the depots and then again on the road while the conscripts marched to their regimental assembly areas in one of the four corps of observations.[40]

During this time, the army was reorganized almost daily. The personnel leaving one depot destined for a regiment would often be diverted in route and sent to another regiment in the same corps, or even to a totally different corps.[41] Even worse was the frequent practice of the infantry depots being a common personnel pool used by almost all branches, with the notable exception of the artillery branch. Officers from the cavalry, train of artillery, engineers, and supply train would scour the depots in search for 'volunteers'. To illustrate, some 1,540 conscripts of the Class of 1813 were originally assigned for duty with the 12th Regiment of the Line. Of these, only 1,100 actually became infantrymen with the that regiment. The remaining 440 draftees were appropriated while in the training center and 'transferred' to the cavalry, train of artillery, and army supply train, or *équipages militaires*.[42]

Obviously, there were many drawbacks to this practice, the worst of which was the loss of morale. Many young men suffered a deflated ego when they were transferred out of the Emperor's infantry, to become privates in the supply train. Undoubtably, there were many who were happy at their reassignment. Others, as we will see later, deliberately sought to get out of infantry service. Typically, the men who went into the cavalry in this manner were volunteers for the branch, but most knew nothing about how to care for their animals.[43]

Another problem in the incessant tapping of the infantry depots by the other branches was the resulting constant numerical errors created from the *comptabilite-hommes*, or head count of the men (already referred to in this work as parade states). Thus, when the parade state of a regiment was taken on a certain date showing so many present and under arms, with others in hospitals, detached, or in route to the regiment, and then some of the men in route were later drawn away to a different unit, their presence would be noted in their new unit on a later date. The later parade states date was often made before the old regiment from which the personnel were taken had a chance to make another report that would reflect its loss of these same men. As a result of this chaos, the double counting of the same men was a frequent error in the early months of 1813. These were noticed by the man who possessed history's keenest eye for detail. Napoleon soon became frustrated by the conflicting daily reports. Finally, he said one day in front of his ministers: "I see so many variants in the reports submitted to me I don't know what to believe."[44] To be certain, the parade states of January, February, and March, 1813, were accurate only with regard to the number of persons present and under arms. The inaccuracies regarding those detached from the regiment, reflects the tulment and confusion of an army described by Clarke as "being created from thin air".[45]

Invariably, the Imperial Guard reconstituted its units in a more orderly and efficient manner, benefitting from its status and the care given it by the Emperor. In addition to the veterans sent to the Guard from the Army of Spain and the other surviving veterans supplied from the old army of 1812, there were many other resources which helped speedily rebuild the infantry arm of this élite corps. Members of the *vétérans*—retired veterans from the Guard—were asked to volunteer again for service in their old units. All *pupilles* (minors) of the Guard age 17 and over became members of the Young Guard infantry, and the 4 superb instructional battalions at Fontainbleau were immediately drafted into the Young Guard.[46]

From this foundation, the manpower of the Young Guard infantry was supplied from a variety of sources. Some 8,000 conscripts of the Class of 1813 were already in the Guard depots by February. Another 10,000 men of the "levy of the four classes" went to the Young Guard while 20,000 youths of the Class of 1814 were selected to report on April 1, 1813, for service in the Young Guard. Finally, of the supplementary levy of 80,000 men, another 24,000 were earmarked for the Young Guard.[47]

The Guard cavalry built its ranks from veterans and true volunteers from the towns and departments near Paris—these volunteers were not those who went into the Guards of Honor regiments. For political reasons, the squadrons which were comprised of these true volunteers were designated as "Young Guard" squadrons of the Grenadiers à Cheval, Chasseurs à Cheval, Empress Dragoons, and Guard Light Lancers.[48]

The artillery of the Imperial Guard rebuilt its companies quickly, as well as added new ones. From the Guard artillery depot at La Fère, two Old Guard *Volante* (Horse

Artillery) and four Old Guard foot companies were quickly reconstituted from existing cadres and veterans from the artillery depots of the Army of Spain. The Old Guard Sappers were raised from marine artificers and from the depot personnel of the line sapper and miner battalions. Meanwhile, the Train of Artillery of the Guard was reconstituted by filling it out with 800 conscripts from the Class of 1813.[49] As has already been mentioned, the artillery of the Young Guard was rebuilt from four artillery companies of the old cohorts. Other Young Guard companies would be formed from personnel arriving from the Army of Spain.[50]

As the masses of conscripts flowed from their depots in France eastward to the military areas bordering the Rhine, there to be incorporated into makeshift battalions, the young soldiers met with their first horrors of war—the wounded, often mutilated survivors of the 1812 campaign. On their return to France, most of these unfortunates had been directed home via Mayence where an enormous catch-all depot had been established for the disabled veterans of the destroyed 1812 army.[51]

It was in and around Mayence that the youths destined for the army saw these poor men. Marshal François Kellermann, the commanding officer at Mayence[52] who oversaw all the activity of the forces at that staging area, had, in January, warned the Minister of War that the location of the general depot for the wounded in Mayence was not a good idea.[53] On February 14, 1813, Marshal Kellermann again denounced the presence of the wounded depot in the same area where the young conscripts were marching to join the army. "All the battalions," he wrote Clarke, "and detachments which arrive here and which are not composed of only conscripts, have before their eyes the sight of these mutilated soldiers, whose morale is generally very bad, and who by their gossip and their contact, can discourage them. When these veterans run into conscripts from their corps or from their Departments, they surround them and tell them anything they feel like saying. The spirit of these young conscripts is so good that, to prevent it from being corrupted, it is necessary that they have the least communication possible with these disabled soldiers, most of whom no longer know discipline and a part of whom teach the others to roam from hospital to hospital and to avoid the service to which these conscripts are called... I regard the maintenance of this general depot [of wounded] in Mayence as impolitic and dangerous."[54]

Only days later, General Lauriston, who was in Magdebourg on the Elbe River, penned a similar warning to Clarke. "I have found in Magdebourg", he wrote on February 20, "a frightful confusion produced by the soldiers of all ranks flowing back from the *Grande Armée*...I believe it should be that the evacuation from Berlin be made through Leipzig and that nobody else should pass through Magdebourg, so that the new soldiers see the least possible sick men with frozen feet."[55] Upon these and other complaints, the war ministry rearranged the evacuation of the wounded as Lauriston recommended.[56]

Since the conscripts of the Class of 1813 had been the first levy to be processed into the new army, they were, by February 21, 1813, almost entirely absorbed into the "advance guard" (the 28 battalions at Erfurt), by the four corps of observation, and the Young Guard.[57] At Erfurt, the battalion strengths were brought up to 700 combatants,[58] but only after the Young Guard first bolstered its ranks with pick of the Class of 1813.[59] At the corps of observation along the Rhine, the Class of 1813 went to form the 4th battalions of the 28 regiments of the army whose 2nd battalions were being formed in Erfurt. Once these 4th battalions had any similitude of organization, all 28 of them were sent into the 32nd Military Division (Hanseatic area) to help passify the populace, be organized into divisions, and to receive training.[60] The divisions which were composed of these 4th battalions were the 2nd Division in I Corps and the 5th Division in II Corps. "These battalions arrive very tired", General Louis de Lauberdière, military commander of the 32nd Military Division headquartered at Osnabrück, wrote to Clarke on April 15, 1813. "I grant them each day special carriages to transport the weakest and the lame... Every moment possible is employed in teaching them to load and aim their muskets."[61]

As the Class of 1813 left the depots, their place was taken by the "levy of the four classes" who were intended to be formed into new battalions around the cadres withdrawn from the Army of Spain.[62] Many men from this levy were directed into the 1st battalions of the regiments of the old 1812 army. However, even after these conscripts reported for duty, the 1st battalions were still too weak, prompting Napoleon to flesh out these battalions with "only tall and strong men"[63] of the Class of 1814, "keeping the weak for the 3rd and 5th [depot] battalions."[64] This seemed like an easy enough way to complete the 1st battalions had it not been for the lack of adequate physical specimens. For example, the commander of the 4th Military District complained that he had only adolescents of moderate height and constitution from which he could choose to complete the 1st battalions. "As things stand," he wrote to Clarke on April 24, "I must inform Your Excellency that it would be impossible to fulfill that condition for more than one company, even though the number of men received from that conscription [of 1814] is more than 800 out of 950."[65]

The war ministry's response was immediate and of vital interest to this study. "Telling you of necessity to complete the 1st battalions with 1814 conscripts, big and strong," replied Clarke on April 29, "it is well understood that these are the biggest and strongest of those who arrive at the depot."[66] Thus, Napoleon's desire to complete the 1st battalions with "tall and strong" men of the Class of 1814 was, in reality, a grammatical difference between the relative and the absolute. As it was to be discovered, the "big and strong" boys of the conscription Class of 1814 were actually small and weak when compared to most mature men. As a result—and as we will see in later chapters—the boys of this and other levies were not physically ready for war, nor were most of them able to contend with the deprivation and demands of army life.

With the arrival of the young conscripts at their destinations, the battalions and detachments were organized into regiments. In the 1st Observation Corps of the Rhine, the newly constituted battalions at first retained their original numerical designation (i.e.- 4th battalion of the 85th Line). The reformed battalions of this corps, as well as those in the 2nd Observation Corps of the Rhine and the Observation Corps of Italy, were often grouped together into provisional, or temporary, regiments consisting of two battalions.[67] This was often the case since the battalions which technically were part of the same regiment were sent to different corps. Occasionally, there were two or more battalions of the same regiment with the same corps. When this occurred, the battalions of the regiment served together.[68]

The rebuilding cavalry arm of the line was forced to improvize more than their counterparts in the infantry. Shortages of trained men and horses were critical.[69] As a result, provisional regiments were often formed from provisional squadrons. This meant that temporary squadrons were often comprised of two companies from different units that, in turn, were converged to form temporary regiments. The inevitable result of the bringing together of disparate elements into a new command was to inhibit the regimental élan and espirit de corps of the cavalry. However, this faulty organization was recognized by the cavalry generals and the temporary regiments eventually disappeared from the army's organization.

Regardless of how the infantry or cavalry regiments were organized, most all of these units of the army, other than the Imperial Guard, suffered from a severe lack of officers. Compounding the problem, the quality of the company level officers seemed to be significantly below the standards previously exhibited in Napoleon's earlier armies.[70] The shortage of officers, along with complaints by general officers regarding officer quality, and returns from the parade states, substantiate this predicament.

Napoleon began to sense the need for officers to lead the new troops as early as January 4, 1813, when he wrote to Clarke: "There are in all those [Spanish] armies many officers, many in unmounted cavalrymen, many in supply trains, many in artillery support units, prefectly useless; order it all brought back to France."[71] The officers of these fragments and other units in Spain formed the cadres of many formations of the new *Grande Armée*.

Also, in an effort to find officers for the young men of the army, promotions were rapidly handed out. At the top of the list were surviving non-commissioned officers of the 1812 army as well as cadets at Saint-Cyr.[72] However, even with liberal promotions being made up to the limit of the law, there were still not enough officers to lead the troops of the line.[73] This situation forced Napoleon to accelerate advancement by taking 100 corporals and promoting them to sublieutenants.[74] Naturally, the hasty promotion of so many so quickly resulted in less qualified personnel in the officer ranks.

That the overall officer quality was not up to the old standards was nowhere more obvious than in the old cohorts. It will be remembered that the cohorts initially had officers comprised of those on retirement, or enforced retirement, or former officers of the army serving in the National Guard.[75] Of these officers, the ones on retirement were usually proven warriors, but older men nevertheless, some of which had lost much of their zeal for active service. The officers on enforced retirement were typically those who just could not hack it with the army and had been sent home. Such then was the officer material of the cohorts as they headed off to war.

It did not take long for the shortcomings of these officers to be brought to the attention of Napoleon and the Minister of War. Among the first to voice his opinion about the poor officers heading the cohorts was Marshal François-Joseph Lefebrve, who wrote the following letter to Clarke on February 1: "I think it necessary to warn you of the disorder which reigns in the marching columns of the cohorts headed for Mayence. I have found the entire route, from Châlons to Paris, covered with soldiers marching alone, in groups, without order and without leaders, belonging to the 1st, 8th, 9th, 12th, 13th, and 14th Cohorts. The last two, 13th and 14th, are the only ones I met yesterday marching in formation with a leader at the head. It must be that the officers of these units are indeed bad to permit such disorder to reign in the marching of their soldiers, that it would be a good deal of trouble to bring back later on the discipline they have been allowed to forget for so long. I did all that was possible to urge the officers to whom I was able to speak, to establish a little more order in their body of men; but they told me it was due to permission given to many individuals from all these cohorts to go home, which makes me fear that there will be the greatest difficulty in gathering them together afterwards."[76] Later that month, Clarke received other disturbing reports concerning the cohorts[77], including one from General Eloir-Laurent Despeaux, commander of the 25th Military Division, who informed the Minister of War of a near mutiny by the disaffected men of the 34th and 35th Cohorts. "I have the honor of informing Your Majesty," Clarke wrote to the Emperor on February 17, "that, according to a report transmitted to me by General Despeaux, it would seem that the 34th and 35th Cohorts, in route for arrival in Paris, are very undisciplined and motivated by the worst morale; that during their journey, the soldiers made bold statements out loud and publicly that, if they were made to go on to Paris, they would kill their officers."[78] Clarke suggested that new officers be sent out from Paris to meet these units, restore order, and lead them through the city. However, Napoleon decided on diverting these cohorts directly from Orleans to Metz, thereby not risking any potential scandal.[79]

Other reports urged the Minister of War and the Emperor to have all the officers from all the cohorts completely replaced and then interviewed to determine whether or not they should be reassigned with the active army.[80] Finally, all these complaints led Napoleon to promise General Lauriston, who was in command of the Observation Corps of the Elbe—a corps composed entirely from the old cohorts—that new officers would soon be made available. "You speak of the bad officers of the cohorts," Napoleon wrote Lauriston on February 8, "I have ordered to gather in Magdebourg a large number of generals, field grade officers, and other officers of all grades. A part of these will be at your disposition, and you will be able to make use of them to replace the officers with whom you are not happy; upon making these changes, your army [corps] will be fine."[81]

The promise of new officers for the former cohorts boosted Lauriston's morale and confidence in the Emperor's plan, as evidenced by the general's February 13 letter to Clarke: "I have just had the 151st Regiment of the Line pass in review. It has a total of 2,522 men, including officers ready for service, and 247 in the area hospital. The men are of the best type, very rigorous, and perfectly well disposed. The non-commissioned officers are somewhat young, but thet want to do well. As for the officers, its always the composition as in the other regiments [formed from the old cohorts]. I shall speak no further of it to Your Excellency. The measures that His Majesty has just taken for the replacement of those who are incapable of serving France will make these new regiments the finest and best of the army."[82]

However, owing to the critical shortage of all officers throughout the army, the plan to replace the old officers of the cohorts with younger, more aggresive, and more attentive ones was a difficult task. This is illustrated in another letter written by Lauriston almost six weeks later. "Your Excellency will permit me," he wrote Clarke on March 26, "to bring to your attention that, in spite of the sending back of 25 officers [from the old cohorts], taking one thing with another by regiment it will be necessary to send back another 25; that I am obligated at each post to have the password repeated like a corporal; that the officers [of the old cohorts] are old and no longer know anything about the service, and what is worse, that I have not yet been able to put a regiment together and have it put through maneuvers...We can get everything from the soldier, but the beginning does not favor discipline."[83]

From all quarters came the hue and cry for more and better officers. From corps commanders, from Imperial aides de camp, from the elderly but still tough-minded Marshal Kellermann, they pleaded with Clarke and Napoleon for qualified officers to lead the new

PROFILE OF THE MAKEUP OF THE
GRANDE ARMÉE OF 1813

Formation	Cadre Makeup	Troop Makeup
Imperial Guard Infantry:		
Old Guard	A, B, K	A, C
Middle Guard	A, B, K	A, C
Young Guard	B, K, L	G, H, I, J, L, N
Imperial Guard Cavalry	A, B, K	A, C, O
Imperial Guard Artillery	A, B, K	A, D, E
Cavalry of the Line	K, M	G, H, J, N
Artillery of the Line	A, B, K, L	D, N
Line and Light Infantry:		
Durutte's Division	A, B	F
The 28 2nd Battalions of Erfurt	A, B, K	A, G
Other 2nd Battalions	A, M	A, G
1st Battalions	K, M	H, J
4th Battalions	K, L, M	G, N
3rd & 5th (depot) Battalions	M	H, I, J
6th, 7th, & 8th Battalions	M	I, J
134th Line Regiment	L	L
"Regiments de Marine"	B	E, I, J
37th Light Infantry Regiment	L	L
Line Regiments 135—156	B	D, G

CODE

A	=	Survivors of 1812—whether of the same unit or transferred from another
B	=	Existing depot personnel
C	=	Selected veterans from Spain
D	=	Old cohorts
E	=	Naval Artillery Corps
F	=	Class of 1812
G	=	Class of 1813
H	=	Levy of the four classes
I	=	Supplementary levy
J	=	Class of 1814
K	=	Cadres from Spain
L	=	Other existing cadres/troops from around the Empire
M	=	Newly created cadre
N	=	Existing units from Spain
O	=	Newly raised volunteer units

troops. It was to little avail. The officer corps of France had perished in Russia. Napoleon could call on the young men of the country to fill the ranks of the new army, but officers could not be easily replaced. Thus, even with every possible source in central Europe turned upside down in search for officers, no matter what promotions were made including those above what regulations officially allowed, there remained serious gaps in the officer corps for both the infantry and cavalry of the line.

Feeling the pressure to send *numbers* of officers to the army, Clarke and his ministers often assigned completely unqualified candidates to the service. Sooner or later, these incompetents were discovered. One such discovery was made by Napoleon himself. Following an inspection on April 27, the Emperor wrote Clarke: "If your office had undertaken to name the most inept officers in France, it would not have succeeded better. These officers are an object of derision for the soldiers...The majority of captains have never been under fire. I am going to be obliged to dismiss and send back all these officers. You also are sending me young people coming from schools and who have not been to Saint-Cyr, so they do not know anything, and it is in the new regiments that you are placing them!"[84] A few days after this reprimand, the first major engagement of the war was fought at Lutzen. The experience at this battle not only frustrated Napoleon by the quality of many of his officers, but also by the lack of qualified officers of most all ranks. "I find myself on the field of battle without officers," the Emperor wrote Clarke on May 5. "Furthermore, the campaign will use a lot of them; it is necessary to have a lot to replace them, without making promotions too fast, which doesn't accomplish the end anyway...if you need officers and non-coms, the Army of Spain is an inexhaustible nursery; I authorize you to bring them in from there."[85] Once again, the Emperor called on the Army of Spain to supply the personnel needed for the *Grande Armée*.

The lack of numbers of officers mentioned by Napoleon was another cry for leadership echoed long before the campaign began by many corps commanders, including Lauriston. Less than two weeks before hostilities commenced, the commander of the V Corps wrote another letter to Clarke, begging that the war ministry send his corps more officers. "...Your Excellency will see," Lauriston wrote on April 13, "that I lack 83 captains and 73 lieutenants...the lack of captains is truly detrimental; these officers are the heart of the companies."[86]

The overall lack of officers, as well as the dirth of quality ones led, in turn, to a less comprehensive training schedule, as well as to isolated incidents of lack of respect and indiscipline. The latter problem—lack of respect and indiscipline—was unique almost exclusively to the old cohorts. As already mentioned, the lack of quality officers in these units was most acute, the episode involving the 34th and 35th Cohorts being the most scandalous. Other cohorts committed undisciplined acts which their leaders did not know how to check,[87] while in other cohorts, the officers simply failed to inspire respect or enforce discipline.[88] Therefore, it is little wonder that Kellermann and Lauriston so urgently sought to obtain new officers for these units.

Outside these specifics instances, which by no means should be construed as normal behavior in the army of 1813, the biggest problem created by the officer crisis was the resulting lower standard of training in many units. Much of the problem of the new units' lack of drill was attributable to the fact that they had been run through the training centers in only 8 to 10 days.[89] This was done despite the fact that the men were suppose to be trained at the depots for at least one month.

The change in policy was pushed by the Ministry of War itself when, in January, it instructed the depot commanders "to watch with greatest care the training and discipline of the 1813 conscripts for whom the veterans must serve as models."[90] However, when it became clear that there were virtually no veterans at the depots to serve "as models", and coupled with the repeated levies for more troops, the ministry began to reprimand the depot commanders for not pushing the conscripts through fast enough![91] Therefore, training took place on the march to the depot, the few days while in the training center, and while on the march to join one of the corps of observation.

As the conscripts marched out of the training centers and off to the frontier, they were moved in stages; each stage was a morning's march of 10 to 15 miles. At the end of this march, there would be a camp (of sorts) already set up where the new soldiers would draw supplies, uniforms, equipment, and arms, based upon the needs of the conscripts and the availability of supplies. During the afternoon, the men would drill for several hours before falling out for an early dinner and bed. The routine would be repeated day after day until the men arrived at their destination.[92]

Once the draftees reported to their regiments, reactions from corps commanders and Imperial aides de camp were sure to follow. When General Doucet first arrived in Erfurt, he noticed that "the training is not very far along."[93] On March 2, another important observation was made concerning the 2nd battalions forming in Erfurt. After a review of the 2nd battalion of the 26th Light Infantry, the following report was sent to Paris: "The battalion has no idea of how to drill, but nine-tenths do reasonably the manual of arms and how to load."[94] On March 16, General Arrighi wrote from Erfurt. "The 2nd battalions from the 17th, 25th, and 72nd Regiments of the Line left today for Magdebourg", the Duke of Padoua informed Clarke. "These three battalions are, of all those which have passed through here, the fartherest behind in their training; it is almost nil."[95] Another opinion of the progress of the 2nd battalions was penned by General Doucet on April 1, when he wrote Clarke that most of the Erfurt battalions considered it "a great honor to attain platoon level training."[96] Arrighi's and Doucet's assessments seem alarming if one considers that the 2nd battalions of Erfurt had all formed around cadres of the survivors of 1812. Also, "eight or ten [battalions] at most"[97] of the 28 being organized in Erfurt were fleshed out by the remainder of the 1812 conscription. These battalions were, by April 1, able to perform battalion level evolutions owing to the more experienced soldiers in their ranks.[98]

It was going to take time to whip the new soldiers of the 2nd battalions into shape—longer than what was at first anticipated. It was therefore decided to send many of the 2nd battalions to the lower Elbe River area, there to be organized into the 4th Division in II Corps.[99] Comments from different reviews made from early March to mid-April clearly point out that the 2nd battalions which comprised the 4th Divison were only able to achieve platoon level drill—a platoon being the same as a company—by the opening of hostilities. With the difficulty of training and molding new battalions, there is little wonder why Napoleon ordered these battalions into the region of the lower Elbe so that they could be out of harms way during the beginning of the campaign.[100]

Not all battalions were like those sent to the lower Elbe; the training level varied from unit to unit. On February 14, the 1st battalion of the 28th Light Infantry was going through its paces in Mayence when it caught Marshal Kellermann's eye, prompting him to write to Clarke that this unit "already executes well all types of firing, and...will be the finest and most prepared of Souham's division."[101] Elsewhere on this same day, Colonel Cavalier of the gendarmarie wrote to his commanding officer, General Jean-Pierre Henry, "that [the voltigeur company] of the 5th Light Infantry Regiment is excellent; they are almost all old soldiers."[102] In the same letter, Colonel Cavalier remarked about the voltigeur companies of the 86th, 121st, and 122nd Regiments of the Line, noting "that these young conscripts absolutely don't know how to use their weapons...."[103]

The groups that progressed most rapidly in their training were the former cohorts and the *marins*. Though never drilled as infantry, and being completely unfamiliar with small arms, the majority of men of the naval artillery corps were already in the military, adults, and "well officered."[104] Once the detachments of *marins* were brought together into their regiments, they immediately displayed an espirit de corps noted by almost all officers who came into contact with them.[105] As a result, the marines possessed high morale and quickly jelled into reliable shock troops, although their expertise with small arms seemed always to be on a level with most of the conscript units.[106]

As for the battalions of the former cohorts, they had already been under arms for almost a year[107] before being incorporated into the army. Due to many poor officers leading these units, some cohorts got off to a slow start in their training, but by April, 1813, the battalion drill of the former cohorts was as good or better than most regiments of the line or light infantry[108] thanks mainly to the quality and maturity of the men. However, if the marines and former cohorts could perform battalion maneuvers by April 1, they both were hard pressed to act in coordinated, regimental drill at that time. They were able to concentrate on this aspect for several weeks before the campaign began. Even with this drill, General Lauriston was unimpressed with the regimental maneuvers of the old cohorts. "His Majesty must reasonably believe," Lauriston wrote Prince Eugène on April 15, "that, from the time the cohorts are brought together into a regiment, there must exist a teamwork in maneuvers and in the makeup of the regiments; that does not exist at all."[109]

Even after the beginning of the spring campaign, there were many examples of recruits coming out of the depots with almost no training. Evidentally, some of the new troops looked so bad in drill while still at the training centers that the populace referred to the army as the "infants of the Emperor."[110] One confidential memo to Clarke seems to confirm this point. "It has been noticed," wrote General Savary, Minister of Police, on May 13, "and I have had several occassions to preceive it myself, that in Paris the conscripts of the new levy exercised on the Champs-Elysées during the hours ordinary given over to public strolling. I realize the need to instruct these young soldiers and it is not about that that I will make the least observation: but that it should positively choose the moment when the avenues of the promenade are covered with people to display there these soldiers still brand new and often half-dressed, this moment, I say, appears to me badly chosen and has many inconveniences, because of the reflections and bad gossip to which it gives rise."[111]

Whatever the problems were for the infantry in preparing for war—from the lack of officers and non-commissioned officers to form cadres, to the insufficient numbers of officers, to the low quality of many of these, often resulting in slower or substandard training—they were only a fraction of the difficulties experienced by those rebuilding the cavalry. The reason why the cavalry was the most brutalized branch of the service during 1812, and why it was the most difficult to restore, is simple enough. Cavalry required two elements—trained men and trained horses[112]—both of which, after Russia, were rare commodities indeed.

Nevertheless, in spite of difficulties, rebuilding of the cavalry had to begin from somewhere. The Emperor started by ordering the regiments be reconstituted around the few survivors of 1812 and cadres withdrawn from Spain. The cadres from Spain consisted of officers and non-coms from regiments of dragoons, chasseurs à cheval, and hussars, along with a single regiment of cuirassiers—the 13th. Among the cuirassier regiments already in the *Grande Armée* , it should be noted that the 14th Cuirassiers, formerly of the Dutch army[113] (not to be confused with the 14th Polish Cuirassiers) had such a poor performance in Russia that the French generals did not want to utilize their depot personnel for any other units. Thus, due to the "undistinguished reputation"[114] of Dutch cavalry, the Ministry of War chose not to draw on the depot or cadres from the 14th (Dutch) Cuirassiers for the rebuilding of any other unit.[115]

Although their numbers were small, the cavalry cadres enthusiastically went about the monumental task of reforming their combat arm. The plea went out for old cavaliers to rejoin the army; the response was very good. Heeding the call, former cavalry officers, non-commissioned officers, and enlisted men from all over the Empire again took their place under the tricolor. Most of these veterans found their way into the cavalry of the Imperial Guard. Paris raised two excellent squadrons totalling 500 men and horses, which Napoleon took into the 2nd Regiment of Light Lancers of the Guard "as a sign of his regard."[116] General Bourcier, in command of the army's general remount depot headquartered at Magdebourg in Northern Germany had, by April 1, managed to scrape together approximately 10,000 veteran cavalrymen[117]—not all mounted—composed of men from more than 60 different regiments.[118] Thus, while Broucier had 10,000 cavalry present and under arms on April 1, they were nothing more than a multitude of small, disparate elements, dispersed all over Northern Germany.

Even with these welcome volunteers, the cavalry arm lacked manpower. With prospects of hostilities looming on the horizon, the Ministry of War had to somehow appropriate more bodies for the mounted service. To accomplish this, Clarke and his ministers silently allowed cavalry officers to tap the infantry depots for manpower.

With small groups of horsemen from dozens of different regiments spread across the countryside, and large numbers of conscripts newly introduced into the cavalry service, it was very difficult for the commanders to train and mold their new commands into combat ready regiments, brigades, divisions, and corps. With the I and II Reserve Cavalry Corps being organized by General de Fay Latour-Maubourg and General Horace Sébastianti respectively, Napoleon ordered the III Reserve Cavalry Corps be formed[119] and eventually led by Arrighi de Casanova. While the general had been useful in his assisting of the formation of the 28 battalions at Erfurt, the expertise of Napoleon's nephew was in the cavalry arm. Initially setting up his headquarters at Metz[120], Arrighi immediately went about the difficult task of forming his corps from fragments of units and various detachments not yet part of any regiment. When, in late April, Clarke inquired as to whether or not the III Reserve Cavalry Corps was ready to join the army for the impending campaign, "regardless of its state of organization, even if it means forming provisional [temporary] regiments",[121] the response was immediate. "If circumstances dictate that we send the army part of the III Cavalry Corps before its organization is fully realized," answered Arrighi on April 23, "we must wait, if possible, until one squadron per regiment has arrived, so that there be a nucleus by division and by brigade...It is also desired that the squadron furnished by each regiment retain their squadron designation, rather than giving them temporary numbers: this latter measure would diminish the zeal and rivaly of the officers, non-commissioned officers, and cavalrymen who, if not sure that they are part of a permanent regiment, do not acquire that espirit de corps so necessary, especially to the conscripts."[122] Hard pressed by Napoleon for more men—especially cavalry—the Ministry of War replied to Arrighi that if his corps was to be fielded, it would have to do so by the "necessary evil"[123] of expediently forming temporary, or provisional, regiments.

The large number of conscripts incorporated into the cavalry to attain numerical strength presented even more of a problem here than in the infantry. While a conscript infantryman had to learn the basics of survival and drill, a conscript cavalryman not only had to acquire a knowledge of how to take care of himself and perform mounted drill, he also had to know how to care for his mount. In this last respect, most of the conscripts taken into the cavalry in 1813 had never been on a horse before, nor groomed an animal. This single fact would lead to many other problems discussed later in this work.

Also complicating the rebuilding of the cavalry was the acute shortage of horses. The requisition for horses in 1813 was made time and time again. Indeed, this is a frequent subject in Napoleon's correspondence as well as the letters from the war ministry.[124] From the four corners of the Empire, officials constantly busied themselves in the procurement of horseflesh and dispatching the animals to the *Grande Armée*, with the horses coming from the Hanseatic area of Germany among the largest groups of animals requisitioned by the army.

As with the infantry, the shortage of officers and non-coms greatly affected the speed at which the new cavaliers learned their trade. As previously mentioned, most of the conscripts which ended up in the cavalry arm in 1813 had never before groomed or mounted a horse. As might be expected, many of the new troopers at first had difficulty just remaining in the saddle during maneuvers.[125] Nevertheless, several hours of drill a day resulted in steady progress right up until the start of the spring campaign.[126]

Rebuilding the artillery of the *Grande Armée* was a far different and easier (if one can use such a term under these conditions) proposition for Napoleon than was the reconstruction of the infantry or cavalry branches. Although the personnel of the artillery service in the 1812 army had suffered greatly, and while most of their animals had perished in the ordeal, resulting in the loss of most of the French guns, caissons, forges, and other mobile equipment, the artillery branch of the Empire was still the cornerstone of Napoleon's military might.

It was not an accident that the artillery of the French Imperial armies had attained this prominence. Before Napoleon took his first command at the head of the Republican Army of Italy in 1796, the artillery of the French armies had a long tradition of pride and excellence, supported by superior schools and a heady officer corps.[127] Since the artillery branch was not nearly as glamorous as the cavalry or even the infantry, it traditionally attracted the hard working, but nevertheless intellectual middle class and poor nobility of France. As a result of its makeup, the artillery lost significantly fewer *émigres* from the Revolution than did any other branch of service.[128] Thus, when Napoleon became First Consul, he inherited an artillery arm which was already very competent. However, the young Napoleon was himself an artillerist of the first order and he sought more from his favorite branch of service than mere competence. Napoleon demanded excellence and got it. The Emperor molded the artillery arm of France into the most efficient and deadly battlefield force in the world.

There were many reasons for the artillery of France being superior to other Continental powers. In addition to those already mentioned, Napoleon's reorganization and subdivision of artillery troop-types into *artillerie à cheval* (horse artillery), *artillerie à pied* (foot artillery), *pontonniers* (pontoniers), *ouvriers* (workers), and *armuriers* (armorors)[129] was a signifigant step forward in the evolution of that combat arm. It was, however, his brilliant creation of the massive *train d'artillerie* (train of artillery) that gave his guns a singular efficiency unmatched by another other nation.[130] The *train d'artillerie* placed the movement of guns and ammunition in the hands of the highly trained soldier-drivers and took it out of the hands of civilian contractors. By 1812, the Emperor routinely "doubled"[131] the first 13 battalions of these personnel for war time activity. It is significant to note that the *train d'artillerie* was so well organized and efficient, that in stark contrast to the complete breakdown of the French logistical system in 1812, the *train d'artillerie* never faltered and the artillery of the *Grande Armée* was always well supplied with ammunition, "even in the depths of Russia."[132]

Another of Napoleon's significant contributions to the French artillery service was his creation and subsequent personal supervision of a large army artillery staff. Artillery officers were specialists, and Napoleon wanted to be sure that their expertise impacted on every level of command. Consequentally, artillery chiefs for divisions (with a rank of *chef de bataillon*), corps (*général de brigade* or *général de division*), and armies (*général de division*) became important positions with the active army.[133] Other artillery officers saw to the quality of the men and materiel coming into the artillery. Among their responsibilites, these officers supervised production quality control of everything related to the artillery branch, the general administration for the nation's artillery, and the all-important education of young officer candidates at the superb artillery schools.[134] Always keeping a ever watchful eye of the activities of the army artillery staff, Napoleon had "a special compartment in his astounding memory"[135] especially devoted to this subject.

It is therefore no surprise that the artillery branch enjoyed an unprecedented popularity among French men looking to enter military service. With its enormous pool of trained officers all over the Empire, the army artillery staff was quickly able to replace the officers who perished in Russia. Also, stocks of guns, materiel, and munitions which had already been manufactured to make good any campaign losses, quickly appeared at the corps of observation as their organization began to take shape.[136]

As in the other branches of the army, the Russian debâcle had taken a deadly toll on the officers, non-coms, and other ranks of personnel in the field companies of artillery. However, with the incorporation of the artillery companies previously part of the cohorts, the army gained approximately 8,000 trained gunners. In addition to these were 571 distinguished veterans of the naval artillery corps which were allowed admittance into the artillery of the Old Guard.[137] Thus, before the end of February, 1813, the artillery service had taken in over 8,500 veteran gunners—enough to flesh out the artillery for the entire new *Grande Armée*.

On the surface, the artillery would seem to have been completely re-created. To be sure, the men who filled the ranks of the artillery companies in the 1813 army were trained, mature men. However, one must remember that, as a group, these 8,500 artillerists were not horsemen and this fact played a part in retarding the reconstruction of the vital, mobile companies of *artillerie à cheval*. Also, even with enough well-drilled personnel to operate the guns, the numbers of animals available to pull the pieces and supporting equipment was *the* primary factor in the delay in employing the artillery—both foot and horse companies—with the army. Where the lack of horseflesh especially took its toll was that it limited the number of companies of *artillerie à cheval* which could be employed. Also, the critical shortage of trained horses also affected the rebuilding of the vital *train d'artillerie*. Since draft horses had to be mature animals, matched in teams and then toughened to become strong enough to pull their load, not any horse could be used for this duty.[138] Thus, the location of the right horses for the *train d'artillerie* was a constant problem that was magnified in the early months of 1813 when not enough animals could be obtained. "His Majesty insists," explained Clarke on April 8, "that sufficient teams for the *train d'artillerie* be procured at once. I authorize whatever means necessary in order to gather another 15,000 horses for the service."[139]

Throughout the first months of 1813, in the midsts of all the pressures, details, and demands which Napoleon had to address in the rebuilding of the *Grande Armée*, the Emperor characteristically remained more concerned with the artillery than anything else. Realizing his serious lack of cavalry and the youth of his infantry, Napoleon sought to strengthen the new army through its artillery. As the campaign opened, the Emperor offered a prophetic statement: "We will fall back on the battles in Eygpt; good infantry, supported by artillery, must be able to sustain itself."[140] Unfortunately for Napoleon, he had very few good infantry on which he could rely although his infantry was to prove itself superior to that of the Allies in the upcoming campaign. The artillery would indeed have to do more than ever before.

Despite all the difficulties raising the army, equipping it, finding enough officers and non-commissioned officers to lead and train the men, most of the troops of the new *Grande Armée* were enthusiastic and eager to serve France. This is born out time and again throughout the letters and reports of the officers and officials which had a hand in the rebuilding of the army. On January 10, 1813, the commandant of the 6th Military Division wrote to the Minister of War: "In general, I have been satisfied with the fine bearing of the troops and the good spirits which animates them...."[141] Later that month, on January 22, the commandant of the 18th Military Division, while on his way to Dijon, inspected the 3rd battalion of the 16th Light Infantry Regiment and informed the Ministry of War as to his findings: "I found it well armed, well dressed, and well equipped. The men are small, but generally healthy enough and they seem to be willing; the officers have assured me that they are very manageable."[142] A few days later, on January 27, General Doucet commented on the parade states of the 2nd battalion of the 103rd Regiment of the Line: "The type of men is good, tractable, and in good spirits."[143] Two weeks later, on February 10, Marshal Kellermann wrote to Clarke about the troops of the 1st battalion, 28th Light Infantry Regiment: "The conscripts are animated by the best will and their training has zeal and untiring activity...."[144] Three days later, on February 13, Lauriston penned the following comment to Clarke regarding the 151st Regiment of the Line: "The men are of the best type, very rigorous, and perfectly well disposed."[145] Another three days had passed when Colonel Cavalier advised General Henry on February 16 that "the men of the 5th Légère [Light Infantry] Regiment are excellent."[146] The following month, Lauriston let Clarke know that he and his staff were getting excellent effort from his regiments when he wrote "we can get everything from the soldier...."[147] Also in March, Marshal Marmont commented that "the regiments of the naval artillery corps act superbly, and inspire the conscripts of the corps."[148] As the army made final preparations for war in April, General Laubardière, commandant of the 32nd Military Division, made the following observation concerning the 4th battalions of the 28 regiments of the old I, II, and III Corps: "All these battalions are French," he wrote Clarke on April 15, "I must say that the young soldiers give promise of courage and good attitude."[149] That same day, Marmont again expressed his pleasure with the *marins* when he commented to Clarke: "These regiments are anxious to prove themselves; their enthusiasm has spread to the rest of the [VI] corps."[150] Further, Marmont described the men of the 37th Light Infantry Regiment as "magnificent."[151] Finally, there is Napoleon's famous comments to Clarke after his review of the same light infantry regiment on the eve of the campaign. "I have just seen the 37th Légère; it is impossible to see a corps with finer soldiers, but impossible, at the same time, to see one with worse officers...."[152] Perhaps it is this last comment penned by the Emperor himself which best describes the difficulties in forming the *Grande Armée* of 1813.

CHAPTER IV
"A Large Gathering of Men"

Hurriedly called to serve, quickly uniformed and armed, pushed through the depots after only a few days, lacking sufficient officers and non-commissioned officers, the youth of France began to congregate in areas along the Rhine River, the Elbe River, and in Northern Italy. The progress of troop concentrations was such that by March 12, 1813, Napoleon had received enough information that he could intelligently organize his forces for the upcoming campaign in Germany. On that day, the Emperor decreed that the so-called "advance guard" and the four corps of observation would drop those titles and that they would return to the general cadre of the *Grande Armée*[1] to be renamed as active *corps d'armée*. Also on that same day, Napoleon decreed that his new army would have 11 infantry corps of the line, 5 reserve cavalry corps of the line, and the all-important Imperial Guard corps "reorganized in great strength."[2] However, there were not enough officers, men, and arms to magically create this entire host. Therefore, some corps were expected to be ready for war before May[3] while others would be brought into the campaign at a later date as their organization allowed.[4]

The bulk of the army consisted of the 11 infantry corps of the line, numbered I through IX, XI, and XII. The I and II Corps, each scheduled to have three infantry divisions, a cavalry brigade, and an artillery reserve, were only beginning to take shape in mid-March and could not be expected to help the army before the end of May. To allow these corps time to come together and to be whipped into a state of combat readiness, Napoleon deemed it prudent to have the I Corps stationed on the lower Elbe in the vicinity of Hamburg as to be safely to the flank and rear of the anticipated front.[5]

The commander of this area was Marshal Davout, under whom the command of I Corps was given to General Dominique Vandamme. Vandamme was a hot blooded, outspoken man, but one of unquestioned loyalty and excellent combat ability. Due to his grating personality, seemingly all but one of Napoleon's marshals found Vandamme impossible to control. However, even Vandamme dared not get crossways with the stern Davout, and thus the general was placed under the orders of the Prince of Eckümhl.[6]

Of the three infantry divisons numbered 1 through 3 that supposedly comprised I Corps in April, only the 2nd Division under General Jean-Baptiste Domonceau was originally supposed to be part of this formation. The 5th Division under General François-Maris Dufour, originally of II Corps, was the other regular infantry division placed under the orders of Vandamme. Both the 2nd and 5th Divisions were composed entirely of 4th battalions, created from the "levy of the four classes" and formed around cadres drawn off from the Army of Spain. To keep these battalions together and to give them time to train, Napoleon thought it made sense to assign all 28 of these 4th battalions into the 2nd and 5th Divisions, and station them on the lower Elbe.

The remaining infantry division of I Corps was little more than a collection of the most dissimilar elements imaginable. Called the "Reserve Division of Hamburg", this formation included all sorts of adhoc units, including *bataillons de marche* drawn from companies of 10 different regiments[7], men of the 5th Flotilla Equipment Train (who no longer had any bridge train to pull), along with a battalion created from former customs police![8]

By the end of April, the cavalry brigade of I Corps consisted on paper of two regiments, namely the French 28th Chasseurs à Cheval and the 17th Lithuanian Uhlans.[9] The reserve artillery companies and most of the supporting companies of engineers, train, and medical services had yet to be formed by the time the spring campaign began.[10]

Like the I Corps, the II Corps could not be ready for war before the end of May. Therefore, Napoleon also ordered it to be organized safely along the middle to lower Elbe River. The commander of II Corps was Marshal Claude-Victor Perrin. A leader who always displayed personal bravery and coolness under fire, Victor was an able tactician and administrator although not a good disciplinarian. This latter aspect of his makeup may somewhat explain his own unwillingness to cooperate with anyone other than Lannes— with whom he was close friends—or the Emperor himself. Despite this fault, Napoleon needed Victor to command II Corps.[11]

As initially planned, the II Corps was to consist of the 4th, 5th, and 6th Infantry Divisions, a cavalry brigade, and an artillery reserve.[12] By March 15, only the 4th Division under General Jean-Louis Dubreton, former colonel of the 5th Light Infantry Regiment,[13] was complete and operating under the orders of the Duke of Belluna. Dubreton's division consisted of a dozen 2nd battalions from Erfurt, and a company of foot artillery.[14] Since Dufour's 5th Division was assigned to I Corps, the 1st Division under General Armand Philippon,[15] originally intended to be part of I Corps, was transferred to II Corps. This division had within its organization the remaining 16 battalions of the 2nd battalions organized at Erfurt. Thus, all the twenty-eight 2nd battalions of the old I, II, and III Corps of the 1812 army were brought together to serve in the new II Corps. However, Victor's corps could not be counted on for some time as it lacked cavalry and reserve artillery. Even worse, the corps had no staff or support services of any sort.[16]

The new III Corps, formerly known as the First Observation Corps of the Rhine, was further along in its organization, owing primarily to the fact that its foundation was 8 regiments—32 battalions—of the old cohorts.[17] Added to these regiments were new battalions of conscripts. In command of III Corps was one of Napoleon's most celebrated lieutenants, Marshal Michel Ney.[18] Insubordinate and quarrelsome when under the orders of anyone other than Napoleon, yet incredibly brave, Ney could inspire the common soldier like few others. Although his tactical skill sometimes failed him, Ney's courage was beyond reproach. In March, Napoleon summoned the Prince of the Moscowa to Germany to command III Corps.[19] When III Corps was formed, it was to have four infantry divisions numbered 8 through 11, a cavalry brigade, and an artillery reserve.[20] The division commanders under Ney were no strangers to war. With General Joseph Souham at the head of the 8th Division, General Antoine-François Brenier de Montmorand commanding the 9th Division, and General Jean-Baptise Girard leading the 10th Division, the III Corps had three, experienced Peninsular generals.[21] The commander of the 11th Division, General Etienne-Pierre-Sylvestre Ricard, was also a Peninsular veteran, as well as a former division commander in Davout's I Corps in Russia.[22] Added to these formations was the 39th Division under the command of General Jean-Gabriel Marchand,[23] consisting of Badenese and Hessian infantry.[24]

The IV Corps, which until the reorganization was known as the Observation Corps of Italy, was under the leadership of General Henri-Gatien Bertrand.[25] Bertrand, a talented engineer officer who had a long association as an Imperial aide to the Emperor, was literally pressed into service as a corps commander in 1813. The new responsibility was a much different experience for Bertrand, who had always been at Napoleon's side, even when

Marshal Victor Perrin, Duke of Belluno

Son of a notable royal family, Victor was born on 7 December 1764 and entered the Royal Army in 1781. A Général de brigade on 13 June 1795, he saw extensive service during the Revolution, most notably in the Army of Italy. He was Chief of Staff to Marshal Lannes in 1806 and commanded I Corps at Friedland on 14 June 1807. Promoted to Marshal of France the following month, Victor saw extensive service in the Peninsula and in Russia. In 1813, he handled II Corps with steady skill. *Musée de l'Armée.*

Count Henri–Gatien Bertrand

Born on 28 March 1773, Bertrand was one of Napoleon's closest friends and was present during most of the major campaigns of the Napoleonic era. An engineer by profession, he masterminded the bridge building over the Danube during the Wagram campaign. Despite not having prior experience, Bertrand was pressed into service as a corps commander in 1813. He performed extremely well at Leipzig. After 1813, Bertrand became Grand Marshal of the Palace. *Musée de l'Armée.*

he masterminded the building of the bridges over the Danube during the Wagram campaign.[26] Evidentally Napoleon thought Bertrand was up to the task of corps command as the Emperor appointed Bertrand without hesitation. As initially planned, Bertrand was to command the IV Corps consisting of four infantry divisions numbered 12 through 15, supposedly augmented with a cavalry brigade and an artillery reserve.[27] However, before the campaign began, Napoleon took two divisions away from IV Corps—namely the 13th and 14th Divisions—in order to create the XII Corps.[28] Of the two divisions which remained, the 12th Division was composed of French and Croatians[29] under the command of one of the best divisional generals in uniform—General Charles-Antoine Morand.[30] Meanwhile, the 15th Division consisted entirely of Italian troops[31], led by the relatively inexperienced Italian General Bernard Peri.[32] By the time hostilities began, the only cavalry to support IV Corps was a single regiment of Neapolitan Chasseurs à Cheval.[33] Also, when the corps moved out for war in late April, the artillery reserve was not yet organized.[34]

The V Corps—formerly the Observation Corps of the Elbe—was commanded by General Jacques de Law de Lauriston.[35] A former Imperial aide de camp to Napoleon, it was Lauriston who formed and commanded the grand battery at Wagram.[36] Like Bertrand, Lauriston, was given command of a corps for the first time in 1813. The V Corps was originally intended to have four infantry divisions numbered 16 through 19, plus an artillery reserve.[37] By April, only three divisions—the 16th, 18th, and 19th—formed entirely of regiments from the old cohorts were seemingly ready for war.[38] The 16th Division was commanded by General Nicholas-Joseph Maison[39] and the 18th Division headed by General Joseph Lagrange.[40] The 19th Division was commanded by 58 year-old General Donatien-Marie-Joseph de Vimeur Rochambeau, veteran of the American Revolutionary War, and former commander of the Army of Saint-Dominique, who was captured in 1803 and spent the following 8 years in a prisoner of war camp, being repatriated in 1811.[41] Thus, when Rochambeau took the reigns of the 19th Division, it was his first field command in 10 years. The remaining infantry division of Lauriston's command—the 17th under General Jaques Puthod—joined the corps in mid-May.[42] As the campaigned opened, the artillery reserve consisted of only single companies of artillery, engineers, and supply train personnel.[43]

With Napoleon's decree, the Second Observation Corps of the Rhine became the VI Corps of the *Grande Armée*. Named to lead this corps was Marshal Auguste-Frédéric-Louis Viesse de Marmont, the Duke of Ragusa.[44] An experienced corps commander and administrator, Marmont was perhaps the key person responsible for developing the tactical artillery doctrine and ordnance of the artillery System Year XI.[45] A superb artillerist in his own right, Marmont was, until 1812, one of Napoleon's favorite lieutenants.[46] With confidence in his command ability, the Emperor sent Marmont to the Peninsula in 1812[47] in the hopes that the Duke of Ragusa could salvage there the French military situation. Marmont began his campaign brilliantly by outmaneuvering Wellington in a series of hard marches. These bloodless victories seemed to have convinced Marmont that his opponent, the Duke of Wellington, did not want to risk battle. While the French marshal sent his army on a march to outflank the British army, Marmont seemed to have dropped his guard near the village of Salamanca. Wellington's keen eye immediately detected the strung out divisions of French and ordered his army to attack. In the ensuing battle, Marmont and his army were surprised and thrashed by Wellington's forces.[48] During this engagement at Salamanca, or known to the French as Arapiles, Marmont was severely wounded and had to return to France to convalesce.[49] Although the Emperor was furious at Marmont for the disaster at Arapiles, every experienced corps leader was needed for the struggle for Germany.

Charles–Antoine–Louis Morand

One of the most capable divisional infantry officers in uniform, Morand distinguished himself at Auerstädt, Eylau, Eckmühl, Wagram, and Borodino. In 1813, Morand brilliantly led his division at Wartenburg on 3 October 1813, and at Leipzig. At Leipzig, he spearheaded the attack of Bertrand's IV Corps which smashed Gyulai's Austrians on the Lindenau front. He continued his distinguished service record in 1814 and again during the Hundred Days.
Musée de l'Armée.

Count J. A. B. L. Lauriston

Born on 1 February 1768, Lauriston was educated at the École militaire in Paris. An artillerist, he saw service during the Revolution in the horse artillery and rose to the rank of Général de division on 1 February 1805. Lauriston was an aide de camp to Napoleon in 1809 and commanded the grand battery at Wagram. He served in Russia during 1812 and was appointed commander of the V Corps of the *Grande Armée* in 1813. Though captured at Leipzig, Lauriston was capable in his 1813 rôle. *Musée de l'Armée.*

With his arm still in a sling,[50] Marmont reported for duty on the Rhine where he organized, trained, and then led the famous VI Corps throughout the 1813 campaign.

The VI Corps was to consist of four infantry divisions, a cavalry brigade, and an artillery reserve.[51] By the end of April, only three infantry divisions—the 20th, 21st, and 22nd—and the artillery reserve were ready for war.[52] Two of Marmont's divison commanders were solid, proven commanders. General Jean-Dominique Compans and General Jean-Pierre-François Bonet, commanding the 20th and 21st Divisions, respectively, were experienced combat officers.[53] To these men were assigned the regiments from the naval artillery corps, each division having two regiments of *marins*. In command of the 22nd Division was General Jean-Parfait Friederichs.[54] His division, as well as the others of VI Corps, was comprised, at least in part, of temporary regiments.[55] The remaining infantry division of the corps—the 23rd—was being formed by General François-Antoine Teste[56] and could not be ready for action for at least two more months.[57] Although there were no corps cavalry in VI Corps by late April, it is no surprise that Marmont had a strong artillery reserve consisting of 24 pieces of ordnance in place for the start of the campaign.[58]

Marshal Marmont, Duke of Ragusa. Painting by Paul Guérin, *Musée de Versailles.*

There were several, smaller corps planned as well. The VII Corps, under the command of the veteran but always difficult General Jean Reynier,[59] was to consist of the 24th and 25th Divisions made up of newly conscripted Saxon infantry, along with the 32nd Division under General Pierre-François-Joseph Durutte comprised entirely of French infantry units formed from the Class of 1812.[60] The Poles were to raise two divisions of infantry—the 26th and 27th—to be the base for the VIII Corps under Polish Prince Pontiatowski,[61] while two divisions of Bavarians, namely the 28th and 29th Divisions, formed the Observation Corps of Bavaria,[62] later known as the IX Corps.[63] Both the VIII and IX Corps were not expected to be ready for service before summer.[64] However, one division of Bavarians was completed in time to take part in the spring campaign, being attached to Oudinot's XII Corps.[65] The X Corps officially did not exist except in name only as its place on the roster of the *Grande Armée* was known as the garrison of Danzig under the order of General Jean Rapp,[66] consisting of three divisions, namely the 7th, 30th—later replaced by the 34th—and the 33rd Divisions. Since this body of troops was not supposed to be an active corps, the title of X Corps was given to this garrison simply for memorial purposes only.[67]

Duchy of Warsaw, Infantry of the Line.

The XI and XII Corps of the new army were major formations. Marshal Etienne-Jacques-Joseph-Alexandre Macdonald, arguably the most loyal of all Napoleon's corps commanders, was given command of the XI Corps,[68] formerly the "advance guard" of the army, consisting of three divisions numbered 31st, 35th, and 36th, a cavalry brigade, and an artillery reserve.[69] The 31st Division under General Philibert Fressinet[70] consisted of five 4th battalions of French infantry plus two Neapolitan regiments.[71] The 35th Division, under the talented leadership of General Maurice-Etienne Gérard,[72] was a combination of French and Italian conscripts.[73] Meanwhile, the 36th Division led by General Henri-François-Marie Charpentier, former chief of staff to Eugène and then Davout,[74] was composed entirely of French infantry.[75] The corps had a cavalry brigade consisting of Italian and Wurzburg troopers but the corps artillery reserve had not yet materialized when the spring campaign opened.[76]

The XII Corps was created when Napoleon determined that a corps command was needed for Marshal Nicholas-Charles Oudinot. A steady, brave, but not a brillant man, Oudinot seemingly always led his troops from the front. By 1813, he had already suffered over 30 wounds at more than 20 battles.[77] A leader such as Oudinot was needed for the new army and in order to give the Duke of Reggio a corps command, the Emperor decided to split IV Corps. Doubtlessly influencing the Emperor's decision must have been the fact that Bertrand was new at corps command and might not be able to handle a full-strength corps of four infantry divisions and supporting troops. Therefore, the 13th and 14th Divisions were transferred from Bertrand's control to Marshal Oudinot.[78] At the head of the 13th Division was General Michel-Marie Pacthod,[79] whose command consisted of temporary regiments of French infantry and a brigade of Neapolitan light infantry.[80] General Lorencz commanded the 14th Division[81] composed of French conscripts and the 2nd battalion of the Illyrian Regiment.[82] Added to these commands was a division of unenthusiastic Bavarian conscripts under General Ragolvich.[83] By April 25, the XII Corps did field a corps artillery reserve of 8 pieces of ordnance, but no cavalry other than the 3 Bavarian chevauleger regiments that were part of General Ragolvich's command.[84]

Marshal Oudinot,
Musée de l'Armée

General Pacthod,
Musée de l'Armée

Further, Napoleon decreed the formation of other Allied infantry divisions. The 37th was to consist of Westphalians, the 38th was to made up of Württembergers, while the 39th Division, composed of Hessians and Badenese infantry, was already with Ney's III Corps when the campaign opened.[85]

In all corps, each infantry division was comprised of 2 or 3 brigades, each brigade typically consisting of 4 to 8 battalions, usually from 2 or 3 regiments. In some instances, such as with the *marins* and the old cohorts, a single regiment of 4 or more battalions was often a brigade. Cavalry brigades varied in size and strength, depending on the number of squadrons present. Ideally, each 1813 line infantry division was to be supported by two companies of foot artillery, each company consisting of eight piece of ordnance of which six were 6-pounder cannon and two were 5 1/2-inch howitzers. Each line infantry corps was suppose to have one of more companies of reserve artillery. These companies usually consisted of eight pieces of ordnance, of which six were 12-pounders and two 6-inch howitzers. Each line cavalry division was suppose to have one company of horse artillery attached. However, owing to the shortage of horses, the deployment of these batteries was slowed significantly.[86]

As the army began to take shape, Napoleon realized that his young infantry "uninstructed and without training"[87] were going to be exposed "to numerous cavalry charges."[88] To prepare his soldiers for this ordeal, the Emperor ordered his corps commanders to divide their training week thusly: two days a week to performing the manual of arms and musket drill; two days a week to target practice and the remaining three days to maneuvers.[89] During the days which maneuver drill occurred, only two battalion evolutions were commonly practiced. The formation change of going from attack column to square and then back to attack column were those recommended by Napoleon to be the most practiced evolutions.[90]

French line or light infantry battalion of 6 companies in attack column with all companies formed.

French guard battalion of 4 companies in attack column.

The Emperor's numerous letters on this subject bear unimpeachable evidence to his concern for the novice infantry which he would soon lead into battle and for the battalion formations which they were to use. The first of these appeared on February 8, when Napoleon wrote General Lauriston the following: "Busy yourself with the instruction of your troops. Above all, maneuvers of change of formation from attack column to square and back are recommended; exercise the battalion in column of attack, the first division [two companies] issuing fire, etc. The most important maneuver is for each battalion being able to promptly form square without hesitation."[91]

To Generals Bertrand and Lauriston and to Marshal Kellermann, the Emperor sent identical letters on March 2, which said: "Recommend to the generals who command your divisions to cause the troops to conduct the manual of arms and musket drill two days per week; that, two days a week, they will conduct live firing at targets; and the remainder of the week in maneuvers. They should deploy in columns of attack [two company front, or one division front] by battalion; they should conduct charges in columns of attack and to deploy with the front division issuing fire as soon as they arrive in the battle line... the center of the division will commence fire by file and will deploy with fire by file... You will also order that they often maneuver by promptly forming into battalion square, deploying the back and rear divisions of the battalion at a distance of a peloton, and firing by file. This is a maneuver which is necessary for the colonels to be well acquainted with, for there must be the least hesitation for the well-being of the troops.

"Finally, order that each company of voltigeurs be instructed to promptly form company square and immediately issue fire by file, allowing the skirmishers time to promptly reunite to resist the cavalry. Make sure enough gunpowder is available for these excercises, and announce that these are the particular maneuvers which I wish to see performed before me."[92]

Later that month, on March 27, Napoleon added more tactical advice to Bertrand: "The square forms itself indistinctively on any division [two companies] of troops in line, parallel or perpendicular to this line, and according to the circumstances and the nature of the terrain; from the Ordonnance given, I think, in 1805, there is an instruction on this subject that does not leave anything to be desired, but it is important to make it known to the soldiers who stay behind the troops to give warning of a potential attack from the rear to stay closer to the third rank, the square being formed to resist the cavalry. It is necessary that the company of voltigeurs always keep a formed reserve on which it can rally, when, being formed as skirmishers, will not be able to resist formed troops.

"The column of attack will always be formed according to the principles of the Ordonnance. However, if the battle line moves forward in this order, the first division [two companies at the head of each battalion], or head division of each column, will have bayonets at the ready. Then arriving where the battle line desires to halt, these head divisions will start firing from two ranks, and the columns will deploy under the protection of these gunshots.

"I would like, for this maneuver, more promptness than the rules state. This means that each peloton has to start firing upon arriving on the battle line...."[93]

On March 13, the Emperor instructed Marshal Ney: "Have a lot of live firing exercises at targets. You should also order a lot of maneuvers, practicing moving into and out from columns of attack with division frontage, and battalion squares, making sure that the battalion chiefs can promptly change into such formation when charged by enemy cavalry."[94]

French Line Infantry Regiment in 1813. *Composition by E. Detaille*
This is a painting of the 36th Line. In August, the 3rd and 4th battalions of the
36th Line formed part of the 2nd Brigade, 1st Division, of Vandamme's I Corps.

Also, Napoleon specifically told Marshal Marmont on April 17: "With regards to maneuvers, I recommend to you these formations to be most important: that is the attack column and battalion square. The battalion chiefs and the captains must be able to perform changes of formation with great rapidity; it is the only way to employ cover against the charging cavalry and to save the entire regiment."[95]

Undoubtably, the corps chiefs did what they could to help the drilling program. A memorandum from Marshal Macdonald to General Charpentier on April 11 states that the battalions of XI Corps were to "continue to be drilled primarily in attack column and square until the men can easily change from one formation to the other. This drill must be repeated until the battalions can perform it in their sleep."[96]

Other letters confirm that Napoleon's drilling instructions were being carried out, with most of the emphasis being placed on changes of formation from attack column to square and back to attack column. General Souham advised Marshal Ney on April 18 that "the battalions have a full day's drill practicing deploying into square and the reforming into attack column."[97] Another one of Marshal Ney's division generals, the veteran General Girard, reported on April 24 one of the most candid observations on record. "The battalions of my division can rapidly deploy from attack column to square and reform into attack column. But God help us if any other formation is asked."[98]

Inflexibility with the choice of formations used by the infantry was something new to the corps and division commanders in Napoleon's army. In earlier years of the Empire, highly-trained Napoleonic infantry were able to not only deploy in many more formations than just attack column and square, they were able to rapidly deploy in a number of other formations as well as effectively maneuver by regiment and by entire brigades. Being able to move in combat in multi-battalion and multi-regimental formations of many combinations offered enormous tactical flexibility and advantages, especially when pitted against opponents whose choice of formations and concept of coordination often times did not go above the regiment.

With the rebuilding of the army in 1813, the French marshals and generals needed time to teach their new infantry multi-battalion maneuvers. This was especially difficult to achieve, owing to the lack of officers and non-commissioned officers, and to the short period of time with which the army had to drill its formations before war broke out. General Lauriston voiced a strong opinion about the level of regimental drill on April 15, when he wrote to Prince Eugène about his regiments, which will be remembered were comprised entirely of old cohorts. "His Majesty must reasonably believe that, from the time the cohorts were brought together into a regiment, there must exist teamwork in maneuvers and in the make-up of the regiments; that does not exist at all."[99] Since all corps commanders were struggling to bring the level of drill up to regimental coordination, brigade drill for the new regiments was impossible. Except for the regiments of the Old and Middle Guard, as well as the 1st Regiments of the Young Guard Tirailleurs and Voltigeurs which were reconstituted with the instructional battalions of Fontainbleau,[100] and veteran 3rd Regiments of the Young Guard Tirailleurs and Voltigeurs, the entire army went to war in late April, 1813, with its infantry only being able to maneuver by battalion.[101]

On the same day that General Lauriston wrote Prince Eugène about his regiments being incapable of regimental-sized drill, Marshal Marmont penned an alarming report to Napoleon's chief of staff, Marshal Berthier. "I believe it is my duty to request you point out to His Majesty," wrote the Duke of Ragusa on April 15, "that he must not consider my army corps, in its present condition, as being at combat readiness. The reasons are numerous:

"1. The corps lacks officers. Well trained veteran troops would not be capable of moving out with such small number of officers, much the more reason with new [troops]...there are about 80 slots in which officers are needed for the corps. His Majesty ordered a large enough number of officers be sent to the two Observation Corps of the Rhine: all have been sent to the First [Observation] Corps [of the Rhine]...If His Majesty wants my troops to be promptly organized, it is necessary that he authorize me to have sent to the corps the individuals for whom he has been sent the reports.

"2. Only the 1st and 2nd Divisions [the 20th and 21st] have their artillery; the 3rd [the 22nd Division] has neither a cannon nor a caisson of ammunition.

"3. I don't have a single cavalryman...these regiments are needed before the corps moves out.

"4. The provisional regiments are, in my estimation, worthless. Their administration is nil; their battalion drill is marginal at best; and they are completely incapable of regimental maneuver. The regiments from the naval artillery corps are further advanced in their drill; their attitude is exceptional. Most all my infantrymen are untested in land combat.

"5. The corps entirely lacks surgeons.

"6. There is only one assistant to the command staff for the entire army corps. There is no quartermaster, neither for the divisions nor for general headquarters.

"Your Highness will sense that there is a large gathering of men here, but there is not an organized army, and that it would be fatal to the well being of His Majesty's service to put these troops in a position of encountering the enemy before being properly prepared for all that is needed."[102]

Marshal Ney's assessment of the army was even more blunt: "The machine no longer has either strength or cohesion: we need peace to reorganize everything...It would be folly to ensconce ourselves in Germany."[103]

These reports, written on the day which Napoleon left Paris for Germany and the army—only 17 days before the Battle of Lützen—were received by the Emperor upon his arrival in Mayence. Not having yet reviewed any troops of the new army, Napoleon quickly feigned to doubt these "stories of gloom."[104] However, inspections at Mayence quickly exposed many weaknesses of the new army's makeup[105] and Napoleon spent eight days in the Rhine city before proceeding to Erfurt, where the Imperial entourage arrived on April 25.[106]

Before his arrival in Erfurt, the Emperor had ordered parade states be taken for the entire *Grande Armée* on April 25, with Napoleon personally inspecting several corps from April 25 through the 27th, including the VI Corps on April 27.[107] Personal inspections by Napoleon were rigorous ordeals. If what Boulart and Marbot tell us in their memoires is true[108]—and there seems to be no reason to doubt either on this point—the officers and men of VI Corps went through a gut-wrenching experience on that April day. No detail was too small to escape Napoleon's attention. What was mentioned to him at these inspections seemed to be carefully stored and instantly available upon recall at a later time. Thus, with an incomparible depth of knowledge concerning his armed forces, and with a memory that virtually defied all human aptitude, Napoleon scrupulously reviewed Marmont's command.

It is not known what conversations the Emperor had with the officers of VI Corps on April 27, but the results of his inspection are preserved in Napoleon's outraged letter to Clarke, his Minister of War. "I have just seen the 37th Light Infantry; it is impossible to see a corps with finer soldiers, but impossible at the same time to see one with worse officers. If your office had undertaken to name the most inept officers in France, it would not have succeeded better; these officers are an object of derision for the soldiers...The majority of the captains have never been under fire...I am going to be obliged to dismiss and to send back all these officers. You also are sending me young people coming from schools and who have not been to Saint-Cyr, so that they don't know anything, and it is in the new regiments that you are placing them!...".[109]

The April 25 parade states for the entire army were immediately and carefully examined by Napoleon. As skirmishes were already signalling the advance of the Russian and Prussian forces into central Germany, the Emperor at last knew the real strength of his army. Amongst the line corps, the Emperor found only the III (Ney), IV (Bertrand), V (Lauriston), VI (Marmont), XI (Macdonald), and XII (Oudinot) in ready enough shape to be pressed into the field. Reynier's Saxon infantry divisions of VII Corps had not yet been reconstituted and therefore his only field formation was the single, weak French 32nd Division under the orders of General Durutte. Meanwhile, the divisions comprising I and II Corps were nowhere near ready to face the enemy.[110]

However, most disappointing was the state of the reserve cavalry corps, which could only field the diminutive I and II Reserve Cavalry Corps commanded respectively by Generals Latour-Maubourg and Sébastiani. The I Reserve Cavalry Corps had, at least on paper, four divisions of cavalry, two of which consisted of light cavalry and two of which were heavy cavalry.[111] The 1st Light Cavalry Division was commanded by General Pierre-Joseph Bruyères, who was one in a long line of distinguished colonels of the 23rd Chasseurs à Cheval.[112] The 3rd Light Cavalry Division was led by General Louis-Pierre-Aimé Chastel, a former officer in the Grenadiers à Cheval of the Guard, who had been promoted to *général de division* in 1812 and served under Grouchy during the Russian campaign.[113] The commander of the 1st Cuirassier Division was General Etienne Tardif de Pommeroux Bordesoulle, an experienced light cavalry officer who was given his first heavy cavalry command in 1813.[114] The 3rd Cuirassier Division was led by veteran heavy cavalry leader General Jean-Pierre Doumerc. Each of the four cavalry divisions of Latour-Maubourg's corps more resembled a weak brigade than they did a division. By late April, there were no horse artillery units assigned to I Reserve Cavalry Corps although three companies totalling 18 pieces of ordnance had joined the corps before the Battle of Bautzen.[115]

Sébastiani's II Reserve Cavalry Corps did manage to have a single company of horse artillery by April 25, but only 3 very small divisions were in the field. In actuality, the 2nd Light Cavalry Division under General Roussel d'Hurbal was hardly the strength of a regiment as it fielded 2 squadrons, for a meager total of 322 officers and other ranks![116] Even with small numbers, the II Reserve Cavalry Corps was needed for active duty. The other reserve cavalry corps would not be ready until sometime in middle or late May.[117]

The Imperial Guard was no where near its former strength, consisting on April 25 of 3 infantry divisions and 2 cavalry divisions. The 1st Guard Infantry Division was under the command of General Pierre Dumoustier, former colonel of the 34th Regiment of the Line.[118] The 2nd Guard Infantry Division was commanded by General Pierre Barrois, a veteran of Spain from 1808 until late December, 1812.[119] Meanwhile, the Old Guard Infantry Division was led by the crusty, distinguished veteran General François Roguet. The Guard cavalry divisions were led by familiar faces. General Charles Lefebvre-Desnoüettes, one of the favorite light cavalry generals in the army, commanded the 1st Guard Cavalry Division, while General Frédéric-Henri Walther, commander of the Grenadiers à Cheval of the Guard, led the 2nd Guard Cavalry Division. The Guard artillery was led by two officers of opposite qualities. General Charles-François Dulauloy, the overall commander of the Guard artillery, was a "grasping, unreliable"[120] man. On the other hand, the Guard horse artillery was commanded by the superb, incomparible horse gunner General Jean-Jacques Desvaux de Saint-Maurice.

Closer inspection of the returns revealed the true numbers of troops ready for combat on April 25, 1813.[121]

III Corps Ney	# of bns/sqd	Strength of inf. & cav.	Average per battalion/sqdrn	Guns	Artillerists, engineers, train, etc
8th Division	16 / --	12,491	781 / --	16	635
9th Division	15 / --	9,488	633 / --	16	564
10th Division	14 / --	8,121	580 / --	16	394
11th Division	14 / --	7,953	568 / --	16	553
39th Division	10 / --	6,950	695 / --	7	250
Corps Cavalry	-- / 7	1,217	--- / 174	--	----
Corps Artillery Reserve				--*	573
Corps Totals:	69 / 7	46,220	652 / 174	71	2,969

*III Corps artillery reserve was in route, but had not yet arrived.

III Corps net strength of 49,189 present and under arms, of which:

45,003, or 91.5% of the corps were infantry,

1,217, or 2.5% of the corps were cavalry, and

2,969, or 6% of the corps were artillerists and other support troops.

III Corps artillery ratio on April 25 was 1 gun for every 693 combatants.

IV Corps Bertrand	# of bns/sqd	Strength of inf. & cav.	Average per battalion/sqdrn	Guns	Artillerists, engineers, train, etc
12th Division	13 / --	9,392	722 / --	16	465
15th Division	13 / --	9,444	726 / --	20	520
Corps Cavalry	-- / 2	515	--- / 257	--	----
Corps Artillery Reserve				--*	455
Corps Totals:	26 / 2	19,351	724 / 257	36	1,440

*IV Corps artillery reserve was in route, but had not yet arrived.

IV Corps net strength of 20,791 present and under arms, of which:

18,836, or 90.5% of the corps were infantry,

515, or 2.5% of the corps were cavalry, and

1,440, or 7% of the corps were artillerists and other support troops.

IV Corps artillery ratio on April 25 was 1 gun for every 578 combatants.

V Corps Lauriston	# of bns/sqd	Strength of inf. & cav.	Average per battalion/sqdrn	Guns	Artillerists, engineers, train, etc
16th Division	7 / --	4,707	672 / --	22	637
18th Division	12 / --	6,931	578 / --	16	421
19th Division	12 / --	7,755	646 / --	22	732
There was no corps cavalry nor any corps artillery reserve at this time.					
Corps Totals:	31 / --	19,393	626 / --	60	1,790

V Corps net strength of 21,183 present and under arms, of which:

> 19,393, or 91.5% of the corps were infantry, and
> 1,790, or 8.5% of the corps were artillerists and other support troops.
> V Corps artillery ratio on April 25 was 1 gun for every 353 combatants.

VI Corps Marmont	# of bns/sqd	Strength of inf. & cav.	Average per battalion/sqdrn	Guns	Artillerists, engineers, train, etc
20th Division	12 / --	8,439	703 / --	16	488
21st Division	12*/ -	8,351*	696 / --	16	425
22nd Division	14 / --	7,677	548 / --	14	403
There was no corps cavalry at this time.					
Corps Artillery Reserve				24	797
Corps Totals:	38* / -	24,467*	644	70	2,113

VI Corps net strength of 26,580* present and under arms, of which:

> 24,467, or 92% of the corps were infantry, and
> 2,113, or 8% of the corps were artillerists and other support troops.
> VI Corps artillery ratio on April 25 was 1 gun for every 350 combatants.

> *There were 5 infantry battalions totalling 3,646 officers and other ranks
> marching with the 21st Division on their way to join the 32nd Division
> of VII Corps when parade states were taken on April 25. These battalions
> are not included in the numbers shown for VI Corps.

VII Corps Reynier	# of bns/sqd	Strength of inf. & cav.	Average per battalion/sqdrn	Guns	Artillerists, engineers, train, etc
32nd Division	5* / --	896*	179 / --	4	62
Corps Totals:	5* / --	896*	179 / --	4	62

VII Corps net strength of 958* present and under arms, of which:

> 896, or 93.5% of the corps were infantry, and
> 62, or 6.5% of the corps were artillerists and other support troops.

> *On May 1, the 5 infantry battalions marching with the 21st Division of VI Corps—which on April 25 totalled 3,646 officers and other ranks— arrived to reinforce the 32nd Division. Also, note that the Saxon divisions of the VII Corps were still reforming and were not present on April 25.

XI Corps Macdonald	# of bns/sqd	Strength of inf. & cav.	Average per battalion/sqdrn	Guns	Artillerists, engineers, train, etc
31st Division	6*/ --	3,383*	554** / --	12	305
35th Division	13 / --	8,755	673 / --	14	554
36th Division	11 / --	8,666	788 / --	24	396
Corps Cavalry	-- / 2	278	--- / 139	--	----
There was no corps artillery reserve at this time.					
Corps Totals:	30* / 2	21,082*	693** / 139	50	1,255

XI Corps net strength of 22,337 present and under arms, of which:

> 20,804, or 93% of the corps were infantry,
> 278, or 1% of the corps were cavalry, and
> 1,255, or 6% of the corps were artillerists and other support troops.
> XI Corps artillery ratio on April 25 was 1 gun for every 447 combatants.

> * Includes one company of Neapolitan Marines consisting of 2 officers and 60 other ranks present and under arms.
> ** This figure does not include the company of marines.

XII Corps Oudinot	# of bns/sqd	Strength of inf. & cav.	Average per battalion/sqdrn		Guns	Artillerists, engineers, train, etc
13th Division	13 / --	8,274	636	/ --	16	592
14th Division	12 / --	8,011	668	/ --	16	627
29th Division	10 / 6	7,538	684	/ 116	16	157
There was no corps cavalry at this time.						
Corps Artillery Reserve					8	1,152
Corps Totals:	35 / 6	23,823	661	/ 116	56	2,371

XII Corps net strength of 26,194 present and under arms, of which:

> 23,127, or 89% of the corps were infantry,
> 696, or 2% of the corps were cavalry, and
> 2,371, or 6% of the corps were artillerists and other support troops.
> XII Corps artillery ratio on April 25 was 1 gun for every 468 combatants.

Imperial Guard	# of bns/sqd	Strength of inf. & cav.	Average per battalion/sqdrn		Guns	Artillerists, engineers, train, etc
1st Gd Inf Div	16 / --	9,429	589	/ --	52*#	2,241
2nd Gd Inf Div	11 / --	7,371	670	/ --	38	2,407
Old Gd Inf Div	8 / 2	3,026	352	/ 106	20	594
1st Gd Cav Div	-- / 8	1,422	---	/ 178	--**	**
2nd Gd Cav Div	-- / 10+	1,913	---	/ 191++	--**	**
Guard Artillery Reserve—in route					***	***
Corps Totals:	35 / 17	23,161	560	/ 209	110	5,242

Imperial Guard net strength of 28,403 present and under arms, of which:

> 19,613, or 69% of the corps were infantry,
> 3,548, or 12.5% of the corps were cavalry, and
> 5,242, or 18.5% of the corps were artillerists and other support troops.
> Guard artillery ratio on April 25 was 1 gun for every 258 combatants.

* This total included 2 companies of Old Guard *Volante* (Horse Artillery) which were later detached for service with the cavalry divisions.
** Old Guard *Volante* companies are included with 1st Guard Infantry Division.
*** There was a single company of Old Guard 12-pdr. foot artillery (8 pieces of ordnance) present with the 1st Guard Infantry Division on April 25; it was later joined by 3 more 12-pdr foot companies, all of which then served as the reserve artillery for the corps.
+ There was a single company of Gendarmes d'élite totalling 53 officers and other ranks present in the 2nd Guard Cavalry Division.
++ This average excludes the company of Gendarmes d'élite.
# The third company of Old Guard *Volante* joined the division prior to the Battle of Lützen, raising the number of guns with the 1st Guard Infantry Division to a total of 58.

I Reserve Cav. Corps	# of sqdms	Strength of cavalry	Average per squadron	Guns	Artillerists & train personnel
1st Lt Cav Div	9	602*	75*	--	----
3rd Lt Cav Div	9	931	103	--	----
1st Cuirass Div	6	753	126	--	----
3rd Cuirass Div	8	646	81	--	----
Corps Totals:	32	2,932	92	--	----

I Reserve Cavalry Corps net strength was 2,932 officers and other ranks.

* Only 8 regiments (each regiment with only a single squadron) filed returns. This strength and average based on the 8 reporting regiments.

The I Reserve Cavalry Corps had a "division de marche" forming in Gotha and Hanau in preparation to move to join the corps. On April 25, this formation totalled 2,194 officers and other ranks.

II Reserve Cav. Corps	# of sqdrns	Strength of cavalry	Average per squadron	Guns	Artillerists & train personnel
2nd Lt Cav Div	3	322	107	--	----
4th Lt Cav Div	11	1,480*	135**	--	----
2nd Cuirass Div	7	768	109	--	----
Corps Artillery				6	125
Corps Totals:	21	2,570	122**	6	125

II Reserve Cavalry Corps net strength was 2,695 officers and other ranks, of which:

        2,570, or 95% of the corps were cavalry, and
        125, or 5% of the corps were artillerists and support personnel.

* The 4 squadrons of the 23rd Chasseurs à Cheval numbered 718 of this total.
** If the 23rd Chasseurs à Cheval are excluded from this calculation, the average squadron strength for the remaining units is only 84 combatants. Marbot's 23rd Chasseurs à Cheval had an average squadron strength of 180 combatants.

Note: On April 25, the III, IV, and V Reserve Cavalry Corps were in the early stages of organization and were not yet ready for active service. There were also many other infantry divisions not shown in this summary that were organizing at this time and joined the army during the course of the campaign. The complete listing of the *Grande Armée* on 25 April 1813 is shown in Appendix A.

Since the various corps which could be called on to fight were in two general areas—the middle Elbe River area and the vicinity of the Main River—Napoleon decided to split the *Grande Armée* in two, each part named for the river around which it organized.[122] The Emperor would be with the Army of the Main, commanded by Marshal Soult, while his step-son, Prince Eugène, commanded the Army of the Elbe.[123] On April 25, Prince Eugène's army (excluding the Old Guard Infantry Division under Rouget which was marching with the Army of the Elbe on its way to join the rest of the Guard present with the Army of the Main) consisted of approximately 53,700 combatants from the V, VII (including the battalions marching with VI Corps destined for the VII Corps), XI Corps, plus Latour-Maubourg's and Sebastiani's frail I and II Reserve Cavalry Corps.[124] On that same day, the Army of the Main numbered approximately 151,000 effectives from the III, IV, VI, and XII Corps, and the Imperial Guard.[125] Excluding the formations being organized and not yet formally in the field, as well as those on the move to join the *Grande Armée*, the Emperor's combat-ready formations on April 25, 1813, numbered roughly 205,000 combatants and 463 pieces of ordnance,[126] representing a gun-to-troop ratio of 1 : 443. This ratio would become more favorable during the campaign as many more artillery companies joined the army while on campaign and as the losses through strategic consumption mounted.

Even with more artillery on the way, the *Grande Armée* still had two seriously debilitating handicaps—its lack of cavalry and its deficient administrative arm. As the army readied itself for war on April 25, only 11,700, or less than 6% of the combatants present and under arms, were cavalry. In previous years of the Empire, the Imperial forces led by Napoleon had always boasted of a numerous cavalry arm which typically comprised of 15% to 20% of the army's combatants.[127] However, regardless of this handicap, Napoleon ordered his young army to war over terrain which was well suited to cavalry because the rich countryside of Saxony was vital in supplying his army with food. Hence, the Emperor's repeated instructions to his corps commanders to have the troops repeatedly drilled in forming square to repulse hostile cavalry should once again be duly noted.

The administrative service, which was expected to provide sustenance for the young soldiers, was still crippled from men and materiel lost in Russia. Count Daru, the director of army administration, realized the inadequacy of his branch before the start of hostilities. "As mentioned in my prior correspondence," Daru wrote to Berthier on April 20, "Your Highness is aware of what I feel is a dangerous shortage of officers, horses, and transports for the [administrative] service. Very little has improved since my last letter...I am of the opinion that His Majesty's well being may be jeopardize if we are to take the field in our present condition."[128] The army's Intendant General, Count Dumas, was equally concerned about the ability of the army's administration. "Sire, without sufficient officers and equipment," Dumas wrote the Emperor on April 16, "the administration of the army cannot be satisfactory. I fear the consequences if we are not able to properly feed our troops."[129] The *Grande Armée* of 1813 would march to war with many questionable characteristics.

Anticipating some of the limitations of his young troops, the Emperor sent a communique to all corps commanders on April 27. "The campaign which we are about to undertake will make it necessary for you to show the best example for all the officers and men...His Majesty believes that leadership will overcome our deficiencies."[130] It is certain that Napoleon reasoned that the French officer corps was to be a critical factor in the upcoming campaign. In this regard, the Emperor was determined to lead by example, and that victory would follow regardless of the army's makeup or shortages. "In war, morale considerations account for three-quarters, the balance of the actual forces only for the other quarter."[131] As the month of April, 1813, came to a close, the great captain who was the author of that well known phrase was about to once again prove that very point.

The Conscripts of 1813. *Lithograph by Raffet.*

CHAPTER V
"Overpowered by Children"

In mid-April, as Napoleon was on his way from Paris to join the army, the Russians and Prussians began crossing the Elbe River below Magdebourg,[1] heralding the renewal of hostilities. The spring campaign of 1813 ushered in a new era in Napoleonic history. The French military was not the only army crippled by the 1812 campaign, or composed almost entirely of conscripts. The Russians, too, had suffered grievous casualties the preceding year. Failing to receive adequate reinforcements to make good their losses, the battalions of the Tsar remained woefully understrength.[2] Meanwhile, the Prussians had been coerced French allies in 1812 and had not escaped the Russian ordeal unscathed. One of Prussia's largest problems in going to war in 1813 was her lack of well-trained infantry, most of her army being reservist, or landwehr, regiments.

Thus, for the first time in Napoleonic history, the spring campaign in Germany pitted opposing armies which were all of questionable combat value. With notable unit exceptions aside, the 1813 armies had low quality infantry, most of which had been conscripted into service, or were volunteers without adequate training. The result of having relatively few well-trained infantry was that the army commanders had to rely more heavily than ever on their artillery arm. The battles of 1813 would dramatically reflect this change.

As expected, the Allied armies fielded superior numbers in the theater of war, but their main advantage—and the one with which Napoleon was gravely concerned—was their numerical superiority in cavalry. When the campaign opened, the Russians and Prussians fielded approximately 25,000 regular cavalry, 11,000 landwehr cavalry, plus another 14,000 Cossacks.[3] To oppose all these horsemen, Napoleon had less than 12,000 cavalry in the saddle, or a French cavalry deficit of about 4 to 1. Although more French cavalry would join the *Grande Armée* during the campaign, this shortcoming would indeed prove to be one of the Emperor's biggest handicaps. Despite the numerical inferiority in the mounted arm, Napoleon's new army still maintained a clear-cut advantage in leadership at the corps, divisional, and brigade level. However, the officers at the regimental, battalion, and company level were typically no where near the equals of those who had once served during the early or middle years of the Empire. Finally, Napoleon's military machine still boasted a distinctive qualitative edge over the Allied armies in its artillery branch—both in officers and well as men. This superiority would be fully exploited by the Emperor many times throughout 1813.

Prior to the major battles of the spring campaign—destined to be fought at Lützen and Bautzen—the pattern of behavior of the French soldiers was established both on and off the battlefield. In the face of the enemy, the young *soldats* behaved well enough, provided that they had immediate artillery support. The first evidence of this is seen at the "siege" of Wittemberg from April 17 to April 24, 1813. During this two week period, some 3,000 French conscripts under the command of Baron La Poype were surrounded and besieged by Wittgenstein's Russian army corps. Behind makeshift earthworks, La Poype's young soldiers repulsed attack after repeated attack. In some cases, the French beat back Russians in excess of four times their own number. Finally, after suffering over 1,000 casualties and 14 days of frustration, Wittgenstein withdrew his corps.[4]

The new French infantry also performed well in other skirmishes leading up to the action at Weissenfels on April 29. In several clashes against Russian cavalry, Cossacks, and Prussian cavalry, the conscripts of Napoleon's army were undaunted by their opponents. In each skirmish, the French *fantassins* would form square and, supported by their artillery, easily drive the Allied horsemen from the field.

Most of the French corps and divisional commanders were well aware of the importance of keeping many cannon around the new infantry regiments for more reasons than just fending off enemy cavalry. Marshal Davout's comment to Prince Eugène on May 1 is indicative of the opinions expressed by many senior officers. "All these battalions [I Corps] are, without exception, recruits, full of high morale; but were they led against enemy artillery without having any [artillery], one would destroy their morale forever and one would be open to great misfortunes."[5] As already seen in prior chapters, Napoleon also realized the importance of his artillery arm, as echoed in his previously mentioned analogy to the Egyptian campaign. "We will fall back on the battles in Egypt," Napoleon said. "Good infantry, supported by artillery, must be able to sustain itself." Thus, the Emperor constantly strove more than anything else to increase the numbers of his cannon in order to make up for the deficiencies of his young soldiers.

The fruit of these labors quickly paid off when, on April 29, Souham's 8th Division of Marshal Ney's III Corps engaged a large corps of Russian cavalry supported by numerous Cossacks near Weissenfels.[6] The confrontation was one of contrasts. The Russians were all mounted troops and a battery of horse artillery; the French possessed only infantry and foot artillery. The Russian cavalry tried to panic the young French infantry with a series of sudden charges that were pressed home with valor. To repulse these horsemen, Souham's men transformed their formations into battalion squares and, with the divisional 6-pounder foot artillery companies working at top speed, withstood charge after charge. With Souham's infantry standing solidly in square, and lacking their own infantry support, the Russian cavalry had little hope for a favorable outcome. However, the Russians remained undaunted and continued to reform their regiments after each repulse.

Sensing that he had the upper hand in the action, Souham ordered his division to advance. The squares moved towards the enemy while the artillerists manhandled their pieces forward in support of the attack. After four hours of fighting, the stubborn Russian cavalry had had enough. With men exhausted and horses spent, assailed by squares of French infantry advancing in checkerboard formation supported by artillery, the Russian horse withdrew leaving the battlefield to Souham and his men.[7]

Although only a minor action in the sense of a Napoleonic battle, the combat at Weissenfels proved that the new French infantry could, if properly readied and deployed in square, easily repulse unsupported cavalry. Souham's assessment of his troops in this combat was one of measured optimisim. "The officers and men of my division behaved with the greatest courage," he reported to the Prince of the Moscowa, "although meeting enemy cavalry and artillery without infantry proved beneficial and to our cause."[8] Eager to show his master the combat quality of his men, Marshal Ney wrote ecstatically to Imperial headquarters about the outcome at Weissenfels. "This engagement," he informed Berthier that evening, "which can be considered a great success by the importance of its effect on morale, does the greatest honor to Souham's division. I have never seen in any body of troops an enthusiasm equal to that of these battalions, finding themselves for the first time before the enemy, moving forward on the cavalry and artillery to the cries of *Vive l'Empereur!* and repeating that cry after the enemy's retreat like a chant of victory. This

Marshal Michel Ney, Prince of the Moscowa

One of the most celebrated—and most criticized—of Napoleon's marshals, Ney was both a blessing and a burden to the Emperor. When under the close supervision of Napoleon, Ney could accomplish almost anything. When left unsupervised—such as in the rôle of an army wing commander— Ney often failed repeatedly. Nevertheless, Ney's unmatched bravery inspired fanatical efforts from his troops. *Musée de l'Armée.*

Count Joseph Souham

One of the older generals of the *Grande Armée*, Souham was born on 30 April 1760, and saw extensive service during the Revolution. His talents were quickly rewarded as he rose to the rank of Général de division by 1793. He fell into disgrace in 1804 for his relations with Moreau, but was reinstated into the service in 1807. During 1813, Souham very ably commanded III Corps, being wounded at Lützen and again at Leipzig. *Musée de l'Armée.*

spectacle was worthy of His Majesty's eyes and must strengthen his opinion of these young soldiers, who became veterans in a single day."[9]

By reading and comparing these two reports, it is easy to see that Souham's cooler head did not let himself get carried away by his victory. Ney, on the other hand, heaped excessive praise on the new troops—soon to be a common occurrance with many marshals, generals, and even Napoleon himself. However, despite Ney's oration, the Prince of the Moscowa knew that one battle did not a veteran make. "A single day is not enough to make a veteran soldier out of a conscript," wrote the great French army historian Camille Rousset. "He [Ney] was well aware that this enthusiastic gallantry, this intoxication of first engagement cannot be confused with the sustained, cold, reasoned courage of every day and of every hour; that this courage doesn't even make up the complete soldier, that other military virtues must be added to it, patience, perseverence, especially obedience and respect for discipline, and that barring a miracle, those virtues, which are not innate in the conscript, cannot be acquired in one day."[10] Upon receiving word of Souham's victory at Weissenfels, the Emperor instructed Berthier on April 30 that: "You will announce to the Viceroy [Prince Eugène] the engagement of the Prince of the Moscowa where the soldiers covered themselves with glory."[11] The spring campaign had started out on the right note for the *Grande Armée*.

The Emperor Directing the Advance of the *Grande Armée*, April 1813.
Composition by Desvarreux.

However, military operations are much more than just combat. After Weissenfels, the Emperor's young soldiers soon discovered some of the true meanings of war—the daily drudgery of campaigning and the deprivation of which it is so much a part. Napoleon's own maxim clearly illustrates what was expected of a good soldier. "The first qualification of a soldier is fortitude under fatigue and privation, courage is only second; hardship, poverty, and want are the best school for the soldier."[12] Thus, it was in conduct off the battlefield that the young soldiers of Napoleon's army would be tested the most severely, and there they would fall woefully short.

From the first day that the divisions and corps moved out for the spring campaign, most of the troop formations of the Emperor's army displayed poor march discipline. Any army of any age had to have strict march discipline if its men were to survive off the battlefield and win on the battlefield. Discipline was needed to insure that the men took care of themselves; discipline was vital to keep the unit together while marching to avoid the temptations of marauding and desertion; and discipline was mandatory to enforce orders up and down the chain of command. Units with sensible, strict discipline, enforced by capable officers and non-coms, inevitably arrived on the battlefield with more men than units with lax leadership and discipline. This was of obvious importance because the more men that arrived on the field of battle, the better the odds for victory.

Considering the shortages in so many of the new French formations of officers and non-commissioned officers, coupled with the young age of most of the conscripts, and the lack of proper administrative support, it is of little surprise that Napoleon's infantry exhibited poor discipline off the battlefield. Such indiscipline was soon brought to the Emperor's attention. On the same day in which he instructed Berthier to advise Prince Eugène of the victory at Weissenfels, Napoleon wrote to Ney about the lack of march discipline in III Corps. "They are complaining," said the Emperor on April 30, "that your troops are committing many disasters so that villages are being abandoned; it is a bad calamity; put things in order there."[13] It was therefore less than one week into the campaign and already there were signs of a serious weakness in the army—poor march discipline resulting in both officers and enlisted men leaving the ranks. It was the ominous beginning of an unfortunate characteristic destined to drain the *Grande Armée* of more and more valuable manpower as the campaign wore on. This loss of men through strategic consumption ultimately proved to be one of the main reasons for Napoleon agreeing to an armistice in June, despite a series of battlefield victories.

Following the action at Weissenfels, the first major engagement of the spring campaign was fought at Lützen on May 2, 1813. The rolling Saxon countryside had been the sight of a famous battle during the Thirty Years' War, where Gustavus Adolphus was killed in 1632 while at the head of his Swedish army.[14] The 1813 Battle of Lützen began about midday[15] when Ney's III Corps, acting as the advance guard[16] of the *Grande Armée*, was assailed by Wittgenstein's army, the lead elements of which were two corps of eager Prussians under the command of Blücher and Yorck.[17] Heavily outnumbered and outgunned, Ney's troops at first put up a stiff resistance. However, after only two hours[18] the Allied attack became too much for Ney's inexperienced conscripts. Initially, they began to lose ground by "slowly falling back while maintaining formation."[19] Soon the combination of retrograde motion and enemy pressure took its toll; battalion after battalion lost cohesion, broke ranks, and fled. The situation was rapidly becoming critical and the entire III Corps was on the verge of collapse when Napoleon arrived on the scene at 2:30 P.M. at the head of Bertrand's IV Corps, Marmont's VI Corps, Macdonald's XI Corps, and the Imperial Guard.[20]

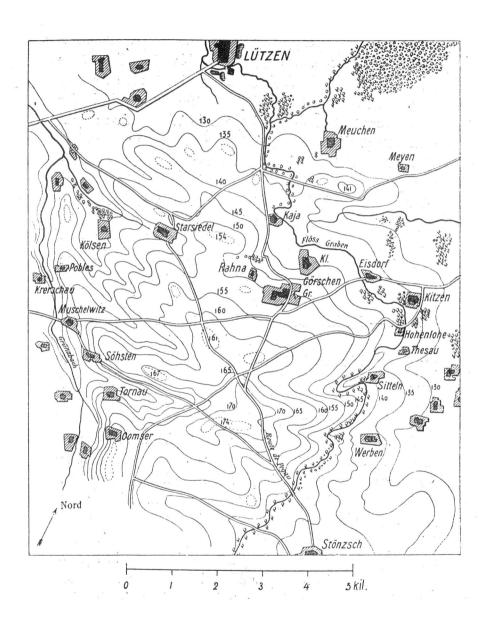

The Battlefield of Lützen, 2 May 1813.

Vive l'Empereur! **Arrival of Napoleon on the battlefield of Lützen.**
Lithograph by Raffet.

First stopping the panic in the infantry battalions of III Corps by placing the cavalry of the Old Guard in the path of Ney's troops,[21] Napoleon then quickly surveyed the battlefield. The Emperor decided to anchor his center with a grand battery of 80 guns consisting of 58 pieces of the Imperial Guard and 22 guns from Marmont's reserve artillery.[22] Napoleon selected General Antoine Drouot to command the grand battery.[23] To provide protection for these guns, a combined arms team consisting of the infantry of the Old Guard and the Imperial Guard cavalry were positioned at the corners and behind the pieces. Once Drouot's grand battery swung into action, Napoleon brought his other corps into the line of battle to vigorously counter attack or to pin the enemy to his present positions.

Never before had Napoleon so constantly exposed himself to enemy fire as he did at Lützen.[24] Rallying troops, leading attacks, directing the fire of artillery companies, the Emperor and his staff seemed to be everywhere that May afternoon. Napoleon's presence animated the troops as they responded to his courage and leadership. Meanwhile, as the other corps took their place in the line of battle, Drouot pushed his 80 guns into "canister range of the enemy"[25] where he recalled that "the deadly blasts from our guns cut down the enemy by the thousands."[26] With the middle of Wittgenstein's line being blown away, Napoleon sensed that the battle was ripe. The Emperor gave the order: *"La Garde au feu!"* [27] Marshal Mortier, assisted by four Imperial aides de camp—Flahaut, Dejean, Lebrun, and Cordineau[28]—led forward 16 battalions[29] of the Middle and Young Guard to break the enemy center. A fifth Imperial aide de camp, the Count of Lobau, placed himself at the head of General Ricard's rallied 11th Division of III Corps. Animated by the leadership of Lobau, these conscripts debouched from the village of Kaja, attacked and pushed back the Prussian Guards between the villages of Rahna and Klein Görschen.[30]

The Emperor rallying the conscripts of the broken battalions from Ney's III Corps at Lützen.

The Guardsmen were formed into four separate columns, each column consisting of one brigade of four battalions and led by an Imperial aide de camp.[31] The introduction of superbly led, fresh reserves into the line of battle, which was being swept by a murderous artillery fire from 80 pieces of ordnance, proved too much for the tiring Allies. General Flahaut de la Billarderie, one of Napoleon's aides de camp, vividly recalled the assault in his after action report. "The Emperor ordered four Imperial aides to accompany the troops of the Guard selected for the attack. I accompanied General Berthezène at the head of the Fusiliers of the Guard. This brave general and his fine troops had earlier attacked and routed the enemy from their positions around Kaja; the men comprising the Fusiliers were all veteran soldiers and their discipline and élan were no match for our adversaries: the Fusiliers were supremely confident of victory.

"The signal to advance being given, our brigade moved out, and eventually passed by the left flank of the grand battery. The discharges from these pieces were deafening and the smoke covered the field, obscuring our view. Our battalions were formed in attack column of two pelotons [companies] width and rapidly traversed the ground already devastated by the day's fighting. We passed over the wreckage of entire regiments which had been cut down by our guns. At times, the enemy dead and wounded were so thick that our men's feet did not touch the ground. My horse hesitated often as it looked for firm footing.

"The enemy could not withstand our advance. They fired a few, sporadic volleys, broke ranks, and fled before our bayonets. His Majesty can be pleased with the soldiers of the Guard who carried this attack into the heart of the enemy line."[32]

Yorck and Blücher's Prussians broke.[33] Soon thereafter, some of the Russians who had not been in the fight as long as the Prussians, likewise gave way.[34] The disorganized retreat by so many low quality troops soon degenerated into a general panic. Within minutes, the center of the Allied army was reduced to a terror-stricken mob and routed from the field.[35] The new *Grande Armée* had won the day.

Napoleon's victory at Lützen was, however, limited due to the lack of cavalry which prevented the Emperor from pursuing *à l'outrance* the defeated foe. As it was, pursuit was left to Marmont's VI Corps.[36] However, Wittgenstein still had plenty of troops under control, but the majority of his remaining infantry were already committed to action on the Allied right flank. He therefore ordered several brigades of Prussian cavalry and divisions of Russian horse to arrest the advance of Marmont[37] to allow the Allied army time to break-away from the engagement. Soon, thousands of Allied cavalry swirled around Marmont's battalions. Attempting to react to this charge, a few of the battalions from provisional regiments in Bonet's 21st Division did not form square[38] and were ridden down. Marmont and his staff narrowly escaped capture[39] before finding refuge in a square of *marins*.[40] Like the battalions from the naval artillery corps, most of the infantry of VI Corps successfully formed square and these fire-ringed bastions repulsed the Allied cavalry, but not before the horsemen achieved their goal of bringing the advance of VI Corps to a halt.[41]

The Young Guard at Lützen, 2 May 1813. *Composition by F. Robiquet.*

Analysis of the French victory soon followed. The first was authored that evening when the Emperor dictated one of his famous bulletins. This report, in part, read: "Our center gave way; a few battalions broke ranks. But these brave youths, at the sight of the Emperor, rallied shouting *Vive l'Empereur!*...His Majesty scarcely knew how to praise the good will, the courage and the boldness of the army. Our young soldiers didn't think of the danger. In this great moment, they revealed all the nobility of French blood... I have been commanding the French armies for 20 years; I have never before seen so much valor and devotion."[42] This praise was superceded the next day when Napoleon issued his famous proclamation to the army: "Soldiers, I am pleased with you! You have fulfilled my expectations! You have made up for everyone by your morale and by your valor... The Battle of Lützen will be placed above the Battle of Austerlitz, of Jena, of Friedland, and of the Moscowa."[43]

The Emperor Saluting the Young Guard at Lützen, 2 May 1813.

The Battle of Lützen placed *above* the famous victories at Austerlitz and Jena? If Napoleon had possessed a cavalry arm to pursue the routed Russians and Prussians like he wanted to, it is entirely likely that the Battle of Lützen would have been an epic triumph to rival his greatest victories. However, it is clear that both the bulletin and the proclamation were gross overstatements. What is certain is that Napoleon's victory at Lützen reestablished the Emperor's military reputation among his adversaries. The 1812 campaign had severely tarnished his prestige, so it was imperative for Napoleon to win his first battle in 1813. Also, the victory at Lützen gave a boost to the morale of the war weary French populace. For the most part, France had been at war for the past 20 years, and the blood tax was already appallingly high. Finally, the Battle of Lützen restored the confidence of many senior French officers whose morale was understandably shaken by the Russian disaster and the difficulties in raising and training an entirely new army.

Following their sovereign's lead, many generals and marshals also heaped praise on their victorious young troops. "Each soldier was a hero," wrote Prince Eugène the evening after Lützen. "All did their duty; not a single man lagged behind, and it was only with difficulty that any could be found to be made to accompany the wounded out of danger."[44] The next day—the same one on which Napoleon issued his famous proclamation—Marshal Ney penned his report to Imperial headquarters, which ended thusly: "The enemy's furious attacks could not dim the determination or break the ranks of these young soldiers. His Majesty has been a witness of the enthusiasm of the troops, and he will have recognized with pleasure in their noble élan that unfailing French valor which can even replace experience."[45]

Like his after action report of Weissenfels, Ney's assessment of his new soldiers at the Battle of Lützen bordered on sheer fantasy. Here was "the bravest of the brave"[46] writing to his commanding officer that the ranks of III Corps were not broken during the battle and that bravery could substitute for experience. There is no denying that the army, including Ney's corps, had behaved bravely at Lützen. However, the conscripts of III Corps—attacked by overwhelming numbers—barely lasted more than two hours before their battalions began to break and dissolve into flight. This fact is undeniably confirmed by a number of reports, the most descriptive of which was made by an officer in the Imperial Guard. Coming upon the hard-pressed soldiers of Ney's III Corps at Lützen at about 2:30 P.M., Major Chlapowski of the 1st (Polish) Light Lancers of the Guard recalled that "the young troops were throwing away their arms which strewed the ground over which we galloped. Half an hour later we halted between the road and the village of Kaye, and deployed in a line facing the village in a field where the remnants of Ney's green troops were still in flight. The Emperor ordered us to bar their passage between our squadrons."[47] This situation, as described by Major Chlapowski, is totally different from the one portrayed in the Prince of the Moscowa's report. Further, the state of affairs as described in Chlapowski's report is verified by many other after action reports.[48] Although the entire III Corps had not collapsed, many of the battalions were broken. What battle was Ney referring to when he said that the enemy attacks could not break the ranks of his troops? Even the bulletin issued by Napoleon after the battle admitted to this development. Perhaps the Russian experience had affected Ney!

Marshal Marmont, whose corps in part consisted of all four regiments of the *marins*, was on the right flank of Drouot's grand battery during the final hours of the battle. Ordered to pursue the beaten foe, Marmont led his corps forward, attracting the full attention of the enemy who committed thousands of cavalry against VI Corps. In contrast to Ney's report, the after action recollection of the Duke of Ragusa penned on May 8 was moderately toned and realistic. "...Then the enemy assembled large forces against mine and above all numerous guns. More importantly, the 150 enemy cannon were aimed solely against my army corps; my troops calmly suffered from their fire with courage and deserve great praise. Compans' division [the 20th] was the most exposed, and deserves the most praise; the ranks, being shelled each moment, would reform with the shouts of *Vive l'Empereur!*

"Immediately after this terrible cannonade, the enemy cavalry sallied forth with a vigorous charge directed against the 1st Regiment de Marine. This excellent regiment, commanded by the brave colonel Emond, displayed, in that moment, that quality good infantry shows against the cavalry, and the efforts of the enemy were in vain against our bayonets. Other charges were likewise conducted and all likewise without success. Thus the beautiful day ended, where the VI Corps had the honor of firing the first cannon shots and the last musket shots. I cannot give too much praise to the troops of the command of whom His Majesty had deigned to entrust me. The soldiers of the navy have shown themselves worthy of the land army to which His Majesty attached them, and the new soldiers go forward firmly in the footsteps of the veterans."[49]

General Bertrand, whose IV Corps arrived on the field of Lützen just before 5 P.M. following a forced march, commented in his after action report that: "Marching to the sound of the guns, IV Corps covered six kilometers in record time; not a man dropped out of ranks; the young soldiers were eager to meet the enemy."[50] Probably the most interesting comment from a corps commander following Lützen came from General Lauriston, who relayed the opponents' reaction. "The information obtained from the inhabitants," he informed Berthier on May 5, "is that the Russian and Prussian officers are humiliated and they say that it is dishonorable for them to be *overpowered by children*."[51]

Certainly, the young French battalions of the *Grande Armée* of 1813 deserved praise for their hard-fought victory at Lützen. However, in spite of all the praise given to them while on the battlefield, Napoleon was not pleased at all with the march discipline of his troops. Perhaps the Emperor knew, or recalled the words, of the famous speech made by de Jaucourt before the Assembly in January, 1792. "A victory won by an undisciplined and badly trained army will cost much more blood than another."[52] Regardless of whether of not the Emperor had read or heard this speech, he knew all too well the self-evident truth of these words.

After Lützen and once again off the battlefield, Napoleon's young army was out of control. The inexperienced officers and non-commissioned officers either did not know how, or care, to hold in check the misconduct of their troops, who had evidently been spoiled by the accolades for their victory. A man of order, Napoleon was incensed by the indiscipline within his army which, in turn, caused the number of combatants to shrink daily. By May 6, the Emperor had seen and heard enough. Napoleon issued a stern order of the day which set forth in no uncertain terms his displeasure with the march discipline of the *Grande Armée*.

"Many soldiers are spreading out right and left into the countryside: others are stragglers. It's the fault of officers who permit their men to quit ranks: it's the fault of the generals who have no rearguard to collect the stragglers. The soldiers permit themselves to unload their weapons by firing their gun instead of using the wad-extractor; others go off into the countryside and shoot cattle. It is a crime, because a shot in war is an alarm signal: it is a crime, because one risks killing or wounding people whom one doesn't see, and becuase finally it's an act of marauding....

"His Majesty orders that every soldier who fires a shot, while marauding, or to unload his weapon, will be punished by imprisonment and demoted. If the shot has wounded or killed someone, the soldier will be punished by death."[53]

Napoleon in Bivouac, 1813. The Emperor typically camped inside a square of the Old Guard infantry, as shown in this *lithograph by Raffet.*

The meaning of the Emperor's order of the day on May 6 may not have fully sunk in with the young troops. Evidence of this exists with Marmont's order of the day on May 8—the same day which he praised his men in his official report on the Battle of Lützen. Marmont's May 8 order of the day reminded the troops to first regain and to then maintain their discipline while off the battlefield. "The Marshal, commander-in-chief of the VI Corps, makes known his unhappiness to the troops under his orders for the disorders they are committing daily. If the good conduct which they upheld on the field of battle is done to earn them the good will of His Majesty, the continuation of the disorders will bring down on them all his sternness."[54]

Despite army and corps orders addressing the problem of march discipline, the consequences of rapid maneuvers and first major battle of the war was already cause for great concern. A far more debilitating kind of loss was already leaving its indelible mark on the new *Grande Armée*: strategic consumption. Napoleon's 1813 army was not unique in that it suffered from soldiers quitting the ranks. Certainly, fatigue and desertion were as old as war itself, and all armies throughout history have suffered to some degree from these factors. However, what was cause for concern was that upon entry into the field, the Emperor's command immediately began to feel the effects of weaklings who could not keep up with their units, or deserters who broke ranks.

There is an alarming report made by the elderly, yet vigilant Marshal Kellermann to Berthier on May 17, in which the former wrote: "I have the honor to inform Your Highness that unattached men from the infantry and the cavalry, weaponless, but completely dressed and equipped, are returning from the army and reentering Mayence, without travel orders nor orders of any kind. I am unaware how these soldiers could leave their corps and come by stages without obstacle this far...Those whose return seems to smack of desertion I shall have arrested...Those unattached, wishing to justify their flight, spread along the route all rumors which would seem to justify it."[55]

Closer inspection by Kellermann during the next two days revealed that most of the "unattached" men in Mayence were simply deserters, some of which openly admitted their guilt, while the vast majority had slipped into the convoys of wounded. Discovering this trick, Kellermann also noticed that most of the wounded returning to Mayence were so slightly injured that they should have never left their corps in the first place![56] "What kind of officers do we have," asked Kellermann to the Major General on May 19, "who allow men, ever so slightly wounded, to either leave their units, or allow these to join or remain in the company of heros who have shed their blood for the colors?"[57]

The answer to this puzzle certainly lies in at least five distinct factors: 1) the army's lack of quality officers and non-coms; 2) the young age and resulting immaturity and physical weakness of many of the new French soldiers; 3) the lack of proper training for the conscripts, including survival in the field; 4) the army's insufficient medical and administrative services; and finally 5) Napoleon's aggressive method of war.

The first three factors have already been discussed in this work. The fourth factor—the lack of proper medical and administrative services—likewise already mentioned earlier, was a result of the Russian campaign which decimated the army's medical and administrative capabilities. Even though Count Daru made a Herculean effort to restore the administrative services, there was only so much that could be accomplished before the resumption of hostilities. As a result, most of the corps began the 1813 campaign with either no one or very few persons on the medical staffs or filling the administrative posts. As it was, the administrative support of the *Grande Armée* was hard-pressed just to provide enough bread for the army, let alone furnish enough personnel to restore all administrative functions such as requisitioning supplies from the surrounding countryside.

As a result, in part or by a combination, of all the first four factors, the majority of the new French army were not able to sustain the rapid marches and rigors of campaign which Napoleon's method of warfare demanded from his soldiers. "The strength of an army," wrote Napoleon in his maxims, "like the power in mechanics, is established by multiplying the mass by the rapidity; a rapid march augments the morale of an army and increases all the chances of victory."[58] Napoleon was arguably the first great captain to introduce true, lightning warfare to the modern world. Napoleon's campaigns of the late 1790s and early 1800s astounded his opponents by rapid marches previously thought impossible. "I have destroyed the enemy merely by marching,"[59] the Emperor said following his triumph at Ulm in 1805. He knew that his army would have to again move fast in 1813. "When an army is inferior in number, inferior in cavalry, and in artillery," Napoleon wrote, "the first deficiency should be supplied by rapidity of movement; the want of artillery by the nature of the maneuver; and the inferiority in cavalry by the choice of position."[60]

Thus, Napoleon's method of warfare always emphasized rapid maneuvers which were bound to bring on extraordinary fatigue, even among the most mature, well conditioned, and well officered body of troops. A significant portion of Napoleon's numerous successes was invariably due to hard, decisive marches designed to compromise the enemy's strategic position. Certainly the most famous of Napoleon's maneuvers—*manoeuver sur le derrières*—was attempted no less than 30 times during his military career.[61]

Therefore, the Emperor's force of activity was beyond the physical capabilities of his young, physically weak, improperly trained, inadequately officered, and improperly nourished army. Once the march orders were given in late April, and the Emperor began pushing his army eastward across Saxony and into Silesia, the wastage—or strategic consumption—was immediate. Warnings that the young conscripts would be unable to stand up to the physical demands of marching day in and day out can be seen as early as February. "Apart from the fact that these young conscripts absolutely don't know how to use their weapons," Colonel Cavalier reported on February 16, "they cannot stand up to the marches it would take in order to win successes...it would be much better to have only 100 men from good troops than the 600 these five companies put forth."[62]

The Conscripts of 1813. *Composition by Bombled.*

In no formation of the *Grande Armée* was the strategic consumption more dramatically illustrated than with the 1st Guard Infantry Division under the orders of General Dumoustier. On April 25, this division numbered 11,670 officers and other ranks present and under arms. Of this number, some 28 officers and 961 men were members of the 2nd Regiments of the Old Guard Grenadiers and Chasseurs which were destined for the Old Guard Infantry Division which they joined before Lützen. Therefore, the division had 10,581 personnel present and under arms on April 25 in units which would still be in the division after Lützen. The vast majority of these men were members of the Young Guard. At the Battle of Lützen, the division suffered 1,069 casualties—304 wounded and 765 killed or missing.[63] Also, the division was reinforced before the battle by the arrival of the third company of Old Guard *Volante*. Yet on May 5, the division had only 7,865 combatants present and under arms with 3,040 in hospitals. Of those in the hospital, only 10% were there as a result of being wounded in combat. The remaining 90%—approximately 2,700 men—were no longer in ranks as a result of these young soldiers simply breaking down from the rigors of a campaign which was less than 10 days old! Therefore, the 1st Guard Infantry Division suffered a strategic consumption loss of approximately 25% from April 25 to May 5.[64]

"Conscripts of the line or conscripts of the Guard, there was not much difference between them," concluded Camille Rousset. "What is said of the one makes the other well enough known."[65] More and better officers and non-commissioned officers did not seem to improve the strategic consumption which drained the Young Guard and the rest of the army as well. The troops were simply too young, and those not strong enough for military service invariably dropped out of ranks in the early stages of the campaign.

This fact is further supported by the daily reports of the generals and marshals, who state in no uncertain terms that the single, main reason for the *Grande Armée's* loss of manpower through strategic consumption was due simply to the fact that the youths in uniform were not old enough to be physically capable of withstanding the kind of stress and fatigue demanded of a Napoleonic army at war. As illustrated at Lützen, the conscripts were capable of battlefield heroics for a single day. However, within the first few days of the 1813 campaign, they also proved to be incapable of completing the trilogy of successful, victorious Napoleonic warfare—lightning marches to fall suddenly upon the enemy, followed by the fighting and winning of a major battle, to be concluded by resuming a rapid march to pursue and destroy the beaten enemy. Had Napoleon had the mature veterans of the army he led in Italy, or at Austerlitz, or at Jena, he would have probably won the 1813 campaign by May 10.

As it turned out, the Emperor was unable to pursue and destroy the Allied army after Lützen owing to his lack of cavalry and to the exhausted state of his young infantry. "The regiments of my corps badly need a good night's rest," wrote Lauriston to Berthier on May 8, "they are full of ardor and good will. The men are vigorous but they do not yet have the experience to undertake a long march."[66] It must be remembered that Lauriston's V Corps consisted entirely of regiments composed of the old cohorts. Thus, its ranks contained older and more mature men than many regiments of other corps who had 18 and 19 year olds populating their ranks. Yet, Lauriston told Berthier less than a week after Lützen that his men are in dire need of rest and cannot sustain themselves by constant marches.

By a combination of blood and strategic consumption, the price of victory at Lützen was not cheap. The III Corps had suffered the most. Of the 49,189 officers and men which were present and under arms on April 25,[67] Ney's May 5 parade states reflected serious losses. The rolls showed that since the campaign began, III Corps had lost 1,533 killed in action, 11,512 wounded, and 2,521 prisoners or missing,[68] for a total loss of 15,566—a casualty rate of 31.6% of the corps! Among the losses, 13,240 were French infantry casualties.[69] The French infantry of III Corps had numbered 38,053 combatants present and under arms on April 25.[70] Therefore, Ney had lost almost 35% of his French infantry after only 10 days!

Other corps had suffered as well. The V and XI Corps, which together on April 25 numbered 43,520 officers and men present and under arms,[71] had together lost only 4,625 killed, wounded, and captured up until May 5.[72] The IV Corps, which consisted of 26 battalions, had only 8 of them report on May 5,[73] and these showed a total casualty figure from Lützen of 500 combatants.[74] The VI Corps which totalled 43 battalions had less than half of them report on May 5.[75] These partial returns reflect a total of 1,730 killed, wounded, and missing[76] from the reporting battalions from VI Corps—obviously just a fragment of the total casualties suffered by Marmont's corps at Lützen. Already mentioned were the losses sustained by the 1st Guard Infantry Division which amounted to 1,069.

Therefore, totalling the *known* casualties for the French army up through May 2, Napoleon suffered 23,490 killed, wounded, or missing at Weissenfels (only Souham's division engaged) and at Lützen. Add to this the unknown, estimated losses of the other formations which did not report on May 5, and it is safe to say that the *Grande Armée* suffered a minimum of 25,000 casualties at the Battle of Lützen.[77] This represents about 18% of the 141,168 combatants of Napoleon's forces which were actually engaged or on the battlefield. By comparison, the Battle of Lützen cost the Russians and Prussians under Wittgenstein at least 20,000 men of the 73,000 engaged,[78] or about 27% of their engaged troops.

Although Napoleon had lost over 25,000 men on the battlefield in the first week of the campaign, and at least another 15,000 to desertion and strategic consumption during this same period,[79] he was determined to remain true to his principals of war. The Emperor continued pursuit of the beaten foe, pushing the *Grande Armée* eastward as fast as his young soldiers and numerically inferior cavalry could manage. Organizing his forces into three pursuit columns, Napoleon remained with center column consisting of the I Reserve Cavalry Corps, VI Corps, XI Corps, and the Imperial Guard. An extemporaneous 'advance guard' of the center column under the command of Prince Eugène was formed from Latour-Maubourg's I Reserve Cavalry Corps and Macdonald's XI Corps. These men first made contact against the Allied rear guard at Colditz on May 5.[80]

The Russians and Prussians were conducting a curiously leisurely crossing of the Mulde River[81] when the alarm was sounded by the approach of Eugène's troops. The Prince quickly sent word to the Emperor of what he had found at Colditz. Immediately, Napoleon and his staff spurred on their horses to meet up with Eugène and ordered the remainder of the column forward at the double quick.[82] The weather was miserable;[83] torrential rains soaked the ground and the combatants making maneuvers extremely difficult and testing the endurance of the men. Once at the front, Napoleon conducted a quick reconnaissance of the enemy positions. In spite of the elements, the Emperor was determined to crush the enemy forces before him and ordered Eugène to attack.[84]

After the action had been underway for some time, a Russian prisoner was brought before Napoleon. A brief interrogation revealed that he was from Miloradovitch's command.[85] This discovery raced through the ranks of the Guard like lightning. During the 1812 campaign, the soldiers of Miloradovitch had been known for their brutality against French prisoners, especially those of the Imperial Guard.[86]

Standing close to Napoleon during the interview was General François Rouget, commander of the Old Guard Infantry Division.[87] After hearing whose command it was before them, Rouget stepped forward and said to the Emperor: "Sire, the veterans who served in Russia cannot stand idle. I beg Your Highness to order me and my men forward."[88] Napoleon glanced at his staff, all of whom gave solemn nods of approval. Turning back to Rouget, the Emperor gave the order: *"La Garde au feu!"* With Rouget at their head, the fur bonnets[89] of the Guard moved forward in the pouring rain. In this instance, the miserable weather worked in favor of the French because the Russian infantry could not put out an effective defensive fire and the Russian cavalry was already occupied by Latour-Maubourg's squadrons. With emotions running high, the Guard soon closed on the Russians "with cold steel"[90] and slaughtered the Tsar's troops "without mercy."[91] Many of the remaining Allied troops on the west bank of the Mulde broke ranks and ran for their lives. In the meantime, the Prussian engineers were able to save their valuable bridge train.

After Colditz, the pursuit of the Prussians and Russians resumed with Napoleon urgently pushing his youthful troops eastward. The Emperor's pressure produced large dividends. Allied morale crumbled as confidence among the Prussian and Russian troops dwindled daily as their retreat continued with no letup in sight. Materially, the most important action took place on May 9 when Napoleon's advancing troops captured intact the Allied pontoon bridges over the Elbe at Dresden.[92] Not one to let up the pressure on his retreating foe, Napoleon ordered his corps commanders to force march their troops across the Elbe and to try and run the Allies to ground. The Emperor wanted to force a decisive battle while he had the strategic initiative and moral superiority.

Three days later, on May 12, some 25 miles northeast of Dresden, another action was fought between the advancing French and the retreating Allies. The XI Corps under Macdonald—acting as the advance guard of the *Grande Armée*—attacked a superior force of Allies acting as a their army's rearguard in and around the town of Bischofswerda.[93] Macdonald's after action report described the combat. "Our troops fought everywhere with tenacity and valor," he told Marshal Berthier on May 13. "The enemy forces were double mine, and nevertheless I beat them and stormed all the formidable positions, and in spite of the maneuvers of 10,000 enemy cavalrymen and 60 pieces of artillery in a grand battery, the city, which is no more,[94] was carried at the bayonet point. The troops of His Majesty covered themselves with glory..." The following day, Macdonald wrote again to the Major General. "My troops are full of ardor; once they are slightly rested, I will be able to dare all and undertake everything."[95]

About this same time, some 250 miles to the northwest, Marshal Davout was busy fighting the insurrection of the Hanseatic Legion.[96] The revolt, which began in early March, was of great concern to Napoleon for many reasons. First, this area was the Emperor's strategic northern flank. He could not hope to fight in Germany without this flank being secure. Second, the area of the Hanseatic league furnished the French army a large portion of its horseflesh. The revolt shut off this vital supply,[97] without which the army could not effectively rebuild its cavalry, transport, and administrative arms. Finally, with the landing of Bernadotte's Swedish army in Swedish Pomerania, the operations of several small Allied "free corps" in the area resulting in the capture of Hamburg, and the rumors of a major Allied offensive through Mecklemburg in conjunction with a British naval landing somewhere in Hanover, it seemed as though Napoleon's strategic left flank was in jeopardy.[98]

In response to this crisis, Napoleon dispatched his most able administrator and trusted lieutenant, the "Iron Marshal,"[99] Louis Davout. The Prince of Eckmühl was instructed by the Emperor in no uncertain terms to crush the insurgents, regain control of Hamburg, and restore the flow of horses to the army, all while organizing the French and French-Allied forces along the lower Elbe River.[100]

To an old warhorse like Davout, his assignment was not what he preferred, but one which he nevertheless tackled with his accustomed sense of duty and thoroughness. As Davout assumed command of the entire 32nd Military Division,[101] a new commander for I Corps was needed. Since no subordinate dared cross the stern Davout, Napoleon assigned the capable but otherwise troublesome General Vandamme to the command of I Corps,[102] which was then organizing along the lower Elbe. Although this corps could not be expected to meet regular enemy formations before June, Vandamme whipped his units into shape by fighting the insurgents and the enemy "free corps." Numerous skirmishes served as confidence builders for the young troops. "I cannot be more pleased with the valor of our troops," Vandamme wrote to Davout on May 13, "and in spite of their youth and inexperience I cannot recall having found more ardor in our old troops."[103]

The minor engagements fought by Vandamme's new battalions were nowhere near the intensity of the desperate fighting being experienced by the corps with the Emperor. This form of warfare resumed at the Battle of Bautzen which was waged on May 20-21, 1813. Being relentlessly pursued, the Allied commanders decided to turn about and risk another major battle against Napoleon.

General Raglowich's 29th (Bavarian) Division, attached to XII Corps, fording the Sprée River at Bautzen, 20 May 1813. *Composition by Philippoteaux.*

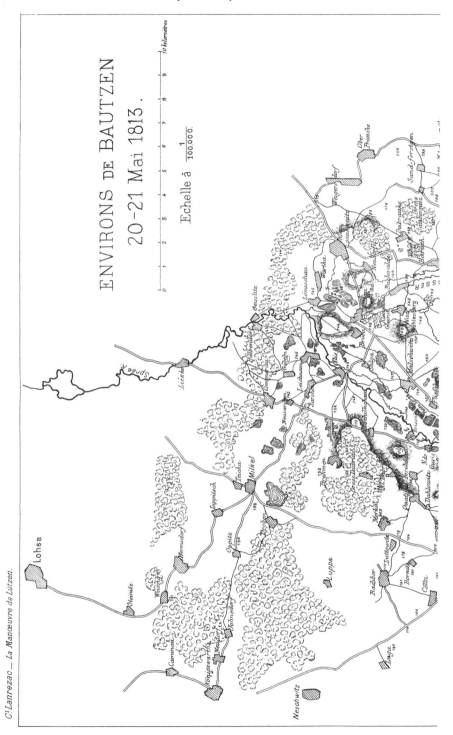

ENVIRONS DE BAUTZEN
20-21 Mai 1813.

Echelle à 1/100.000.

C.Lanrezac _ La Manœuvre de Lützen.

94

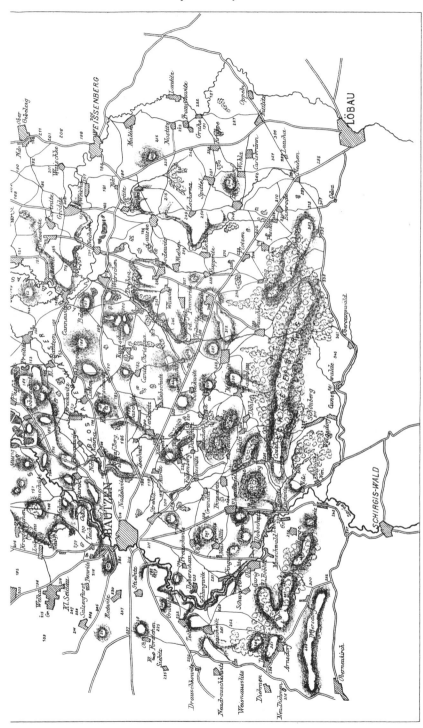

NANCY-PARIS, BERGER-LEVRAULT & CIE ÉDITEURS

N° 13. — ENVIRONS DE BAUTZEN (20-21 MAI 1813).

The Allied army consisted of approximately 96,200 combatants and 622 guns.[104] To increase combat effectiveness, the Prussians and Russians dug in facing west, their batteries commanding the Sprée River and the village of Bautzen.[105] The position was a strong one, and Napoleon had no intention of repeating the bloody operational plan used at Borodino; there would be no headlong frontal attack. With more manpower and guns concentrated on the field of battle than his opponents, the Emperor instead decided to fix the enemy in his positions by launching a series of controlled, frontal attacks designed only to distract and to pin the enemy.[106] These attacks would come from the 109,000 combatants and 355 guns in the corps directly under Napoleon, consisting of IV, VI, XI, XII, I Reserve Cavalry and the Imperial Guard. Meanwhile, Marshal Ney, acting as an army wing commander at the head of 77,000 officers and men supported by 221 guns in five other corps—II, III, V, VII and the II Reserve Cavalry Corps—would fall upon the enemy right flank and rear.[107] When Ney's attack was fully developed, the entire army would vigorously attack, rupture the Allied line, and seal the victory.

****

General Franquemont and the Württembergers at the Battle of Bautzen, 21 May 1813. *Composition by R. Knötel.*

Napoleon's *Grande Armée* at Bautzen[108]

Corps	Division	Commander	# of bns/sqd	Officers present	Other ranks and under arms
IV Corps—		Bertrand	Strengths as of 10 May 1813		
	12th Division	Morand	13	257	9,291
	15th Division	Peri	13	282*	9,936*
	38th Division**	Franquemont	8	105	4,438
	Neapolitan Cavalry		2	18	363
	Württemberg Cavalry		8	37	989
	Corps Reserve Artillery				605†
	Corps Totals:			699	25,017 and 49 guns

* The 15th Division suffered a total of 2,862 casualties in the combat of Königswartha on May 19. Including these losses, as well as attrition through strategic consumption, the approximate strength of Bertrand's IV Corps at Bautzen was 22,000 combatants and 49 pieces of ordnance.

** The 38th Division consisted entirely of Württembergers.

† Officers in units of the artillery reserve are included in this figure.

VI Corps—Marmont. No strength returns for this corps exist between 25 April and 20 May 1813. Therefore, using the April 25th returns, less an estimated 2,500 for casualties at Lützen and another estimated 3,000 lost through strategic consumption, the VI Corps had approximately 21,000 combatants in ranks supported by 70 pieces of ordnance on May 20, 1813.

Corps	Division	Commander	# of bns/sqd	Officers present	Other ranks and under arms
XI Corps—		Macdonald	Strengths as of 15 May 1813		
	31st Division	Fressinet	7	92	2,496
	35th Division	Gérard	12	197	5,926
	36th Division	Charpentier	11	193	5,944
	Corps Cavalry included with 35th Division totals.				
	Corps Totals:			482	14,366 and 52 guns

After deducting about 1,400 combatants estimated to have fallen out of ranks through strategic consumption between May 15 to May 20, the XI Corps had approximately 13,500 officers and other ranks present and under arms at Bautzen supported by 52 pieces of ordnance.

Corps	Division	Commander	# of bns/sqd	Officers present	Other ranks and under arms
XII Corps—		Oudinot	Strengths as of 14 May 1813		
	13th Division	Pacthod	13	238	9,357
	14th Division	Lorencez	12	194	6,878
	29th Division	Raglovich	10	163	6,205
	Bavarian Cavalry		3	24	741
	Corps Reserve Artillery				439[†]
	Corps Totals:			616	23,620 and 50 guns

[†] Officers in units of the artillery reserve included in this figure.
After deducting about 1,200 combatants estimated to have fallen out of ranks through strategic consumption between May 14 and May 20, the XII Corps had approximately 23,000 effectives in ranks at Bautzen with 50 pieces of ordnance.

Corps	Division	Commander	# of bns/sqd	Officers present	Other ranks and under arms
Imperial Guard—		Mortier	Strengths as of 15 May 1813		
	1st Yg.Gd. Div.	Dumoustier	14	213	7,544
	2nd Yg.Gd. Div.	Barrois	10	139	4,765
	Old Guard Div.	Rouget	8	123	3,355
	Guard Cavalry	Lef-Desn	12		2,982[†]
	Guard Cavalry	Walther	18		3,774[†]
	Guard Reserve Artillery				1,970[†]
	Corps Total:			475	24,390 and 116 guns

[†] Officers are included in this figure.
After deducting about 800 combatants estimated to have fallen out of ranks through strategic consumption between May 15 and May 20, the Imperial Guard had approximately 23,500 officers and other ranks present and under arms at Bautzen supported by 116 pieces of ordnance.

Corps	Division	Commander	# of sqdrns	Officers present	Other ranks and under arms
I Reserve Cavalry Corps—		Latour-Maubourg	Strengths as of 15 May 1813		
	1st Lt Cav Div	Bruyère		103	2,167
	1st Cuirass Div	Bordesoulle		111	2,046
	3rd Cuirass Div	Doumerc		82	1,635
	Corps Total:			296	5,818 and 18 guns

There were many squadrons de marche in route to this corps on May 15. It is estimated that the strategic consumption suffered by the corps would have cancelled out the reinforcements received. Thus, the I Reserve Cavalry Corps had approximately 6,000 combatants in the saddle (and with the 3 accompanying artillery companies) at Bautzen along with 18 guns.

Total strength of troops (present and under arms) directly under Napoleon's command present and engaged at the Battle of Bautzen numbered approximately 109,000 combatants supported by 355 guns. Therefore, the gun-to-troop ratio for these formations at this battle was 1 gun for every 307 combatants.

Ney's Army Wing at Bautzen— troops engaged at the battle[109]

Corps	Division	Commander	# of bns/sqd	Officers present and under arms	Other ranks
V Corps—		Lauriston	Strengths as of 16 May 1813		
	16th Division	Maison	8	174	4,175
	17th Division*	Puthod	12	232	6,787
	18th Division	Lagrange	10	211	4,928
	19th Division	Rochambeau	12	216	6,882
	3rd Lt Cav Div[†]	Guyon	8	55	1,492
	Corps Totals:			888	24,264 and 99 guns

* The 17th Division joined the corps on the field of battle on May 21; the division had 16 guns.

[†] The 3rd Light Cavalry Division was attached to V Corps at this time. This cavalry division had no artillery attached.

Deducting the 1,821 casualties V Corps suffered at the combat of Eichberg on May 19, and allowing for another 300 combatants lost through strategic consumption from May 16 to May 20, the V Corps had approximately 23,000 officers and other ranks present and under arms at Bautzen, supported by 99 pieces of ordnance.

Corps	Division	Commander	# of bns/sqd	Officers present and under arms	Other ranks
III Corps—		Souham	Strengths as of 16 May 1813		
	8th Division	Souham	16		12,227[†]
	9th Division	Delmas	16		9,671[†]
	10th Division	Albert	14		9,887[†]
	11th Division	Ricard	14		9,660[†]
	39th Division	Marchand	12		9,463[†]
	Corps Cavalry	Laboissière	9		1,269[†]
	Corps Reserve Artillery				800[†]
	Corps Totals+:				30,000* and 84 guns

[†] The III Corps returns for May 16 show only the *total* strength of the formations, including those who are in hospitals, previously captured since the start of the campaign, or temporarily detached. Therefore, these figures are far in excess of the number of officers and men actually present and under arms.

* Considering the 15,566 casualties suffered by III Corps at Weissenfels and Lützen (some of the men who were lightly wounded no doubt returned to ranks) and estimating the strategic consumption losses up to May 20 at 5,000, the strength of the corps at Bautzen probably did not exceed 30,000 combatants; there were 84 pieces of ordnance present at the battle with III Corps.

Corps	Division	Commander	# of bns/sqd	Officers present	Other ranks and under arms
VII Corps—		Reynier	Strengths as of 16 May 1813		
	32nd Division	Durutte	7*	136	4,097
	Saxon Division	von Sahr	8	117	6,000
	Saxon Cavalry		2	11	290
	Corps Totals:			264	10,387 and 16 guns**

* The 5 battalions marching with VI Corps in late April, along with the remnants of the old division, combined to form 7 battalions.
** Of this total, 4 guns belonged to the 32nd Division and 12 guns belonged to the Saxon foot artillery of von Sahr's division.
Deducting 700 combatants lost through strategic consumption from May 16 to May 20, the strength of VII Corps at Bautzen was approximately 10,000 officers and other ranks present and under arms along with 16 pieces of ordnance.

The strength of the troops under Ney's command who were present and engaged at the Battle of Bautzen numbered approximately 63,000 officers and other ranks supported by 199 guns. Thus, Ney's corps engaged at Bautzen had a gun-to-troop ratio of 1 gun for every 317 combatants.

Troops of Ney's Army Wing not engaged at the Battle of Bautzen[110]

Corps	Division	Commander	# of bns/sqd	Officers present	Other ranks and under arms
II Corps—		Victor	Strengths as of 16 May 1813		
	1st Division	Philippon	12		6,500†
	4th Division	Dubreton	10		5,500†
	Corps Total:				12,000† and 16 guns
	† Totals, including officers.				

Corps	Division	Commander	# of sqdrns	Officers present	Other ranks and under arms
II Reserve Cavalry Corps—Sébastiani			Strengths as of 16 May 1813		
	2nd Lt Cav Div	Roussel	6	41	901
	4th Lt Cav Div	Exelmans	6	61	980
	2nd Cuirass Div	Wathier	6	61	871
	Corps Totals:			168	2,752 and 6 guns

Taking into account losses through strategic consumption, the total strength of formations under Ney's command not engaged at the Battle of Bautzen numbered approximately 14,000 officers and other ranks with 22 pieces of ordnance.

Thus, the entire army wing under the orders of the Prince of the Moscowa numbered approximately 77,000 combatants present and under arms on May 20, along with 221 guns.

Combining the strength of the corps under Ney and those under Napoleon, the French army at Bautzen numbered a grand total of 186,000 combatants present and under arms supported by 576 guns. Of these, some 172,000 were engaged, along with 554 pieces of ordnance.

****

It was a plan worthy of the "Emperor of Battles", and would have undoubtedly resulted in the complete annihilation of the Allied army had Ney not botched the flanking maneuver. The Prince of the Moscowa was out of his depth as an army wing commander and his failure to fully envelope the Allied flank allowed the Prussians and Russians time to escape Napoleon's trap after a loss of approximately 20,000 combatants.[111] For the Emperor, Bautzen turned out to be another hollow victory, which carried a price tag of 12,000 Frenchmen *hors de combat*.[112]

Considering the relative inexperience of the army, the combat performance of Napoleon's new soldiers during the period of the Battle of Bautzen was remarkable. One such example occurred the day before Bautzen, when Lauriston's corps thrashed Yorck's Prussians at Eichberg. In this combat, Lauriston's command—which numbered about 25,000 combatants—attacked and convincingly defeated a numerically superior force of Prussians. For the loss of 1,821 casualties, the V Corps killed, wounded, or took prisoner some 5,000 of the enemy.[113]

Losses Suffered by V Corps at the Combat of Eichberg, 19 May 1813[114]

Formation	Killed Officers	Others	Wounded Officers	Others	Prisoners Officers	Others	Horses Killed	Wounded
Corps staff	----	----	1	----	----	----	----	----
151st Line Regt	4	36	6	156	----	1	----	----
153rd Line Regt	----	48	10	163	----	----	----	----
134th Line Regt	2	49	3	201	----	80	----	----
154th Line Regt	1	32	19	393	----	79	----	----
155th Line Regt	3	25	14	270	----	24	----	----
135th Line Regt	2	10	7	145	----	----	----	----
149th Line Regt	----	----	----	----	----	----	----	----
150th Line Regt	----	----	----	----	----	----	----	----
Artillery	----	1	----	8	----	----	8	8
1st C à Cheval	----	3	----	7	----	----	8	12
2nd C à Cheval	----	----	1	6	----	----	1	3
3rd C à Cheval	----	----	----	5	----	----	7	5
9th C à Cheval	----	----	----	1	----	----	3	2
19th C à Cheval	----	----	----	2	----	----	----	3
2nd and 3rd combined Italian C à Cheval	----	----	----	3	----	----	3	3
Corps Totals:	12	204	61	1,360	----	184	30	36

For their conduct at Bautzen, Napoleon conferred special merit on the VI Corps, especially the 37th Light Infantry Regiment—which will be remembered as composed of the old veterans from the departmental and city militias and guards—and the 4th Regiment de Marine.[115] Also, the infantry and artillery of the Imperial Guard were singled out for their effectiveness and bravery. Accodring to Drouot, the artillery of the Guard "provided IV Corps and the infantry of the Guard with the firepower that helped make possible our victory"[116] while the infantry of the Guard "swept over the enemy",[117] carrying several positions in the center of the Allied line.

The day after Bautzen, on May 22, the cavalry of the Imperial Guard, supported by the I Reserve Cavalry Corps, was unleashed against the retreating Russians and Prussians. Covering the retreat of the Allied army were several thousand of their own cavalry. The French cavalry attacked and, spearheaded by both regiments of the Guard light lancers, drove the Prussian and Russian cavalry from the field. "General Lefebvre-Desnoëttes, at the head of 1,500 Polish and Red Lancers of the Guard," read the May 24th Bulletin of the *Grande Armée*, "charged and routed the enemy cavalry...The Red Lancers of the Guard is composed mainly of volunteers from Paris and its suburbs. General Lefebvre-Desnoëttes and General Colbert, their colonel, give them great praise...In the small skirmish of the 22nd at Reichenbach, we acquired the certitude that our young cavalry is, in equal number, superior to that of the enemy."[118]

IMPERIAL GUARD Cavalry	Casulaties Suffered in the Combat on 22 May					
	Officers			Other Ranks		Horses
	Killed	Wounded	Prisoners	Wounded	Killed or Prisoners	Killed
Lancers of Berg	—	1	—	7	11	5
1st (Polish) Light Lancers	—	1	—	77	9	8
2nd (Red) Light Lancers	—	2	2	80	11	11
Chasseurs à Cheval	—	2	—	2	—	7
Mamelukes	—	—	—	7	1	1
Gendarmes d'élite	1	—	—	1	—	2
Guard Horse Artillery	—	—	—	5	1	9
	1	6	2	179	33	43

Although the May 24th bulletin did not go to the lengths of excessive praise as did the one honoring the infantry following Lützen, it was, however, a true statement only if confined to the cavalry of the Imperial Guard, to the heavy cavalry of the line, and to a few select light cavalry regiments. A honest and more indicative sign of the combat effectiveness of most of the cavalry of the line during the spring campaign can be seen in Marshal Macdonald's after action report of May 27.

Pursuing the beaten enemy following the combat at Reichenbach, Macdonald's advance guard of the *Grande Armée*, consisting of his own XI Corps and General Latour-Maubourg's I Reserve Cavalry Corps,[119] came upon a strong Russian rearguard at Pilgramsdorf near Goldberg. Wishing to press the retreating army, Macdonald ordered his troops to attack. "I chased them [the Russians] from the heights of Pilgramsdorf", Macdonald reported to Berthier at 6 P.M. that evening, "they again took up a very favorable position on the rolling hills and in the defiles which surround Goldberg. A new battle was

General Colbert and the Red Lancers of the Guard

joined in which the first brigade of cavalry [of the 1st Light Cavalry Division] and a few squadrons of the second brigade [of the 1st Cuirassier Division] took part, supported by some infantry squares; but it is with sorrow that I tell Your Highness that only the cuirassiers did their duty well; the rest turned tail on three consecutive charges. I led the third crying *"Vive l'Empereur!"* I was cowardly abandoned, having gained one of the enemy's cavalry points. It was only the fire and firmness of our squares which saved me. The cavalry generals did all they could to keep their troops in order, to rally them, and to insure a complete victory, but in vain."[120]

General Bruyères, commander of the 1st Light Cavalry Division, reported that same evening. "The young, inexperienced troopers which comprised, for the most part, the first brigade of my division, were unable to close with the enemy, despite the urging from myself and their officers. Only the 7th Hussars, which are mostly old soldiers, did not panic."[121] General Bordesoulle, commanding officer of the 1st Cuirassier Division recalled: "I rode with General Quinette de Cernay; the Duke of Tarentum led the charge. Our men maintained good order and overturned several regiments of the enemy who then fled before us when we discovered that we had not been accompanied by our light cavalry."[122]

One of the reasons for the line cavalry's ineffectiveness was detailed by General Latour-Maubourg. "I must inform Your Highness," the commander of the I Reserve Cavalry Corps wrote to Berthier on May 30, "that the 1st Divisions of Light Cavalry and of Cuirassiers have decreased in a tangible and distressing way, either by the horses sent back to the remount depots or by those which died of fatigue...The causes of this large number of horses left behind is due in part to tiring marches which took place over some time, but even more to the ineptitude of most of the cavalrymen forming the newly arrived detachments and who, in great part, have been taught how to ride as they left France."[123] This opinion was seconded by General Bourcier from his headquarters in Magdebourg. "Most of the animals being returned to the depot from the army," he wrote Clarke on May 28, "are no longer serviceable due to ignorance and neglect of our young cavalrymen, who simply don't know how to properly care for their mounts."[124]

The next significant action fought by the French cavalry during the spring campaign took place on June 7 at Leipzig. The city was full of sick and wounded, and its streets were choked by numerous stragglers from the army. Charged with the protection of Leipzig was Napoleon's nephew, General Arrighi de Casanova. The Duke of Padoua's ad-hoc command consisted of his own newly-forming III Reserve Cavalry Corps numbering only 1,500 effectives, a cavalry "regiment de marche" of 500 troopers from various cavalry depots, and a "pitiful",[125] extemporaneous brigade of 1,500 infantry "laggards from all the regiments of the *Grande Armée*."[126]

Determined on capturing the Saxon capitol from Arrighi was Russian General Woronzow at the head of a provisional corps consisting of one weak division of infantry numbering only 2,000 effectives, two divisions of cavalry which counted 3,000 sabres, and a force of 1,200 Cossacks. The engagement which followed was described by Arrighi late that evening. "Although our young cavalrymen did everything in good order and were not taken by surprise," Arrighi wrote Berthier, "the enemy attacked in such force, at all points at once, that we had several posts taken after a stiff defense...I recognized, however, on this occasion, in spite of the high morale or our cavalrymen, that they still need time to acquire the instruction they lack, the skill of their trade, to be in a position to test themselves advantageously against cavalry such as we have had before us today, and that it is necessary that it always be supported by infantry."[127]

As previously illustrated, the young French infantry displayed admirable traits on the battlefield, gaining a series of victories over their Allied counterparts. Nevertheless, throughout the spring campaign, the Emperor's infantry continually got into trouble off the battlefield because of poor march discipline. As a result, this cost Napoleon much more than just the loss of troops due to straggling and desertion. Poor march discipline led, in turn, to several outpost skirmishes between French and enemy forces, often resulting in disastrous consequences for the Emperor's infantry.

One such episode occurred on May 19, the day before the start of the Battle of Bautzen. Bertrand's IV Corps was marching east, approching Königswartha, when the advance guard of the corps, consisting of the 15th Division, bivoucked about noon after its day's march.[128] This division consisted entirely of Italian troops under the command of fellow countryman General Bernard Peri. There had been no bread or food provisions issued to the division since the 16th.[129] The following three days, the officers and men had lived off what had been foraged; by the 19th, they were at their limit of endurance. Once camp was made, Peri allowed his hungry command to fan out across the countryside in search of food. This practice was acceptable to some degree only if conducted under the cover of friendly cavalry and the infantry's own outpost guards. However, the corps had no supporting cavalry and Peri did not take the precaution to scout a nearby wood before allowing his division to break ranks and forage. This lack of security proved costly.

A strong force of Russian cavalry, acting as the advance screen of the Allied army which was digging in at Bautzen, saw the foraging infantry, called for and patiently awaited reinforcements; then struck suddenly.[130] The dispersed Italians could not defend themselves as the enemy cavalry rode them down. Within minutes, Peri's division lost 2,862 combatants, including 1,289 taken prisoner.[131] When one considers that the 15th Division had a total of 10,934 officers and other ranks present and under arms on April 25, which had been reduced through marching to 10,218 on May 10, the losses sustained at Königswartha represented 26% of the division's April 25 strength, or 28% of the command's May 10 strength.

Another telling incident of the indiscipline exhibited by Napoleon's infantry off the battlefield happened on May 26 at Milchersdorf near Hainau. The day before this combat, General Lauriston sent a prophetic letter to the Major General. "I must call Your Highness' attention to the route march conduct of the troops. The lack of distribution of provisions for several days brings the soldier to dare everything in order to obtain food. There are far fewer laggards as soon as a city or village is seen. The generals do everything they can to stop this disorder; the small number of officers inhibits these efforts, all the more since the officers themselves seek food. Your Highness must be convinced of the care that I shall bring to bear in stopping this disorder which increases from day to day."[132]

Whatever Lauriston planned to do in correcting the march indiscipline in his corps was no doubt hastened by the costly events of the following day. About 4 P.M. on May 26, General Nicolas-Joseph Maison, commanding the 16th Division in Lauriston's V Corps, halted his command at the village of Milchersdorf. As was the accustomed habit, part of the division immediately disbanded and fanned out over the countryside to look for food. The infantry were supposed to be protected by the cavalry of General Louis Chastel's 3rd Light Cavalry Division. However, the cavalry halted its march about a mile shy of Milchersdorf while the infantry pushed on to the village. The split in the march formations of these divisions must have undoubtably occurred through the need for the cavalry to obtain forage for the horses from the nearby fields while the infantrymen sought food in and around the Milchersdorf.

After much of the French infantry had already broken ranks and were scouring the village and surrounding area for food and drink, General Ziethen attacked with his Prussian cavalry. This mounted assault was made by a formidable force consisting of 3 regiments of

General Maison's 16th Division under attack at Milchersdorf, near Hainau, 26 May 1813. *Composition by R. Knötel.*

cuirassiers, 2 regiments of the Prussian Guard cavalry, supported by 3 more regiments of Silesian hussars and uhlans. The scattered infantry of Maison's command were helpless to resist this onslaught and were mercilessly ridden down by the high-spirited Prussian cavalry. Had the 16th Division not bivouacked around the buildings of the village where the men sought refuge from Ziethen's horsemen, it is entirely likely that Maison's entire command might have perished.[133]

However, the gun shots alerted the nearby 18th Divison. General Joseph Lagrange, commander of the division, immediately ordered his men to march to their comrades assistance. Placing himself at the head of the 155th Regiment of the Line,[134] Lagrange gave instructions for the regiment to form battalion squares and advance. The arrival of these well-led infantry deployed in square soon drove the Prussian cavalry away, but not before Ziethen's command had exacted fearful losses on the French.

Maison's division was wrecked. The 151st Regiment of the Line suffered 616 casualties—including 399 prisoners—out of a total of the 1,006 who were present at the start of the day. The 153rd Regiment of the Line lost 344 officers and men, including one of its entire grenadier companies. The division's company of sappers was "entirely carried off".[135] All together, the combat at Milchersdorf, or Hainau, cost the 16th Division 1,001 infantry, its sapper company, plus 5 pieces of artillery.[136]

The losses sustained in this and some of the other minor engagements stemmed, to some degree, from the fact that the administrative branch of the army was not able to provide bread or effectively requisition supplies for many of the troops. Although the people in charge of the administration of the army were experienced and capable, they simply did not have the materiel means, nor personnel required, to either bake and efficiently distribute bread, or to place at the disposition of the corps commanders the administrators necessary to effectively requisition supplies from the countryside. Failure to provide the means to feed the hungry French soldiers led to the brigade and division generals taking chances with larger and larger forage parties, which sometimes led to disasters as seen at Milchersdorf (Hainau) and at Königswartha.

Despite these setbacks, virtually every single engagement of the spring campaign was won by Napoleon's young troops. The 5th Division under Dufour won an action at Zollenspicker on May 6, and was victorious at Tettenborn on May 9 and again on May 12.[137] Oudinot's XII Corps performed well and flogged the Prussians at Hoyerswerda on May 28 and again beat the same opponents at Luckau on June 4.[138] "My squares were formed and well disposed," Oudinot wrote Berthier of the action at Luckau. "The young troops of His Majesty have shown in all circumstances a lot of courage and they stayed very calm while forming squares."[139] Numerous other skirmishes and combats produced similar results. Invariably, most of the combats involved French infantry against Allied cavalry, or French infantry fighting a combination of Allied cavalry and infantry.

Thus, except for the ambushes at Milchersdorf and Königswartha, and the failure of the cavalry outside Goldberg and Leipzig, both major and minor battles from late April to early June saw a repeated series of successes by French arms. The Prussians and Russians were no match for the Emperor and his imperfect instrument of war.

Of course, with success came its price tag—and it was high. The combat casualties sustained by Napoleon's forces from late April to early June were significant. However, it was the fatigue of the daily marches that drastically reduced the ranks of the young infantry and cavalry of the *Grande Armée*. Lauriston again voiced his opinion on this matter in a letter to Berthier on May 27. "The harvest of a moment's rest is needed to reorganize my army corps, which the last three night's marches have greatly reduced. The soldier is not yet accustomed to these sorts of fatigue. He fights like a lion, but he very badly needs to be supervised in the matter of discipline."[140]

The former cohorts composed of mature men were suffering, but the battalions comprised of younger soldiers fared even worse. Perhaps the best evidence of this is a letter from Marmont to Berthier on May 29. "Your Highness may recall my letter of 15 April which, in part, described the situation in the provisional [temporary] regiments. I am compelled to report that the deficiencies in the administration of the provisional [temporary] regiments is such that, unless the youths comprising the battalions which make up these formations can be rested and then transferred into the regiments of which they are organizationally part, they can not be counted on to conduct any more marches, let alone fight."[141]

Upon close inspection, the losses sustained by the *Grande Armée* from April 29 to June 4 were severe. Considering those lost in battle, the Imperial army had suffered more than 55,000 killed, wounded, and captured.[142] What proved more alarming was that another 90,000 troops overloaded the field hospitals[143]—casualties of strategic consumption. Despite these losses, Napoleon's army won both major engagements of the spring campaign and was driving the enemy forces out of Germany. However, the pursuit of the Russian and Prussian army across Saxony and into Silesia totally outstripped the meager capabilities of the army's administrative branch. By June 1, 1813, two corps of the *Grande*

Armée were down to their last cartridges and their resupply trains were no where to be found—they had fallen victim to the thousands of Cossacks marauding rear areas and lines of communication. This forced Napoleon to assign more and more active combat units to protecting the supply trains[144] that otherwise could have been with their corps.

These troubling factors, plus the deaths of Marshal Bessières and Grand Marshal Duroc—"sacrificed to fruitless victories"[145]—served to diminish the enthusiasm of many of Napoleon's marshals and generals. Baron Fain, one of the Emperor's secretaries, observed how the strain of constant wars "had ravaged these souls of iron."[146]

"Sire, I have felt sorrowful and I am still experiencing sorows," Bertrand wrote the Emperor on June 4. "But I beg Your Majesty to be persuaded that I will be forever a man of honor and one of the most beloved and devoted servants to an august person."[147] The officers as well as the young soldiers of the *Grande Armée* were in need of rest which was brought about by the Armistice of Pleischwitz.

Death of Marshal Bessières, 1 May 1813. *Composition by Boutigny.*

Colonel, French Line Infantry Regiment, 1813.
Composition by Édouard Detaille.

CHAPTER VI
"This Armistice Stops the Progress of My Victories"

On the same day that Marshal Oudinot fought the Prussians at Luckau, and three days before Arrighi defended Leipzig from Woronzow's Russians, an armistice was concluded between the warring sides at Pleischwitz on June 4. The reasons why Napoleon consented to a cessation of hostilities were both political and military. Politically, the Emperor was worried about Austria joining the coalition. There were already serious rumblings coming from Vienna, and in order to better prepare for the unwanted event should Austria enter the war, Napoleon had dispatched Prince Eugène back to Northern Italy in May to organize a new army to defend that important part of the Empire.[1]

There is no doubt that the main considerations for agreeing to an armistice were military. It is quite clear that the Emperor was extremely concerned about the insufficiency of his cavalry as well as to the overall condition of the army. This is born out in two important letters, the first of which was dated May 29 from Hughes Bernard Maret, Minister of Foreign Affairs, to Armand Augustin Caulaincourt, Duke of Vicenza, the minister negotiating the terms of the armistice. "An armistice which is not at least two and one-half months is of no service to the Emperor," wrote Maret, "as that is the time needed to reestablish his cavalry."[2]

The second document—a letter from Napoleon to Clarke—also confirms the Emperor's concern about his cavalry. "You will see, by the news in the *Moniteur*," Napoleon informed his Minister of War on June 2, " that we are negotiating an armistice. It would be possible that it is signed today or tomorrow. This armistice stops the progress of my victories. I decided upon it for two reasons: my lack of cavalry which prevents me striking telling blows, and the hostile position of Austria...Communicate the substance of this letter to the minister of the War Ministry and redouble efforts on behalf of the cavalry, artillery, and the infantry on the march in the various directions I have ordered. If I am to do it, I shall wait until September to strike heavy blows. I wish to be then in a position to crush my enemies...."[3]

Napoleon has been criticized by many historians for having agreed to the June armistice.[4] His forces had won every major engagement—and most of the minor ones— since the start of the campaign. The Emperor had pushed his army relentlessly eastward, driving before it the disheartened troops of the Tsar[5] along with the defeated, though still aggresive, Prussians.[6] Napoleon had reestablished his reputation over his opponents despite overall numerical inferiority, the fact that the *Grande Armée* had very few cavalrymen, and despite enormous wastage through strategic consumption.

However, Napoleon's advance across Saxony and into Silesia had become a logistical nightmare. The march of the *Grande Armée* had outstripped the meager transport and administrative services. As a result, most of the corps were low on ammunition while two others had only the cartridges in their pouches.[7] All the corps were on one-quarter bread rations[8] as transport convoys requiring larger and larger escorts had to battle the menacing Russian Cossacks that roamed the countryside. As a result, the lack of nourishment led to serious difficulties in trying to keep the young men strong enough just to keep them in ranks.[9]

Thus, to put the army back in order (the reader should never forget that, above all else, Napoleon was a man of order), to strengthen its numbers, and restore its administration, Napoleon agreed to the armistice. In so doing, it is interesting to note that not one of the Emperor's corps commanders or confidants advised him against this move. It was a decision that seemingly met with approval from all levels of command and government. Therefore, it is certainly reasonable to postulate that, by the summer of 1813, most of the people surrounding Napoleon desired a cessation of hostilities and were hoping that the armistice would lead to a permanent peace.

These hopes notwithstanding, the ministers and commanders still went about their duties in improving the *Grande Armée*. "The condition of the regiments which make up the III Army Corps," wrote Marshal Ney to Berthier on June 10, "deserves the Emperor's full attention. All have need of reinforcements, particularly officers and non-coms, for it is impossible to find in the actual cadres subjects to replace those that have been lost. It would take around 80 captains, 100 lieutenants, and at least 140 sergeant-majors, sergeants, or quarter-masters to reorganize the battalions. Without this help, what remains cannot be counted on; the incentives of the organization lose each day their force, instruction becomes impossible, and discipline is destroyed."[10]

Ney's III Corps had suffered heavily in the five weeks from April 27 to June 4, 1813. Of the 49,189 officers and other ranks who were present and under arms on April 25, only 24,581—half the corps—were still in ranks by May 31.[11] The latter figure includes several companies of artillery, engineers, and other support units which reinforced the corps before Bautzen.[12] The reduction of the effectives within the ranks of III Corps dramatically illustrates the losses incurred within the line corps of the *Grande Armée* during the spring campaign.

Oudinot's XII Corps, which on April 25 boasted 26,194 combatants in ranks, was reduced by May 14 to 23,620 officers and other ranks present and under arms. These numbers were reduced to 13,818 present by June 4.[13] Of the remaining troops, some 717 were General Beaumont's cavalry which had been attached to the corps after May 14. Therefore, of the same units which comprised XII Corps in late April, only 13,101 remained with the colors—a loss of 50%.[14]

"The three divisions of the IV Corps have suffered a lot during May 18, 20, and 21," Bertrand wrote the Emperor on June 4. "I am sending to the deputy chief of staff a report on the conditions of the soldiers as well as the report on the battle of the 21st in which the IV Corps participated. I beg Your Majesty to send help to the IV Corps."[15]

Once the fighting stopped, the reaction effect "well known to doctors"[16] occurred almost immediately. Following weeks of stress, fatigue, and violent emotions, within a few days after hostilities temporarily ended, there were "crowds of sick"[17] choking the hospitals.[18] In almost every line corps, the sick were a minimum of 33% of the total effectives. Some corps had as many as 50% of their people on the sick lists.[19]

The number of men which flooded the hospitals was alarming in another respect—many were there because of self-inflicted wounds. Reports of voluntary mutilation were noted in almost every report of every head surgeon in the army.[20] In a dispatch to Marshal Oudinot on June 9, the head surgeon of the XII Corps believed that "the self-inflicted wounds are only found among the youngest soldiers of the corps."[21] The Duke of Reggio passed this information on to Berthier the same day, adding that "the Emperor needs to address this matter at once."[22]

Action was not long in coming. Napoleon immediately ordered an investigation by instructing one of his most able and trusted administrators, Count Pierre Daru, to carefully interview every single wounded man in every hospital of every corps in the entire army![23] For this prodigious task, Daru sought and received the assistance of Count Mathieu Dumas, the Intendant General of the *Grande Armée*. Together, Daru, Dumas, and their staffs turned up some shocking statistics.

There were literally thousands of men who had been wounded only in the hand. On June 13, Daru reported that, in the Dresden hospitals alone, there were 2,128 of these persons.[24] Some corps commanders did not wait for Daru to visit, and held their own inspections. The VI Corps seemed to have had less of a problem than most. On July 2, Marshal Marmont wrote to the Major General: "I have scrupulously reviewed the record of all the men wounded in the hand, and in regard to each of them I made an inquiry in their regiment. His Majesty will learn doubtlessly with pleasure that only a quarter are suspected of having wounded themselves; I have come to the certainty that out of 404 men wounded in the hand, 295 have been by the enemy, and the result of my interrogation is all the less suspect since I have noticed, in general, among the officers and the non-coms of the companies, a spirit of strictness which does them honor."[25]

What to do with thousands of cowards who had self-inflicted wounds was soon decided. Since men with mutilated hands could not continue to serve in the cavalry, infantry, or artillery, they were transferred either to the train of artillery (*train d'artillerie*) or to the supply train (*equipage militaires*).[26] The men who had deliberately maimed themselves found grueling labor behind a team of horses.

Another major problem was the lack of money[27] with which to pay the army. In the spring, most of the country's defense funds had been used to equip and arm the hosts of new soldiers, as well as procure horses and new mobile equipment. By June, both the officers and men of the *Grande Armée* were completely impoverished as they had not been paid at all that year.[28] With hostilities temporarily abated, the army's morale suffered from the lack of pay. To partially correct this situation, Napoleon issued a general order on June 27,[29] authorizing that all ranks were to immediately receive backpay for the first four months of the year. Also, officers were to receive their pay for May.

Along with the backpay, the Emperor decreed that target practices be organized in every corps, with progressively bigger prizes for the best marksman at the company, battalion, regimental, brigade, division, and corps levels.[30] "The objective," explained Napoleon on July 23, "is, not only to train the troops, but also to provide a little gaiety and interest in the camps. Indeed, it is proper that all sorts of games and everything that can cause competetion be established."[31]

The money and shooting competetions were welcomed, and both served to help improve morale. Neither, however, solved the biggest problem facing the Emperor's army—the lack of food. Since the beginning of the armistice, most of Napoleon's troops were stationed in lower Silesia. The Emperor wanted to use the weeks of peace to rebuild his infantry, and to improve and increase his cavalry. While these were being accomplished, Napoleon ordered the building of hut camps to shelter the men and to spare them the daily troubles of foraging. No longer allowed to forage for food and drink, the French were reduced to requisitioning supplies from a hostile, local populace, complimented by the army's bakeries.

COMPARISON OF STRENGTHS FOR III CORPS
FOR THE PERIOD 25 APRIL TO 31 MAY 1813

III CORPS

	# (bns)	25 April Officers	25 April Other Ranks	31 May Officers	31 May Other Ranks	% casualties & strategic consumption suffered during this period
8th Division— Général de division Count Souham						
1st Brigade: Général de brigade Chasseraux						
6th Provisional Light Infantry	(2)		1,662[†]	32	622	61%
10th Provisional Light Infantry	(2)	36	1,541	30	570	62%
14th Provisional Regt. of the Line	(2)	39	1,558	19	696	55%
19th Provisional Regt. of the Line	(2)	37	1,258	21	523	58%
2nd Brigade: Général de brigade Chemineau						
21st Provisional Regt. of the Line	(2)	32	1,572	25	643	58%
24th Provisional Regt. of the Line	(2)	34	1,555	11	678	57%
22nd Regiment of the Line	(4)	79	3,088	49	1,139	62%
Divisional artillery and train			387[†]	7	188	50%
Engineers			187[‡]	3	148	19%
8th Division Totals*			13,065[†]		5,404[†]	59%

[†]Includes officers.
*Excludes staff and equipage.

	# (bns)	25 April Officers	25 April Other Ranks	31 May Officers	31 May Other Ranks	% casualties & strategic consumption suffered during this period
9th Division— Général de division Brenier (Delmas)						
1st Brigade: Général de brigade Anthing						
2nd Provisional Light Infantry	(2)	35	1,177	24	436	62%
29th Light Infantry Regiment	(1)	19	659	24	595	9%
136th Regiment of the Line	(4)	77	2,709	56	1,209	55%
2nd Brigade: Général de brigade Grillot						
138th Regiment of the Line	(4)	86	2,709	46	874	67%
145th Regiment of the Line	(4)	92	1,925	69	1,536	20%
Divisional artillery and train		5	349	7	254	26%
Engineers		3	178	3	82	53%
9th Division Totals*			10,023[†]		5,215[†]	48%

[†]Includes officers.
*Excludes staff and equipage.

	# (bns)	25 April Officers	25 April Other Ranks	31 May Officers	31 May Other Ranks	% casualties & strategic consumption suffered during this period
10th Division— Général de division Baron Girard (Albert)						
1st Brigade: Général de brigade Gorie						
4th Provisional Light Infantry	(2)	38	1,012	29	517	48%
139th Regiment of the Line	(4)	98	2,353	56	1,076	54%
2nd Brigade: Général de brigade Van Dedem						
140th Regiment of the Line	(4)	78	2,537	50	1,252	50%
141st Regiment of the Line	(4)	82	1,932	55	857	55%
Divisional artillery and train		7	358	8	218	38%
Engineers		not present		3	82	---
10th Division Totals*			8,486[†]		4,118[†]	51%

†Includes officers.
*Excludes staff and engineers.

11th Division— Général de division Baron Ricard
1st Brigade: Général de brigade Tarayre

9th Light Infantry Regiment	(2)	27	1,218	21	508	58%
17th Provisional Regt. of the Line	(2)	33	1,376	28	610	55%
18th Provisional Regt. of the Line	(2)	29	1,139	21	503	55%

2nd Brigade: Général de brigade Dumoulin

142nd Regiment of the Line	(4)	89	2,008	56	1,054	47%
144th Regiment of the Line	(4)	94	1,940	60	1,090	43%
Divisional artillery and train		3	367	16	270	23%
Engineers		2	181	2	147	19%
11th Division Totals*			8,506†		4,386†	48%

†Includes officers.
*Excludes staff and equipage.

39th Division— Général de division Count Marchand
1st Brigade: Général de brigade Stockhorn

1st Baden Regiment of the Line	(1)	14	664	12	463	30%
3rd Baden Regiment of the Line	(2)	29	1,658	23	1,110	33%

2nd Brigade: Général de brigade Prince Emile of Hesse-Darmstadt

Hesse-Darmstadt Leib-Garde Fusiliers	(2)	19	1,315	25	841	35%
2nd Hesse-Darmstadt Musketeers	(2)	37	1,242	24	649	47%
Hesse-Darmstadt Leib-Garde Regiment	(2)	30	1,250	27	672	45%
Divisional artillery and train		4	246	9	336	---
39th Division Totals*			6,508†		4,191†	36%

†Includes officers. *Excludes staff and equipage.

III Corps Cavalry Brigade— Général de brigade Laboissière

10th Hussars, 1st—3rd squadrons	(3)	32	685	26	692	---
Baden Light Dragoons, 1st—4th sqdrns	(4)	26	474	9	290	40%
Cavalry Brigade Totals*			1,217†		1,017†	16%

†Includes officers. *Excludes staff and equipage.

III Corps Artillery Reserve—

2 companies of Foot Artillery	not present		8	344	---
2 companies of Horse Artillery	not present		8	231	---
Engineers (Sappers), 3 companies	7	387	5	245	36%
Artillery Reserve Totals*		394†		841†	---

†Includes officers. *Excludes staff and equipage.

III CORPS TOTALS:

	49,189†#	24,581†**	50%
	71 guns	84 guns	

† Includes officers.
# Includes staff and equipage.
** Excludes staff, equipages, and reserve artillery companies present on May 31 which were not with the corps on April 25.

In theory, there was merit to this plan. The country was rich and could support friendly troops. However, the populace of lower Silesia had no love for the French and thus cooperated very little with the requisition requests made by the Emperor's agents.[32] "Our agents," wrote Count Daru on July 1, "after receiving virtually no supplies from the most modest requests, are forced to demand much in order to receive very little."[33] As a result, Napoleon's soldiers continued to experience undernourishment, even though they were no longer on active campaign.

Responding to Napoleon's directive, it is interesting to note Marshal Ney's reply. "I will order the target practice," the Prince of the Moscowa informed Berthier on July 25. "As for the games to be established in the camps to provide gaiety and competetion for the soldiers, I think what would better produce a similar effect would be to line up his pay and especially to feed him more abundantly. The ration has not always been complete, and the men who compose my army corps are at an age where one eats the most and where the entire ration is not even sufficient. The soldier has not stopped working on his barracks and exercising, and it would be very urgent that he be granted additional bread."[34]

For many years, the daily bread ration for a French soldier was 28 ounces. A decree in 1810 reduced the ration to 24 ounces per day.[35] Naturally, this bread allowance was supposed to be supplemented by supplies obtained either through foraging or requisition. However, with the 1813 administrative system incapable of supplying the needed bread, many of the troops were deprived of their most basic ration. Add to this the unwillingness of the German population to provide Napoleon's troops with requested requisitions, and one begins to see how the Emperor's young soldiers were on the verge of starvation during the armistice.

This point is clearly born out in the correspondence of the corps commanders. Two days following Ney's complaint about the lack of bread for III Corps, Marshal Marmont sent a similar letter to the Major General. "Since the establishment of the VI Corps in the Bunzlau circle," the Duke of Ragusa wrote on July 27, "the means of subsistance have been so difficult that it was necessary several times to reduce the ration [of bread]; but circumstances called for it. Today, our situation is changing; in four of five days we will be out of all trouble, and the harvest which is under way will give us the greatest resources. However, it does not alter the fact that many of my troops, especially the youngest, are undernourished. What bread is delivered is mostly rye which is not nearly as desirable as wheat.

"It is well documented," Marmont concluded, "that the nourishment of 24 ounces of bread is not sufficient for the young soldiers who have not reached their full growth and who are exercising six or seven hours a day, especially not getting and being unable to get neither wine nor beer regularly, and not even brandy to substitute for the lack of better subsistance. It seems to me well documented that the gloom of the troops, about which His Majesty is taking such useful and wise measures, will not disappear until the soldiers have more strength, and they will have more strength when they eat more."[36]

Other corps commanders wrote similar letters as well. Bertrand noted in a July 31 letter to Berthier that "the soldiers are constantly hungry. If hostilities are to resume shortly, how can His Majesty expect IV Corps to sustain marches on an empty stomach? The *ordonnateur* [organizing officer] does what he can, but the results are wholly lacking."[37]

Lauriston offered his opinion as well. "I have just reviewed the V Corps," he wrote Berthier on August 1. "I am very satisified with the progress of the training, but I cannot be more displeased with our lack of subsistance. It was the reason why so many dropped out of ranks in the last campaign. If something is not done at once to correct the situation, a similar circumstance cannot help but be repeated."[38]

Marshal Victor likewise voiced his concern over the lack of food and pay, and the impact on his young troops. "I am convinced about the inconveniences caused by the reduction of the bread ration to 24 ounces," Victor wrote to Berthier on August 5. "It is recognized by all officers that this last amount is not sufficient to nourish a young soldier who is still growing, especially when that soldier is endlessly, as today, busy with tiring exercises and drinks only water. It can be seen every day that a great number of these young men are suffering from hunger and that their bodies, which would be strengthened by better nourishment, are visibly weakened and soon put out of serviceable condition...The army will soon be fine and very good, if I can judge other corps by the expectations given me by the II Corps; but, to have it thus, I am of the opinion that the pay must be brought up to date as soon as possible and the bread ration must be 28 ounces instead of 24."[39]

Macdonald added his voice to those of the other corps commanders in calling for more food for his troops. "I herein submit the parade states for XI Corps taken this morning," the Duke of Tarentum informed Berthier on August 1. "The officers and men of my corps are generally in good spirits, but most are constantly hungry. I attribute this to the fact that the ration of bread is too small, if and when we receive it, and that the requisitioned supplies are not surrendered by the local populace. If we are to remain in camps, my soldiers are going to have to be supplied, or soon they will not be fit for duty."[40]

These pleas, laced with some prophetic insights, were to no avail. The administrative branch of the army had a job too big to handle and the Imperial treasury was all but bankrupt.

While the corps commanders were worrying about feeding and paying their troops, they were also faced with another challenge—improving the training of the soldiers while increasing the size of their regiments. Throughout the spring campaign and the armistice, new conscripts of the various levies continued to pour into the training centers. Acknowledging that the previous regulation to keep the recruits in the depots for four weeks of training was an impossibility, the Ministry of War officially reduced the training period to only two weeks.[41] This, too, was a useless regulation. The flood of conscripts was simply too great; most men remained in the depots only 8 to 10 days.

In vain, the officers and non-commissioned officers of the training centers tried to whip the recruits into enough shape so they could conform to the Ministry's circular that all troops were suppose to arrive in Mayence "already trained in battalion movements."[42] The absurdity of this expectation cannot be overstated too strongly. How were the instructional personnel of the training centers supposed to meet up on the road to the depot with a group of young men—mostly 18 and 19 year-olds—and take them in a matter of *days* from being totally unfamiliar with any aspect of military life to being "already trained in battalion movements?" For the Ministry of War to forecast such a transformation totally defies any sense of military logic or rationale.

From the reports penned during the first four months of 1813 and discussed earlier in this work, it should have been clear to Clarke and his ministers that it took new recruits several weeks just to be able to achieve platoon—or company—level drill, and at least several months to reach battalion level maneuvers. Therefore, the Ministry of War's requirement, or expectation, that the depot officers deliver to Mayence new troops with the equivalent of two months training was sheer fantasy, unless of course the training centers were going to keep the men of the various levies for at least two months. Naturally, that did not happen. Therefore, masses of uniformed and armed, but virtually untrained, conscripts choked the roads heading east to the Rhine and on into Germany where they joined the *Grande Armée*.

Ever since the embryonic stages of the 1813 army's organization, there were temporary, or provisional, regiments of line or light infantry. These regiments were formed by taking separate battalions from two different regiments and combining them for field operations. In some instances, three battalions from separate regiments were combined into temporary, or provisional, demi-brigades. In every division and corps in which the temporary regiments were present, the division and corps commanders continually protested as to the existance and combat worth of these makeshift formations.

General Joseph Souham, commander of the 8th Division, was among the strongest critics of the provisional regiments. "With the exception of the 22nd Regiment of the Line," Souham wrote Ney on June 15, "my entire division is comprised of temporary regiments. These units, which only appeared through the haste of organizing the army for the last campaign, must be abolished and the battalions reorganized into the regiments of which they are part. Only in this way can the battalions of the same regiment be brought together to develop the administration and espirit de corps so essential for making war. I urge Your Highness to inform His Majesty of this unfortunate arrangement and to seek an immediate remedy."[43] Ney took up the matter with Imperial headquarters.

"There are in the III Corps," the Prince of the Moscowa informed the Major General on July 11, "twenty-five battalions forming temporary regiments whose administration is extremely neglected....The depots of the units of which they are momentarily a part send them nothing, no doubt because they fear the incorporation of these battalions into the regiments whose number they bear and to which they belong. I can, furthermore, assure your most Serene Highness that the welfare of the Emperor's service would require that this incorporation be made the soonest possible time; this would even be, as it seems to me, the only way of remedying the disorders of all kinds which reign in the temporary regiments and which one can attribute solely to the mistaken forming of these units."[44]

Marshal Marmont, who had written Berthier on April 15 about the "worthless"[45] value of the temporary regiments, wrote again on this matter during the armistice. "Your Highness is no doubt aware as to the problems connected with the temporary regiments," the Duke of Ragusa wrote on June 29. "The dissolution of these formations, and the reuniting of these battalions with their parent regiment, should be ordered at once."[46]

The many complaints regarding the temporary regiments had already persuaded the Ministry of War to abolish these formations. Only two days after the armistice was signed, Clarke wrote to Berthier, authorizing him to reduce and reorganize "as many as soon as possible, the number of temporary regiments, by incorporating into the same divisions the battalions of the same regimental number."[47]

Extensive reorganization was realized among the battalions comprising the temporary regiments raised before the spring campaign. Of the 52 temporary regiments in the active line corps of the army on April 25, only 16 remained in existence when hostilities resumed in mid-August.[48] The temporary regiments were completely eliminated in the I, II, IV, and XII Corps. The VI and XI Corps each reduced their number of temporary regiments by two.

However, the abolishment of old temporary regiments did not encompass those in the IX Corps (formerly the Observation Corps of Bavaria), and the newly-formed XIV Corps. In both these corps, many temporary regiments were formed during the summer out of necessity to group the disparate battalions. Attempts at dissolving the temporary regiments in both these corps, as well as in some of the temporary regiments in the older corps, were halted in early August. The reason for this was "the fear of disorganizing, at the moment of resumption of hostilities, the divisions and corps"[49] which contained the

Number of Temporary, or Provisional, Regiments of French Line and Light Infantry in the Active Corps of Napoleon's *Grande Armée* of 1813

Corps—Division		Number on 25 April	Number on 15 August	Change in the Number of Temporary Regiments
I Corps	1st Division	8	0	-8
	2nd Division	8	0	-8
	23rd Division[1]	not formed	0	0
II C.	4th Division	6	0	-6
	5th Division	6	0	-6
	6th Division	not formed	0	0
III C.	8th Division	6	6	0
	9th Division	1	1	0
	10th Division	1	1	0
	11th Division	2	1	-1
IV C.	12th Division	2	0	-2
	15th Division	0	0	0
V C.	16th Division	0	0	0
	17th Division	0	0	0
	18th Division	0	0	0
	19th Division	0	0	0
VI C.	20th Division	2	2	0
	21st Division	2	0	-2
	22nd Division	3	3	0
VII C.	or VIII Corps	0	0	0
IX C.[2]	51st Division	not formed	4	+4
	52nd Division	not formed	5	+5
	53rd Division	not formed	1	+1
	54th Division	not formed	5	+5
XI C.	31st Division	2	2	0
	35th Division	0	0	0
	36th Division	2	0	-2
XII C.	13th Division	1	0	-1
	14th Division	0	0	0
XIII C.	3rd & 40th Divs	not formed	0	0
	50th(-) Division	not formed	0	0
XIV C.	42nd Division	not formed	5	+5
	43rd Division	not formed	2	+2
	44th Division	not formed	4	+4
	45th Division	not formed	5	+5
Totals:		52	47	-5

[1] Originally part of VI Corps, transferred to I Corps.
[2] Formerly known as the Observation Corps of Bavaria.
Note: Eugène's Army of Italy is not included in the above calculations.

battalions comprising the temporary regiments. This is why, for example, of the 10 temporary regiments in III Corps on April 25, all but one of those temporary regiments still remained when the fall campaign began.[50]

Many of the new conscripts were used as replacements and fed into existing units. In this manner, the losses of the spring campaign were made good during the armistice. Therefore, by August 15, many of the French line and light infantry battalions were up to full strength, while the cavalry regiments were substantially reinforced.[51]

In addition to the conscripts assigned to existing units, there were a great number who were assigned to newly-forming battalions around Mayence, Dresden, and Hamburg. Before the spring campaign began, Napoleon had ordered the formation of an observation corps at Mayence. Later, the name was changed to the Observation Corps of Bavaria and placed under the orders of Marshal Augereau, the Duke of Castiglione. With so many recruits pouring into Mayence, this corps grew to include six new French infantry divisions.

On August 4, the Emperor decided to split this observation corps in two. He therefore ordered four French infantry divisions—the 42nd, 43rd, 44th, and 45th—to become the XIV Corps[52] of the *Grande Armée* under the command of Marshal Gouvion Saint-Cyr. Marshal Augereau retained the 51st and 52nd Divisions to which was added the 53rd and 54th Divisions and the Duke of Castigilone's command was then renamed the IX Corps.[53]

Further reorganization of the army took place throughout the summer. In June, Napoleon informed Marshal Davout that the 1st and 2nd Divisions of I Corps under Vandamme would be recalled for service in the Dresden area.[54] On July 1, the move was formally ordered. The Emperor wanted Vandamme to have three infantry divisions so in addition to those adready part of I Corps, the 23rd Division under Teste, formerly of Marmont's VI Corps, was transferred to Vandamme's command.[55]

This left Davout to hold Hamburg with the 3rd and 40th Divisions, the Danish Auxiliary Division, and other, disparate forces of the government of Hamburg, under the nominal command of General Hogendorp. The active divisions under Davout's orders were designated as the XIII Corps.[56]

All the new French divisions raised during the summer had to be formed around cadres drawn from somewhere. Where could these cadres come from? After the pool of personnel from the remnants of the 1812 army, the Army of Spain, and the independent units from across the Empire were consumed, Napoleon had to turn to the military schools to find young officers for the new battalions. These institutions were scraped to the bottom. Saint-Cyr produced over 450 sub-lieutenants for the new army, bringing with them "the spirit of bravery and devotion."[57]

However, due to the unprecedented demand for officers, the academies were forced to reduce their officer candidates' time at the institutions to a mere two months.[58] Thus, the new officers had very little training before receiving their commissions. This is confirmed in the June 18 letter from the Inspector General of Military Schools to Berthier. "The 150 students [of Saint-Cyr] who are going to leave will be preferable to the preceding promotion of 240. They will at least have a knowledge of arithmetic with a notion of other classic courses, although they will have acquired it in two months."[59]

The pressing into service of young, enthusiastic, but nevertheless relatively untrained officers was due, of course, to the incredible number of conscripts being called to the colors. Throughout the armistice, the numerical progression of the French army increased substantially as dozens of newly formed battalions appeared on the roster sheets without any corresponding increase in morale or perceivable combat value. Virtually all the line and light infantry battalions raised during the summer were formed around scratch-built cadres, comprised primarily of the youths of the Class of 1814, then expediently thrown together into provisional regiments. The continued practice of forming new provisional, or temporary, regiments was continued despite the vehement protests made by virtually every corps and divisional commander in the army.

During this time, Napoleon was especially interested in augmenting the strength of his cavalry and the Young Guard. Virtually every means to increase their numbers was sought as new regiments of Young Guards were raised,[60] along with more squadrons within the cavalry regiments, while replacements into the existing formations made good the losses from the spring campaign.

The continued call for more soldiers to the ranks of the Young Guard began to worry the Minister of War. On July 21, Clarke communicated his feeling in this respect to the Emperor. "It is necessary to insist on this point [stop increasing the Young Guard] because it is unnerving the army."[61] However, even though Napoleon had earmarked 54,250 of the "best conscripts"[62] of the various levies for duty with the Young Guard, the Ministry of War found it to be a near impossible order to execute owing to the lack of quality recruits.[63] When the numbers going into the Young Guard began to slow down because of this fact, the Emperor immediately responded with reprimands.[64] The floodgates immediately opened and into the ranks of the Young Guard poured the conscripts of the various levies, regardless of physique.

"The 15 regiments of Tirailleurs and of Voltigeurs," wrote General Marie-François-August Caffarelli du Falga, the commander of the Imperial Guard in Paris, in a letter to Clarke on June 6, "each have more than 1,800 men made up of the weakest and most sickly which the conscription produced."[65] If there was any optimism about the new Young Guard regiments, it was the fact that the best officers and non-commissioned officers available were hand-picked by the Emperor.[66]

While some infantry regiments increased in size by the addition of new battalions, the existing battalions had their spring campaign losses replenished. A few infantry regiments actually reduced the number of battalions by consolidating survivors into fewer, stronger battalions. The practice of reducing the number of battalions was common in the more veteran regiments, such as those formed from the cohorts, as the officers did not want an infusion of conscripts into their regiments just to keep the same number of war battalions. That is why, for example, in V Corps, the line regiments reduced their war battalions from 4 to 3. Simiarly, the regiments of III Corps which were also formed from the cohorts used the armistice to consolidate the survivors of 4 battalions and the depot personnel into 3 war battalions with no depot battalion remaining.[67]

In contrast, another group of veterans increased their number of war battalions with the addition of conscripts from their regimental depots. In VI Corps, the 1st Regiment of the Naval Artillery Corps (1st Regiment de Marine) increased the number of its war battalions from 4 to 5 with all depot personnel—mainly conscripts of the Class of 1814—composing the 5th battalion. The 2nd Regiment de Marine maintained their 6 war battalions, while the 3rd and 4th Regiments of *Marins* each increased by one the number of war battalions in their regiments by ordering all depot personnel into the field as the 3rd battalion. Therefore, while the troops of the Naval Artillery Corps had 14 war battalions during the spring campaign, they fielded 17 war battalions for the fall campaign, the extra personnel for these battalions all coming from the emptying out of the regimental depots composed mainly of young conscripts.[68]

The cavalry's numbers were likewise increased during the armistice. New squadrons were stamped out with much the same rapidity in which the infantry battalions were formed. However, most of the troopers—once conscripted into service—were volunteers, and their officer material was markedly better. "Most of the officers and non-commissioned officers passing through the depot on the way to the army," wrote General Broucier to Clarke on June 10, "are veterans of the earlier wars and are eager to serve His Majesty."[69] Owing to this and the fact that most of the new men were fed into existing regiments, the regimental espirit de corps and élan so essential to the cavalry arm was more easily restored.

The armistice also allowed the artillery branch to increase the numbers of ordnance in the army. For the troops of the line, the desired artillery support was for each infantry division to be supported by 2 companies of foot artillery, each company consisting of six 6-pounder guns and two 51/2-inch howitzers, for an ideal total of 16 guns per division. Each line infantry corps was supposed to have at least two companies of reserve foot artillery and one company of horse artillery in the corps artillery reserve. Ideally, the reserve foot companies each consisted of six 12-pounder guns and two 6-inch or 51/2-inch howitzers. Each horse artillery company fielded four 6-pounder guns and two 51/2-inch howitzers. Further, each division of cavalry in the army's cavalry reserve was to be supported by one company of horse artillery.[70]

The summer also allowed some division commanders to try and resurrect the infantry's regimental artillery. In 1809, Napoleon had decreed that each regiment of line and light infantry was to have a company of regimental artillery consisting of two pieces of ordnance, typically captured Austrian 3 pounder guns or French Gribeauval 4 pounder cannon.[71] By the time of the Russian campaign, virtually all of the French line and light infantry regiments of the *Grande Armée* each had their own regimental guns.[72] With the difficulties associated with rebuilding the 1813 army, the reestablishment of the regimental artillery companies was not top priority, but some divisional commanders saw to it that their French regiments had the additional firepower.

As these companies began to reform, it became obvious that there were next to no more small-caliber cannon remaining—these pieces had perished in the depths of Russia while most of the remaining 3 or 4 pounder guns had already been melted down to cast new 6 pounder field pieces. In searching for guns for the regimental artillery companies, Davout's chief of staff reported that "there are only 2 pieces of 8 [pounders] and 2 pieces of 4 [pounders] belonging to the old [Gribeauval] artillery system in the entire 32nd Military Division."[73]

Since there were almost no 3 or 4 pounder cannon remaining, it was decided to arm the regimental artillery companies with 6 pounder guns.[74] Therefore, the regimental companies that saw service in 1813 served larger caliber pieces than ever before.

Looking at the parade states for the *Grande Armée* on 15 August 1813, it is evident that most of the line infantry divisions raised before the spring campaign were fully staffed with artillery personnel and ordnance. But primarily because of the lack of horses, the infantry divisions raised during the summer were less uniform in their artillery support.

Meanwhile, the artillery of the Imperial Guard was increased to an unprecedented establishment of 16 companies of Young Guard foot artillery, each company consisting of eight pieces of ordnance, of which six were 6-pounder guns and two were 51/2-inch howitzers. Also, the Old Guard Horse Artillery, the *Volante*, was once again increased to its full establishment of 6 companies, each company consisting of 6 pieces of which four were 6-pounder guns and two were 51/2-inch howitzers.[75]

The foot artillery of the Old Guard was also returned to its full strength establishment of six companies. Two companies each had six 6-pounder guns and two 51/2-inch howitzers. The remaining four companies were the Emperor's famous "Beautiful Daughters", each company consisting of six 12-pounder guns and two 6-inch howitzers.[76]

When the fall campaign opened, the artillery of the Imperial Guard consisted of the following ordnance:

Designation	Number of companies	Consisting of: 12-pdrs.	6pdrs.	6" h	51/2" h
Old Gd Foot	6	24	12	8	4
Old Gd Horse	6		24		12
Young Gd Foot	16		96		32
Totals—	28	24	132	8	48

Thus, the total ordnance belonging to the companies of the Imperial Guard numbered 212 pieces. In addition, the horse artillery company from the Grand Duchy of Berg fielding four 6-pounder guns and two 51/2-inch howitzers served in the Imperial Guard Corps, bringing the total number of ordnance operating with the Imperial Guard in August to 218 pieces.[77]

Throughout the summer, the commanders and troops worked hard at improving the training level of the army. The results varied significantly from corps to corps. Undoubtably the highest level of training proficiency for all arms existed in the Imperial Guard. This body of troops, consisting of the best men and officers which France could still boast, had no equal among the Continental adversaries. Nevertheless, it was not the same Guard which had been forged in the battles of the late Republic and throughout the early to middle Empire. While the Old and Middle Guard infantry and cavalry were proven veterans, any unusual factors concerning the training expertise in the Imperial Guard invariably originated with the new regiments of the Young Guard.

By the resumption of hostilities, the Young Guard infantry were capable of brigade maneuvers[78]—a feat which they could not perform before the armistice.[79] Among these regiments, there is little question that the best formations were the 3rd Voltigeurs and the 3rd Tirailleurs. Other Young Guard infantry regiments which were solidly rebuilt from existing cadres and developed into above-average units were the 1st and 2nd Regiments of Voltigeurs and Tirailleurs, as well as the Flanker Grenadiers. The remaining Young Guard regiments were, as already mentioned, formed from masses of conscripts built around cadres drawn from a variety of sources. Despite these problems, the improvement in the drill and training level of the Young Guard infantry made "considerable progress during the armistice."[80]

Like so many of the Young Guard infantry regiments that were newly raised in 1813, the new squadrons of cavalry belonging to the Young Guard were no where near the equals to the senior regiments of the Guard. There seems to be relatively few comments on these new squadrons, other than those made by their divisional and corps commanders.[81] In all cases, the opinions expressed about the Young Guard squadrons reeked of measured cynicism. "The squadrons belonging to the Young Guard," General Nansouty remarked to Berthier on August 1, "have shown dramatic improvements in their maneuvers. They now only have to prove themselves [in combat]."[82] "The Young Guard cavalrymen are well disposed," wrote General Ornano on August 5, "and their training is satisfactory. The officers realize that the first battles will fully measure their worthiness."[83]

Less optimistic were the observations concerning the new cavalry regiments comprising the Guards of Honor. General Dejean, one of Napoleon's aides de camp, was nominally the commander of the Guards of Honor Cavalry Division. Following a review of the different regimental assembly areas, Dejean penned this truthful report back to the Emperor on August 6. "I have just concluded my inspection of the regiments comprising the Guards of Honor. Although I am pleased with the efforts of the officers, I can hardly say the same about the rest. While there are a few patriotic volunteers in the ranks, most of the enlisted men are not well disposed. They do not respond to discipline and their conduct is derisible, and they are scorned by the rest of the army. I must inform Your Majesty that the greater portion of these regiments cannot be considered as combat ready. Once brought into the field, most of the men will no doubt find a way to quit the ranks. It is my opinion that once this occurs, they will be worth much more than they are now, since only the troops wanting to serve Your Highness will remain."[84]

There were no such negative reports about the Guard artillery. On the contrary, the generals were enthustiastic about their commands. "The horse artillery of the Guard, " General Desvaux de Saint-Maurice wrote to the Emperor on August 1, "has been completely restored to its former organization...The officers have an average of 17 years in the service and the gunlayers have an average of 14 years.

"I am completely satisfied with the maneuvers of these companies. From a full gallop, we are able to come to a stop and fire our first round in less than a minute...Our ammunition is plentiful and the animals are strong and well cared for.

"Your Majesty may be assured that the horse artillery of the Guard is ready to uphold its tradition...."[85]

General Drouot also voiced his feeling about the Guard artillery in an August 6 letter to Berthier. "The artillery of the Old Guard is fully restored and the Young Guard companies are filled out. All companies have at least double ammunition provisions, with both the foot and horse companies of the Old Guard having triple ammunition."[86]

Among the infantry troops of the line, those of Marmont's VI Corps showed the most improvement in their training and maneuvers.[87] Coordinated brigade drills, including being able to perform difficult "brigade in line"[88] maneuvers were evidence of the training progress made by the infantry of VI Corps. No doubt, some of the credit for this progress must be attributed to the more mature men and homogeneous units which comprised much of Marmont's command.

Other corps were not as far along in their training. For example, the notes shown on the August 1 parade states for Victor's II Corps—which was a two day affair beginning on July 31 and concluding on August 1—mention that the training of the troops was "merely a cut above mediocre."[89] This assessment, no doubt expressed in relative terms compared to previous French Imperial armies, perhaps best describes the majority of the troops comprising Napoleon's *Grande Armée* of 1813.

Regardless of the level of training, the army readied itself for campaigning in mid-August as hostilities resumed. On August 15, parade states for the army revealed the strength of the active corps of Napoleon's *Grande Armée* as follows:[89]

****

Count Antoine Drouot

One of the finest gunners produced by Napoleonic France was born in Nancy on 11 January 1774. Drouot attended the Châlons Artillery School, where he graduated at the top of his class. Commander of the foot artillery of the Guard in 1808, he served with distinction at Wagram and Borodino. During 1813 and 1814, he ably commanded large grand batteries at numerous battles. Highly respected by his fellow officers, Drouot was known as the "Sage of the Army." *Musée de l'Armée.*

Baron Desvaux de Saint-Maurice

The premier horse gunner of the *Grande Armée* was born in Paris on 26 June 1775. Desvaux was educated at the Châlons Artillery School, and saw extensive service during the Revolution. Colonel of the 6th Horse Artillery Regiment in 1803, Desvaux's abilities during the 1809 campaign earned him a promtion to Général de brigade and commander of the superb Guard Horse Artillery. He served with great distinction throughout his career until his death at Waterloo.

125

Napoleon's *Grande Armée*
as of
15 August 1813

Imperial Guard Mortier/Nansty.	# of bns/sqd	Strength of inf. & cav.	Average per battalion/sqdrn	Guns	Artillerists, engineers, train, etc
Old Gd Inf Div	10 / --	4,805	480 / --	8	217
1st Yg Gd Div	14 / --	8,590	614 / --	24	783
2nd Yg Gd Div	14 / --	8,186	585 / --	24	850
3rd Yg Gd Div	12 / --	8,037	670 / --	24	545
4th Yg Gd Div	12 / --	7,894	658 / --	24	640
1st Gd Cav Div	-- / 22	4,028	--- / 183	---	---
2nd Gd Cav Div	-- / 24	4,984	--- / 208	---	---
Guards of Honor	-- / 20	5,037	--- / 252	---	---
Horse Artillery of the Guard with the Guard cavalry				24	794
Guard Artillery Reserve				90	6,358
Corps Totals:	62 / 66	51,561	--- / ---	218	10,187

Imperial Guard net strength of 61,748 present and under arms, of which:

> 37,512, or 61% of the corps were infantry,
>
> 14,049, or 23% of the corps were cavalry, and
>
> 10,187, or 16% of the corps were artillerists and other support troops.
>
> Guard artillery ratio on August 15 was 1 gun for every 283 combatants.

I Corps Vandamme	# of bns/sqd	Strength of inf. & cav.	Average per battalion/sqdrn	Guns	Artillerists, engineers, train, etc
1st Division	14 / --	9,626	688 / --	16	303
2nd Division	14 / --	10,226	730 / --	16	309
23rd Division	14 / --	9,725	695 / --	14	321
27th Division(-)	4 / 8	2,689	360 / 156	6	166
Corps Cavalry	-- / 4	835	---- / 209	---	---
Corps Artillery Reserve				28	1,144
Troops in route		1,432			
Corps Totals:	46 / 12	34,533	--- / ---	80	2,243

I Corps net strength of 36,776 present and under arms, of which:

> 32,451, or 88% of the corps were infantry,
>
> 2,082, or 6% of the corps were cavalry, and
>
> 2,243, or 6% of the corps were artillerists and other support troops.
>
> I Corps artillery ratio on August 15 was 1 gun for every 460 combatants.

II Corps Victor	# of bns/sqd	Strength of inf. & cav.	Average per battalion/sqdrn	Guns	Artillerists, engineers, train, etc
4th Division	15 / --	9,969	665 / --	16	388
5th Division	14 / --	9,376	670 / --	14	305
6th Division	13 / --	8,253	635 / --	16	265
Corps Cavalry	-- / 6	781	--- / 130	---	---
Corps Artillery Reserve				20	1,054
Troops in route		1,539			
Corps Totals:	42 / 6	29,918	--- / ---	66	2,012

II Corps net strength of 31,930 present and under arms, of which:

29,137, or 91% of the corps were infantry,
781, or 2% of the corps were cavalry, and
2,012, or 7% of the corps were artillerists and other support troops.

II Corps artillery ratio on August 15 was 1 gun every 484 combatants.

III Corps Ney	# of bns/sqd	Strength of inf. & cav.	Average per battalion/sqdrn	Guns	Artillerists, engineers, train, etc
8th Division	15 / --	8,000	533 / --	12	269
9th Division	13 / --	6,616	509 / --	16	289
10th Division	11 / --	5,230	475 / --	16	295
11th Division	13 / --	6,299	485 / --	12	314
39th Division	10 / --	5,443	544 / --	12	355
Corps Cavalry	-- / 11	1,659	--- / 151	---	---
Corps Artillery Reserve				42	2,226
Troops in route		3,355			
Corps Totals:	62 / 11	36,602	--- / ---	110	3,748

III Corps net strength of 40,350 present and under arms, of which:

34,837, or 86.5% of the corps were infantry,
1,765 or 4.5% of the corps were cavalry, and
3,748, or 9% of the corps were artillerists and other support troops.

III Corps artillery ratio on August 15 was 1 gun every 367 combatants.

IV Corps Bertrand	# of bns/sqd	Strength of inf. & cav.	Average per battalion/sqdrn	Guns	Artillerists, engineers, train, etc
12th Division	11 / --	7,112	647 / --	16	447
15th Division	14 / --	7,588	542 / --	12	499
38th Division	8 / ---	3,479	435 / --	6	115
Corps Cavalry	-- / 8	763	--- / 95	6	117
Corps Artillery Reserve				24	1,625
Troops in route		834			
Corps Totals:	33 / 8	19,776	--- / ---	64	2,803

IV Corps net strength of 22,579 present and under arms, of which:

19,013, or 84.5% of the corps were infantry,

763, or 3% of the corps were cavalry, and

2,803, or 12.5% of the corps were artillerists and other support troops.

IV Corps artillery ratio on August 15 was 1 gun every 353 combatants.

V Corps Lauriston	# of bns/sqd	Strength of inf. & cav.	Average per battalion/sqdrn	Guns	Artillerists, engineers, train, etc
16th Division	9 / --	6,826*	758 / --	24	418**
17th Division	13 / --	7,860*	605 / --	20	375**
19th Division	12 / --	9,369*	781 / --	22	303**
Corps Artillery Reserve				26	1,218
Troops in route		1,445			
Corps Totals:	34 / --	25,500*	--- / --	92	2,314**

V Corps net strength of 27,814 present and under arms, of which:

25,500*, or 92% of the corps were infantry, and

2,314**, or 8% of the corps were artillerists and other support troops.

V Corps artillery ratio on August 15 was 1 gun every 302 combatants.

* Includes regimental artillery company personnel.

**Excludes regimental artillery company personnel.

VI Corps Marmont	# of bns/sqd	Strength of inf. & cav.	Average per battalion/sqdrn	Guns	Artillerists, engineers, train, etc
20th Division	14 / --	8,194	585 / --	16	450
21st Division	14 / -	8,335	595 / --	16	480
22nd Division	14 / --	6,184	442 / --	16	484
Corps Cavalry	--./ 8	907	---- / 113	6	122
Corps Artillery Reserve				32	1,462
Corps Totals:	42 / 8	23,620	---- / ---	86	2,998

VI Corps net strength of 26,618 present and under arms, of which:

22,713, or 85.5% of the corps were infantry,
907, or 3.5% of the corps were cavalry, and
2,998, or 11% of the corps were artillerists and other support troops.

VI Corps artillery ratio on August 15 was 1 gun every 310 combatants.

VII Corps Reynier	# of bns/sqd	Strength of inf. & cav.	Average per battalion/sqdrn	Guns	Artillerists, engineers, train, etc
24th Division	10 / --	5,967	597 / --	12	452
25th Division	9 / --	5,072	564 / --	12	359
32nd Division	14*/ --	10,504	727* / --	12	447
Corps Cavalry	-- / 13	1,521	---- / 117	12	327
Corps Artillery Reserve				6	558
Troops in route		376			
Corps Totals:	33*/13	23,440	--- / ---	54	2,143

* The number of battalions present excludes the detachments present with the 32nd Division.

VII Corps net strength of 25,583 present and under arms, of which:

21,919, or 86% of the corps were infantry,
1,521, or 6% of the corps were cavalry, and
2,143, or 8% of the corps were artillerists and other support troops.

VII Corps artillery ratio on August 15 was 1 gun every 474 combatants.

VIII Corps Poniatowski	# of bns/sqd	Strength of inf. & cav.	Average per battalion/sqdrn	Guns	Artillerists, engineers, train, etc
26th Division	8 / --	4,466	558 / --	18	413
27th Div(-)	2 / --	1,165	582 / --	9	205
Corps Cavalry	-- / 6	1,182	--- / 197	---	---
Corps Artillery Reserve				9	541
Corps Totals:	10 / 6	6,813	--- / --	36	1,159

VIII Corps net strength of 7,972 present and under arms, of which:

> 5,631, or 71% of the corps were infantry,
> 1,182, or 15% of the corps were cavalry, and
> 1,159, or 14% of the corps were artillerists and other support troops.
> VIII Corps artillery ratio on August 15 was 1 gun every 221 combatants.

IX Corps Augereau	# of bns/sqd	Strength of inf. & cav.	Average per battalion/sqdrn	Guns	Artillerists, engineers, train, etc
51st Division	12 / --	9,223	769 / --	12*	480
52nd Division	11 / --	8,342	758 / --	12*	482
53rd Division—still forming					
54th Division—still forming					
No corps cavalry, although the V *bis* Reserve Cavalry Corps later attached to IX Corps.					
Corps Artillery Reserve				14*	598
Corps Totals:	23 / --	17,565	--- / --	38*	1,560

IX Corps net strength of 19,125 present and under arms, of which:

> 17,565, or 92% of the corps were infantry, and
> 1,560, or 8% of the corps were artillerists and other support troops.
> *No artillery materiel returns given; therefore, these are best estimates.
> Estimated IX Corps artillery ratio on August 15 was 1 gun every 503 combatants.

X Corps in garrison at Danzig—see Appendix D for details.

XI Corps Macdonald	# of bns/sqd	Strength of inf. & cav.	Average per battalion/sqdrn	Guns	Artillerists, engineers, train, etc
31st Division	14/ --	7,653	547 / --	20	661
35th Division	13 / --	6,727	518 / --	22	658
36th Division	11 / --	6,145	559 / --	20	512
Corps Cavalry	-- / 7	1,165	--- / 166	--	---
Corps Artillery Reserve				38	1,170
Corps Totals:	38 / 7	21,690	--- / ---	100	3,001

XI Corps net strength of 24,691 present and under arms, of which:

> 20,525, or 83% of the corps were infantry,
> 1,165, or 5% of the corps were cavalry, and
> 3,001, or 12% of the corps were artillerists and other support troops.
> XI Corps artillery ratio on August 15 was 1 gun every 247 combatants.

XII Corps Oudinot	# of bns/sqd	Strength of inf. & cav.	Average per battalion/sqdrn	Guns	Artillerists, engineers, train, etc
13th Division	9 / --	4,141	460 / --	16	322
14th Division	11 / --	7,027	638 / --	16	346
29th Division	10 / --	4,446	444 / --	18	512
Corps Cavalry	-- / 10	1,187	--- / 118	---	---
Corps Artillery Reserve				16	963
Corps Totals:	30 / 10	16,963	--- / ---	66	2,143

XII Corps net strength of 19,106 present and under arms, of which:

> 15,776, or 83% of the corps were infantry,
> 1,187, or 6% of the corps were cavalry, and
> 2,143, or 11% of the corps were artillerists and other support troops.
> XII Corps artillery ratio on August 15 was 1 gun every 289 combatants.

XIII Corps Davout	# of bns/sqd	Strength of inf. & cav.	Average per battalion/sqdrn	Guns	Artillerists, engineers, train, etc
3rd Division	14 / --	9,232	659 / --	16	446
40th Division	14 / --	9,929	709 / --	12	232
50th Div.(-)	6 / --	3,654	609 / --	9	194
Danish Div.—					
infantry	13 / --	8,115	624 / ---	32	362
cavalry	-- / 10	1,199	--- / 120	included above	
Corps Artillery Reserve				6	1,045
Corps Totals:	47 / 10	33,563	--- / ---	75	2,279

XIII Corps net strength of 35,842 present and under arms, of which:

> 32,364, or 90.5% of the corps were infantry,
> 1,199, or 3.5% of the corps were cavalry, and
> 2,279, or 6% of the corps were artillerists and other support troops.

XIII Corps artillery ratio on August 15 was 1 gun every 478 combatants.

XIV Corps Saint-Cyr	# of bns/sqd	Strength of inf. & cav.	Average per battalion/sqdrn	Guns	Artillerists, engineers, train, etc
42nd Division	14 / --	10,799	771 / --	14*	459
43rd Division	13 / --	9,823	756 / --	14*	421
44th Division	12 / --	7,996	666 / --	14*	501
45th Division	12 / --	8,087	674 / --	14*	414
Corps Cavalry	-- / 12	2,231	--- / 186	---	---
Corps Artillery Reserve				28*	1,818
Corps Totals:	51 / 12	38,936	--- / ---	84*	3,613

XIV Corps net strength of 42,549 present and under arms, of which:

> 36,705, or 86.5% of the corps were infantry,
> 2,231, or 5% of the corps were cavalry, and
> 3,613, or 8.5% of the corps were artillerists and other support troops.
> *Artillery materiel for XIV Corps for this date not shown in the returns; therefore, this is best estimate.

XIV Corps artillery ratio on August 15 was 1 gun every 507 combatants.

I Reserve Cav. Corps	# of sqdrns	Strength of cavalry	Average per squadron	Guns	Artillerists & train personnel
Latour-Maubourg					
1st Lt Cav Div	22	4,092	186	--	---
3rd Lt Cav Div	19	3,906	206	--	---
1st Hv Cav Div	22	3,226	147	--	---
3rd Hv Cav Div	21	2,965	141	--	---
Corps Artillery Reserve				36	968
Troops in route		3,283	---	--	---
Corps Totals:	84	17,472	---	--	968

I Reserve Cavalry Corps net strength was 18,440 officers and other ranks, of which:

17,472, or 95% of the corps were cavalry, and
968, or 5% of the corps were artillerists and support personnel.

I Reserve Cavalry Corps artillery ratio on August 15 was 1 gun for every 512 combatants.

II Reserve Cav. Corps	# of sqdrns	Strength of cavalry	Average per squadron	Guns	Artillerists & train personnel
Sébastiani					
2nd Lt Cav Div	19	3,236	170	--	---
4th Lt Cav Div	20	3,122	156	--	---
2nd Hv Cav Div	13	2,082	160	--	---
Corps Artillery Reserve				18	545
Troops in route		1,913			
Corps Totals:	52	10,353	---	18	545

II Reserve Cavalry Corps net strength was 10,898 officers and other ranks, of which:

10,353, or 95% of the corps were cavalry, and
545, or 5% of the corps were artillerists and support personnel.

II Reserve Cavalry Corps artillery ratio on August 15 was 1 gun every 605 combatants.

III Reserve Cav. Corps	# of sqdrns	Strength of cavalry	Average per squadron	Guns	Artillerists & train personnel
Arrighi de Casanova					
5th Lt Cav Div	10	2,067	206	--	---
6th Lt Cav Div	6	1,361	227	--	---
4th Hv Cav Div	11	1,571	143	--	---
Corps Artillery Reserve				24	385
Troops in route		2,279			
Corps Totals:	27	7,278	---	24	385

III Reserve Cavalry Corps net strength was 7,663 officers and other ranks, of which:

7,278, or 95% of the corps were cavalry, and
385, or 5% of the corps were artillerists and support personnel.

III Reserve Cavalry Corps artillery ratio on August 15 was 1 gun every 319 combatants.

IV Reserve Cav. Corps Kellermann	# of sqdrns	Strength of cavalry	Average per squadron	Guns	Artillerists & train personnel
7th Lt Cav Div	8	1,326	166	6	112
8th Lt Cav Div	16	2,642	165	6	169
Corps Totals:	24	3,968	---	12	281

IV Reserve Cavalry Corps net strength was 4,249 officers and other ranks, of which:

  3,968, or 94% of the corps were cavalry, and
  281 or 6% of the corps were artillerists and support personnel.

IV Reserve Cavalry Corps artillery ratio on August 15 was 1 gun every 354 combatants.

V Reserve Cav. Corps L'héritier	# of sqdrns	Strength of cavalry	Average per squadron	Guns	Artillerists & train personnel
9th Lt Cav Div	11	1,749	159	--	---
5th Hv Cav Div	7	1,050	150	--	---
6th Hv Cav Div	5	884	177	--	---
Corps Artillery Reserve				3	95
Troops in route		1,725			
Corps Totals:	21	5,408	---	3	95

V Reserve Cavalry Corps net strength was 5,503 officers and other ranks, of which:

  5,408, or 98% of the corps were cavalry, and
  95, or 2% of the corps were artillerists and support personnel.

V Reserve Cavalry Corps artillery ratio on August 15 was 1 gun every 1,834 combatants.

V *bis* Reserve Cav. Corps Milhaud	# of sqdrns	Strength of cavalry	Average per squadron	Guns	Artillerists & train personnel
9th *bis* Lt Cav	5	1,201	240	--	---
5th *bis* Hv Cav	6	1,496	249	--	---
6th *bis* Hv Cav	6	1,144	191	--	---
Corps Totals:	17	3,841	---	--	---

V *bis* Reserve Cavalry Corps net strength was 3,841 officers and other ranks, of which:

  3,841, or 100% of the corps were cavalry.

Army of Italy Prince Eugène	# of bns/sqd	Strength of inf. & cav.	Average per battalion/sqdrn	Guns	Artillerists, engineers, train, etc
1st Division	12 / --	7,473	623 / --	18	698
4th Division	11 / --	6,426	584 / --	20	656
2nd Division	11 / --	6,706	610 / --	18	562
3rd Division	11 / --	6,758	614 / --	16	518
5th Division	12 / --	6,687	557 / --	16	683
6th Division	12 / 1	7,158	584 / 149	14	775
7th Division	14 / --	10,792	771 / --	8	184
Cav. Division	-- / 26	4,916	--- / 189	12	368
Army Artillery Reserve				44	1,391
Army Totals:	83 / 27	56,916	--- / ---	166	5,835

Army of Italy net strength of 62,751 present and under arms, of which:

      51,851, or 83% of the army were infantry,

      5,065, or 8% of the army were cavalry, and

      5,835, or 9% of the army were artillerists and other support troops.

Army of Italy artillery ratio on August 15 was 1 gun for every 378 combatants.

Summary of the *Grande Armée* on 15 August 1813 Napoleon	Total of all combatants present and under arms	Guns
Imperial Guard	61,748	218
I Corps	36,776	80
II Corps	31,930	66
III Corps	40,350	110
IV Corps	22,579	64
V Corps	27,814	92
VI Corps	26,618	86
VII Corps	25,583	54
VIII Corps	7,972	36
IX Corps	19,125	38
XI Corps	24,691	100
XII Corps	19,106	66
XIII Corps	35,842	75
XIV Corps	42,549	84
I Reserve Cavalry Corps	18,440	36
II Reserve Cavalry Corps	10,898	18
III Reserve Cavalry Corps	7,663	24
IV Reserve Cavalry Corps	4,249	12
V Reserve Cavalry Corps	5,503	3
V *bis* Reserve Cavalry Corps	3,841	---
Total of the active corps in the *Grande Armée*	473,277	1,262

Of the above total, some 351,648, or 74% of the army were infantry,
77,152, or 16.5% of the army were cavalry, and
44,477, or 9.5% of the army were artillerists, etc.
Grande Armée artillery ratio on August 15 was 1 gun for every 375 combatants.

Prince Eugène's Army of Italy	62,751	166

Grand total of all active corps in the theater of war	536,028	1,428

Including Eugène's army, of the above total, some
403,499, or 75% of the troops were infantry,
82,217, or 15.5% of the troops were cavalry, and
50,312, or 9.5% of the troops were artillerists, etc.
Combined armies artillery ratio on August 15 was 1 gun for every 375 combatants.

****

In addition to the active field formations listed, there were tens of thousands of troops in garrisons and depots around Germany (see Appendix D for details). Including all these men, the grand total of those present and under arms amounted to 20,505 officers and 623,666 other ranks, plus 2,033 staff personnel, for a combined total of 656,204 combatants.[90]

On paper, the *Grande Armée* looked impressive. It had been miraculously rebuilt through the organizational genius and indefatigable energy of Napoleon. However, appearances were deceptive. The Emperor's instrument was nothing close to the superb war machine which he had led in earlier years to victory after victory. Once the fall campaign began, its shallow veneer would soon be worn through, exposing the true weaknesses of the *Grande Armée* of 1813.

Marines of the Guard. *Painting by Édouard Detaille. Musée de l'Armée.*

CHAPTER VII
"Withdraw Me From This Hell"

With the accession of Austria to the Allied coalition, Napoleon's position in Germany worsened significantly. In addition to the large army which Austria contributed to the Allied war effort, tipping the numerical advantage to the coalition forces by a ratio of three to two, her entry into the war suddenly exposed Napoleon's strategic right flank.

For the fall campaign of 1813, the Allies confronted Napoleon with large armies. Operating in front of Berlin was the Army of the North consisting of 120,000 Russians, Prussians and Swedes, headed by the timid and mediocre Crown Prince of Sweden, Jean Baptiste Bernadotte. In Silesia were another 95,000 Russians and Prussians commanded by the irrepressible Marshal Blücher. The largest Allied army was the Army of Bohemia numbering 240,000 Austrians, Russians, and Prussians, under the cautious leadership of Austrian General Schwarzenberg. Meanwhile, a fourth Allied army—the Polish Reserve Army—under the command of General Benningsen was plodding towards Germany with another 60,000 Russians.[1]

The vastness of the 1813 theater of war, and the different approaches which the Allies could utilize, made Napoleon's position in Saxony and Silesia very difficult to defend. Regardless of geographical difficulties and numerical inferiority, the Emperor was resolved not only to defend Germany, but to defeat in turn each of the Allied armies. To accomplish both goals, Napoleon decided to adopt a central position strategy and form the *Grande Armée* into two wings and a reserve.

The northern wing—opposite Bernadotte's army—consisted of the IV, VII, and XII Corps, plus the III Reserve Cavalry Corps, all totalling approximately 75,000 combatants supported by 208 pieces of ordnance. These troops were given the title Army of Berlin and were under the command of Marshal Oudinot. The much larger southern wing—known as the Army of the Bober—was posted in Silesia, initially under the orders of Marshal Ney. This powerful wing consisted of the III, V, VI, and XI Corps, and the II Reserve Cavalry Corps, numbering 130,000 officers and other ranks with 406 pieces of ordnance. Most of the remaining troops formed the army reserve under the personal direction of the Emperor himself. The reserve consisted of the I, II, VIII, XIV Corps, the I, IV, and V Reserve Cavalry Corps, along with the Imperial Guard, all of which numbered 209,000 combatants and 538 pieces of ordnance. In order to guard all the approaches of the Bohemian mountains, the reserves were subsequently placed in two lines with the I, II, VIII, and XIV Corps comprising the first line, while the I, IV, and V Reserve Cavalry Corps along with the Imperial Guard acting as the second line.[2]

Napoleon's initial plan of campaign was to stand on the strategic defensive in the south while ordering Marshal Oudinot to march on Berlin in coordination with Marshal Davout's XIII Corps debouching from the Hamburg area. Together, with two small independent divisions based from Magdebourg, these forces were expected to engage and either hopefully destroy or neutralize the numerically superior Allied Army of the North. Meanwhile, the Emperor would await the advance of both the Army of Silesia and Army of Bohemia. Once these movements were detected, Napoleon reasoned that he could fully

utilize his central position in and around Dresden by analyzing the most advantageous situation, swiftly turn his troops on and crush one of these armies, and then turn them about to quickly annihilate the other Allied army.[3]

The Allies, however, were not planning to cooperate with Napoleon's campaign design. The Army of the North was to defend Berlin while the Allied focus of attention centered on Silesia and southern Saxony. It was here that the Allies decided to initially advance in Silesia and gain the attention of the French Army of the Bober. This movement, however, was only planned to be a feint. The real blow was to be delivered by the massive Army of Bohemia. After Blücher had fully occupied the French attention along the Bober River, Schwarzenberg's army was to debouch from the mountains for which it was named, advance along a broad front on the west bank of the Elbe River, seize Leipzig, and cut Napoleon's communications with France.[4] To help accomplish this goal, the Allied commanders further agreed that anytime a single Allied army would find itself on its own and up against forces commanded by Napoleon, that Allied army commander would retreat while the other Allied armies assumed the offensive. Battle would be offered to Napoleon only if two or more of the Allied armies were concentrated.[5] In this manner, the Allies planned to defeat Napoleon and liberate Germany.

The designs of both sides resulted in a series of battles in late August and early September that may be broadly categorized as the first phase of the fall campaign for Germany. Among the first actions of the fall campaign was a combat on August 17 near Goldberg, in which General Lauriston's V Corps, supported by portion of the XI Corps cavalry under General Alexandre Montbrun, met the advancing troops of Blücher's Army of Silesia. After this action, Lauriston penned the following opinion of the light cavalry which formed the cavalry brigade of XI Corps. "They are children who are seeing the enemy for the first time," Lauriston wrote Marshal Berthier on August 17. "These young men are well intentioned, but so inexperienced that they are always defeated, because they fall off their horses."[6] Three days later, on August 20, another action was fought around Goldberg between the same two adversaries. In this minor engagement, the infantry of V Corps man-handled the Russian infantry, while the cavalry from XI Corps likewise defeated both Russian and Prussian cavalry, and rode down a regiment of Russian infantry as well. "Our cavalry charged," Lauriston reported to the Major General on August 23, "broke three squares, repulsed some cavalry charges, and covered itself with glory...The field of battle showed six Russians for one Frenchman."[7]

Blücher's tantalizing advance, coupled with the inactivity of the Austrians, convinced Napoleon to take to the offensive against the Army of Silesia. Riding eastward, the Emperor ordered the Army of the Bober into the attack.[8] The Army of the Bober suddenly shifting of gears from neutral into a rapid advance could mean only one thing— Napoleon was with or close to these troops. Blücher's staff immediately recognized this and ordered its own Army of Silesia to retreat.[9]

As Napoleon followed Blücher's retreating army further eastward, the Emperor received a desperate appeal for help from Marshal Gouvion Saint-Cyr,[10] commander of the XIV Corps who had remained in and around Dresden. Schwarzenberg's army had suddenly debouched from the mountains of Bohemia and was already on the west side of the Elbe River. The Austrian general was intent on taking the city and getting astride the lines of communication for the Army of the Bober. Schwarzenberg probably would have taken Dresden had it not been for the superior command ability of Saint-Cyr, whose delaying action slowed the Allied advance in time for the Emperor to react.

Napoleon swiftly countermarched back to Dresden.[11] The Emperor also decided to take Marshal Ney with him, and therefore left Marshal Macdonald in command of the Army of the Bober[12] with strict orders that will be discussed later. Countermarching with the Emperor were four powerful corps, including Marshal Mortier's Imperial Guard, Latour-Maubourg's I Reserve Cavalry Corps, Victor's II Corps, and Marmont's VI Corps.[13] When ordering the march back to Dresden, Napoleon decided to switch the VI Corps from the Army of the Bober into the army reserve[14] in order that he could fully utilize this powerful body of troops.

In order to reach Dresden in time to save Saint-Cyr, the formations under Napoleon conducted a series of hard, forced marches. The Guard arrived in Dresden after marching 125 miles in four days "not on good roads, but alongside them."[15] When Latour-Maubourg's, Victor's and Marmont's troops arrived at Dresden, they did so after covering 130 miles during the same four days.[16] Sustained marches like these were brutalizing tests of endurance, and thousands of the Emperor's hungry soldiers dropped along the roadside from exhaustion.[17]

Although their numbers dwindled and their stomachs ached from lack of food, the army's morale did not diminish. They were confident that the Emperor would lead them to victory. As these footsore troops of the *Grande Armée* arrived outside Dresden, the corps commanders halted their columns long enough for the troops to change into their dress uniforms.[18] This transformation completed, the men resumed their march into Dresden with bands playing and the throats of tens of thousands singing the famous Napoleonic war song *The Victory Is Ours*.[19] Too late did Schwarzenberg realize that Napoleon was upon him.

Napoleon's Arrival at Dresden. *Painting by Philippoteaux.*

****

Napoleon's *Grande Armée* at Dresden[20]

Corps	Division	Commander	# of bns/sqd	All ranks present and under arms
Imperial Guard—		Mortier	Strengths as of 15 August 1813	
	Old Gd Inf Div	Friant	10	5,022
	1st Yg Gd Div	Dumoustier	14	9,373
	2nd Yg Gd Div	Barrois	14	9,036
	3rd Yg Gd Div	Delaborde	12	8,582
	4th Yg Gd Div	Roguet	12	8,534
	1st Guard Cav	Lef-Desn	22	4,028
	2nd Guard Cav	Ornano	24	4,984
	Guard Horse Art with Cavalry			794
	Guard Artillery Reserve			6,358
	Corps Total:			56,711 and 218 guns

After deducting about 4,700 combatants estimated to have fallen out of ranks through strategic consumption between August 15 and August 25, the Imperial Guard had approximately 52,000 officers and other ranks present and under arms at Dresden supported by 218 pieces of ordnance.

Austrians Assault the *Grande Armée* at Dresden, 26 August 1813.
Bibliothèque nationale.

Corps	Division	Commander	# of bns/sqd	All ranks present and under arms
II Corps(-)—		Victor	Strengths as of 15 August 1813	
	4th Division	Dubreton	15	10,357
	5th Division(-)	Dufour	7	4,819
	6th Division	Vial	13	8,518
	Corps Cavalry	Hammerstein	6	781
	Corps Artillery Reserve			1,054
	Troops in route			1,539
	Corps Total:			27,068 and 70 guns

After deducting about 5,000 combatants estimated to have fallen out of ranks through strategic consumption between August 15 and August 25, the II Corps had approximately 22,000 officers and other ranks present and under arms at Dresden supported by 70 pieces of ordnance.

Corps	Division	Commander	# of bns/sqd	All ranks present and under arms
VI Corps—		Marmont	Strengths as of 15 August 1813	
	20th Division	Compans	14	8,644
	21st Division	Lagrange	14	8,815
	22nd Division	Friederichs	14	6,668
	Corps Cavalry	Normann	8	907
	Corps Artillery Reserve			1,462
	Corps Total:			26,618 and 86 guns

After deducting about 3,100 combatants estimated to have fallen out of ranks through strategic consumption between August 15 and August 25, the VI Corps had approximately 24,500 officers and other ranks present and under arms at Dresden supported by 86 pieces of ordnance.

Corps	Division	Commander	# of bns/sqd	All ranks present and under arms
XIV Corps(+)(-)—		Saint-Cyr	Strengths as of 25 August 1813	
	from 23rd Div	O'Meara	8	5,502*
	42nd Division—detached—with Vandamme's I Corps			
	43rd Division	Claparède	13	10,244
	44th Division	Berthezène	12	8,497
	45th Division	Razout	12	8,501
	Corps Cavalry	Pajol	12	2,231
	Corps Artillery Reserve			1,818
	Corps Total:			36,793 and 70 guns

* Strength of O'Meara's Brigade of the 23rd Division as of 15 August 1813. The XIV Corps had approximately 36,500 officers and other ranks present and under arms at Dresden supported by 70 pieces of ordnance.

Corps	Division	Commander	# of sqds	All ranks present and under arms
I Reserve Cav Corps(-)—Latour-Maubourg		Strengths as of 15 August 1813		
	1st Lt Cav Div—detached—with Vandamme's I Corps			
	3rd Lt Cav Div	Chastel	19	3,906
	1st Hv Cav Div	Bordesoulle	22	3,226
	3rd Hv Cav Div	Doumerc	21	2,965
	Corps Artillery Reserve			968
	Troops in route			3,283
	Corps Total:			14,348 and 36 guns

After deducting about 2,300 combatants estimated to have fallen out of ranks through strategic consumption between August 15 and August 25, the I Reserve Cavalry Corps had approximately 12,000 officers and other ranks present and under arms at Dresden supported by 36 pieces of ordnance.

Taking into account the estimated losses through strategic consumption, the total strength of the formations under Napoleon at the Battle of Dresden numbered approximately 147,000 officers and other ranks present and under arms supported by 480 pieces of ordnance.

Note: The army's strategic consumption rate was extremely high at the very start of the campaign as whose who were not fit or eager for duty soon dropped out of ranks.

****

The Battle of Dresden was a desperate, prolonged struggle which raged in and around the city for two days. On August 26, the day was won mainly by the conscripts of the XIV Corps and Young Guard as they denied the Allies access into Dresden. During the fighting on that day, there were several notable actions in which the vicious counterattacks of the Young Guard put to flight enemy formation after enemy formation. The two battalions of the 1st Tirailleurs charged and routed six Prussian battalions, capturing several hundred prisoners in the process, while the 3rd Voltigeurs captured an entire enemy battalion with its standard.[21]

The battle of August 27 was won by the French cavalry and horse artillery. Throughout that fateful day, torrential rains made small arms fire virtually impossible. With infantry being unable to defend themselves, cavalry and mobile artillery dominated the battlefield.

The most notable events of the second day at Dresden involved the I Reserve Cavalry Corps of Latour-Maubourg, led by Marshal Murat. Under the direction of the King of Naples, the French horse attacked and utterly destroyed the left flank of the Army of Bohemia. Time and again, squares of Austrian infantry were picked apart by French lancers or mowed down by French horse artillery.[22]

145

When the rain storms began the night of the 26th, the Emperor had ordered his artillery companies to be double-teamed[23] in order for them to be able to move over the muddy countryside. This foresight rewarded Napoleon handsomely. One entire division of Austrian infantry surrendered to General Bordesoulle. With the Austrians standing solidly in square in the pouring rain and the French heavy cavalry poised nearby to charge, the French cavalry general called upon the Austrians to surrender. The Austrian response was that the cuirassiers by themselves could not force the infantry to lay down its arms. Bordesoulle then ordered his horsemen to uncover a horse artillery company which was unlimbered and ready to fire. The Austrians surrendered at once.[24]

General Auguste-Daniel Belliard, chief of staff to Murat during the Russian campaign and again serving in the same role in the 1813 fall campaign, wrote to Berthier as soon as the battle ended. "I think you can be satisfied with us. The cavalry truly produced marvels. The King [of Naples] himself led the first squadrons against the squares, and that was needed to give spirit to our young men who thereafter could not be held back."[25]

That same evening, Murat excitedly reported to Napoleon of the cavalry's victory. "Sire, today's engagement gives the greatest honor to Your Majesty's cavalry...All the squares were broken. I must tell Your Majesty, to the glory of your cavalry, that the triple ranks of bayonets of these masses were broken by sabre strokes, in spite of the most stubborn resistance that infantry has ever achieved...This day's results are glorious for Your Majesty's forces. Your cavalry has taken around 15,000 prisoners, 12 pieces of artillery, and 12 flags, a lieutenant general, two generals, and a large number of superior officers of all grades, and I can absolutely assure Your Majesty that the enemy has at least 7,000 to 8,000 more men out of combat in killed, wounded, or missing. I hope to have gathered tomorrow all the cannons and equipment which the enemy left behind in the Tharand Gorge."[26]

The Battle of Dresden had cost the Allies dearly. Including killed, wounded, missing, and captured, Schwarzenberg's army lost more than 38,000 men; Napoleon had suffered barely 10,000 casualties.[27] Clearly demonstrated at this battle were two important points. Firstly, Napoleon could still move his army with astounding rapidity. The second was that when infantry muskets were wet and unable to fire, the cavalry, and to a lesser degree, the artillery, were decisive.

This second point was vividly demonstrated on another battlefield the same day that Napoleon was pounding Schwarzenberg. When the Emperor left the Army of the Bober on August 23 to hasten back to Dresden, he had left Marshal Macdonald in command with specific orders to push the enemy beyond the village of Jauer and then to stand on the defensive and prevent Blücher's army from marching either to Berlin to join up with Bernadoote, or to Bohemia to join up with Schwarzenberg.[28]

On August 25, Macdonald began his move on Jauer. The Duke of Tarentum marched with his army in three columns. The northern column consisted of Souham's (formerly Ney's) III Corps and Sébastiani's II Reserve Cavalry Corps. The center column was comprised of the XI Corps under General Gérard, and the southern column consisted of Lauriston's V Corps. The northern and center columns were maneuvering within 2 miles of each other, but Lauriston was more than 8 miles away from XI Corps.[29]

****

Marshal Murat, King of Naples.
Painting by Gèrard. Musée de Versailles.

Macdonald's Army of the Bober
at Katzbach[30]

Corps	Division	Commander	# of bns/sqd	All ranks present and under arms
III Corps—		Souham	Strengths as of 15 August 1813	
	8th Division	Brayer	15	8,269
	9th Division	Delmas	13	6,905
	10th Division	Albert	11	5,525
	11th Division	Ricard	13	6,613
	39th Division	Marchand	10	5,798
	Corps Cavalry	Laboissière	11	1,659
	Corps Artillery Reserve			2,226
	Troops in route			3,355
	Corps Totals:			40,350 and 110 guns

After deducting about 4,000 combatants estimated to have fallen out of ranks through strategic consumption between August 15 and August 25, the III Corps had approximately 36,000 officers and other ranks present and under arms at the Katzbach supported by 110 pieces of ordnance.

Corps	Division	Commander	# of bns/sqd	All ranks present and under arms
V Corps—		Lauriston	Strengths as of 15 August 1813	
	16th Division	Maison	9	7,244
	17th Division	Puthod	13	8,235
	19th Division	Rochambeau	12	9,672
	Corps Artillery Reserve			1,218
	Troops in route			1,445
	Corps Totals:			27,814 and 92 guns

After deducting about 2,800 combatants estimated to have fallen out of ranks through strategic consumption between August 15 and August 25, the V Corps had approximately 25,000 officers and other ranks present and under arms at the Katzbach supported by 92 pieces of ordnance.

Corps	Division	Commander	# of bns/sqd	All ranks present and under arms
XI Corps—		Gérard	Strengths as of 15 August 1813	
	31st Division	Ledru	14	8,314
	35th Division	Gérard	13	7,385
	36th Division	Charpentier	11	6,657
	Corps Cavalry	Montbrun	7	1,165
	Corps Artillery Reserve			1,170
	Corps Totals:			24,691 and 100 guns

After deducting about 2,700 combatants estimated to have fallen out of ranks through strategic consumption between August 15 and August 25, the XI Corps had approximately 22,000 officers and other ranks present and under arms at the Katzbach supported by 100 pieces of ordnance.

Corps	Division	Commander	# of sqdrns	All ranks present and under arms
II Reserve Cavalry Corps(-) Sébastiani			Strengths as of 15 August 1813	
	2nd Lt Cav Div	Roussel	19	3,236
	4th Lt Cav Div	Exelmans	20	3,122
	2nd Hv Cav Div	Saint-Germain—did not cross the Katzbach with 6 guns		
	Corps Artillery Reserve			545
	Troops in route			1,913
	Corps Totals:			8,816 and 12 guns

After deducting about 800 combatants estimated to have fallen out of ranks through strategic consumption between August 15 and August 25, or in the artillery company attached to the 2nd Heavy Cavalry Division, the II Reserve Cavalry Corps had approximately 8,000 officers and other ranks present and under arms at the Katzbach supported by 12 pieces of ordnance.

Taking into account the estimated losses through strategic consumption, the total strength of the formations under Macdonald at the Katzbach numbered approximately 91,000 officers and other ranks present and under arms supported by 314 pieces of ordnance.

****

The following day—August 26—most of Lauriston's corps and all of Gérard's troops crossed the rain-swollen Katzbach River near Goldberg and were waiting for Souham and Sébastiani to close up on their left. However, the march of these formations was delayed by the miserable roads and countryside which had been turned into a huge quagmire from the heavy rains. Meanwhile, Blücher turned his army about and was moving northwest, thinking that the French would stop their advance before attempting to cross the Katzbach.[31]

Suddenly, a violent storm, much like the one which would prove so debilitating to the Army of Bohemia the next day at Dresden, hit this area of Silesia in full force. In a blinding, wind-driven rain and hail that reduced visibility to only several hundred yards,[32] the opposing armies stumbled into contact. Lauriston wasted little time in ordering his regiments into the attack. The infantry of V Corps quickly rolled up Langeron's Russians,[33] but had to suspend their offensive and form squares when hordes of enemy cavalry arrived to assist their hard-pressed comrades. Amidst the wind, rain, and hail, "out of 500 loaded muskets, not 10 shots per battalion went off."[34] Unable to defend themselves, the infantry of V and XI Corps suffered heavy casualties at the hands of the Allied horsemen.

Finally, Sébastiani's light cavalry divisions arrived on the field. In General Exelmans' division, Colonel Chamans' 7th Chasseurs à Cheval defeated a brigade of Prussian cavalry[35] while the 23rd Chasseurs à Cheval under Colonel Marbot and the 24th Chasseurs à Cheval led by Colonel Schmidt charged and routed another three regiments of Prussian horsemen.[36] After defeating these cavalry, the 23rd Chasseurs à Cheval came upon some Prussian infantry formed in square. Both sides were at a stand still as the infantry could not fire their muskets and drive off the French cavalry but the chasseurs could not break the bayonet-armed Prussians with their swords. To Marbot's assistance rode Colonel Perquit at the head of the 6th Light Lancers. Outreaching the Prussian bayonets, the 6th Light Lancers inflicted "terrible execution"[37] and broke the defenseless infantry.

The success of Sébastiani's cavalry was, however, only short-lived. More than 20,000 Allied horsemen soon flooded the battlefield, enfilading and overturning most of the French light cavalry regiments. With most of his troops already in full flight, Macdonald joined Marbot's 23rd Chasseurs à Cheval—the only regiment of Sébastiani's corps which had maintained good order—and ordered the army to retreat to Goldberg.[38]

The Battle of Katzbach was a French disaster. The Army of the Bober lost 15,000 men and 36 artillery pieces.[39] Blücher's losses were probably about 5,000.[40] Suffering the most was Laursiton's proven infantry who were simply unable to defend themselves in the elements against the numerous enemy cavalry.

Count Maurice Etienne Gérard

Born in Damvilliers on 4 April 1773, Gérard was one of the multitudes of citizens that volunteered in 1791. By 1794, he was a demi-brigade commander under Bernadotte. Gérard's association with Bernadotte continued into 1809, when Gérard became chief of staff of IX (Saxon) Corps. Greatly distinguishing himself at Wagram, Gérard also saw duty in Russia with Davout's I Corps. Gérard performed well in 1813, as both a division commander as well as at the head of XI Corps. *Musée de l'Armée.*

**Retreat of the Army of the Bober from the
Battle of Katzbach, 26 August 1813.**
Composition by R. Knötel.

The following day, Macdonald had the unpleasant task of informing Imperial headquarters of his defeat. He included in his report the following: "The army will march tomorrow to take up its position on the Bober ordered by His Majesty, except, however, the post at Hirschberg which, in the present circumstances, I will not occupy, except to come back when the army is recovered from the awkward situation in which it finds itself, caused by the sad events and by the frightful weather which is not abating and which does more harm to His Majesty's troops than the arms of his enemies."[41]

A few hours later—in the middle of the night—the Duke of Tarentum learned that a single regiment of Prussian hussars had put to flight 14 of his disorganized, dispirited battalions who were unable to fire their weapons in the continuing downpour. Perhaps Macdonald had alerted Berthier to such possible routs when Macdonald concluded his report several hours before learning of this lastest misfortune: "The soldier is disgusted by the marches and the bad weather, and discouraged because he cannot fire his weapon."[42] Meanwhile, Lauriston reported to the Major General that "the engagement at Katzbach has ruined the V Corps."[43]

The dispirited Army of the Bober retired to Bunzlau. While this retreat was being carried out, Macdonald sent two more reports to Berthier. "The enemy has only weakly pursued," he told the Major General on August 29, "but his light cavalry, the bogy of deserters, showed up everywhere with horse artillery...Our troops are in a pitiful state, soaked with rain for 24 consecutive hours, marching in mud halfway up the leg, crossing overflowing torrents. In this state, the generals cannot prevent the soldier from looking for shelter, his musket being useless to him...Things being what they are, it would be to compromise the army to have it undertake to do anything before being rallied, rested, and its weapons put back in working order."[44]

Later that evening, Macdonald wrote another dispatch to Imperial headquarters. Macdonald had just learned of the virtual destruction of Puthod's isolated 17th Division, which had been attacked and driven back against a river where most of its men had no choice but to surrender. "I have the sorrow to inform Your Highness that the rains have occasioned a succession of disasters which cut me to the heart. Puthod's division is no longer. Its remnants were overthrown this evening in the floods at Lowenberg, without it having been possible to reestablish passage for the men...I shall attempt tomorrow to hold the line of the Bober, but I can only regroup behind the Queiss [River], where I will choose a position for giving battle, if yet the generals succeed in rallying their multitude of stragglers. Many have crossed the Queiss without it having been possible to stop them...His Majesty knows the circumstances...I could not foresee nor control the elements; they are the cause of all our misfortunes, for the check suffered by the cavalry was slight in proportion to the strength of the army, and would have been very repairable without a continual deluge for three days and nights...It has not been possible for me to know yet the state of our losses and the number of combatants I still have."[45]

Macdonald's defeat on the Katzbach was just one of two disasters suffered by French forces during the month of August. When Marshal Marmont learned of his sovereign's plan of campaign, he offered Napoleon these prophetic words on the Emperor's birthday. "I strongly fear that the day where Your Majesty will have gained a victory and believed he'd won a decisive battle, he'll only learn that he lost two of them."[46] Less than three weeks later, Marmont's prediction came true. Napoleon's victory at Dresden on August 26-27 was offset by Macdonald's debâcle and by the events at Külm on August 30.

Following the triumph at Dresden, Napoleon sent Marmont's VI Corps and Saint-Cry's XIV Corps, less the 42nd Division, to pursue of the retreating enemy, while ordering

Vandamme's I Corps, augmented by General Mouton-Duvernet's 42nd Division and General Corbineau's light cavalry from I Reserve Cavalry Corps, to fall on the enemy left flank.

On August 28 and 29, the pursuit produced handsome results. Marshal Marmont reported the following to Berthier on the evening of August 29: "Six battalions [of the VI Corps] alone involved and without artillery have chased before them, in a completely remarkable way, very superior forces, that is to say, have overrun 12,000 to 15,000 enemy infantry with 12 artillery pieces who were in a very strong position. I have never seen braver troops with greater spirit; as much care was needed to moderate it as elsewhere was necessary to instill it."[47]

Another report filed by Marmont commended his troops for their victory at the August 28 engagement at Dippoldiswalda: "Particular praise goes to General Lagrange and General Compans, the 32nd Light Infantry, the 1st and 4th Regiments de Marine; and the 37th Light Infantry deserve high praise in particular."[48] The Journal of the VI Corps mentioned that in the action at Falkenhayn on August 29, "the 37th Light Infantry Regiment, the 4th Regiment de Marine, and the 1st battalion of the 2nd Regiment de Marine...covered themselves with glory"[49] for routing the enemy. Also reporting on the combat at Falkenhayn, General Lagrange wrote: "A special attack force consisting of two battalions of the 37th Light Infantry, the entire 4th Regiment de Marine, and the 1st battalion of the 2nd Regiment de Marine, was assembled under the command of Chef de bataillon Durand, an officer of great distinction. The élan of our troops could not have been greater, for they attacked and routed the entire enemy force, capturing 12 guns and several hundred prisoners."[50]

During the same two days, events likewise went well for Vandamme and the I Corps. On the 28th, the leading elements of I Corps arrived at Hellendorf and found the Russian II Corps under Eugen of Württemberg ready and deployed for battle. In the action that followed, the six battalions comprising General Quiot du Passage's brigade of the 23rd Division attacked and mauled two divisions of Russian infantry. "We arrived at Hellendorf," Vandamme reported to Berthier late that evening, "and the enemy fought in vain against our brave young men; they were overthrown everywhere and put in full flight...I have about 4,000 or 5,000 enemy troops in front of me. I attack then tomorrow at dawn and march on Toeplitz with the entire I Corps, if I do not receive a countermarching order. All of our troops conducted themselves perfectly and rivaled each other in zeal and ardor."[51]

It was the last dispatch received from Vandamme. On the 29th, he continued his attack against an ever-growing number of Russians. At Külm the following day—August 30—the roles reversed dramatically. The Allies, numbering some 44,000 combatants including the powerful Russian Imperial Guard, attacked Vandamme, whose reinforced corps numbered approximately 40,000 officers and other ranks present and under arms.[52] After the action was in full swing, a corps of Prussians numbering 10,000 men under General Kleist suddenly stumbled out of the Bohemian mountains in which they had been lost for the past two days. The unexpected appearance of these Prussians placed them directly in Vandamme's rear—the only possible retreat route open to the French.[53]

Trapped and outnumbered, Vandamme turned his corps around, intent on attacking and breaking through Kleist's corps. Fighting with desperate ferocity, Vandamme's men trampled the Prussians underfoot by overrunning eight batteries (64 pieces) of artillery, bayoneting 600 artillerists, and scattering two brigades of infantry. Finally, Vandamme's path was blocked at Peterswalde; the French had no choice but to abandon their guns and other mobile equipment and escape as best they could into the rugged Saxon forests.[54]

During these operations, General Mounton-Duvernet's 42nd Division of XIV Corps was attached to I Corps. When the Battle of Külm began, the 42nd Division numbered 12 battalions and one company of foot artillery (two battalions and a company of artillery had been detached prior to the battle) totalling just over 7,000 combatants.[55] The division had only 4,000 men with no guns, caissons, or wagons remaining on the 2nd of September. "My division will have lost 3,000 men in these two fatal days," Mouton-Duvernet wrote to Marshal Mortier. "One can be no prouder than I am of my young people and of the majority of the officers; they covered themselves with glory."[56]

The defeat at Külm destroyed the I Corps. Excluding the elements of the 27th Division, Vandamme's command in mid-August was almost 34,000 strong. Of these, only 8,400 were remaining under the colors on September 2.[57] Further, I Corps lost at Külm all its guns, caissons, wagons, along with its outspoken commanding officer, General Vandamme, who was taken prisoner.[58] In Vandamme's place, the Emperor appointed his long-time, distinguished aide de camp, General Mouton, the Count of Lobau.[59] Lobau at once set about his difficult task of reorganizing the survivors and restoring the morale of I Corps.

General Georges Mouton, Count of Lobau

Georges Mouton, the Count of Lobau, displayed all the essentials of an Imperial aide de camp. Tenaciously brave, unquestionably loyal, and tactically expert, Lobau had a long, distinguished combat record as one of Napoleon's Imperial aides. In 1813, Lobau would prove himself again. At Lützen, he led the rallied conscripts of 11th Division and bested the Prussian Guard. He was promoted to aide-major général of the Imperial Guard in July, and then to the command of I Corps in September. At the head of I Corps, he won the combat of Giesshübel on 15 September. Ordered to remain in Dresden, Lobau was taken prisoner on 11 November 1813 when the city fell. *Bibliothèque Nationale.*

While the drama at Külm unfolded, Macdonald continued to fall back in the wake of his defeat on the Katzbach. By August 31, the remnants of Macdonald's army had finally rallied in Lauban on the west bank of the Queiss River. In the opening 15 days of the campaign, the corps comprising the Army of the Bober had suffered staggering losses. For example, the III Corps numbered some 40,350 combatants on August 15. Excluding the 39th Division, the III Corps had 34,907 effectives on this date. Of this later number, only 22,224 remained on August 31—a casualty and strategic consumption wastage of 36% in only 16 days![60]

Lauriston's valuable V Corps had been injured even worse. Of the more than 27,800 officers and other ranks supported by 92 artillery pieces present on August 15, slightly more than 7,000 combatants and 42 guns could still be counted on the last day of the month.[61] This translates into an utterly staggering casualty and strategic consumption loss of almost 75% of the corps. However, many who were not present at the end of August were stragglers that eventually rejoined the colors.

The defeat at Katzbach and subsequent 40 mile retreat back to the Queiss River seemed to totally demoralize many of the young troops in the Army of the Bober. As morale sank, desertion rose, and the leaders of the army began to plead for assistance. "It would be necessary in order to rebuild the confidence and morale of the army," General Lauriston informed Marshal Berthier on August 31, "that His Majesty might be able to send a corps like that of the Young Guard to join us; that movement would bring in a great number of deserters. However, there is no discouragement; the troops feel that they are superior to the enemy in combat, and if we joined battle against them with all our troops assembled, I am sure of success."[62] It is interesting to note that this letter was written by a general officer whose command had lost 75% of its effectives in only two weeks. Despite the disaster at Katzbach and the effects of the retreat to the Queiss, Lauriston's confidence remained very high indeed.

In contrast, and perhaps in some respects more realistic, was Marshal Macdonald's letter of that same date to Berthier. "Tonight, I will fall back to Goerlitz, where there is a fine position covered by the Neisse [River]. There, I shall see the whole army reunited; I will know its strength and I will determine its situation, but I do think that it is still too soon to risk an engagement; that's not how I am thinking. I think, on the contrary, it would take an engagement where one might find an isolated enemy corps; but it would be foolhardy to fight against a much stronger army and for which the elements have procured decided advantages. Besides, our supply of small arms cartridges is exhausted; they have all been used or spoiled...Already, 7,000 or 8,000 men may have returned to ranks; there must be still twice that number [of stragglers] as far as Dresden. What is unusual is that there is neither terror nor fear. The soldier sought shelter, and, in that, he was imitating all too well the example of his officers...."[63]

In the meantime, Napoleon ordered Prince Poniatowski's VIII Corps to join the Army of the Bober.[64] This was accomplished when the Poles arrived at Goerlitz on September 1. That evening, Macdonald sent another communiqué to the Major General. "I must have here," the Duke of Tarentum wrote from Goerlitz, "judging by appearances, some 60,000 to 70,000 men, many without weapons, and entire corps without ammunition. The enemy is gathering up the marauders whom no discipline is able to restrain, or, to put it more truthfully, there is an extreme half-heartedness in all ranks."[65]

Defeat and retreat was affecting many of the officers as well as the men. Already decided that the army could not hold the Queiss River line even with the addition of Poniatowski's Poles, Macdonald ordered another withdrawal. On September 2, the Army of the Bober fell back another 18 miles to the Neisse River.[66]

During the last day of August and the first two days of September, the Duke of Tarentum was able to review each corps in his army. Following this series of inspections, Macdonald sent the following report to Berthier. "It was my view to remain in position at Goerlitz," Macdonald wrote from Noslitz on September 2. "But I must declare that the luke-warmness of the leaders, the indiscipline, the marauding, the lack of weapons for perhaps 10,000 men, and no munitions are motives enough to convince His Majesty to bring his army closer to this one, with the impact of giving it a stronger composition and of revitalizing morale. I am made indignant by the lack of zeal and interest the officers exhibit in serving him [Napoleon]. I expend thereon all the energy, all the strength of character of which I am capable, and it is needed in the very painful circumstances in which I have found myself. I am neither seconded, nor imitated. I beg Your Highness, earnestly, to solicit from His Majesty another commander-in-chief for this army and to put me in charge of only the XI Corps. I will set an example of obedience, of zeal, and of devotion for the others to follow."[67]

That same day, General Lauriston wrote to Napoleon with his optimistic assessment of the Army of the Bober. "The III Corps is still sound and vigorous. The cavalry of II Reserve Cavalry Corps is good; despite the defeat on the 26th, the old cavaliers are not disadvantaged. The XI Corps is still sufficient...The V Corps is the most reduced...Sire, we are not discouraged. A word and especially a glance from Your Majesty would electrify all heads and would inspire boundless courage. It is needed that we feel the effect of your presence; bring us close enough to you so that the army appears to move each day according to your direct orders."[68]

Responding to these pleas, Napoleon rode to Goerlitz, arriving on September 5, at the head of VI Corps and the Guard.[69] Knowledge of the Emperor's movement was all that was needed to persuade Blücher to retreat, thereby avoiding direct confrontation with Napoleon with only a single Allied army. With the Army of Silesia out of reach, Napoleon returned to Bautzen on September 6. After the 24 hours that the Emperor was with Macdonald, Napoleon left the Duke of Tarentum in command of the Army of the Bober, publicly giving Macdonald "the greatest marks of esteem."[70]

Baron R. J. I. Exelmans

Born on 13 November 1775, Exelmans served as a volunteer in the 3rd battalion of the Meuse in 1791 under Oudinot. He transferred to the cavalry and was an aide de camp to Général Broussier and then to Marshal Murat during the years 1799 through 1808. Exelmans then transferred into the Guard Cavalry until his promotion to Général de division in 1812. In 1813, he ably commanded the 4th Light Cavalry Division in Sébastiani's II Reserve Cavalry Corps. *Musée de l'Armée.*

The Mêlée at Hagelberg, 27 August 1813. Hand-to-hand combat between Prussian landwehr and the 19th Regiment of the Line (Division Girard). *Composition by R. Knötel*

COMPARISON OF STRENGTHS FOR III CORPS
FOR THE PERIOD 15 AUGUST TO 31 AUGUST 1813

III CORPS

	# (bns)	15 August Officers	15 August Other Ranks	31 August Officers	31 August Other Ranks	% casualties & strategic consumption suffered during this period
8th Division— Général de division Count Souham						
1st Brigade: Général de brigade Brayer						
6th Provisional Light Infantry	(2)	44	1,202	16	602	50%
10th Provisional Light Infantry	(2)	42	1,273	37	769	39%
14th Provisional Regt. of the Line	(2)	46	791	44	448	41%
19th Provisional Regt. of the Line	(2)	43	1,024	15	335	67%
2nd Brigade: Général de brigade Charrière						
21st Provisional Regt. of the Line	(2)	41	1,147	35	587	48%
24th Provisional Regt. of the Line	(2)	38	787	29	416	40%
22nd Regiment of the Line	(3)	52	1,416	39	963	32%
Divisional artillery and train		6	263	incl.	at end	---
8th Division Totals[†][*]		306	7,640	215	3,720	51%

[†]Excludes troops in route to join their regiments.
[*]Excludes staff, artillerists and artillery train.

	# (bns)	15 August Officers	15 August Other Ranks	31 August Officers	31 August Other Ranks	%
9th Division— Général de division Delmas						
1st Brigade: Général de brigade Anthing						
2nd Provisional Light Infantry	(2)	41	795	42	601	23%
29th Light Infantry Regiment	(2)	42	745	36	434	40%
136th Regiment of the Line	(3)	76	1,536	65	1,411	8%
2nd Brigade: Général de brigade Vergez						
138th Regiment of the Line	(3)	63	1,467	67	990	31%
145th Regiment of the Line	(3)	78	1,776	58	1,213	31%
Divisional artillery and train		9	280	incl.	at end	---
9th Division Totals[†][*]		300	6,319	268	4,649	26%

[†]Excludes troops in route to join their regiments.
[*]Excludes staff, artillerists and artillery train.

	# (bns)	15 August Officers	15 August Other Ranks	31 August Officers	31 August Other Ranks	%
10th Division— Général de division Baron Albert						
1st Brigade: Général de brigade Van Dedem						
4th Provisional Light Infantry	(2)	47	728	46	632	13%
139th Regiment of the Line	(3)	78	1,903	70	1,455	23%
2nd Brigade: Général de brigade Suden						
140th Regiment of the Line	(3)	59	1,381	64	915	32%
141st Regiment of the Line	(3)	67	967	64	1,000	---
Divisional artillery and train		6	289	incl.	at end	---
10th Division Totals[†][*]		251	4,979	244	4,002	19%

[†]Excludes troops in route to join their regiments.
[*]Excludes staff, artillerists and artillery train.

11th Division— Général de division Baron Ricard

1st Brigade: Général de brigade Tarayre

9th Light Infantry Regiment	(2)	40	674	32	494	26%
17th Provisional Regt. of the Line	(2)	40	866	32	570	34%
50th Regiment of the Line	(2)	44	976	37	577	40%
65th Regiment of the Line	(1)	19	294	21	239	17%
2nd Brigade: Général de brigade Dumoulin						
142nd Regiment of the Line	(3)	72	1,455	59	1,452	1%
144th Regiment of the Line	(3)	78	1,741	76	1,454	16%
Divisional artillery and train		7	307	incl.	at end	---
11th Division Totals[†]*		293	6,006	257	4,786	20%

[†]Excludes troops in route to join their regiments.
*Excludes staff, artillerists and artillery train.

39th Division— Général de division Count Marchand

By August 31st, the 39th Division was no longer part of III Corps, and therefore has been excluded from this computation.

III Corps Cavalry Brigade— Général de brigade Laboissière

10th Hussars, 1st—6th squadrons	(6)	49	1,132	48	742	33%
Baden Light Dragoons, 1st—5th sqdrns	(5)	14	464	18	382	16%
Cavalry Brigade Totals[†]*		63	1,596	66	1,124	28%

[†]Excludes troops in route to join their regiments.
*Excludes staff.

III Corps Artillery Reserve—

4 companies of Foot Artillery	11	312	incl.	below	---
2 companies of Horse Artillery	6	174	incl.	below	---
All artillerists on 31 August			52	795	---
All artillery train personnel on 31 August			24	1,053	---
All equipage	10	722[††]	11	797	---
Engineers (Sappers), 4 companies	13	546	11	124	76%
Imperial Gendarmes	2	44	2	42	4%

[††]Includes troops in route.

III CORPS TOTALS:

34,907[†]*	22,224[†]*	36%
110 guns	86 guns**	

[†]Includes officers.
*Excludes staff.
**It must be remembered that 39th Division was no longer present with III Corps on August 31 and therefore the 12 artillery pieces in that division were also not present.

However, the marshal found little comfort in just the Emperor's words—Macdonald needed the means to wage war. In response to these materiel needs, the Emperor on September 3 dispatched to the Army of the Bober four large convoys. The first consisted of 55 caissons, of which 24 were loaded with small arms cartridges, another convoy had 4,000 muskets and 6,000 pairs of shores. The third convoy was laden with more ammunition while the fourth convoy had another 5,000 muskets.[71]

These materiels had not yet arrived on September 5 when Macdonald dictated the following letter. "I feel a great deal of sorrow," he told Berthier, "that His Majesty again puts upon me a burden which I am in no position to bear. The munitions of war were lacking and they have not been replaced. I made known the true situation of this army and it has not been rectified. It has neither strength, nor body, nor organization. Your Highness can nevertheless assure the Emperor that I shall do everything humanly possible with such elements."[72]

During Napoleon's journey from Dresden to Goerlitz and then back to Bautzen, he saw roads and towns choked with thousands of stragglers. The lost manpower from the army, and the disorders caused by deserters and marauders, outraged the Emperor. As a result, he issued the following proclamation:[73]

> Every soldier who deserts his flag, betrays the first of his duties.
>
> As a consequence, His Majesty orders:
>
> Article 1. Every soldier who deserts his flag without legitimate cause will be subject to decimation. To this effect, as soon as 10 deserters are returned, the generals commanding the army corps will have them draw lots, and will have one shot.
>
> Article 2. The Major General is charged with the execution of the present order.
>
> Bautzen. 6 September 1813
>
> Napoleon

While events in Silesia and southern Saxony occupied the attention of Napoleon and Macdonald, another important series of events began to unfold on the road to Berlin. The Emperor had given command of the Army of Berlin to Marshal Oudinot. With the IV, VII, XII Corps, and the III Reserve Cavalry Corps, the Duke of Reggio was under orders to coordinate an offensive with Davout coming from Hamburg and Girard's and Lanusse's divisions from Magdebourg against Bernadotte's Army of the North. The combination of these French-Allied forces were supposed to either defeat Bernadotte's forces, or at least keep the Army of the North on the defensive and prevent these troops from marching southward in coordination with any other Allied offensive. It was an overly ambitious plan—one far exceeding the capabilities of the young, outnumbered, widely separated commands—and certainly beyond the talents of Oudinot.

Despite these factors, Oudinot marched on Berlin. A number of minor actions—all won by Oudinot's Franco-Allied troops—drove in Bernadotte's outposts. In the meanwhile, Girard and Lanusse marched their divisions east from Magdebourg, defeating the Allied forces at Lübnitz on August 27, while Davout struck out from Hamburg, driving before him the Swedish corps under General Wegesack.[74]

These minor reverses shook Bernadotte's nerve. The Crown Prince of Sweden was ready to abandon Berlin to Oudinot when the Prussian General Bülow flatly refused to give up the city without a battle.[75] This came on August 23. Oudinot's army was advancing through broken country that offered few connecting roads for lateral communication and support. As a result, each of the corps under Oudinot was virtually on its own, pushing slowly forward without adequate cavalry screens. Suddenly, at about 3 P.M., General Bülow, commanding a corps of 38,000 Prussians, attacked Reynier's VII Corps of 18,000 men near Gross-Beeren. In another downpour of rain which seemed to typify the weather conditions of the battles fought during the fall campaign, the Saxon infantry under Reynier collapsed after an unequal struggle against overwhelming numbers of enemy. Unable to hold the field, Reynier ordered a retreat.[76]

Gross-Beeren cost the VII Corps 3,000 combatants and 13 artillery pieces.[77] Bülow lost about 1,000 officers and men.[78] The diluvial rains again proved harmful to the French army. "Muskets no longer worked," Marshal Oudinot wrote in his report on August 26, "and the soldiers were reduced to their bayonets."[79] Although not a major battle, Gross-Beeren unnerved the Saxon infantry and light cavalry from which they never recovered. Reynier's confidence in the Saxons was likewise affected and he strongly advised Marshal Oudinot to retreat.

The setback at Gross-Beeren and Reynier's assessment of the Saxons persuaded the cautious Oudinot to call off his offensive. He ordered the Army of Berlin to retreat some 50 miles back to Wittemberg on the Elbe River, despite the protestations of his other corps commanders. One of the most noteworthy objections was made by Napoleon's long-time friend, General Bertrand, commander of IV Corps, who wrote to Berthier on August 31. "I am not afraid to say that although the IV Corps may have a few hundred men less, it is all the more fearsome for the enemy: it has the highest morale. In the movements that we made, be it forward or backward, or on the flanks, it is noteworthy, for the soldiers as well as for the officers, that the enemy never tried anything successfully, that we were always superior, we fought only when we chose to, for as long as we judged it profitable and in positions we selected. The IV Corps has become used to maneuvering calmly before the enemy, and it is really more valuable than when it left Sprottau [at the end of the armistice]."[80]

With the Army of Berlin's withdrawal, Girard and Lanusse, who had advanced eastward from Magdebourg, suddenly found themselves isolated and attacked by swarms of enemy cavalry and Cossacks. By September 3, the two divisions had fought their way back to Magdebourg, but only after losing 1,200 of the original 6,400 men fielded by these small commands. Upon seeing these troops return to the city after an absence of two weeks, General Jean Lemarois, military governor of Magdebourg, wrote the following observation to Marshal Berthier on September 4. "Lanusse's division returned last night scarcely 3,000 men strong, part of whom were without weapons, knapsacks, shakos, in all in such a tattered state that one would think that they fought a six month campaign."[81] With the retreats of Oudinot and the Magdebourg divisions, Davout had little choice but to turn back to Hamburg.[82]

Oudinot's failed offensive greatly displeased Napoleon for he felt that the Allied Army of the North could not be given a chance to be free to move south in hopes of coordinating movements with Blücher's Army of Silesia. The Emperor responded by dispatching Marshal Ney to assume command of the Army of Berlin with orders to march on the Prussian capital, thereby forcing Bernadotte into a major battle. On September 3, the Prince of the Moscowa arrived at the army's camp below Wittemberg. Ney's force of personality on the commanders was immediate, as evidenced by the General Charles Lebrun, the Duke of Plaisance's letter to Napoleon. "Sire, the Prince of the Moscowa arrived yesterday morning," the commander of I Corps wrote on September 4. "He immediately made plans to march forward; he is to leave tomorrow. It can already be seen that here is a leader...."[83]

That same day, Bertrand wrote to the Major General: "Your Highness, the Prince of the Moscowa reviewed IV Corps today, and then gave an electrifying speech. Every soldier was moved to the depths of his soul. He will march tomorrow to seek out the enemy and to destroy him."[84]

The Army of Berlin struck camp on September 5—it did not have to march far to find the enemy and a major battle. On September 6, Ney's forces encountered Bernadotte's army at the village of Dennewitz.[85] The superior numbers of Allied cavalry and Cossacks prevented the French cavalry from detecting the presence of the large bodies of Allied infantry. Without full knowledge of the dangers which lay ahead, Ney aggressively pushed his army into a deadly ambush.

****

Ney's Army of Berlin at Dennewitz[86]

Corps	Division	Commander	# of bns/sqd	All ranks present and under arms
IV Corps—		Bertrand		Strengths as of 15 August 1813
	12th Division	Morand	11	7,559
	15th Division	Fontanelli	14	8,087
	38th Division	Franquemont	8	3,594
	Corps Cavalry	Briche	8	880
	Corps Artillery Reserve			1,625
	Troops in route			834
	Corps Totals:			22,579 and 64 guns

After deducting about 2,500 combatants estimated to have fallen out of ranks through strategic consumption between August 15 and September 5, the IV Corps had approximately 20,000 officers and other ranks present and under arms at Dennewitz supported by 64 pieces of ordnance.

Corps	Division	Commander	# of bns/sqd	All ranks present and under arms
VII Corps—		Reynier		Strengths as of 15 August 1813
	24th Division	de Lecoq	10	6,419
	25th Division	de Sahr	9	5,431
	32nd Division	Durutte	14	10,951
	Corps Cavalry	de Lindenau	13	1,848
	Corps Artillery Reserve			558
	Troops in route			376
	Corps Totals:			25,583 and 54 guns

After deducting about 10,500 combatants estimated to have fallen out of ranks through strategic consumption and combat casualties between August 15 and September 5, as well as 13 guns lost at Gross Beeren, the VII Corps had approximately 15,000 officers and other ranks present and under arms at Dennewitz supported by 41 pieces of ordnance.

Corps	Division	Commander	# of bns/sqd	All ranks present and under arms
XII Corps—		Oudinot	Strengths as of 15 August 1813	
	Staff and administrative personnel			184
	13th Division	Pacthod	13	4,463
	14th Division	Guilleminot	11	7,373
	29th Division	Raglovich	10	4,958
	Corps Cavalry	Baumont	7	1,165
	Corps Artillery Reserve			963
	Corps Totals:			19,106 and 66 guns

After deducting about 3,100 combatants estimated to have fallen out of ranks through strategic consumption between August 15 and September 5, the XII Corps had approximately 16,000 officers and other ranks present and under arms at Dennewitz supported by 66 pieces of ordnance.

Corps	Division	Commander	# of sqdrns	All ranks present and under arms
III Reserve Cavalry Corps—Arrighi			Strengths as of 15 August 1813	
	5th Lt Cav Div	Lorge	10	2,067
	6th Lt Cav Div	Fournier	6	1,361
	4th Hv Cav Div	Defrance	11	1,571
	Corps Artillery Reserve			385
	Troops in route			2,279
	Corps Total:			7,663 and 24 guns

After deducting about 600 combatants estimated to have fallen out of ranks through strategic consumption between August 15 and September 5, the III Reserve Cavalry Corps Corps had approximately 7,000 officers and other ranks present and under arms at Dennewitz supported by 24 pieces of ordnance.

Taking into account the estimated losses through strategic consumption and previous combat casualties at Gross Beeren, the total strength of the formations under Ney at Dennewitz numbered approximately 58,000 officers and other ranks present and under arms supported by 195 pieces of ordnance.

****

In the ensuing battle, Bertrand's IV Corps and Durutte's 32nd Division of VII Corps fought with great skill and determination.[87] However, these troops were not enough to stem the hordes of Allies. Once again, the Saxon infantry was the first to give way, then followed by the Saxon light cavalry. The more solid formations finally broke from increased enemy pressure, but not without first putting up a fierce fight. The infantry of IV Corps and the French *fantassins* of VII Corps probably would have perished completely if it had not been for a timely charge by Defrance's dragoons of Arrighi's III Reserve Cavalry Corps.[88]

Despite these heroics, Ney's army was finished. Panic set in among the young soldiers and they ran from the field. In a few short hours, the Army of Berlin lost over 20,000 men, of which over 13,000 were taken prisoner. Also lost were 53 guns, 412 caissons and wagons, and 4 standards.[89] The Allied victory carried a price tag of 10,500 Prussians and another 1,500 Russians; the Swedish losses were extremely minor as Bernadotte kept these divisions on a short leash and consequentally they saw only limited action.[90] Dennewitz had ruptured Napoleon's left flank in Saxony. Ney's army turned into a fleeing rabble as it headed back to Torgau; it was not a happy withdrawal.

Morale of the young troops sank to a new low. The XII Corps, which on August 15 numbered just over 19,100 combatants, lost thousands of dispirited soldiers who simply deserted. On September 7, Oudinot's command numbered slightly more than 4,000 soldiers still with the colors.[91] The depressing state of affairs reduced the usually frank and optimistic Bertrand to writing vague nonsense. "The troops behaved [at Dennewitz] in diverse circumstances of the day," Bertrand informed Berthier on September 9, "first enthusiastically, then with the calmness which characterizes well disciplined armies."[92]

The 29th (Bavarian) Division at Dennewitz, 6 September 1813.
Composition by R. Knötel.

The following day, Marshal Ney assessed that his army was incapable of standing at Torgau and ordered it to cross to the left bank of the Elbe and retreat to Wurzen, which was about two-thirds the way from Torgau to Leipzig. Fed up with his predicament, the bravest of the brave[93] penned the following stressful letter to Berthier. "It is my duty to declare to Your Highness," Ney wrote from Wurzen on September 10, "that it is impossible to draw on a good part of the IV, VII, and XII Corps in the actual state of their organization. These corps are reconstituted on paper, but they are not in fact; each of the corps commanders almost does what he judges suitable for his own security. Things are at a point where it is very difficult for me to obtain a parade states report. The morale of the generals, and of the officers in general, is singularly shaken. To command thus is no more than to half command, and I would rather be a grenadier. I beg you, monseigneur, to obtain from the Emperor, either that I, alone, be General-in-Chief, with the generals of the divisions on the wing only under my orders, or that His Majesty prefer to withdraw me from this Hell. I do not need, I think, to speak of my devotion; I am ready to shed all my blood, but I wish that it be usefully. In the actual state of affairs, only the presence of the Emperor would be able to reestablish the whole army, because all wills yield to his genius, and petty vanities disappear before the majesty of the throne."[94] Napoleon responded by ordering Ney to turn his army around, reestablish it on the east bank of the Elbe, and march back to Torgau.[95]

The very next day, On September 11, a small action vividly demonstrated just how badly shaken Marshal Ney's army had become. "The XII Corps," the Prince of the Moscowa reported to Berthier, "which yesterday was marching on Domitzch, ran into a few Cossacks; the troops gave in to such a panic-stricken terror that it was very difficult to rally them...."[96] On September 13, Ney wrote again to the Major General. "In order that all the army corps which are near Torgau may usefully become part of the Berlin expedition, it is desirable that they join up at the soonest possible moment with forces which the Emperor will lead there...If it is necessary that they emerge through Torgau and force the crossing of the Elster, while the Emperor arrives via Luckau, otherwise the dejection of the troops is such that a new check is to be feared."[97]

However, Napoleon believed that Ney was too apprehensive about his situation and had Berthier send a strong message[98] to this end. The Emperor's sharp rebuke was not taken well by Ney, and the Prince of the Moscowa immediately fired his reply back to Berthier on September 15. "His Majesty, you tell me, finds that in seeing monsters, one invents them, and that in many things, he finds that I am going too fast. In truth, the mistrust has reached such a point that I no longer know what to do to please His Majesty. A commanding general, according to good sense, cannot be a machine so compromised as not to be able to take measures which circumstances require. Obliged to justify them, there is always time to rectify the errors which may slip in. Instead of consideration, it is with ill-temper that I'm treated, and, I dare say it, unjustly."[99]

Despite the exchange between Napoleon and Ney, there can be absolutely no doubt that the Army of Berlin had been grievously damaged by the Battle of Dennewitz. After reviewing IV Corps on September 15, General Bertrand noted the following to Berthier. "The events of the past few weeks are beginning to take its toll on the IV Corps as well as on the other corps. We have lost many men."[100] In his report of September 15, General Reynier concluded that the VII Corps "will require considerable reorganization and reinforcements, preferrably Frenchmen."[101] Evidently, the apathetic Saxon infantry and light cavalry that comprised the majority of VII Corps made such an unfavorable impression on their army commander that Ney predicted on September 12 that: "It is very probable that the Saxons, particularly the light cavalry, could switch arms against us

Count J. L. E. Reynier

Swiss by birth, Reynier was one of Napoleon's most loyal corps commanders. During the Revolution, he served as chief of staff to Souham and then to General Moreau. He saw extensive service in Italy from 1804 through 1808 after which he saw duty in Spain and in Russia. His peers considered him difficult to get along with but respected his loyalty. Captured at Leipzig, he was exchanged in February 1814 and died a few days later of exhaustion. *Musée de l'Armée.*

whenever they get a chance."[102] Oudinot's XII Corps was still trying to rally its remaining troops. As a result of the losses among the infantry corps, Arrighi's III Reserve Cavalry Corps was the most solid formation in the Army of Berlin.

Similar stories of defeats in minor engagements continued to arrive at Imperial headquarters almost daily. The Allies, deciding to exploit the broad theater of war and their superior numbers of mounted troops, launched a series of raids aimed at raising havoc along Napoleon's lines of communication. These excursions into the French-held countryside resulted in the Allies capturing thousands of French stragglers, ambushing messengers as well as columns of reinforcements, and destroying numerous, vital supply convoys. French garrrisons at Weissenfels and Merseburg were captured by Prussian General Thielemann on September 12 and 14, netting the Allies more than 3,000 prisoners and 26 guns.[103] Further north, a raid by Walmoden, spearheaded by the Russo-German Legion, ambushed and mauled a French task force near the Gärda River on September 16. The French command, led by General Pécheux, consisted of five infantry battalions, one cavalry squadron, and six guns; it lost all its guns, some 500 killed and wounded, along with another 800 taken prisoner.[104]

By mid-September, Allied cavalry—mainly Prussian landwehr—supported by thousands of Cossacks, were menacing French lines of communication on the west bank of the Elbe River. Since Napoleon wanted to keep his main forces on the east side of that river, the Emperor was forced to order approximately 17,000 troops, including a division of Young Guard cavalry under Lefebvre-Desnoëttes (see Appendix J), to conduct a series of sweeps through the Saxon countryside[105] with the purpose of engaging and destroying the Allied nuisance. This operation did relieve the pressure on the lines of communication, but met with only limited success as the Allied cavalry were not fully neutralized. There were simply too many of them.

The stories of the setbacks suffered by the Emperor's lieutenants, the disheartening news concerning the persistent hunger suffered by the soldiers, and the turmoil in the rear areas, was cause for grave concern not only among the marshals and generals, but also within the Emperor's cabinet as well. Following receipt of the Dennewitz defeat, Napoleon's Minister of Foreign Affairs, Hughes-Bernard Maret, the Duke of Bassano, sent a confidential letter to the Minister of War, General Henri Clarke. The content of this lengthy piece of correspondence is vital to any understanding of Napoleon's predicament in 1813. "Events are piling up in such a way that granting His Majesty happy and brilliant odds, it's an act of prudence, however, to foresee the opposite. I believe I must, my dear Duke, speak plainly and confidentally with you. The Russian army is not our most dangerous enemy. It has suffered great losses, has not been reinforced, and, aside from its cavalry, which is rather numerous, it is playing only a subordinate role in the on-going struggle. But Prussia has made great efforts; excitement carried to a very high degree has favored the position taken by its sovereign; his armies are numerous, his generals, officers, and soldiers are very spirited. Still, Russia and Prussia together would only have offered weak obstacles to our armies; but the inclusion of Austria has extremely complicated the question.

"Our army, whatever the price the victories gained may have cost it, is still fine and numerous; but the generals and the officers, weary of war, no longer have that momentum which caused them to do great things. The theater is too extended. The Emperor is victorious every time he is present, but he can't be everywhere, and the leaders who command alone rarely come up to his expectations. You know what happened to General Vandamme; the Duke of Tarentum has suffered setbacks in Silesia, and the Prince of the Moscowa has just been beaten marching on Berlin.

"In such circumstances, my dear Duke, and with the Emperor's genius, we can still hope for everything; but it may also be that contrary events can impact on events in a harmful way. It is not to be greatly feared, but we must regard it as possible and neglect nothing which prudence demands.

"I present you this picture so that you may know everything and act accordingly. You would do well to see to it that the border strongholds be put into good condition and to gather therein a great deal of artillery; for in that category we often undergo rather sensitive losses. You should have a secret understanding with the Director General of the Commissary to have extraordinary supplies in the Rhine strongholds, in short, in order to prepare everything needed in advance, so that, in an unusual circumstance, His Majesty not experience new difficulties and that you not be caught napping. You are aware that, if I write to you thus, it is that I have carefully reflected on that which is going on beneath my eyes, and that I have assured myself that in doing so nothing which His Majesty might disapprove. A great success can change everything and put matters back in the propitious situation in which the immense advantage won by the Emperor at Dresden had placed them."[106]

By the last week of September, Napoleon began to fully realize the enormous difficulties of his situation. His young army was starving; many of the army's leaders lacked the confidence to act independently; strategic consumption was up dramatically as hunger and bad weather turned marches into torturing endurance tests which the undernourished men and horses could not withstand; and the lines of communication were in chaos from a combination of enemy cavalry and tens of thousands of deserters who roamed the Saxon countryside. "I was informed," Ney wrote to Berthier on September 13, "that a large number of deserters, about 6,000 [from the Army of Berlin], who, from the beginning of the battle [at Dennewitz] threw away their guns in order to run faster, and they fled to Leipzig."[107] The deserters found their way into the columns of sick and wounded as they moved west to Mayence. In these columns, the self-inflicted "wounds on the hands"[108] were seen more and more often.

To further help clean up in the rear areas, the general depot of cavalry was ordered to relocate westward towards Fulda.[109] Consisting of 8,000 men, 6,000 horses, and much mobile equipment,[110] once on the march, this vulnerable column stretched for miles. Thus, towards the Rhine moved a seemingly never-ending column of men and horses to which was added convoys of sick and wounded soldiers.

As might be expected, this column attracted "the scum of the army".[111] Bands of deserters, turned outlaw, would chase away the train drivers, steal the horses and wagons, and sell them to the people in the countryside.[112] With no Imperial Gendarmes and few officers present, it was next to impossible to control these brigands. The general in charge of the relocation move was General Noirot, who wrote to Berthier on September 20 of his difficulties. "I have only a small number of good officers; the rest of them are excessively bad, without knowledge, without subordination, without honor, and without courage. I even have to tell Your Highness about several of them who have cowardly abandoned their troops in the face of the enemy, and fled spreading fear."[113]

General Dalton added his voice to the events taking place in the rear areas in connection with the relocation of the cavalry depot. "It is the model of the perfect rout, and this gives a terrible impression to the inhabitants as to the situation within the army, as they do not know that these are only the scum of the army. There was no more disorder in the path of the Berezina."[114]

With his rear areas in complete turmoil, and after considering several plans, Napoleon opted for a retreat to the west bank of the Elbe River, retaining strong bridgeheads at 7 vital cities. This move was designed to get his rear areas and lines of communication in order, and "wait for the Allies to come and be killed."[115] While this move was being accomplished, the Emperor again looked carefully at the strength of his rapidly depleting army. To offset the staggering losses through strategic consumption as well as future casualties, and despite all the problems associated with organizing new troops, Napoleon decided to call up even more men.

On September 27, Count Daru wrote to the Minister of War: "I have the honor of informing Your Excellency that His Majesty has just signed the *senatus-consulte* which orders the call to active duty of 280,000 conscripts to whit; 160,000 from the conscription of 1815, and 120,000 from earlier classes. I am joining to this letter a copy of the decree which sets the distribution of these 120,000 and the means of executing this levy. I am going to make known to Your Excellency the observations which His Majesty ordered me to transmit.

"Your Excellency will note that His Majesty has leaned heavily on the sound departments. He deems it suitable that you make it known in writing to the prefects that it is the true Frenchmen who must sustain the struggle in which we are engaged...

"His Majesty wishes that you arrange matters that no conscript has to make a round trip; thus, a man from Meurthe, for example, must not go to Brittany, then come back to the Rhine, when he is outfitted. To this purpose, the Emperor orders that Bretons be sent to bases in Brittany, Normans to bases in Normandy, and so forth, and plan it so that no conscript marches more than a week in order to arrive at his base. Your Excellency will realize that it makes no difference that the conscripts are assigned to bases located in their own province, since they are not to remain there more than a month and soon after they must report to the Rhine...

"As for the distribution of the conscripts by branch of service, His Majesty attaches less importance to it because, according to the method we've adopted, we can transfer from one base to another...The intention of His Majesty is that each department furnishes one-tenth for the Imperial Guard, which will make 12,000 men."[116]

Two weeks later, on October 7, the Senate formally approved the measure. The 120,000 men of this *senatus-consulte* amounted to yet another supplementary levy of the Classes of 1808 through 1814. All these men were to report to their depots between November 8 and November 23 and could not be expected to join the army before the New Year.[117]

In the meantime, Clarke searched everywhere for more men. He cleaned out the depots, the hospitals, and even the prisons! The cadres around which these men were formed were drawn exclusively from conscripts which had themselves deserted, been captured, and returned to duty. The regiments organized in this manner were among the most pitiful formations imaginable. "According to your orders," wrote the commander of the 25th Military Division to Clarke on October 5, "the 123rd, 124th, and 127th Regiments of the Line are to be composed of refractory conscripts. These men are arriving daily at the bases assigned them, but they almost all arrive in impaired health which can only be blamed on the time they spent in prison, and on the little care the officers escorting them gave them while in route...992 have already entered the 123rd, and only 513 of these are present and fit for duty; 315 are in the hospital, and 134 of those present are so weak that the regimental colonel is calling for their discharge...there still are in the pool of refractory conscripts, a few men I have been unable to believe I am to include, because they will never be able to bear arms; they are deformed, small, puny, and several among them are crippled. If these men are not discharged, they will die in the hospital, as happens daily...."[118]

The ill-health of the men comprising these regiments was further confirmed by the colonel commanding the "general depot of insubordinates and deserters"[119] in Strasbourg, who wrote: "The detachment which arrived today was in a pitiful state; out of 114 men of which it was composed, 45 had to be sent immediately to the hospital, being almost dead."[120]

Other means to increase the size of the army included returning to the ranks those who had deserted but had not been arrested. However, most of these men were useless. From Erfurt, General Dalton observed that the deserters as well as the "unfortunate wounded and sick that arrive in Erfurt pass through a thousand dangers. Followed by parties of Cossacks...they wander from village to village, surviving most of the time on unripened fruits. They arrive in a state of exhaustion and are pitifully diseased...."[121]

On September 25, the Emperor wrote from Dresden to Marshal Kellermann at Mayence, asking him to "stop the deserters and stragglers who were leaving the army in large numbers."[122] Kellermann was then ordered to first lock up these deserters, then "give them clothes, equipment, muskets, and to send them back to Leipzig in *bataillons de marche*."[123]

Thus, instead of trying every possible means to tackle the food and subsistance distribution problem, the Emperor chose instead to raise more troops and press newly formed or reformed units composed of deserters into the field. The addition of these formations added little, if any, to the real combat effectiveness of the *Grande Armée*.

Meanwhile, for the soldiers "who, by duty and by honor"[124] remained loyal to the colors by remaining in ranks, their most serious difficulty was just finding enough food not only to stay alive but to maintain good health. Part of the problem was that the insecurity of the rear areas forced Napoleon to concentrate his corps more closely than normal in order to provide his men protection. Naturally, the consequences of this was that the difficulties involving foraging and requistions increased proportionally.

The single biggest problem was that the administration of the army could not locate or provide enough rations. Only one week following the victory at Dresden, Marshal

Saint-Cyr indicated the discouragement within the ranks of XIV Corps due to the troops not receiving enough food. "We cannot keep them in the camps," Saint-Cyr wrote Berthier on September 3. "They leave in order to find something to help them sustain life, and I am afraid, in a very few days, of a complete breakdown in discipline and organization if we cannot give them some subsistence. The countryside is in ruin, and even the supply of potatoes is running out."[125]

For days in a row, the troops would not receive a single ounce of food, other than what they could find on their own. Jean-Baptiste Barrès, a captain and company commander in the 3rd battalion of the 47th Regiment of the Line in General Compans' 20th Division of Marmont's VI Corps, wrote on September 2nd: "For six days we had been without food. I ate nothing but the strawberries and bilberries which abounded in the woods."[126]

The longer the campaign continued, the more acute the lack of food became. On September 13, Marshal Victor voiced his complaints about the shortage of food for II Corps. "The soldiers can only remain with their regiments if they have food. If they are fed, we can overcome all difficulties." Victor ended his report with the following conclusion. "The general administration of the army is the only thing that can stop this misery that weighs down II Corps."[127]

But there was virtually no food to be found. Saxony's bountiful resources had played out. The *ordonnateurs* could not even find enough grain for the army's bakeries. On September 13, Napoleon reluctantly approved the reduction in the daily allotment of bread to a meager 8 ounces,[128] augmented with as much rice or potatoes as possible.

The news struck the army like a thunderbolt. "Without food, the army is melting away," General Bertrand wrote Berthier on September 15, "and the administration cannot seem to reverse the unfortunate trend that provides the soldier with less and less every day."[129] The Count of Lobau added his voice to those pleading for more subsistence. "Everywhere hunger cries misery," the commander of I Corps wrote to Berthier on September 20, "and the disintegration of the army is scary."[130]

Général de brigade Raymond de Montesquiou, Duke of Fezensac, was in command of the 2nd Brigade of the 1st Division in Lobau's I Corps. He observed the following about his young soldiers: "It is not on the battlefields that soldiers go through the severest ordeals: French youth has an instinct for bravery. But a soldier must be able to endure hunger, fatigue, and bad weather...we have known men like this; but it is asking too much of young fellows whose constitution is barely formed and who, to start with, do not have the military spirit, the loyalty to the colors, and the moral energy which doubles a man's strength while doubling his courage."[131]

With hunger cries coming from all quarters, Napoleon finally wrote the following to Daru on September 23. "The army is not being fed. It would be an illusion to see otherwise. Twenty-four ounces of bread, one ounce of rice, and 8 ounces of meat are insufficient for the soldier. The rules of all time gave to each soldier in time of war 28 ounces of bread, and this was considered insufficient even when the soldier could add vegetables and potatoes found in the country. Today, you give him only 8 ounces of bread, 3 ounces of rice, and 8 ounces of meat. The soldier survives only with the consumption of meat...The 3 ounces of rice that we give him could be discontinued if we would give him 24 ounces of bread...One ounce of rice and 24 ounces of bread would form a good ration; one ounce of rice would represent the 4 ounces of bread that is missing to go from 24 to 28. The potatoes and the vegetables found by the soldier in the country would be equivalent to the 2 ounces of vegetables that we are supposed to give him...To make it easier for the administration, we could give him the 24 ounces in 16 ounces of bread and 8 ounces of grains of wheat...The III, the V, and the XI Corps have not received rice for 5 days; their soldiers' bread ration has been reduced to 8 ounces. I would like to be able to order that all the corps receive the ration of 24 ounces of bread and one ounce of rice...."[132]

Napoleon was not able to give such an order. Sustenance of every kind—rice, potatoes, and grains to make bread—had been exhausted. The administration of the army, seemingly incompetent in this plight, was powerless to change that which it could not control. As a result, the amount of food available to feed the army continued to dwindle. On October 13, the Emperor reduced the official ration to only 6 ounces.[133] The painful suffering within Napoleon's army grew.

Those who remained in ranks, weakened by lack of subsistence, were no longer capable of performing the marching feats Napoleon expected of his soldiers. With less nutrition and increased demand for physical activity, strategic consumption rose sharply. In the last half of the month of September, the army lost 1,000 men a day to non-battle factors. In the first 15 days of October, the rate of wastage rose to more than 1,700 combatants a day! Thus, in the 30 days preceding the Battle of Leipzig, Napoleon suffered more than 40,000 non-battle casualties.[134] Strategic consumption was eviscerating Napoleon's *Grande Armée* of 1813.

Wastage of the *Grande Armée* of 1813. *Composition by Bombled.*

171

Napoleon at Leipzig. *Composition by R. Knötel.*

CHAPTER VIII
"Malbrouck s'en va-t-en en guerre"

As Napoleon ordered the *Grande Armée* to withdraw onto the west bank of the Elbe River, he was still confident of victory, his numerous difficulties notwithstanding. Dresden's close proximity to the Bohemian mountains made it too vulnerable as a central position base. The Emperor therefore decided to switch his center of operations to Leipzig from which he would again attempt to implement his strategy of the central position[1] to defeat the numerous Allied armies.

However, the losses sustained by the Imperial forces in the first 45 days of the fall campaign suggested to Napoleon that before the next series of slugging matches began, a reorganization was prudent in order to maximize the army's efficiency, both in manpower as well as in leadership. Therefore, after taking a hard look at his war machine, Napoleon initiated many changes.

To protect his southern flank, the Emperor decided to leave the reorganized survivors of I Corps under the Count of Lobau, and Saint Cyr's XIV Corps, to hold Dresden. Napoleon reasoned that he would again need the city as a base of operations against Schwarzenberg after he had defeated the other Allied armies.[2] The remainder of the army was ordered to concentrate towards Leipzig. In the corps which constituted Napoleon's mobile command in October of 1813, notable changes were made when compared to the August organization. Of the line infantry corps, only Victor's II and Marmont's VI were judged sound enough not to warrant tampering.[3] The remainder of the line infantry corps had their composition altered to some degree.[4]

Marshal Ney's former command, the III Corps, which had been under the able guidance of General Souham for the latter part of the spring campaign and for most all of the fall campaign, lost two of its five infantry divisions to the reorganization. General Albert's 10th Division was assigned to Lauriston's V Corps, which had lost the entire 17th Division in late August. Also, General Marchand's 39th Division, consisting in part of Napoleon's most reliable German infantry—the solid regiments from Hesse-Darmstadt—was allocated to Macdonald's XI Corps, increasing the infantry complement of the Duke of Tarentum's corps to 4 infantry divisions.

The IV Corps, whose morale was temporarily shaken at Dennewitz, had recovered its poise by October and was left intact. However, to help make good a portion of the losses suffered since the start of the fall campaign, Napoleon ordered some of the survivors of XII Corps be sent to General Bertrand's command. Included in these troops were the 137th Regiment of the Line, along with General Wolff's brigade of Westphalian and Hessian cavalry.

Other survivors of XII Corps—namely, the 13th Division—were transferred to Reynier's VII Corps, which had suffered heavy casualties and a high desertion rate among its Saxon infantry and light cavalry contingents. As a result, the 24th Division was disbanded and its survivors merged with those of the 25th Division, which was retained as an active division of the corps. Durutte's 32nd Division, though reduced in size, was still considered a valuable formation and was left untouched.

Poniatowski's tough but small VIII Corps was augmented with the addition of two infantry regiments. The best known of these formations was the famous Vistula Legion,[5] which had reconstituted two of its battalions following the 1812 campaign, and was formerly part of the garrison of Wittemberg.[6] The Vistula infantry were added to the 1st Brigade of the 26th Division. Meanwhile, the 4th Polish Infantry Regiment—which, like the Vistula Legion, was pulled out of the garrison at Wittemberg—reinforced the portion of the 27th Division that was with VIII Corps.[7]

The XII Corps, whose morale had been shattered by the defeat at Dennewitz, was disbanded and its survivors distributed as previously mentioned. The disbanding of XII Corps left Marshal Oudinot temporarily without a command, so Napoleon further decided to reorganize the infantry of the Imperial Guard.[8]

Consequently, the four divisions of the Young Guard were split into two corps. The 1st and the 3rd Divisions, both consisting entirely of Voltigeurs, were placed under the command of Oudinot and named the I Young Guard Corps. Meanwhile, Marshal Mortier was ordered to take command of the II Young Guard Corps, consisting of the 2nd and 4th Divisions composed of Tirailleurs and Flankers.

The remaining Guard infantry were separated into the 1st and 2nd Old Guard Divisions. The 1st Old Guard Division, under the incomparable divisional leadership of General Friant, consisted of the four senior regiments of the Old Guard infantry. These superb regiments had been substantially reinforced since the start of the fall campaign with qualified personnel, and on the eve of the Battle of Leipzig their battalion strengths averaged 782 officers and other ranks present and under arms.

Also receiving reinforcements was the newly created 2nd Old Guard Division, commanded by the steady General Curial. This division was composed of the splendid Middle Guard regiments, along with the Italian Vélites, the Saxon Grenadier Guard battalion formerly of VII Corps, the reorganized single battalion of the Westphalian Fusilier Guards which had been transferred from XI Corps, and the new Guard battalion from the Grand Duchy of Warsaw.[9]

Ordered to concentrate with the main army were all of the corps constituting the reserve cavalry. Among these, the I Reserve Cavalry Corps, under the very capable leadership of General Latour-Maubourg, was by far the biggest and the best of the line cavalry formations. The heart of the corps was comprised of the regiments of heavy cavalry, most notably the French cuirassiers and the Saxon heavy cavalry. Perhaps it should be noted here that a world of difference existed in the loyalty to Napoleon of the Saxon heavy cavalry when compared to the rest of their countrymen. Following the defeat of Prussia in 1806, and especially from the 1809 Danube campaign on, the superb regiments of Saxon heavy horse—namely the Garde du corps and the Zastrow Cuirassiers—identified very closely with Napoleon and always displayed a fierce pride and devotion in serving the Emperor. Even after the *Grande Armée's* defeat at Leipzig and subsequent retreat back to France, the Saxon heavy cavalry remained steadfastly loyal to Napoleon. When the Allies issued heavy-handed reprisals against Saxony due to the heavy cavalry's continued service to France, Napoleon thought it best to discharge these devoted followers. The Saxon cavalrymen finally agreed to quit the army and return to their homeland following the strongest of protests and an emotion-charged farewell.[10]

While Napoleon was reorganizing his army and reconcentrating northward towards Leipzig, the Allies likewise developed a new plan. Benningsen's Russians—the Polish Reserve Army—had finally arrived in Bohemia. With these additional forces present along side Schwarzenberg's massive Army of Bohemia, it was decided that this large host would move north towards Leipzig. Meanwhile, further to the east, Blücher's Army of Silesia

The Emperor conducting a personal reconnaissance, 1813.
(Baron Gourgaud is on foot on the far left). *Composition by R. Knötel.*

would march north to join forces with Bernadotte's Army of the North located at Wittemberg, approximately 40 miles northeast of Leipzig. Once together, these armies would push southward towards Leipzig.[11] The battles which resulted from these maneuvers can be broadly categorized as the second phase of the fall campaign. These combats, which culminated in the cataclysm at Leipzig, and then finally, the campaign's epilog at Hanau, marked the end of the struggle for Germany.

As Napoleon's converging corps made for Leipzig, news of the advance by Blücher's and Bernadotte's armies presented the Emperor with an opportunity to crush these Allies north of the city before Schwarzenberg's and Benningsen's armies could arrive. Maneuvering north past Leipzig, forced marches on empty stomachs pushed the soldiers of the *Grande Armée* to their limit, and the troops were not able to move as fast as Napoleon needed them to march. As a result, the Allies—who were near Düben—caught wind of Napoleon's advance and scrambled to the west, crossing the Mulde River and continuing on to the Saale River.[12] During this retreat, a sharp clash took place on October 9 between Sacken's Russian corps of the Army of Silesia, which was acting as the army's rear guard, and Sébastiani's II Reserve Cavalry Corps. In the fight which ensued, Sébastiani's horsemen cut one brigade of Russian infantry to pieces and captured a large portion of Blücher's baggage trains.[13]

The next day, Augereau's conscripts of the IX Corps and Milhaud's V *bis* Reserve Cavalry Corps, who were marching eastward towards Leipzig, smashed a slightly smaller Allied force of Austrians and Prussians under Liechtenstein and Thielemann.[14] Further north on October 11, General Delmas—commanding the 9th Division—attacked and destroyed an entire division of Prussians at Dessau, capturing some 2,000 prisoners in the process.[15] Meanwhile, Reynier's VII Corps, temporarily reinforced with Dombrowski's

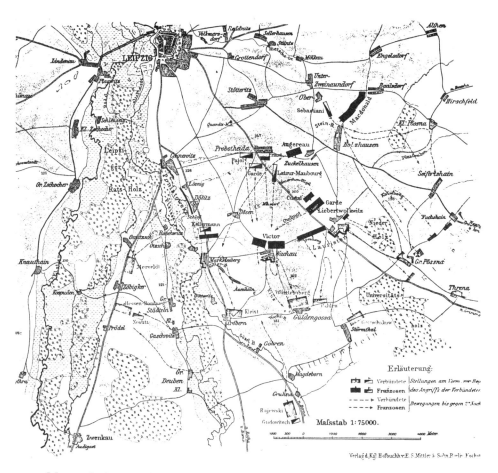

Map of the southern front (Wachau) at Leipzig, 16 October 1813.

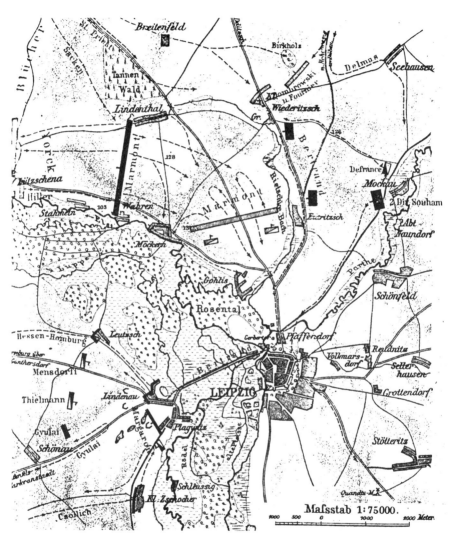

Map of the northern front (Möckern and Lindenau) at Leipzig, 16 October 1813.

27th Polish Division, fought the remainder of the same Prussian corps. After a brief but bloody battle, the entire Prussian corps was put to flight and sent "streaming headlong north into Berlin."[16]

Despite these small victories, Napoleon's central position was becoming more critical by the day. The Emperor's maneuvers against the lines of communication of the Army of Silesia had not caused Blücher and his staff to call retreat, which was in direct disobedience to the orders given them by the timid Bernadotte.[17] Instead, the Prussian staff ordered the army to move southward against Napoleon's rear and his base of operations at Leipzig.

By October 12, Napoleon realized that Saint-Cyr was blockaded by Ostermann's Corps of Russians from Benningsen's army and that at least one Allied army—Bohemia— was coming up on Leipzig from the south (at this time, it is not clear if Napoleon knew that the Polish Reserve Army was also on the way). Blocking the advance of the massive Army of Bohemia south of Leipzig was a far smaller force under Marshal Murat, who was just barely holding his own in preventing the enemy from capturing the city and cutting the *Grande Armée's* communications with France.

The Emperor also knew that Blücher's temporarily immobilized army was licking its wounds from the engagements of the 9th and 11th. Therefore, from his current position north of Leipzig, Napoleon decided to turn his army about and march southward to the city. Once there, together with the troops under Murat and the various other independent commands which had coalesced around Leipzig, the Emperor planned to crush Schwarzenberg before Benningsen and Blücher could reach the field. Further, Napoleon believed that he would not have to contend with the Army of the North as he predicted that the overly conservative Bernadotte would let his army simply "prance in place".[18] Thus, along muddy roads and on empty stomachs, Napoleon's weary army trudged back to Leipzig to meet its destiny.

Years after the battle, the *Grande Armée's* position at Leipzig was caustically described by Marshal Marmont as being "at the bottom of a funnel."[19] To state it simply, Napoleon's precarious situation at Leipzig was a case of the strategy of the central position gone bad. The massive Allied armies were too close. With his significant numerical inferiority, Napoleon could not hold off the Allies on one front by trading space for time and still have enough troops to crush his enemies on another. Nevertheless, the Emperor, overly anxious to come to grips and crush his foes—and confident of victory despite the many difficulties—accepted battle on the most unequal of terms.

****

Napoleon's *Grande Armée* at Leipzig[20]

Imperial Guard	# of bns/sqd	Strength of inf. & cav.	Average per battalion/sqdrn	Guns	Artillerists, engineers, train, etc
		Strength returns as of 15 October 1813			
1st Old Gd Div	8 / --	6,255	782 / --	8	*
2nd Old Gd Div	9 / --	4,664	518 / --	8	*
1st Yg Gd Div	12 / --	6,044	504 / --	24	*
2nd Yg Gd Div	10 / --	5,470	547 / --	24	*
3rd Yg Gd Div	12 / --	4,731	394 / --	24	*
4th Yg Gd Div	14 / --	5,521	394 / --	24	*
1st Gd Cav Div	-- / 15	1,483	--- / 99	---	---
2nd Gd Cav Div	-- / 11	1,551	--- / 141	---	---
3rd Gd Cav Div	-- / 15	3,224	--- / 215	---	---
Guards of Honor	-- / 20	901	--- / 45	---	---
Horse Artillery of the Guard with the Guard cavalry				24	670
Guard Artillery Reserve				90	6,418*
Corps Totals:	65 / 61	39,844	--- / ---	218	7,088

Imperial Guard net strength of 46,932 present and under arms, of which:

> 32,685, or 70% of the corps were infantry,
> 7,159, or 15% of the corps were cavalry, and
> 7,088, or 15% of the corps were artillerists and other support troops.
> * All artillerists and support personnel included in the total for the Guard Artillery Reserve.
> Guard artillery ratio on October 15 was 1 gun for every 215 combatants.

II Corps Victor	# of bns/sqd	Strength of inf. & cav.	Average per battalion/sqdrn	Guns	Artillerists, engineers, train, etc
		Strength returns as of 25 September 1813			
4th Division	12 / --	5,437	453 / --	16	205
5th Division	8 / --	4,175	522 / --	8	174
6th Division	12 / --	6,097	508 / --	16	376
Corps Artillery Reserve				14	1,180
Corps Totals:	32 / --	15,709	--- / ---	54	1,935

II Corps net strength of 17,644 present and under arms, of which:

> 15,709, or 89% of the corps were infantry,
> 1,935 or 11% of the corps were artillerists and other support troops.
> II Corps artillery ratio on September 25 was 1 gun every 327 combatants.

After deducting about 1,044 combatants estimated to have fallen out of ranks through strategic consumption between September 25 and October 15, the II Corps had approximately 16,600 officers and other ranks present and under arms at Leipzig supported by 54 pieces of ordnance.

III Corps Souham	# of bns/sqd	Strength of inf. & cav.	Average per battalion/sqdrn	Guns	Artillerists, engineers, train, etc
		Strength returns as of 1 October 1813			
HQ and administration		376			
8th Division	15 / --	4,442	296 / --	12	*
9th Division	13 / --	4,235	326 / --	13	*
11th Division	13 / --	4,357	335 / --	12	*
Corps Cavalry	-- / 11	1,065	--- / 97	---	---
Corps Artillery Reserve				22	3,069*
Corps Totals:	41 / 11	14,475	--- / ---	59	3,069*

III Corps net strength of 17,544 present and under arms, of which:

> 13,410, or 76.5% of the corps were infantry,
> 1,065 or 6% of the corps were cavalry, and
> 3,069, or 17.5% of the corps were artillerists and other support troops.

> III Corps artillery ratio on October 1 was 1 gun every 297 combatants.
> * All artillerists and support personnel included in the total for the
> Corps Artillery Reserve.

After deducting about 844 combat casualties and combatants estimated to have fallen out of ranks through strategic consumption between October 1 and October 15, the III Corps had approximately 16,700 officers and other ranks present and under arms at Leipzig supported by 59 pieces of ordnance.

IV Corps Bertrand	# of bns/sqd	Strength of inf. & cav.	Average per battalion/sqdrn	Guns	Artillerists, engineers, train, etc
		Strength returns as of 15 October 1813			
12th Division	16 / --	5,705	357 / --	16	*
15th Division	7 / --	1,859	266 / --	6	*
38th Division	3 / 8	1,168	320 / 25	---	---
Corps Cavalry	-- / 7	221	--- / 32	6	*
Corps Artillery Reserve				8	871*
Corps Totals:	26 / 15	8,953	--- / ---	36	871

IV Corps net strength of 9,824 present and under arms, of which:

> 8,524, or 87% of the corps were infantry,
> 429, or 4% of the corps were cavalry, and
> 871, or 9% of the corps were artillerists and other support troops.

> IV Corps artillery ratio on October 15 was 1 gun every 273 combatants.
> * All artillerists and support troops included with the returns for the
> Corps Artillery Reserve.

V Corps Lauriston	# of bns/sqd	Strength of inf. & cav.	Average per battalion/sqdrn	Guns	Artillerists, engineers, train, etc
		Strength returns as of 1 October 1813			
10th Division	11 / --	3,635	330 / --	10	*
16th Division	9 / --	3,747	416 / --	10	*
19th Division	12 / --	3,696	308 / --	10	*
Corps Cavalry	-- / 8[†]	935[†]	--- / 117	---	---
Corps Artillery Reserve				23	1,918*
Corps Totals:	32 / 8	12,013	--- / --	53	1,918

V Corps net strength of 13,931 present and under arms, of which:

        11,078 or 79% of the corps were infantry,

         935, or 7% of the corps were cavalry, and

        1,918, or 14% of the corps were artillerists and other support troops.

        V Corps artillery ratio on October 1 was 1 gun every 263 combatants.

        * All artillerists and support troops included with the returns for the
          Corps Artillery Reserve.

        [†] These horsemen were Dermoncourt's light cavalry brigade from
          the Chastel's 3rd Light Cavalry Division of I Reserve Cavalry Corps.

After deducting about 631 combatants estimated to have fallen out of ranks through strategic consumption between October 1 and October 15, the V Corps had approximately 13,300 officers and other ranks present and under arms at Leipzig supported by 53 pieces of ordnance.

VI Corps Marmont	# of bns/sqd	Strength of inf. & cav.	Average per battalion/sqdrn	Guns	Artillerists, engineers, train, etc
		Strength returns as of 1 October 1813			
20th Division	14 / --	5,079	363 / --	16	*
21st Division	14 / -	5,543	396 / --	16	*
22nd Division	14 / --	4,720	337 / --	16	*
Corps Cavalry	-- / 8	935	---- / 117	6	*
Corps Artillery Reserve				28	3,027*
Corps Totals:	42 / 8	16,277	---- / ---	82	3,027

VI Corps net strength of 19,304 present and under arms, of which:

        15,342, or 79.5% of the corps were infantry,

         935, or 5% of the corps were cavalry, and

        3,027, or 15.5% of the corps were artillerists and other support troops.

        VI Corps artillery ratio on October 1 was 1 gun every 235 combatants.

        * All artillerists and support troops included with the returns for the
          Corps Artillery Reserve.

After deducting about 904 combatants estimated to have fallen out of ranks through strategic consumption between October 1 and October 15, the VI Corps had approximately 18,400 officers and other ranks present and under arms at Leipzig supported by 82 pieces of ordnance.

VII Corps Reynier	# of bns/sqd	Strength of inf. & cav.	Average per battalion/sqdrn	Guns	Artillerists, engineers, train, etc
		Strength returns as of 1 October 1813			
13th Division	9 / --	see 32nd	--- / --	8	*
25th Division	9 / --	3,679	409 / --	12	*
32nd Division	6 / --	8,290**	553† / --	6	*
Corps Cavalry	-- / 13	868	---- / 67	6	*
Corps Artillery Reserve				20	960*
Corps Totals:	24 / 13	12,837	--- / ---	52	960

VII Corps net strength of 13,797 present and under arms, of which:

      11,969, or 87% of the corps were infantry,

        868, or 6% of the corps were cavalry, and

        960, or 7% of the corps were artillerists and other support troops.

      VII Corps artillery ratio on October 1 was 1 gun every 265 combatants.

      * All artillerists and support troops included with the returns for the Corps Artillery Reserve.

      ** This total is for both the 13th and 32nd Divisions.

      † This average is for both the 13th and 32nd Divisions.

After deducting about 997 combat casualties and combatants estimated to have fallen out of ranks through strategic consumption between October 1 and October 15, the VII Corps had approximately 12,800 officers and other ranks present and under arms at Leipzig supported by 52 pieces of ordnance.

VIII Corps Poniatowski	# of bns/sqd	Strength of inf. & cav.	Average per battalion/sqdrn	Guns	Artillerists, engineers, train, etc
		Estimated strength returns as of 14 October 1813			
26th Division	10 / --		--- / --	18	---
27th Div(-)	4 / --		--- / --	9	---
Corps Cavalry	-- / 6		--- / --	---	---
Corps Artillery Reserve				9	---
Corps Totals:	14 / 6	6,000	--- / --	36	1,000

VIII Corps net strength of 7,000 present and under arms, of which:

      5,400, or 77% of the corps were infantry,

        600, or 9% of the corps were cavalry, and

      1,000, or 14% of the corps were artillerists and other support troops.

      VIII Corps artillery ratio on October 14 was 1 gun every 194 combatants.

IX Corps Augereau	# of bns/sqd	Strength of inf. & cav.	Average per battalion/sqdrn	Guns	Artillerists, engineers, train, etc
		Strength returns as of 15 October 1813			
51st Division	7 / --	4,350	621 / --	6	*
52nd Division	6 / --	4,297	716 / --	6	*
Corps Artillery Reserve				--	539*
Corps Totals:	13 / --	8,647	--- / --	12	539

IX Corps net strength of 9,186 present and under arms, of which:

       8,647, or 94% of the corps were infantry, and

        539, or 6% of the corps were artillerists and other support troops.

       IX Corps artillery ratio on October 15 was 1 gun every 767 combatants.

       * All artillerists and support troops included with the returns for the

       Corps Artillery Reserve.

XI Corps Macdonald	# of bns/sqd	Strength of inf. & cav.	Average per battalion/sqdrn	Guns	Artillerists, engineers, train, etc
		Strength returns as of 1 October 1813			
HQ and administration		370			
31st Division	12 / --	5,573	464 / --	20	*
35th Division	13 / --	3,941	303 / --	22	*
36th Division	11 / --	4,776	434 / --	20	*
39th Division	10 / --	5,112	511 / --	12	*
Corps Cavalry	-- / 7	496	--- / 71	--	---
Corps Artillery Reserve				24	2,903*
Corps Totals:	46 / 7	20,268	--- / ---	98	2,903

XI Corps net strength of 23,171 present and under arms, of which:

      19,772, or 85% of the corps were infantry,

        496, or 2% of the corps were cavalry, and

      2,903, or 13% of the corps were artillerists and other support troops.

      XI Corps artillery ratio on October 1 was 1 gun every 236 combatants.

      * All artillerists and support troops included with the returns for the

      Corps Artillery Reserve.

After deducting about 1,171 combatants estimated to have fallen out of ranks through strategic consumption between October 1 and October 15, the XI Corps had approximately 22,000 officers and other ranks present and under arms at Leipzig supported by 98 pieces of ordnance.

I Reserve Cav. Corps	# of sqdrns	Strength of cavalry	Average per squadron	Guns	Artillerists & train personnel
Latour-Maubourg		Strength returns as of 1 September 1813			
1st Lt Cav Div	22	3,500	159	--	---
3rd Lt Cav Div	13†	2,167†	170	--	---
1st Hv Cav Div	22	2,757	125	--	---
3rd Hv Cav Div	21	2,252	107	--	---
Corps Artillery Reserve				36	1,128
Corps Totals:	78	10,676	---	--	1,128

I Reserve Cavalry Corps net strength was 11,804 officers and other ranks, of which:

> 10,676, or 90% of the corps were cavalry, and
> 1,128, or 10% of the corps were artillerists and support personnel.

I Reserve Cav Corps artillery ratio on September 1 was 1 gun for every 328 combatants.
> † One brigade of the 3rd Light Cavalry Division was with Lauriston's
> V Corps.

After deducting about 2,676 combat casualties and combatants estimated to have fallen out of ranks through strategic consumption between September 1 and October 14, the I Reserve Cavalry Corps had approximately 8,000 officers and other ranks present and under arms at Leipzig supported by 36 pieces of ordnance.

II Reserve Cav. Corps	# of sqdrns	Strength of cavalry	Average per squadron	Guns	Artillerists & train personnel
Sébastiani		Strength returns as of 1 October 1813			
HQ and administration		73			
2nd Lt Cav Div	19	2,121	112	--	---
4th Lt Cav Div	20	2,377	119	--	---
2nd Hv Cav Div	13	1,819	140	--	---
Corps Artillery Reserve				12	402
Corps Totals:	52	6,390	---	12	402

II Reserve Cavalry Corps net strength was 6,792 officers and other ranks, of which:

> 6,390, or 94% of the corps were cavalry, and
> 402, or 6% of the corps were artillerists and support personnel.

II Reserve Cavalry Corps artillery ratio on October 1 was 1 gun every 566 combatants.

After deducting about 792 combat casualties as well as combatants estimated to have fallen out of ranks through strategic consumption between October 1 and October 14, the II Reserve Cavalry Corps had approximately 6,000 officers and other ranks present and under arms at Leipzig supported by 12 pieces of ordnance.

III Reserve Cav. Corps	# of sqdrns	Strength of cavalry	Average per squadron	Guns	Artillerists & train personnel
Arrighi de Casanova		Strength returns as of 15 September 1813			
5th Lt Cav Div	12	1,425	119	--	---
6th Lt Cav Div	8	1,202	150	--	---
4th Hv Cav Div	13	1,510	116	--	---
Corps Artillery Reserve				9	494
Corps Totals:	33	4,137	---	9	494

III Reserve Cavalry Corps net strength was 4,631 officers and other ranks, of which:

4,137, or 89% of the corps were cavalry, and

494, or 11% of the corps were artillerists and support personnel.

III Reserve Cavalry Corps artillery ratio on September 15 was 1 gun every 515 combatants.

After deducting about 631 combat casualties as well as combatants estimated to have fallen out of ranks through strategic consumption between October 1 and October 14, the III Reserve Cavalry Corps had approximately 4,000 officers and other ranks present and under arms at Leipzig supported by 9 pieces of ordnance.

IV Reserve Cav. Corps	# of sqdrns	Strength of cavalry	Average per squadron	Guns	Artillerists & train personnel
Sokolnicki*		Estimated strengths as of 14 October 1813			
7th Lt Cav Div	8		125	6	---
8th Lt Cav Div(-)	8		125	6	---
Corps Totals:	16	2,000	---	12	250

IV Reserve Cavalry Corps net strength was 2,250 officers and other ranks, of which:

2,000, or 89% of the corps were cavalry, and

250 or 11% of the corps were artillerists and support personnel.

IV Reserve Cavalry Corps artillery ratio on October 14 was 1 gun every 188 combatants.

*The IV Reserve Cavalry Corps under Sokolnicki, and the V Reserve Cavalry Corps under Pajol, were both under the orders of Kellermann (the younger) at the Battle of Leipzig. This was a temporary command arrangement designed to make use of Kellermann's talents.

V Reserve Cav. Corps[†]	# of sqdrns	Strength of cavalry	Average per squadron	Guns	Artillerists & train personnel
Pajol*		Estimated strength returns as of 14 October 1813			
9th Lt Cav Div	14		119	--	---
5th Hv Cav Div	15		120	--	---
6th Hv Cav Div	13		119	--	---
Corps Artillery Reserve				3	160
Corps Totals:	42	5,000	---	3	160

V Reserve Cavalry Corps net strength was 5,160 officers and other ranks, of which:

      5,000, or 97% of the corps were cavalry, and

       160, or 3% of the corps were artillerists and support personnel.

V Reserve Cavalry Corps artillery ratio on October 14 was 1 gun every 1,720 combatants.

    [†] The V Reserve Cavalry Corps under L'hértier and the V *bis* Reserve Cavalry Corps under Milhaud were combined on October 12 to form this corps. When the amalgamation took place, L'hértier and Milhaud assumed the heavy cavalry divisional commands; General Pajol was named as the new corps commander.

    *The IV Reserve Cavalry Corps under Sokolnicki, and the V Reserve Cavalry Corps under Pajol, were both under the orders of Kellermann (the younger) at the Battle of Leipzig. This was a temporary command arrangement designed to make use of Kellermann's talents.

Independent Divisions	# of bns/sqd	Strength of inf. & cav.	Average per battalion/sqdrn	Guns	Artillerists, engineers, train, etc
		Strength returns as of 15 October 1813			
27th Div(-)*	4 / 8	2,850	--- / --	12	250
Lefol	4 / --	2,229	557 / --	---	---
Margaron	7 / --	4,320	617 / --	15	483
Totals:	15 / 8	9,399	---- / ---	27	733

Independent divisions net strength of 10,132 present and under arms, of which:

      8,800, or 87% of the corps were infantry,

       599, or 6% of the corps were cavalry, and

       733, or 7% of the corps were artillerists and other support troops.

Independent divisions artillery ratio on October 15 was 1 gun every 375 combatants.

    * Formerly attached to I Corps in mid-August, this division was under the command of General Dombrowski.

Summary of the *Grande Armée* Napoleon	Battle of Leipzig Total of all combatants present and under arms	Guns
Imperial Guard	46,932	218
II Corps	16,600	54
III Corps	16,700	59
IV Corps	9,824	36
V Corps	13,300	53
VI Corps	18,400	82
VII Corps	12,800	52
VIII Corps	7,000	36
IX Corps	9,186	12
XI Corps	22,000	98
I Reserve Cavalry Corps	8,000	36
II Reserve Cavalry Corps	6,000	12
III Reserve Cavalry Corps	4,000	9
IV Reserve Cavalry Corps	2,250	12
V Reserve Cavalry Corps	5,160	3
Total of the active corps in the *Grande Armée* at Leipzig	198,152	772
Independent Divisions	10,132	27
Grand total of all troops of the *Grande Armée* at Leipzig	208,284	799

Due to casualties and strategic consumption suffered between October 14 and when all the troops eventually reached the battlefield, Napoleon never had all the above manpower available on the same day.

Grande Armée's artillery ratio on October 14 was 1 gun for every 260 combatants.

****

Arrayed against Napoleon's forces were not just the Army of Bohemia approaching Leipzig from the south and west, but all four Allied armies coming from the south, west, and north. Together, they were an impressive collection of men and guns. To the south and west of Leipzig was Schwarzenberg's Army of Bohemia, boasting some 195,950 combatants and 786 guns.[21] Also south of the city was Benningsen's Polish Reserve Army, less Ostermann's corps, numbering 33,875 officers and men supported by 134 pieces of ordnance.[22]

North of Leipzig, Blücher pushed his Army of Silesia to the battlefield, arriving with 63,861 effectives and 310 guns.[23] Eventually added to the Allied forces north of the city were the late-arriving corps from the Army of the North who Bernadotte could not restrain from marching to the sound of the guns. The troop formations of the Army of the North contributed 67,416 combatants and 226 pieces of ordnance to the Allied cause.[24]

Thus, the Allies converged on Leipzig from three sides, their armies totalling some 361,102 soldiers and 1,456 guns—an artillery ratio of 1 gun for every 248 combatants. Naturally, not all of these men or guns were on the field of battle at the same time. Nevertheless, these numbers produced frightening odds which proved too much for Napoleon and the *Grande Armée* of 1813.

The massive confrontation at Leipzig was the largest battle of the 19th Century. Known as the "Battle of Nations", it consisted of a series of separate, desperate battles waged throughout October 16th, resumed again on the 18th, and finally concluding on the 19th. For the battles on the 16th, Napoleon assumed personal command of the southern battle front, known as the combat at Wachau. The Allies attacked on this front shortly after dawn. By 11 A.M., all their columns—which had been committed to battle in a disjointed, uncoordinated manner—had been ground to a halt by the Emperor's stubborn troops.

Ordering a counteroffensive, Napoleon planned on rupturing and rolling up Schwarzenberg's line. To blast a hole through which fresh formations could attack, the Emperor ordered General Drouot forward at the head of the Artillery Reserve of the Guard. Drouot's grand battery of 84 guns moved out and unlimbered in front of Eugen of Württemberg's II Russian Corps. The French guns belched a murderous fire which blew apart Eugen's formations. After enduring this bombardment, the survivors of Eugen's command were then mercilessly ridden down and sabred by two corps of cavalry under Marshal Murat, consisting of Latour-Maubourg's I Reserve Cavalry Corps and the Imperial Guard cavalry. So successful and devastating was the French cavalry's attack, that General Bordesoulle's squadrons, spearheaded by the Saxon Garde du Corps and Zastrow Cuirassiers, completely pierced the Allied center by first overturning Pahlen's Russian light cavalry and then sabering their way through the Russian grenadiers and foot guards of Grand Duke Constantine's corps, capturing 26 guns in the process.[25] This attack almost reached Allied army headquarters before the exhausted horsemen were counterattacked by the Russian heavy cavalry. However, the progress of the Emperor's infantry supports had been outstripped by the cavalry's quick advance. Thus, unsupported and with their horses blown, the French and Saxon heavy cavalrymen had no choice but to retire.

As the French horsemen withdrew, the Allied cavalry pursuit carried them into Drouot's grand battery. Upon seeing the withdrawal of Latour-Maubourg's squadrons, Drouot ordered his flanking artillery company commanders to drag their pieces backwards until the grand battery formed a giant, imperfectly shaped circle. From this defensive posture, Drouot's guns mowed down the Allied horsemen as they tried to assault the pieces.[26] With no hope for infantry support of their own, the Allied horsemen broke off and retired back to what could be determined was their own lines.

The principal reason why the French infantry had failed to advance with Latour-Maubourg's cavalry was that a separate Austrian cavalry attack against Marshal Oudinot's I Young Guard Corps had arrested the advance of Oudinot's command, forcing them into square. With Oudinot halted, Napoleon ordered a counterstroke with the service squadrons of the Old Guard cavalry. These 800 superb horsemen, consisting of four total squadrons— one each from the Old Guard Grenadiers à Cheval, the Old Guard Chasseurs à Cheval, the 1st Old Guard (Polish) Light Lancers, and Guard Dragoons—were led forward by General Letort with the mission to break the enemy cavalry and allow Oudinot to resume his advance. In the charge which followed, the Guard cavalry service squadrons scored a brilliant victory against the Austrian horse, including the capture of 190 officers and men of the famous Vincent Chevaulegers.[27]

In other notable action on the Wachau front on the 16th was the combat at Dölitz. It was here that Meerveldt's Austrian II Corps—consisting of 14,129 infantry and cavalry with 50 guns[28]—was trying to cross the Pleisse River in an attempt to drive in Napoleon's right flank. However, Poniatowski's Poles, along with the aid of Lefol's independent division, had contained this advance to a small bridgehead over the Pleisse at Dölitz. About mid-afternoon, Napoleon dispatched General Curial's 2nd Old Guard Division to assist Poniatowski in driving Meerveldt's Austrians back across the river. In the short action which followed, the Guard infantry stormed Dölitz, drove the outclassed enemy into the river, and captured Meerveldt himself along with 2,000 Austrian infantry.[29]

Fighting on the 16th also took place north of Leipzig, known as the combat of Möckern. This front pitted Blücher's entire army against Marmont's VI Corps—the *Grande Armée's* best line formation—reinforced with Dombrowski's 27th Division, and then later, Delmas' 9th Division. What's notable about the struggle on this front is how the French and Polish forces, outnumbered almost 3 to 1, were able to first check and then counterattack Blücher's forces before finally being overwhelmed and driven back.

The scene of the most savage fighting on this front was in and around the village of Möckern itself. The defense of this area was entrusted to General Lagrange's 21st Division, which on October 16 numbered approximately 5,300 infantry supported by 16 guns. The village provided the hinge on which the Duke of Ragusa's defensive line rested, and as such, was the focal point of the Prussian attack. For the task of capturing Möckern, Blücher assigned his best corps—the I Prussian Corps under General Yorck numbering 21,149 infantry and cavalry, along with 104 pieces of ordnance.[30]

The Polish infantry of VIII Corps counterattacking at Leipzig.
Lithograph by Raffet.

The ensuing combat was described in detail by Marmont. "The enemy army marched at me rapidly; his forces appeared to get larger and larger as they came forward, as if they had sprung from the ground.

"The enemy assault was initially directed against the village of Möckern; the village was attacked with vigor, and my fire could not dissipate the fighting of the enemy; the village was defended by the troops of my 2nd Division [the 21st Division] under the orders of General Lagrange. The 2nd Regiment de Marine, was charged with the defense of this post, and fought with vigor and tenacity; they hung on for a long time, lost it, then retook it again; but the enemy redoubled his efforts by sending more troops to capture this point. Then, I ordered a change of facing by brigade, and the troops immediately executed an oblique move by forming 6 lines in echelon, that by so doing, we were placed in a position to keep the village under our control, the village being the focal point of the entire battle. The 37th Light Infantry Regiment and the 4th Regiment de Marine were successively sent into the village; these men retook the entire village and defended it with all the courage you would expect from good troops.

"The fighting continued with the same stubborness and tenacity for more than three hours. The enemy suffered enormously heavy casualties caused by the advantageous positioning of our artillery; but new enemy forces were coming all the time and renewed their attack time and again: a simultaneous explosion of four caissons belonging to 12-pdr. guns, caused one of our reserve batteries to cease fire for an instant, happening at the same time that the enemy was launching an attack, which proved decisive. I decided to send some of the troops of the 1st Division [20th Division], who formed in echelon the center, and directed these to assist those already engaged against the enemy, who was moving against the center of our line.

"The battle took on a new character, and our masses of infantry found themselves, for one moment, less than 30 paces from the enemy. No action was more lively; in a few moments, I was wounded and my uniform riddled; the situation began to deteriorate rapidly.

"It was in this situation, that the enemy made a furious cavalry charge in which several battalions belonging to the 1st and to the 3rd Regiments de Marine were literally crushed.

"Nevertheless, we continued fighting without retreating until nightfall; then we moved to the rear."[31]

Elsewhere on the 16th, there was fighting west of the city, known as the combat of Lindenau. The Austrian III Corps under Gyulai—numbering 20,526 infantry and cavalry, supported by 50 pieces of ordnance[32]—attacked the French outposts guarding Napoleon's sole line of retreat. General Margaron's independent division, consisting of 4,320 infantry and 15 guns,[33] was guarding this area and was barely managing to hang on when Marshal Ney—commander of the northern and western fronts of the battlefield— ordered Bertrand and the IV Corps to Lindenau. Despite being outnumbered two to one, Bertrand wasted little time in putting in his assault. The 9,800 men and 36 guns of the IV Corps counterattacked and easily threw back Gyulai's troops.[34]

Thus, the 16th ended with the French gaining a limited victories in the south at Wachau and in the west at Lindenau, while suffering a setback at Möckern. In these separate combats, the *Grande Armée* utterly destroyed the Russian II Corps, hammered the Austrian II Corps, capturing its commander officer—all while severely shaking Kleist's II Prussian Corps, inflicting heavy casualties on Klenau's IV Austrian Corps and Yorck's I Prussian Corps.

There was a lull in the battle on the 17th as both sides called in their outlying troops. During the day, Napoleon fully realized that all the Allied armies were present or quickly approaching the battlefield. With the presence of so many of the enemy, Napoleon knew that he could no longer entertain the possibility of offensive warfare. Therefore, shortly after midnight on October 18, the Emperor ordered the army withdrawn back into a more defensible perimeter nearer Leipzig, leaving a heavy outpost line where his corps stood on the 16th.

The battle of the 18th was one of attrition. The Allies had no plan other than headlong frontally assaults all along the north, east, and south sides of the concentric French positions around Leipzig.[35] However, Napoleon organized his defense so well that most of the Allied attacks were shattered.

In the south, the number of effective corps which Schwarzenberg could rely upon had been reduced considerably after the combat at Wachau and Dölitz on the 16th. Thus, for the attack on the 18th, the only unshaken troops that Schwarzenberg had available were the Austrian reserves under Prince Hessen-Homburg, consisting in part of the Austrian grenadier corps and heavy cavalry, and Barclay's Russians. These included the Russian Imperial Guard and the Prussian Guards. These formations—the élite of all the Allied armies—advanced and attacked with all their might.

Meeting the fury of these assaults, for the most part, were different line formations of the *Grande Armée*. The assaults by the Austrian reserve corps—all together numbering 16,357 infantry, 3,417 cavalry and 48 guns[36]—were put in around the village of Lössnig, where they were stopped cold and decisively repulsed by Poniatowski's diminutive, heroic corps of Poles. Another column of the reserve corps, attacking from the west across the Pleisse River at Connewitz, ran heads-down into the muzzles of Drouot's Artillery Reserve of the Guard backed up by Oudinot's I Young Guard Corps. The Emperor's "Beautiful Daughters" blew apart the attacking columns and Oudinot's Voltigeurs dispersed the weakened formations and sent them scurrying back across the river.[37]

The attacks by the Austrian reserves were virtually spent when Barclay finally got his 35,000 men and 250 guns moving up the Pommsen Road to attack the village of Probstheyda—the key position to Napoleon's southern line. This area was held by Victor's II Corps, who, with Drouot's Guard guns that had relocated to this area following the repulse of the Austrians at Connewitz, broke furious assault after Russian assault. Seeing that the men of Victor's command were exhausted, the Emperor ordered the II Corps be pulled out of the line and replaced with Lauriston's V Corps. Back came the Russians for more, and these assaults were again turned back. Gathering up all his available formations, Barclay mounted another, massive attack of six infantry divisions against Probstheyda. This powerful force consisted of the two line divisions of Wittgenstein's Russian I Corps, and the infantry of Grand Duke Constantine's Reserve Corps—consisting of two divisions of grenadiers and the two divisions of Russian Imperial Guards with the Prussian Guards attached. These columns rolled forward, threatening to engulf Lauriston's command.

Witnessing this danger, Napoleon rode to the head of Curial's 2nd Old Guard Division and personally led it forward in a counterattack.[38] Falling in along side the 2nd Old Guard Division was Friant's 1st Old Guard Division; Drouot's gunners worked at top speed to lend as much fire support as possible. With the Emperor at their head, the senior divisions of the Imperial Guard counterattacked and "covered [themselves] with glory",[39] throwing back the Allies in disorder. Following this heavy handed repulse, no more Allied assaults were mounted against Probstheyda.

Meanwhile, on the east side of the French defensive perimeter, Benningsen—reinforced with more than a corps of Austrians from Schwarzenberg—attacked westward, but the assault was skillfully stalled by Macdonald and Sebastiani's outnumbered troops. These

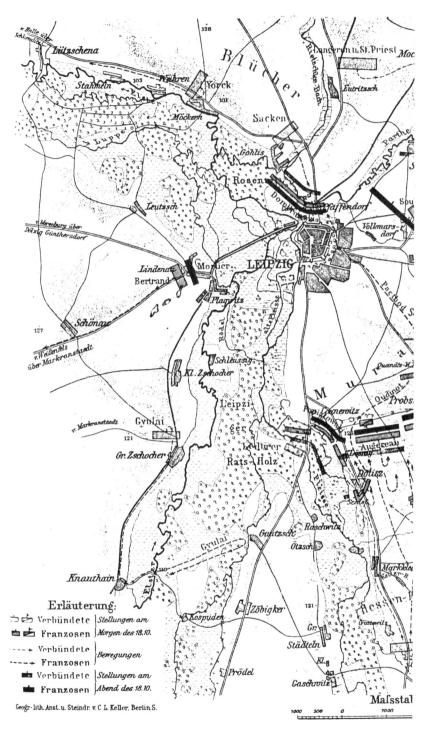

Erläuterung:

Verbündete	Stellungen am
Franzosen	Morgen des 18.10.
Verbündete	
Franzosen	Bewegungen
Verbündete	Stellungen am
Franzosen	Abend des 18.10.

Geogr-lith.Anst.u. Steindr. v. C L Keller, Berlin S.

Maßstab

1000   500   0   1000

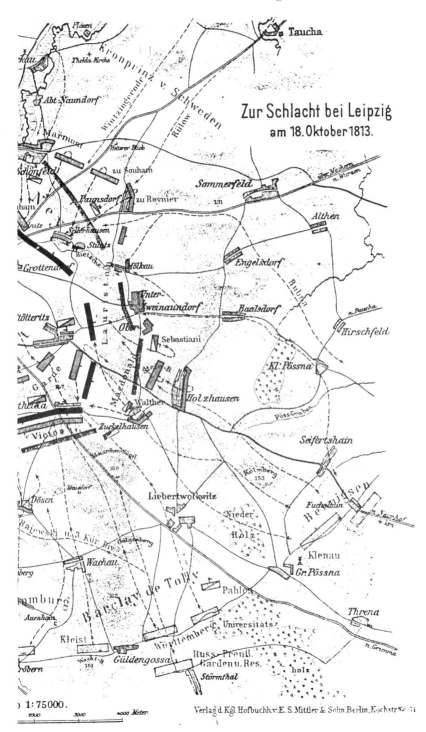

Zur Schlacht bei Leipzig
am 18. Oktober 1813.

1 : 75000.

Verlag d. Kgl. Hofbuchh. v. E. S. Mittler & Sohn. Berlin. Kochstr.

Napoleon leading the counterattack of the Imperial Guard at Probstheyda during the Battle of Leipzig, 18 October 1813.

formations calmly fell back until they linked up with Reynier's VII Corps,[40] which comprised the eastern end of the northern defensive perimeter.

Action on the northern front of Leipzig on October 18 started late in the day, but was a savage, bloody struggle nevertheless. In between the times that Blücher and Bernadotte launched their series of sledge-hammer assaults—virtually all of which were defeated or stalled—most of the Saxon 25th Infantry Division, along with the light cavalry of VII Corps—a total force of perhaps 4,000 men—defected to the Allies.[41] This temporarily left a hole in the line which was plugged before the Allies initiated their sundown attacks.

The Allied attacks in the north were focused on the village of Schönefeld, which was defended by Marmont's VI Corps, with Delmas' 9th Division from III Corps attached. Marmont described the action at Schönefeld in the following words: "The enemy deployed 150 artillery pieces at the same time that they were attacking the village of Schönefeld with the strongest vigor: seven times the enemy was able to take over the largest portion of the village, and seven times they were driven off. Once again [as on the 16th], it was the 2nd Division [21st Division] commanded by General Lagrange, and a detachment of the III Corps [Delmas' 9th Division] that had the glory of defending the village, and no troops acted in such a heroic way, being so outnumbered as they were.

"I do not know any praise too great for these deserving troops, so brave and devoted, even though they had a lot of casualties two days before, they still fought with great courage."[42]

When Napoleon realized that the Allies were trying to use their overwhelming numbers to drive in his defensive perimeter on the east side of the Pleisse-Elster River line,

General Letort at the head of the Service Squadrons of the Guard during their famous charge at Leipzig, 16 October 1813.

he knew that he would have to secure his route of retreat to the west. To accomplish this, he ordered General Bertrand to sally forth from Lindenau and attack Gyulai's Austrians who were blocking the *Grande Armée's* line of communication with France. To take Bertrand's place at Lindenau and the guard the army's rear, Napoleon dispatched Marshal Mortier's II Young Guard Corps. Once Mortier was up, Bertrand suddenly attacked the numerically superior Austrians. The French and Italians of IV Corps went through Gyulai's troops like a hot knife through butter, scattering the Austrian III Corps, which ran pell-mell in opposite directions. Some of Gyulai's men retreated southward and crossed the Elster River, while others fled north across the Luppe River.

Thus, the battle of the 18th came to a close with the Allies making only a few, unimportant gains while losing far more men than the French army. However, Napoleon had no desire to continue a battle of attrition on such a confined front. Besides, the plentiful artillery ammunition of the *Grande Armée* was virtually exhausted. The Emperor had no alternative but to retreat from Leipzig. As the Emperor quit the city and rode west, he was heard whistling the tune "Malbrouck s'en va-t-en en guerre"[43] ("Marlborough Goes Off to War"), no doubt recalling the verse in which the Duke of Marlborough got his English army surrounded on three sides by the French at the Battle of Malplaquet, and how the song ironically applied to his own situation. In spite of all that had happened to him and the *Grande Armée*, Napoleon maintained his sang-froid exterior.

However, despite Napoleon's coolness under duress, the withdrawal from Leipzig became confused, and the only bridge over which the army could safely pass onto the west bank of the Elster River was blown up long before it was in any danger of falling into enemy hands.[44] This demolition—ordered by Napoleon to be fired only *after* the last Frenchman had quit Leipzig and crossed over the river—was done while the bridge was still crowded with retreating soldiers and there were still several corps of the army on the east bank of the Elster in Leipzig!

This shocking, criminally incompetent act turned Napoleon's and the *Grande Armée's* brilliant defensive performance into cataclysmic defeat. Left stranded in Leipzig were Lauriston's V Corps, a portion of Reynier's VII Corps, Poniatowski's VIII Corps, and part of Macdonald's XI Corps. The soldiers which were trapped in the city had but three choices: fight to the death, surrender, or try to swim to safety. Thousands jumped in the Elster and made it to the west bank, including Marshal Macdonald. Many others, however, were not as fortunate. Poniatowski, Dumoustier, and many others drowned in their attempt to swim to safety.[45] Others simply surrendered. However, many of the most fanatic— including most of Poniatowski's Poles—were killed fighting to the last man.[46]

The premature demolition of the Elster bridge cost Napoleon dearly. In addition to 38,000 combat casualties—of which 15,000 wounded were captured while in their hospitals in Leipzig—approximately 15,000 able-bodied men in Leipzig fell into Allied hands, along with 325 guns, 900 caissons and wagons, 28 eagles and standards, and 36 generals. Among the high brass captured were Lauriston and Reynier. Best estimates for the entire battle place the *Grande Armée's* casualties at approximately 53,000 killed, wounded, and captured, plus another 4,000 Saxon defectors, making for a total of approximately 57,000 total combatants lost at Leipzig.[47] Allied casualties were between 50,000 and 60,000, although some estimates place the Allied losses as high as 80,000.[48]

Retreating to Erfurt while beating off the pursuing Allies, Napoleon's army arrived on the 23rd and found sorely needed supplies[49] with which it could replenish its ammunition and fill the empty stomachs. On this day, the Emperor learned of Bavaria's defection to the Allies and the impending defection of the rest of the Confederation of the Rhine.[50] The army would have to force march its retreat to the Rhine.

The troops moved out on the 24th amidst a constant, cold rain, and with almost no food. Only the hardiest of souls remained in ranks. Tens of thousands deserted to find something to eat; starving animals dropped in their traces. Defeat and hunger totally demoralized the young soldiers. The army's numbers dwindled rapidly.[51] By October 29, the advance guard of the *Grande Armée*, consisting of Sébastiani's cavalry, was outside the village of Hanau, which stands on the angle between the Main River and a smaller tributary known as the Kinzig River, less than 30 miles from the Rhine River and Mayence.

In the path of the retreating French army was an ad-hoc Austro-Bavarian corps numbering approximately 43,500 men under the command of the Bavarian General Wrede.[52] Wrede believed that a French force of less than 20,000 were approaching the town. Confident that his army could defeat the much smaller French force, Wrede deployed his troops with their backs to the Main and with the Kinzig cutting through the center of his position.

However, while he may have had significant numerical superiority, Wrede seriously compromised the corps with his deployment, as well as underestimated the quality of his opposition. On the 30th, Napoleon appeared in front of Hanau with a force of approximately 17,000 men, with another 13,000 following close behind.[53] Of those present, the Emperor had the 1st and 2nd Old Guard Divisions, the Imperial Guard Cavalry Corps, the Artillery Reserve of the Guard, Sébastiani's II Reserve Cavalry Corps, and the II Corps under Victor and the survivors of XI Corps with Macdonald at their head. After a reconnaissance of Wrede's poorly chosen positions, Napoleon commented about his opponent: "I could make him a Count, but I could never make him a general."[54] The Emperor ordered his troops into the attack, despite a glaring numerical inferiority.

The center of Wrede's line was held by 10,000 Bavarian infantry, anchored by a farm, and supported by many guns. The enemy position presented a formidable obstacle to the fatigued troops under Macdonald. To help break the enemy line in this sector, the Emperor called upon General Cambronne to lead forward his regiment—the 2nd Old Guard Chasseurs à pied. Ordering his troops to advance with plugged muskets, Cambronne's bearskins charged and routed the Bavarians, who ran for the cover of the massed Austrian artillery in front of Hanau.[55]

Meanwhile, Drouot collected 50 guns from the Artillery Reserve of the Guard— including the companies of "Beautiful Daughters"—and formed a grand battery.[56] Backed up by the General Nansouty's Guard horse and Sébastiani's cavalry, Drouot advanced his guns through a wood opposite the Bavarian left flank. Once clear of the woods, Drouot's guns quickly swung into action, their deadly fire dismounting 28 of the enemy's guns, and blowing apart the static squadrons of Bavarian cavalry holding that area of the field.

As Wrede was sending infantry and cavalry reinforcements to the threatened sector, Sébastiani charged and broke the enemy horse, but was in turn driven back to Drouot's grand battery by recently arrived, fresh Bavarian cavalry. However, the Bavarian success was short-lived. The Guard cavalry, spearheaded by the Old Guard Grenadiers à Cheval under General Laferrière-Levêque, ferociously counterattacked. The "Gods", the Polish lancers, and the Guards of Honor cut their way through the outmatched Bavarian lighthorsemen. Meanwhile, the Guard Dragoons charged and broke three battalion squares of enemy infantry as the Old Guard Chasseurs à Cheval broke and captured two entire Bavarian battalions. The impetus of the Guard cavalry's charge disintegrated Wrede's entire command of the left bank of the Kinzig. The remnants of two Bavarian infantry brigades broke and fled, ruthlessly pursued by the Guard cavalry to the river, where the men comprising this hapless mob were cut down, or drowned, while a few managed to swim to safety.[57]   *Overleaf: General Drouot at Hanau, 30 October 1813.*

With Wrede's forces cleared of the left bank of the Kinzig, the *Grande Armée* continued its retreat to the Rhine, leaving Bertrand's IV Corps behind as the rear guard. Bertrand's infantry took Hanau on the 31st, officially ending the battle. The action cost Napoleon's army less than 1,000 combat casualties, but stragglers lost on the 30th and 31st raised the overall French losses for these two days to over 10,000. Wrede suffered battle casualties of some 9,250 killed, wounded, or captured.[58] The following day—November 1, 1813—the *Grande Armée* crossed the Rhine at Mayence. The long, costly campaign for Germany was finally over.

Charge of the Old Guard Grenadiers à Cheval at Hanau, 30 October 1813.
Composition by R. Knötel.

CHAPTER IX
"I Need Men Not Children"—Historical Analysis

As the *Grande Armée* crossed over onto the west bank of the Rhine River—most of the soldiers once again setting foot on their native soil—Napoleon immediately began to ascertain what troops remained and how he could reorganize them for the defense of France. For this, a series of rigorously held parade states were conducted between the 1st and 15th of November. The findings could not have pleased the Emperor.

When the fall campaign for Germany began in mid-August, Napoleon had 473,277 combatants in all the active corps of the *Grande Armée*. After deducting Davout's XIII Corps in front of Hamburg, the Emperor's mobile field army on August 15, 1813, amounted to 437,435 officers and other ranks present and under arms. This number excluded the 2,144 officers and 58,787 other ranks in garrison at Danzig, Stettin, Custrin, Glogau, Madgebourg, Wittemberg, Erfurt, and Wurzburg.

When the November parade states were authenticated, the returns for the army showed only 74,855 men of all ranks still with the colors.[1] Thus, among the active corps of the army, Napoleon lost no less than 362,580 people in only a three month period of time. These losses reflect that Napoleon's *Grande Armée* of 1813 suffered an incredible casualty and strategic consumption ratio of 83% in only 90 days—an average loss of over 4,000 men per day from all causes.

Add to these losses the 55,000 officers and men who were killed, wounded, or captured during the brief spring campaign, along with the casualties and strategic consumption suffered by Davout's XIII Corps and the two Magdebourg divisions during the fall campaign. When these numbers are totalled, the entire 1813 campaign in Germany cost Napoleon the services of more than 425,000 combatants.

Considering the relatively short period of time that active campaigning was in progress, the losses seem even more horrific. For all pratical purposes, the combined 1813 spring and fall campaigns in Germany totalled only 17 weeks of fighting. Including the battle casualties, this translates into an average loss suffered by the *Grande Armée* of 25,000 men per week—a staggering loss of life and incomprehensible level of human suffering by any means of measurement.

These, however, were just the French army's losses. When one takes into consideration the fallen men in the Allied armies, the total loss of manpower in 1813 exceeds 750,000 men. Thus, when both sides combine their casualties and strategic consumption wastage, the 17 weeks of warfare resulted in an average loss of over 44,000 participants per week!

Further, if one adds in the mind-boggling casualties and wastage suffered by the opposing armies during the 1812 Russian campaign, the losses for all sides within a 16 month period from June 1812 to the end of October 1813 soar to well over 1,250,000. Allowing for the fact that not all of the strategic consumption losses were fatalities, what can clearly be seen from these figures is that the flower of European manhood—especially that of France and Russia—had nevertheless been consumed by these campaigns, which were the most hellish of the Napoleonic wars.

COMPARISON OF STRENGTHS FOR NAPOLEON'S *GRANDE ARMÉE* FOR THE PERIOD 15 AUGUST TO 15 NOVEMBER 1813

GRANDE ARMÉE

Corps	Commanding officer(s)	15 August All Ranks	15 November All Ranks	% casualties & strategic consumption suffered during this period
Imperial Guard	Mortier, Nansouty, et al	61,748	20,501	67%
I Corps	Vandamme/Lobau	36,776	† *	100%
II Corps	Victor	31,930	6,622	79%
III Corps	Ney/Souham	40,350	3,163#	92%
IV Corps	Bertrand	22,579	9,454**	58%
V Corps	Lauriston	27,814	4,699	83%
VI Corps	Marmont	26,618	15,721††	41%
VII Corps	Reynier	25,583	†††	100%
VIII Corps	Poniatowski	7,,972	†††	100%
IX Corps	Augereau	19,125	***	100%
XI Corps	Macdonald/Gérard/Macdonald	24,691	3,167	87%
XII Corps	Oudinot	19,106	††††	100%
XIV Corps	Saint Cyr	42,549	†	100%
I Res. Cav. Corps	Latour-Maubourg	18,440	3,097	83%
II Res. Cav. Corps	Sébastiani	10,898	3,052	72%
III Res. Cav. Corps	Arrighi de Casanova	7,663	1,922	75%
IV Res. Cav. Corps	Kellermann/Sokolnicki	4,249	***	100%
V & V *bis* Res. CCs	L'héritier/Milhaud/Pajol	9,344	3,457	63%
Total for all active corps of the *Grande Armée*, minus Davout's XIII Corps at Hamburg		437,435	74,855	83%

† Surrendered at Dresden on November 11.
†† Includes the 8th Division formerly of III Corps.
††† Perished at Leipzig.
†††† Disbanded before Leipzig—survivors to IV and VII Corps, and included in those returns for November 15.
# Does not include the 8th Division, which was transferred to VI Corps on November 7.
* No returns for Dombrowski's 27th Div.(-); presumed disbanded, or perished at Leipzig.
** Does not include troops in route on November 15.
*** Disbanded after Leipzig.

The number of losses sustained by the entire *Grande Armée* of 1813 are, generally speaking, representative of those suffered by the individual regiments in the Emperor's service. Naturally, regiments which completely perished at Leipzig increase the casualty rate for the whole army. Nevertheless, a study of casualties and strategic consumption suffered by individual regiments that survived Leipzig provides the reader with some general parameters as to percentage losses incurred during the fall campaign.

136th Regiment of the Line, III Corps
Losses in 1813

	Officers	Others
Total strength reporting for duty on the Rhine, 27 February 1813	84	2800
Reserves, detachments, and depot of the Regiment	2	580
Total Officers and Other Ranks which served with the Regiment		3,466

Battle and Date	Officers				Others				Grand
	K	W	P	Total	K	W	P	Total	*Total*
Lützen, 2 May	5	5	—	10	143	780	—	923	933
Bautzen, 21 May	2	3	—	5	22	400	—	422	427
Bunzlau, 21 Aug.	1	—	—	1	1	3	—	4	5
Katzbach, 26 Aug.	—	—	—	—	—	29	—	29	29
Retreat from Silesia,									
27 Aug.—7 Sept.	—	—	2	2	8	11	400	419	421
Leipzig, 16–19 Oct.	4	8	1	13	33	300	70	403	416
	12	16	3	31	207	1,523	470	2,200	
Malingerers in hospital									
in Germany	—	—	2	2	—	—	514	514	516
Deserters and others	—	—	7	7	—	—	—	—	7
Total Casualties	12	16	12	40	207	1,523	984	2,714	= 2,754
Present and Under Arms									
on 10 Nov. 1813	—	—	—	46	—	—	—	666	= 712
									3,466

% Casualties suffered by the 136th Regiment of the Line in 1813 was 79%.

K=Killed   W=Wounded   P=Prisoner

Regiments de Marine, VI Corps
Losses in 1813

	Regiments				
	1st	2nd	3rd	4th	Total
Effectives sent to Germany	5,357	5,588	2,753	3,640	17,338
Killed	1,166	635	324	287	2,412
Remained in hospital in Germany	2,271	2,058	1,360	1,602	7,291
Prisoners or remained in the rear	815	64	366	1,074	2,319
Passed into the Artillery of the Guard	198	200 (?)	71	102	571
Left at Erfurt	350	734	—	—	1,084
Effectives on 2 November 1813	557	1,897	632	575	3,661

% Casualties suffered by the Regiments de Marine in 1813 was 79%.

For example, a careful look at the army returns in August and again in November suggests that the average casualty and strategic consumption ratio incurred by the majority of line infantry and cavalry regiments, as well as most Young Guard infantry regiments, was generally in the 70-79% range. The best Young Guard regiments—the 3rd Voltigeurs and 3rd Tirailleurs—had losses "only" in the 50-56% range. Excluding the Guards of Honor and Gendarmes d'élite, the often-used, hard-fighting Imperial Guard cavalry corps experienced a loss rate of 57% between August 15 and November 1. Artillery companies still surviving in November suffered less severely, their loss rate being in the neighborhood of 30-39%. The best artillery companies of the army—the Old Guard Horse Artillery—lost an average of only 8% of its August 15 effectives, despite fighting in three major battles and numerous smaller actions.[2]

Losses among general officers of the *Grande Armée* were equally crippling. Considering only corps commanders, Napoleon lost the services of 8 of these valuable leaders during 1813. Latour-Maubourg was grievously wounded at Leipzig. Lauriston and Reynier were captured at the same battle, where a wounded Poniatowski drowned trying to swim across the Elster to safety. Vandamme was taken prisoner at Külm, and his replacement, the Count of Lobau, was interned along with Saint-Cyr when Dresden capitulated on November 11, 1813. The loss of these men, as well as dozens of other generals who were killed, wounded, of captured in 1813, plus the death of the irreplaceable Bessières, further eviscerated Napoleon's already depleted pool of lieutenants.

Thus, with the surviving officers and men of his command, Napoleon reorganized his forces in preparation to meet the impending Allied invasion of France, which signalled the start of the 1814 campaign. The curtain had fallen on Napoleon's *Grande Armée* of 1813.

****

The failure of Napoleon's *Grande Armée* of 1813 was, ironically enough, summed up by the Emperor himself shortly after Leipzig. As the vanquished great captain rode west from that fateful field of battle, he was heard murmuring: "I need men not children...men are needed to defend France."[3] Napleon's defeat in the 1813 campaign offers the modern student a moral which is as ageless as armed conflict itself: "one does not improvise soldiers; one does not improvise armies."[4]

The hastily-formed *Grande Armée* of 1813, miraculously raised and energetically organized in record time, and then brilliantly led on the battlefield by its commander-in-chief, was nevertheless the Achilles' heel which Napoleon Bonaparte could not overcome. The army's weaknesses were legion; its strengths were few.

Of the *Grande Armée's* strengths, the French artillery immediately comes to the fore as the outstanding combat arm of any Continental army. Quickly rebuilt after the 1812 debâcle thanks to its massive strength, depth of organization, and quality personnel, the French artillery was proficient, expertly commanded, and well cared for. As such, the Emperor's guns proved their superiority on battlefield after battlefield throughout 1813.

The leadership of the 1813 French cavalry arm while on the battlefield is worthy of praise. Time and again, the French cavalry generals overachieved despite inferior numbers and many troopers who were novice horsemen.

Also commendable was the leadership and skill of the majority of infantry generals when they were suitably motivated and properly supervised. Considering what little they had to work with, many generals produced battlefield results which come close to magical. Therefore, when compared to the performance level of their adversaries, and when under the eyes of the Emperor, the French command team performed extremely well.

Generally speaking, when considering the deficiencies in training, the young age of most of the soldiers, and the conditions in which they had to quickly adapt in order to survive, the battlefield enthusiasm and combat performance of most all of the Franco-Allied soldiers was most commendable. Although the Saxon infantry and light cavalry went over to the Allies at Leipzig, the battle hardly turned on their defection. As a rule, the army's young soldiers seemed always capable of accomplishing feats on the battlefield above those which one might expect, especially if the Emperor was watching!

Invariably, the units which consistently displayed superior skill on the battlefield were those comprised of veteran, or mature troops. The line infantry regiments formed from the cohorts were solid and reliable, but they could not match the tenacity, skill, and élan of troops such as the 37th Light Infantry Regiment, or the regiments raised from the naval artillery corps (Regiments de Marine). As one might expect, the regiments of the Middle and Old Guard proved their superiority over the opposition time and again.

Naturally, the greatest strength of the *Grande Armée* was the organizational genius and superior battlefield direction given it by Napoleon himself. His sheer force of personality won the Battle of Lützen, and the planned turning maneuver at Bautzen was classically Napoleonic. His foresight at Dresden resulted in his artillery being able to move about the battlefield—undoubtably one of the biggest reasons for his victory. The Emperor's plan of battle at Leipzig made the best of his position; up to the moment of the premature demolition of the bridge over the Elster River, the *Grande Armée* inflicted far more battle casualties at Leipzig than they suffered. Finally, Napoleon did not hesitate a moment and crushed the Austro-Bavarian forces at Hanau, despite being outnumbered two to one.

Within the realm of actual battlefield performance during 1813, Napoleon was clearly superior to his opponents in every single engagement at which he was present. The catastrophic, early demolition of the Leipzig bridge notwithstanding, the 1813 campaign once again proved that Napoleon was the "Emperor of Battles."

When considering the 1813 *Grande Armée* in relation to its foes, one cannot help but be struck by the fact that the quality of the opposition was less than impressive. The Russian army, beaten down by the campaign of the preceding year, displayed an uninspired battlefield presence. Despite large numbers, the Austrians were extremely lackluster in their combat effectiveness against Napoleon's new troops. Only the Prussians, led by their rejuvenated general staff and motivated by the territorial imperative, showed signs of aggressiveness. However, the vast majority of Prussian soldiers were so ill-trained and poorly equipped, that they were at a disadvantage in most situations where their numbers and those of the French were close to equal.

However, battlefield performance by officers, men, and ordnance was not all there was to Napoleonic warfare. Many other aspects associated with military campaigning dramatically impacted the French war machine, exposing the fatal weaknesses of Napoleon's *Grande Armée* of 1813.

The army seemed to lack everything—except guns and artillerists. When the 1812 *Grande Armée* perished, so did the heart of the French infantry officer corps. Napoleon and his ministers could call hundreds of thousands of young men to the colors, but infantry officers could not as easily be found. Without enough officers—or without qualified officers—to set proper examples for the men, the result was that the overall march discipline of the army was appallingly poor. This, in turn, meant that when the Emperor put his troops in motion with orders for hard, forced marches, strategic consumption began to immediately impact on the strength of the army.

Going hand-in-hand with the lack of infantry officers was also the absence of qualified non-commissioned officers. These men, so necessary to the learning process of young recruits, were sorely lacking. This shortage, coupled with that of the officers, impacted the army's strategic consumption rate.

The lack of veteran troops, as well as the shortage of mature adults, also had an obvious impact on the army's march discipline. Older men usually had more self-control to deal with hardships, as well as more innovative ways of finding or obtaining food.

Lack of sustenance—a problem throughout the spring campaign—increased dramatically the longer the armies remained in Saxony. The countryside had been stripped bare by the opposing armies. The shortage of food was something that the young soldiers and inexperienced officers did not know how to handle. As a result, multitudes quit ranks in search of subsistence; many did not return.

The formation of temporary, or provisional, regiments of line and light infantry was a necessary expedient which resulted in a large collection of troops without corresponding combat value. In reading over hundreds of after-action and inspection reports, it is interesting to note that not a single word of praise for these ad-hoc formations is ever mentioned. Thus, the opinions expressed by the corps and divisional commanders concerning the worthlessness of the temporary , or provisional, regiments cannot be overemphasized too strongly.

The bankrupt Imperial treasury could not pay the army, which was hardly good for morale. Although attempts to meet some back pay were made during the armistice, lack of funds likewise resulted in equipment shortages for recruits. However, somehow enough muskets could always be found before the men entered the field.

The staggering number of animals lost in Russia resulted in a serious shortage of horseflesh throughout 1813. Due to this deficiency, the cavalry arm, the transport arm, and the horse artillery of the *Grande Armée* were unable to sufficiently rebuild. The cavalry shortage cost Napoleon a chance to throw a quick knockout blow to the Allies following the Battle of Lützen, as well as prevented the much-needed gathering of information and scouting for the army, which especially proved fatal to Macdonald at the Katzbach, and to Ney at Dennewitz.

If Marshal Macdonald's, Marshal Ney's, Baron Fain's, and Maret's observations are accurate concerning the lack of zeal by many of the French general officers—and there seems to be ample evidence to support, for the most part, these claims *when the generals were not under the direct supervision of Napoleon*—there can be little wonder as to why the separate army wings not under direct command of the Emperor were defeated. Maret's analysis of the 1813 campaign in Saxony remains as lucid as anyone since then has been able to describe. The theater of war was too big; Napoleon won battles if he was present, but he simply could not be everywhere at once; and where he was not, the collective skill of the generals outside his control was not able to do great, or even ordinary things.

Other French general officers had little trouble in speaking truthfully about their devotion, but calling for peace nevertheless. General Decaen was one of these generals. In his December 15, 1813, letter to Clarke, he wrote: "After having one more time thought, with calm and reflection, about the problems concerning France at this time, and looking at the means available to face these problems, I have to speak out loud, but this is not a sign of weakness.

"My heart is still full of zeal and dedication with which I have constantly served the Emperor; I beg to try to persuade His Majesty that there are true hopes for the salvation in negotiations for peace, especially if these negotiations are done rapidly and if hostilities end.

"If the Emperor could gather all the French population around him, he could hear the shouts from everywhere: 'Sire, give us peace!' We need to prevent our enemies from taking advantage of the weaknesses of His Majesty's armies...."[5]

Thus, we come to the final weakness of Napoleon's *Grande Armée* of 1813, which, ironically, was also its strongest asset—the Emperor himself. It is impossible that Napoleon did not hear, read, or understand the hundreds of messages being received at Imperial headquarters from all points of the Empire, from all ranks of officers, concerning the multitude of problems facing the new army. There had to have come a time, either while the spring campaign was underway, or during the armistice, when the original faults of the army's organization—primarily the creation of the temporary regiments, the critical shortages of food, as well as the serious lack of cavalry, and the numerous, general faults of the young troops—which had been concealed by the victories of Lützen and Bautzen, could no longer have been ignored.

When these many shortcomings were made clear—and there can be no mistake that they were—Napoleon, instead of seizing the stroke of luck which enabled him to win the Battles of Lützen and of Bautzen by calling a permanent halt to the fighting, got carried away by ambition and went on fighting, the accession of Austria to the Allied cause notwithstanding. He called more men to the tricolor, which only compounded the problem to feed and train those already in uniform. Once the armistice ended, the army found itself engrossed in an almost impossible mission to defeat the numerous Allied armies. The battlefield genius of the great captain was no longer enough to overcome the faults of the army's organization and catastrophe followed.

Napoleon's self-determination and incessant attempts to bend events to shape his own will perhaps best describes his own personality, as well as provides the student with the central explanation as to why he went on fighting against seemingly insurmountable odds. In a letter to his brother, Joseph, Napoleon wrote: "Your character and mine are opposed. You like to cajole people and obey their ideas. *Moi*, I like for them to please me and obey mine."[6]

APPENDICES

SITUATION
of the
GRANDE ARMÉE
25 April 1813

His Majesty
The Emperor Napoleon I, commanding in person

The Emperor's Military Household
Général de division Count Duroc, Duke of Frioul, Grand Marshal of the Palace

Aides-de-Camp to His Majesty
Général de division Lebrun, Duke of Plaisance
Général de division Mouton, Count of Lobau
Général de division Count Durosnel
Général de brigade Baron Dejean
Général de division Count Hogendorp
Général de division Count Gueheneuc
Général de brigade Baron Corbineau
Général de division Count Flahaut de la Billarderie
Général de brigade Baron Drouot
Colonel of Engineers Barnard

Ordnance Officers Attending His Majesty
Chef d'escadron Baron Gourgaud, chief ordnance officer
Captain Baron Atthalin
Captain de Caraman
Captain Baron Desaix
Captain d'Hautpoul
Captain Lamezan
Captain Baron Laplace
Captain Baron de Lauriston
Captain Pailhou
Captain Saint-Jacques

Staff of the Military Household
1st Chamberlain—Count de Turenne
Prefect of the Palace—Baron Beausset
Sergeant-major of the Palace—Canouville
Secretary to the Cabinet—Baron Fain
Secretary to the Cabinet—Baron Mounier
Secretary Intrepreter—Lelorgne d'Ideville

The Imperial Staff
Major General of the Army—Marshal Berthier, Prince of Neuchâtel and of Wagram

Chief of the General Staff
Chief of the General Staff—Général de division Count Bailly de Monthion

Situation of the Grand Armée—25 April 1813
Deputy Chiefs of the General Staff
Général de brigade Baron Guilleminot
Colonel Lssan, Inspector General of Baggagemasters of the Army
Chef de bataillon Margerin, Baggagemaster of the Principal General Quarters
Lieutenant Coignet, Baggagemaster of the Lesser General Quarters
Général de brigade Radet, Commander of the Imperial Gendarmes
Colonel Bonne, Chief of the Topograpical Service

Artillery
Général de division Count Sorbier, Commander of the Artillery
Général de division Count Ruty, Chief of Staff
Général de brigade Baron Neigre, Director of the Artillery Parks
Général de brigade Baron Bouche, Commander of the Bridge Train

Engineers
Général de brigade Rogniat, Commander of the Enginners
Colonel Montfort, Chief of Staff

Equipage
Général de brigade Baron Picard, Inspector General of the Equipage Park

General Administration of the Army
Count Daru, Director of the Administration of the Army
Count Dumas, Intendent General of the Army

Notes: This situation does not include the infantry regimental artillery companies that were in service with the French army. For a complete listing of which regiments still fielded regimental artillery, complete with ordnance details, consult Appendix D, "Situation of the *Grande Armée* 15 August 1813."

Also, this situation does not include the company and regimental designations of the artillery and other support troops. These designations are given beginning in Appendix D.

Finally, the number of officers and other ranks are listed if the return provided this breakdown. Otherwise, the strength given includes both officers and other ranks.

ARMY OF THE MAIN
Marshal Soult, Duke of Dalmatia
Marshal Mortier, Duke of Treviso, commanding the infantry
Marshal Bessières, Duke of Istria, commanding the cavalry
Général de division Count Dulauloy, commanding the artillery
Général de brigade Kirgener, commanding the engineers

	Number of Battalions/ Squadrons	Present & Under Arms Off. - Others

IMPERIAL GUARD (-)

1st Guard Infantry Division— Général de division Baron Dumoustier

1st Brigade: Général de brigade Berthezène		
2nd Old Guard Grenadiers à pied, 1st battalion*	(1)	13 - 525*
2nd Old Guard Chasseurs à pied, 1st battalion*	(1)	15 - 436*
Middle Guard Fusilier Grenadiers, 1st battalion	(1)	14 - 514
Middle Guard Fusilier Chasseurs, 1st battalion	(1)	14 - 624
*destined for the Old Guard Division of the Army of the Elbe		
2nd Brigade: Général de brigade Lanusse		
1st Young Guard Voltigeurs, 1st and 2nd battalions	(2)	27 - 1,310
6th Young Guard Voltigeurs, 1st and 2nd battalions	(2)	29 - 1,089
3rd Brigade: Général de brigade Tindal		
1st Young Guard Tirailleurs, 1st and 2nd battalions	(2)	19 - 1,354
6th Young Guard Tirailleurs, 1st and 2nd battalions	(2)	1,033
7th Young Guard Tirailleurs, 1st and 2nd battalions	(2)	1,368
Divisional artillery and train:		
One company of Old Guard foot artillery, consisting of 6 12-pdr. guns and 2 51/2-inch howitzers; two companies of Old Guard horse artillery, each company consisting of 4 6-pdr. guns and 2 51/2-inch howitzers; and four companies of Young Guard foot artillery, each company consisting of 5 6-pdr. guns and 3 51/2-inch howitzers—total of 52 pieces of ordnance.		1,610
Sappers and Miners attached to the 1st Guard Division	3 cos	99
Guard Equipage	4 cos	8 - 524

1st Guard Cavalry Division— Général de division Count Lefebvre-Desnouëttes

Light Lancers of Berg, 1st squadron	(1)	185
1st (Polish) Guard Light Lancers, 1st, 2nd, and 3rd squadrons	(3)	531
2nd (Red) Guard Light Lancers, 1st, 2nd, 3rd, and 4th sqdrns	(4)	706

2nd Guard Cavalry Division— Général de division Count Walther

Old Guard Chasseurs à Cheval, 1st, 2nd, 3rd, and 4th sqdrns.	(4)	745
Old Guard Grenadiers à Cheval, 1st, 2nd, and 3rd squadrons	(3)	545
Guard Dragoons, 1st, 2nd, and 3rd squadrons	(3)	507
Gendarmes d'élite	(1/2)	53

Imperial Guard Artillery Reserve—

Three 12-pdr. companies of Old Guard foot artillery, one 6-pdr. company of Old Guard horse artillery, one-half company of Duchy of Berg horse artillery, pontoniers, ouvriers, and *Marins* of the Guard—in route.

III CORPS
Marshal Ney, Prince of the Moscowa

8th Division— Général de division Count Souham

1st Brigade: Général de brigade Chasseraux

6th Provisional Light Infantry Regiment, consisting of:	(2)	1,662
2nd battalion, 6th Light Infantry Regiment		
3rd battalion, 25th Light Infantry Regiment		
10th Provisional Light Infantry Regiment, consisting of:	(2)	36 - 1,541
3rd battalion, 16th Light Infantry Regiment		
1st battalion, 28th Light Infantry Regiment		
14th Provisional Regiment of the Line, consisting of:	(2)	39 - 1,558
4th battalion, 34th Regiment of the Line		
3rd battalion, 40th Regiment of the Line		
19th Provisional Regiment of the Line, consisting of:	(2)	37 - 1,258
5th battalion, 66th Regiment of the Line		
3rd battalion, 122nd Regiment of the Line		

2nd Brigade: Général de brigade Chemineau

21st Provisional Regiment of the Line, consisting of:	(2)	32 - 1,572
3rd battalion, 59th Regiment of the Line		
4th battalion, 69th Regiment of the Line		
24th Provisional Regiment of the Line, consisting of:	(2)	34 - 1,555
3rd battalion, 88th Regiment of the Line		
3rd battalion, 103rd Regiment of the Line		
22nd Regiment of the Line, 1st, 3rd, 4th, and 6th bns.	(4)	79 - 3,088

Divisional artillery and train:

Two companies of foot artillery, each company consisting of		387
6 6-pdr. guns and 2 5 1/2-inch howitzers—total of 16 pieces of ordnance.		

Engineers:

Spanish Sapper Battalion	1 co.	187
Equipage	1 co.	61

9th Division— Général de division Baron Brenier de Montmorand

1st Brigade: Général de brigade Anthing

2nd Provisional Light Infantry Regiment, consisting of:	(2)	35 - 1,177
3rd battalion, 2nd Light Infantry Regiment		
3rd battalion, 4th Light Infantry Regiment		
29th Light Infantry Regiment, 1st battalion	(1)	19 - 659
136th Regiment of the Line, 1st, 2nd, 3rd, and 4th bns.	(4)	77 - 2,709

2nd Brigade: Général de brigade Grillot

138th Regiment of the Line, 1st, 2nd, 3rd, and 4th bns.	(4)	86 - 2,709
145th Regiment of the Line, 1st, 2nd, 3rd, and 4th bns.	(4)	92 - 1,925

Divisional artillery and train:

Two companies of foot artillery, each company consisting of		5 - 349
6 6-pdr. guns and 2 5 1/2-inch howitzers—total of 16 pieces of ordnance.		

Engineers:

Spanish Sapper Battalion	1 co.	3 - 178
Equipage	1 co.	1 - 28

10th Division— Général de division Baron Girard

1st Brigade: Général de brigade Goris

4th Provisional Light Infantry Regiment, consisting of	(2)	38 - 1,012
4th battalion, 5th Light Infantry Regiment		
4th battalion, 12th Light Infantry Regiment		
139th Regiment of the Line, 1st, 2nd, 3rd, and 4th bns.	(4)	98 - 2,353

2nd Brigade: Général de brigade Van Dedem Van de Gelder

140th Regiment of the Line, 1st, 2nd, 3rd, and 4th bns.	(4)	78 - 2,537
141st Regiment of the Line, 1st, 2nd, 3rd, and 4th bns.	(4)	82 - 1,923

Divisional artillery and train:

Two companies of foot artillery, each company consisting of		7 - 358
6 6-pdr. guns and 2 5 1/2-inch howitzers—total of 16 pieces of ordnance.		
Equipage	1 co.	1 - 28

11th Division— Général de division Baron Ricard

1st Brigade: Général de brigade Tarayre

9th Light Infantry Regiment, 3rd and 4th battalions	(2)	27 - 1,218
17th Provisional Regiment of the Line, consisting of	(2)	33 - 1,376
4th battalion, 43rd Regiment of the Line		
3rd battalion, 75th Regiment of the Line		
18th Provisional Regiment of the Line, consisting of	(2)	29 - 1,139
3rd battalion, 50th Regiment of the Line		
4th battalion, 65th Regiment of the Line		

2nd Brigade: Général de brigade Dumoulin

142nd Regiment of the Line, 1st, 2nd, 3rd, and 4th bns.	(4)	89 - 2,008
144th Regiment of the Line, 1st, 2nd, 3rd, and 4th bns.	(4)	94 - 1,940

Divisional artillery and train:

Two companies of foot artillery, each company consisting of		3 - 367
6 6-pdr. guns and 2 5 1/2-inch howitzers—total of 16 pieces of ordnance.		

Engineers:

Spanish Sapper Battalion	1 co	2 - 181
Equipage	1 co.	?

39th Division— Général de division Count Marchand

1st Brigade: Général de brigade Stockhorn

3rd Baden Regiment of the Line, 1st and 2nd battalions	(2)	29 - 1,658
1st Baden Regiment of the Line, 1st battalion	(1)	14 - 664

2nd Brigade: Général de brigade Prince Emile of Hesse-Darmstadt

Hesse-Darmstadt Leib-Garde Fusilier Regt., 1st & 2nd bns	(2)	19 - 1,315
2nd Hesse-Darmstadt Musketeers, 1st and 2nd battalions	(2)	37 - 1,242
Hesse-Darmstadt Leib-Garde Regiment, 1st and 2nd bns.	(2)	30 - 1,250

3rd Brigade:
    Frankfurt "Zweyer" Regiment, 2nd battalion   (1)   16 - 676
    Divisional artillery and train:
        Baden foot company, consisting of 4 6-pdr. guns   3 - 127
        Hesse-Darmstadt foot company, consisting of 3 6-pdr. guns   1 - 119

III Corps Cavalry Brigade— Général de brigade Laboissière
    10th Hussars, 1st, 2nd, and 3rd squadrons   (3)   32 - 685
    Baden Light Dragoons, 1st, 2nd, 3rd, and 4th squadrons   (4)   26 - 474

III Corps Artillery Reserve—
Artillery reserve companies and train—in route
Engineers   3 cos   7 - 387
Equipage   1 co   2 - 127
Gendarmerie   2 - 48

IV CORPS
Général de division Count Bertrand

12th Division— Général de division Count Morand
1st Brigade: Général de brigade Bellair
    13th Regiment of the Line, 1st, 2nd, 3rd, 4th, and 6th bns.   (5)   105 - 3,084
    3rd Provisional Light Infantry Regiment, consisting of   (2)   36 - 1,301
        3rd battalion, 3rd Light Infantry Regiment
        4th battalion, 8th Light Infantry Regiment
2nd Brigade: Général de brigade Sicard
    2nd Provisional Croatian Infantry Regiment, consisting of   (2)   45 - 1,633
        2nd battalion, 3rd Croatian Regiment
        1st battalion, 4th Croatian Regiment
    23rd Regiment of the Line, 1st, 2nd, 4th, and 6th bns.   (4)   53 - 3,135
    Divisional artillery and train:
        Two companies of foot artillery, each company consisting of   6 - 341
        6 6-pdr. guns and 2 5 1/2-inch howitzers—total of 16 pieces of ordnance.
    Equipage   1 co.   1 - 117

15th Division— Général de division Peri
1st Brigade: Général de brigade Martel
    1st Italian Regiment of the Line, 3rd and 4th battalions   (2)   45 - 1,551
    4th Italian Regiment of the Line, 1st, 2nd, 3rd, and 4th bns   (4)   75 - 2,488
2nd Brigade: Général de brigade St. Andrea
    6th Italian Regiment of the Line, 3rd and 4th battalions   (2)   45 - 1,669
3rd Brigade: Général de brigade Moroni
    Milan Guard Battalion   (1)   21 - 805
    7th Italian Regiment of the Line, 1st, 2nd, 3rd, and 4th bns   (4)   78 - 2,667
    Divisional artillery:
        Two companies of Italian foot artillery, each company consisting of   14 - 506
        6 6-pdr. guns and 2 5 1/2-inch howitzers, and one company of Italian horse
    artillery, consisting of 3 6-pdr. guns and 1 5 1/2-inch howitzer—total 20 pieces.

IV Corps Cavalry Brigade—

2nd Neapolitan Chasseurs à Cheval, 1st—4th squadrons	(4)	20 - 945

On 25 April 1813, the other cavalry regiments that were to be
part of IV Corps were still organizing along the lower Elbe River.

IV Corps Artillery Reserve—

Artillery reserve companies and train—in route
Engineers:

Italian Sappers & *Marins*	3 cos	8 - 319
Equipage	1 co.	2 - 126

VI CORPS
Marshal Marmont, Duke of Ragusa

20th Division— Général de division Count Compans

1st Brigade: Général de brigade Cacault

1st Regiment de Marine, 1st, 2nd, 3rd, and 4th battalions	(4)	79 - 3,269
3rd Regiment de Marine, 1st and 2nd battalions	(2)	35 - 1,441

2nd Brigade: Général de brigade Joubert

25th Provisional Regiment of the Line, consisting of
  3rd battalion, 47th Regiment of the Line
  3rd battalion, 86th Regiment of the Line
	(2)	21 - 1,110

20th Provisional Regiment of the Line, consisting of
  5th battalion, 66th Regiment of the Line
  3rd battalion, 122nd Regiment of the Line
	(2)	26 - 1,250

32nd Light Infantry Regiment, 2nd and 3rd battalions	(2)	26 - 1,182

Division artillery and train:

Two companies of foot artillery, each consisting of		8 - 292
6 6-pdr. guns and 2 51/2-inch howitzers—total of 16 pieces of ordnance.		
5th Principal Train Battalion		0 - 102
10th *bis* Train Battalion		1 - 85

21st Division— Général de division Count Bonet

1st Brigade: Général de brigade Buquet

2nd Regiment de Marine, 1st through 6th battalions	(6)	105 - 3,225
4th Regiment de Marine, 1st and 2nd battalions	(2)	30 - 1,486

2nd Brigade: Général de brigade Jamin

37th Light Infantry Regiment, 1st, 2nd, and 3rd battalions	(3)	44 - 2,707
Spanish Regiment Joseph Napoleon, 1st battalion	(1)	12 - 742

Provisional Brigade:

3rd battalion, 36th Light Infantry Regiment	(1)	18 - 626
3rd battalion, 131st Regiment of the Line	(1)	16 - 763
3rd battalion, 132nd Regiment of the Line	(1)	17 - 647
3rd battalion, 133rd Regiment of the Line	(1)	18 - 820
2nd battalion, Wurzburg Regiment	(1)	18 - 703

Divisional artillery and train:

Two companies of foot artillery, each consisting of		7 - 233
6 6-pdr. guns and 2 51/2-inch howitzers—total of 16 pieces of ordnance.		
4th *bis* Train Battalion		1 - 108
12th Principal Train Battalion		1 - 85

Situation of the Grand Armée—25 April 1813

22nd Division— Général de division Baron Friederichs

1st Brigade: Général de brigade Ficatier

23rd Light Infantry Regiment, 3rd and 4th battalions	(2)	15 - 1,280
11th Provisional Regiment of the Line, consisting of	(2)	20 - 992
4th battalion, 1st Regiment of the Line		
2nd battalion, 62nd Regiment of the Line		
13th Provisional Regiment of the Line, consisting of	(2)	29 - 1,303
3rd battalion, 14th Regiment of the Line		
4th battalion, 16th Regiment of the Line		

2nd Brigade: Général de brigade Coëhorn

16th Provisional Regiment of the Line, consisting of	(2)	32 - 1,101
6th battalion, 26th Regiment of the Line		
6th battalion, 82nd Regiment of the Line		
121st Regiment of the Line, 3rd and 4th battalions	(2)	17 - 1,135
15th Regiment of the Line, 3rd and 4th battalions	(2)	23 - 851
70th Regiment of the Line, 3rd and 4th battalions	(2)	23 - 856

Divisional artillery and train:

Two companies of foot artillery, one consisting of	
6 6-pdr. guns and 2 5 1/2-inch howitzers, and the other consisting of	7 - 208
5 6-pdr. guns and 1 5 1/2-inch howitzer—total of 14 pieces of ordnance.	
8th Principal Train Battalion	0 - 57
12th *bis* Train Battalion	1 - 80
14th Principal Train Battalion	1 - 49

VI Corps Reserve Artillery—

One company of horse artillery, consisting of	3 - 101
4 6-pdr. guns and 2 5 1/2-inch howitzers	
3rd *bis* Train Battalion	0 - 69
One company of horse artillery, consisting of	2 - 82
3 6-pdr. guns and 1 5 1/2-inch howitzer	
3rd *bis* Train Battalion	1 - 65
One company of foot artillery, consisting of	4 - 122
6 12-pdr. guns and 2 6-inch howitzers	
10th *bis* Train Battalion	1 - 105
One company of foot artillery, consisting of	5 - 124
6 12-pdr. guns and 2 6-inch howitzers	
6th *bis* Train Battalion	1 - 112

Corps reserve artillery had a total of 24 pieces of ordnance.

THE ARMY OF THE ELBE
Prince Eugène de Beauharnais, Viceroy of Italy

V CORPS
Général de division Count Lauriston

16th Division— Général de division Baron Maison
1st Brigade: Général de brigade Avril

151st Regiment of the Line, 1st, 2nd, and 3rd battalions	(3)	90 - 1,812

2nd Brigade: Général de brigade Penne

153rd Regiment of the Line, 1st, 2nd, 3rd, and 4th bns. (4)   82 - 2,723

Divisional artillery and train:

Two companies of foot artillery, each consisting of   7 - 506
6 6-pdr. guns and 2 5$_{1/2}$-inch howitzers, and one company
of horse artillery, consisting of 4 6-pdr. guns and 2 5$_{1/2}$-inch
howitzers—total of 22 pieces of ordnance.

Engineers   1 co   3 - 121
Equipage   1 co.   ?

18th Division— Général de division Count Lagrange
1st Brigade: Général de brigade Charrière

134th Regiment of the Line, 1st and 2nd battalions   (2)   46 - 1,529
154th Regiment of the Line, 1st, 2nd, 3rd, and 4th bns.   (4)   78 - 2,011

2nd Brigade: Général de brigade Suden

155th Regiment of the Line, 1st, 2nd, 3rd, and 4th bns.   (4)   81 - 1,937
3rd Foreign Regiment (Irish Legion), 1st and 2nd bns.   (2)   45 - 1,204

Division artillery and train:

Two companies of foot artillery, each consisting of   5 - 416
6 6-pdr. guns and 2 5$_{1/2}$-inch howitzers—total of 16 pieces of ordnance.

Equipage   1 co.   ?

19th Division— Général de division Rochambeau
1st Brigade: Général de brigade Lacroix

135th Regiment of the Line, 1st, 2nd, 3rd, and 4th bns.   (4)   72 - 2,408

2nd Brigade: Général de brigade Lafitte

149th Regiment of the Line, 1st, 2nd, 3rd, and 4th bns.   (4)   81 - 2,434

3rd Brigade: Général de brigade Harlet

150th Regiment of the Line, 1st, 2nd, 3rd, and 4th bns.   (4)   77 - 2,683

Divisional artillery and train:

Two companies of foot artillery, each consisting of   7 - 610
6 6-pdr. guns and 2 5$_{1/2}$-inch howitzers, and one company
of horse artillery, consisting of 4 6-pdr. guns and 2 5$_{1/2}$-inch
howitzers—total of 22 pieces of ordnance.

Engineers   1 co   3 - 112
Equipage   1 co.   ?

XI CORPS
Marshal Macdonald, Duke of Tarentum

31st Division— Général de brigade Baron* Fressinet

11th Provisional Demi-brigade, consisting of	(2)	39 - 1,206
4th battalion, 27th Light Infantry Regiment		
4th battalion, 20th Regiment of the Line		
13th Provisional Demi-brigade, consisting of	(3)	39 - 1,381
4th battalion, 5th Regiment of the Line		
4th battalion, 11th Regiment of the Line		
4th battalion, 79th Regiment of the Line		
Neapolitan Vélites, 1st battalion	(1)	31 - 625
Neapolitan *Marins*	1 co	2 - 60

Divisional artillery and train:

   Two companies of foot artillery, each consisting of   10 - 295
   four 6-pdr. guns and 2 5 1/2-inch howitzers—total of 12 pieces of ordnance.
* Awarded title "Baron of the Empire" on 3 May 1813.

35th Division— Général de division Baron Gérard

1st Brigade: Général de brigade Le Sénécal

6th Regiment of the Line, 3rd, 4th, and 7th battalions	(3)	42 - 1,358
112th Regiment of the Line, 1st, 2nd, 3rd, and 4th bns.	(4)	79 - 2,885

2nd Brigade: Général de brigade Zucchi

2nd Italian Light Infantry Regiment, , 3rd and 4th battalion	(2)	44 - 1,315
5th Italian Regiment of the Line, 1st, 2nd, 3rd, and 4th bns	(4)	90 - 2,942

Divisional artillery and train:

   Two companies of foot artillery, one consisting of   14 - 475
   6 6-pdr. guns and 2 5 1/2-inch howitzers, and another
with 5 6-pdr. guns and 1 5 1/2-inch howitzer—total of 14 pieces of ordnance.
Engineers:

Italian Sappers	1 co.	3 - 62

36th Division— Général de division Count Charpentier

1st Brigade: Général de brigade Simmer

14th Light Infantry Regiment, 3rd and 4th battalions	(2)	46 - 1,384
22nd Light Infantry Regiment, 1st, 2nd, 3rd, and 4th bns.	(4)	81 - 268

2nd Brigade: Général de brigade Meunier

14th Provisional Demi-brigade, consisting of	(3)	55 - 2,287
3rd battalion, 67th Regiment of the Line		
6th battalion, 10th Regiment of the Line		
6th battalion, 20th Regiment of the Line		
15th Provisional Demi-brigade, consisting of	(2)	40 - 1,505
4th battalion, 3rd Light Infantry Regiment		
4th battalion, 102nd Regiment of the Line		

Divisional artillery and train:

   Three companies of foot artillery, each consisting of   7 - 389
   6 6-pdr. guns and 2 5 1/2-inch howitzers—total of 24 pieces of ordnance.

XI Corps Cavalry Brigade—

4th Italian Chasseurs à Cheval, 1st squadron	(1)	8 - 131
Würzburg Chevaulegers, 1st squadron	(1)	8 - 131*

* Identical strength returns for both cavalry regiments.

Situation of the Grand Armée—25 April 1813

Old Guard Division*— Général de division Baron Roguet

1st Brigade: Général de brigade Rottembourg

1st Old Guard Grenadiers à pied, 1st battalion	(1)	16 - 437
1st Old Guard Chasseurs à pied, 1st battalion	(1)	15 - 448
2nd Young Guard Voltigeurs, 1st battalion	(1)	17 - 515
2nd battalion	(1)	11 - 500

2nd Brigade:

Vélites of Turin	(1)	16 - 303
Vélites of Florence	(1)	17 - 202
Italian Royal Guard Chasseurs à pied	(1)	27 - 160
Hessian Leib-Garde Fusiliers, detachment	(-)	12 - 117

Italian Guard Cavalry:

Tuscan Guards of Honor	(1/2)	3 - 51
Turin Guards of Honor	(1/2)	2 - 65
Italian Guards of Honor	(1/2)	1 - 22
Italian Guard Dragoons	(1/2)	2 - 67

Divisional artillery and train:

One Old Guard foot company, consisting of
6 6-pdr. guns and 2 5½-inch howitzers; one
Italian Royal Guard foot company, consisting of   12 - 551
4 6-pdr. guns and 2 5½-inch howitzers; and
one Italian Royal Guard horse artillery company, consisting
of 4 6-pdr. guns and 2 5½-inch howitzers—total of 20 pieces of ordnance.

Engineers of the Guard   1 co.   1 - 30

* The Old Guard Division was marching with the Army of the Eble, on its way to join up with the other Imperial Guard units in the Army of the Main.

I RESERVE CAVALRY CORPS
Général de division Baron Latour-Maubourg

1st Light Cavalry Division— Général de division Baron Bruyères

1st Brigade:

7th Hussars	(1)	7 - 109
9th (Hamburg) Light Lancers	(-)	2 - 20
8th Hussars	(1)	6 - 93
7th (1st Vistula Legion) Light Lancers	(-)	3 - 25
16th Chasseurs à Cheval	(1)	6 - 119

2nd Brigade: Général de brigade Cambraceres

1st Light Lancers	(1)	5 - 124
3rd Light Lancers	(1/2)	3 - 57
5th Light Lancers	(-)	2 - 21
8th (2nd Vistula Legion) Light Lancers	(-)	?

3rd Light Cavalry Division— Général de division Baron Chastel

1st Brigade: Général de brigade Van Merlen

6th Chasseurs à Cheval	(1)	7 - 144
25th Chasseurs à Cheval	(1)	4 - 105
6th Hussars	(2)	168
8th Chasseurs à Cheval	(1)	4 - 79
Portuguese Legion Chasseurs à Cheval	(1/2)	3 - 68

2nd Brigade:

9th & 19th Chasseurs à Cheval	(detached)	
2nd & 3rd Italian Chasseurs à Cheval	(1)	6 - 87
1st Chasseurs à Cheval	(1)	4 - 117
2nd Chasseurs à Cheval	(1/2)	2 - 86
3rd Chasseurs à Cheval	(-)	1 - 46

1st Cuirassier Division— Général de division Baron Bordesoulle

1st Brigade: Général de brigade Berkheim

2nd Cuirassiers	(1)	6 - 145
3rd Cuirassiers	(1)	5 - 105
6th Cuirassiers	(1)	6 - 96

2nd Brigade: Général de brigade Quinette

9th Cuirassiers	(1)	5 - 168
11th Cuirassiers	(1)	6 - 129
12th Cuirassiers	(1/2)	3 - 79

3rd Cuirassier Division— Général de division Baron Doumerc

1st Brigade: Général de brigade Thouard

4th Cuirassiers	(1/2)	3 - 41
7th Cuirassiers	(1/2)	3 - 53
14th (Dutch) Cuirassiers	(-)	1 - 2

2nd Brigade:

7th Dragoons	(1)	6 - 113
23rd Dragoons	(1)	6 - 119
28th Dragoons	(1)	5 - 114
30th Dragoons	(1)	8 - 126
Provisional Dragoon Regiment	(-)	2 - 24

VII CORPS

Général de division Count Reynier

32nd Division— Général de division Baron Durutte

1st Brigade: Général de brigade Devaux

35th Light Infantry Regiment, 1st battalion	(1)	15 - 132
36th Light Infantry Regiment, 4th battalion	(1)	19 - 213

2nd Brigade: Général de brigade Jarry

131st Regiment of the Line, 4th battalion	(1)	14 - 287

3rd Brigade: Général de brigade Brayer

133rd Regiment of the Line, 4th battalion	(1)	18 - 103
132nd Regiment of the Line, 4th battalion	(1)	11 - 84

Division artillery and train:

One company of foot artillery totalling 4 pieces of ordnance.		2 - 60

Note: On 1 May this division was reinforced by the 3,648 men who marched with Bonnet's division of the VI Corps. The 24th (Saxon) and 25th (Saxon) Divisions of VII Corps were still forming.

II CORPS
Marshal Victor, Duke of Belluno

4th Division— Général de division Dubreton
1st Brigade: Général de brigade Ferriere

37th Provisional Light Infantry Regiment, consisting of	(2)	31 - 1,314
2nd battalion, 24th Light Infantry Regiment		
2nd battalion, 26th Light Infantry Regiment		
38th Provisional Regiment of the Line, consisting of	(2)	39 - 1,040
2nd battalion, 11th Light Infantry Regiment		
2nd battalion, 2nd Regiment of the Line		
39th Provisional Regiment of the Line, consisting of	(2)	37 - 1,204
2nd battalion, 19th Regiment of the Line		
2nd battalion, 37th Regiment of the Line		

2nd Brigade: Général de brigade Brun

40th Provisional Regiment of the Line, consisting of	(2)	44 - 1,307
2nd battalion, 4th Regiment of the Line		
2nd battalion, 56th Regiment of the Line		
41st Provisional Regiment of the Line, consisting of	(2)	32 - 1,311
2nd battalion, 18th Regiment of the Line		
2nd battalion, 46th Regiment of the Line		
42nd Provisional Regiment of the Line, consisting of	(2)	41 - 1,120
2nd battalion, 72nd Regiment of the Line		
2nd battalion, 93rd Regiment of the Line		

Divisional artillery and train:

One company of foot artillery, consisting of	4 - 161

6 6-pdr. guns and 2 5½-inch howitzers—total of 8 pieces of ordnance.

Note: The II Corps was to consist of the 4th, 5th and 6th Divisions, but the 5th was with Vandamme in I Corps and the 6th was still forming in Wesel. The corps had no staff or services. Victor also had the 1st Division, I Corps under his orders.

Forces Organizing on the Lower Elbe

I CORPS
Général de division Vandamme, Count of Unsebourg

2nd Division— Général de division Dumonceau
1st Brigade:

29th *bis* Provisional Light Infantry Regiment, consisting	(2)	1,154
4th battalion, 7th Light Infantry Regiment		
4th battalion, 13th Light Infantry Regiment		
30th *bis* Provisional Light Infantry Regiment, consisting	(2)	417
4th battalion, 15th Light Infantry Regiment		
4th battalion, 33rd Light Infantry Regiment		
31st *bis* Provisional Regiment of the Line, consisting of	(2)	1,070
4th battalion, 17th Regiment of the Line		
4th battalion, 30th Regiment of the Line		

Situation of the Grand Armée—25 April 1813

32nd *bis* Provisional Regiment of the Line, consisting of	(2)	1,057
4th battalion, 33rd Regiment of the Line		
4th battalion, 48th Regiment of the Line		
2nd Brigade:		
33rd *bis* Provisional Regiment of the Line, consisting of	(2)	983
4th battalion, 12th Regiment of the Line		
4th battalion, 21st Regiment of the Line		
34th *bis* Provisional Regiment of the Line, consisting of	(2)	1,281
4th battalion, 85th Regiment of the Line		
4th battalion, 108th Regiment of the Line		
35th *bis* Provisional Regiment of the Line, consisting of	(2)	1,319
4th battalion, 25th Regiment of the Line		
4th battalion, 57th Regiment of the Line		
36th *bis* Provisional Regiment of the Line, consisting of	(2)	1,399
4th battalion, 61st Regiment of the Line		
4th battalion, 111th Regiment of the Line		
Divisional artillery and train:		
One company of foot artillery, consisting of		2 - 111
6 6-pdr. guns and 2 5½-inch howitzers—total of 8 pieces of ordnance.		

5th Division— Général de division Baron Dufour

1st Brigade:		
37th *bis* Provisional Light Infantry Regiment, consisting	(2)	1,366
4th battalion, 26th Light Infantry Regiment		
4th battalion, 24th Light Infantry Regiment		
38th *bis* Provisional Light Infantry Regiment, consisting	(2)	1,354
4th battalion, 11th Light Infantry Regiment		
4th battalion, 2nd Regiment of the Line		
39th *bis* Provisional Regiment of the Line, consisting of	(2)	871
4th battalion, 19th Regiment of the Line		
4th battalion, 37th Regiment of the Line		
2nd Brigade:		
40th *bis* Provisional Regiment of the Line, consisting of	(2)	778
4th battalion, 56th Regiment of the Line		
4th battalion, 4th Regiment of the Line		
41st *bis* Provisional Regiment of the Line, consisting of	(2)	912
4th battalion, 18th Regiment of the Line		
4th battalion, 46th Regiment of the Line		
42nd *bis* Provisional Regiment of the Line, consisting of	(2)	678
4th battalion, 72nd Regiment of the Line		
4th battalion, 93rd Regiment of the Line		
Divisional artillery and train:		
One company of foot artillery, consisting of		5 - 115
6 6-pdr. guns and 2 5½-inch howitzers—total of 8 pieces of ordnance.		

Reserve Div of Hamburg— Général de division Baron Carra Saint-Cyr

1st Brigade: Général de brigade Prince of Reuss		
152nd Regiment of the Line	(1)	20 - 535
"Bataillon de Marche"	(1)	11 - 337
5th Flotilla Equipment Battalion	(1)	13 - 436
Customs Police Battalion	(1)	33 - 436

2nd Brigade: Général de brigade Raymond de Montesquiou, Duke of Fezensac

152nd Regiment of the Line	(2)	20 - 578
"Bataillons de Marche"	(2)	18 - 970
Divisional artillery: ?		?

Cavalry Brigade: Général Beuermann

28th Chasseurs à Cheval	(1)	4 - 95
17th Polish (Lithuanian) Uhlans	(2)	18 - 250

II CAVALRY CORPS
Général de division Count Sébastiani de la Porta

2nd Light Cavalry Division— Général de division Roussel d'Hurbal
1st Brigade: Général de brigade Maurin

11th Chasseurs à Cheval	(1)	7 - 88
12th Chasseurs à Cheval	(1)	7 - 123
2nd Light Lancers	(1)	4 - 93

4th Light Cavalry Division— Général de division Baron Exelmans
1st Brigade: Général de brigade Gérard

4th Chasseurs à Cheval	(1)	8 - 104
7th Chasseurs à Cheval	(1)	10 - 140
20th Chasseurs à Cheval	(2)	9 - 177
6th Light Lancers	(-)	2 - 25

2nd Brigade:

11th (Dutch) Hussars	(1)	5 - 96
23rd Chasseurs à Cheval	(4)	28 - 690
24th Chasseurs à Cheval	(2)	10 - 176

2nd Cuirassier Div— Général de div. Watier, Count of Saint-Alphonse
1st Brigade:

1st Carabiniers	(1)	6 - 85
2nd Carabiniers	(1)	7 - 98
1st Cuirassiers	(2)	16 - 225

2nd Brigade:

5th Cuirassiers	(1)	6 - 93
9th Cuirassiers	(1)	6 - 97
10th Cuirassiers	(1)	10 - 119

Divisional artillery and train:

One company of horse artillery, consisting of	2 - 123

4 6-pdr. guns and 2 5 1/2-inch howitzers—total of 6 pieces of ordnance.

from V CORPS
17th Division— Général de division Puthod
1st Brigade: Général de brigade Vachot

146th Regiment of the Line, 1st, 2nd, 3rd, and 4th bns.	(4)	80 - 2,210
147th Regiment of the Line, 1st, 2nd, 3rd, and 4th bns.	(4)	74 - 2,531

2nd Brigade: Général de brigade Pastol

148th Regiment of the Line, 1st, 2nd, 3rd, and 4th bns.	(4)	64 - 2,183

Divisional artillery and train:

Two companies of foot artillery, each consisting of   7 - 231
5 6-pdr. guns and 1 5½-inch howitzer—total of 12 pieces of ordnance.

from IV CORPS

remainder of IV Corps Cavalry— Général de division Baron Fresia

1st Brigade: Général de brigade Briche

19th Chasseurs à Cheval	(1)	?
2nd Neapolitian Chasseurs à Cheval		—already with IV Corps

2nd Brigade: Général de brigade Stedman

13th Hussars		?
14th Hussars		?

3rd Brigade: Général de brigade Jacquet

Italian Dragoons "Napoleon", 1st—4th sqdrns.	(4)	28 - 885
1st Italian Chasseurs à Cheval, 1st squadron	(1)	?

IV Corps Artillery Reserve—

Artillery and train:
One company of foot artillery, consisting of
6 12-pdr. guns and 1 5½-inch howitzer, along with   7 - 235
one company of horse artillery, consisting of 4 6-pdr.
guns and 2 5½-inch howitzers—total of 13 pieces of ordnance.

XII CORPS
Marshal Oudinot, Duke of Reggio

13th Division— Général de division Count* Pacthod

1st Brigade: Général de brigade Pourailly

1st Light Infantry Regiment, 4th battalion	(1)	18 - 836
7th Regiment of the Line, 3rd battalion	(1)	17 - 609
4th battalion	(1)	14 - 589
12th Provisional Regiment of the Line, consisting of		
4th battalion,65th Regiment of the Line	(1)	10 - 709
4th battalion, 42nd Regiment of the Line	(1)	15 - 670
23rd Provisional Regiment of the Line, consisting of		
4th battalion, 67th Regiment of the Line	(1)	13 - 828
8th battalion, 67th Regiment of the Line	(1)	15 - 819

2nd Brigade: Général de brigade Gruger

4th Neapolitan Light Infantry Regiment, 1st battalion	(1)	29 - 629
2nd battalion	(1)	13 - 641
3rd battalion	(1)	16 - 518

Divisional artillery and train:

Two companies of foot artillery, each consisting of		6 - 301
6 6-pdr. guns and 2 5½-inch howitzers—total of 16 pieces of ordnance.		
Engineers	1 co.	4 - 132
Equipage	1 co.	2 - 147

*Awarded title "Count of the Empire" on 20 May 1813.

14th Division— Général de division Baron Lorencz
1st Brigade: Général de brigade Leclerc

52nd Regiment of the Line, 3rd battalion	(1)	18 - 720
4th battalion	(1)	17 - 587
137th Regiment of the Line, 1st battalion	(1)	18 - 729
2nd battalion	(1)	12 - 740
3rd battalion	(1)	15 - 789
4th battalion	(1)	15 - 774

2nd Brigade: Général de brigade d'Henin

18th Light Infantry Regiment, 2nd battalion	(1)	16 - 580
6th battalion	(1)	15 - 520
156th Regiment of the Line, 1st battalion	(1)	20 - 727
2nd battalion	1)	20 - 736
3rd battalion	(1)	19 - 748
4th battalion	(1)	15 - 771
Illyrian Regiment, 2nd battalion	(1)	22 - 674

Divisional artillery and train:

Two companies of foot artillery, each consisting of		5 - 337
6 6-pdr. guns and 2 51/2-inch howitzers—total of 16 pieces of ordnance.		
Engineers	1 co	4 - 132
Equipage	1 co	2 - 147

XII Corps Artillery Reserve—
Artillery and train:

One company of foot artillery, consisting of		4 - 188
6 12-pdr. guns and 2 6-inch howitzers—total of 8 pieces of ordnance.		
Engineers	2 cos	5 - 371
Equippage	4 cos	8 - 576

Attached to XII CORPS:
29th Division— Général de division de Raglowich
1st (Infantry) Brigade: Général Beckert

1st Bavarian Light Battalion	(1)	13 - 641
3rd Bavarian Regiment of the Line	(1)	17 - 572
4th Bavarian Regiment of the Line	(1)	16 - 812
8th Bavarian Regiment of the Line	(1)	21 - 652
13th Bavarian Regiment of the Line	(1)	12 - 570

2nd (Infantry) Brigade: Général de brigade Maillot de la Traille

2nd Bavarian Light Battalion	(1)	9 - 548
5th Bavarian Regiment of the Line	(1)	21 - 711
7th Bavarian Regiment of the Line	(1)	21 - 711
9th Bavarian Regiment of the Line	(1)	18 - 764
10th Bavarian Regiment of the Line	(1)	6 - 843

Cavalry Brigade: Général Seyssel d'Aix

Bavarian Chevaulèger Regiment	(2)	9 - 217
Bavarian Chevaulèger Regiment	(2)	7 - 213
Bavarian Chevaulèger Regiment	(2)	8 - 242

Divisional artillery and train:

Two companies of Bavarian foot artillery, each consisting of		6 - 151
6 6-pdr. guns and 2 51/2-inch howitzers—total of 16 pieces of ordnance.		

Other Units Forming on the Lower Elbe

38th Division— Général de division de Franquemont
1st Brigade: Général de brigade Neuffer

1st Württemberg Regiment of the Line, 1st and 2nd bns	(2)	1434
2nd Württemberg Regiment of the Line, 1st and 2nd bns	(2)	1434

2nd Brigade: Général de brigade Stockmayer

9th Württemberg Light Infantry battalion	(1)	715
10th Württemberg Light Infantry battalion	(1)	715

Cavalry Brigade: Général de brigade Jell

1st Württemberg Chevaulègers, 1st, 2nd, 3rd, and 4th sqdrns	(4)	580
2nd Württemberg Chevaulègers, 1st, 2nd, 3rd, and 4th sqdrns	(4)	580

Divisional artillery and train:
Two companies of Württemberg foot artillery, each consisting of   291
4 6-pdr. guns and 2 7-pdr. howitzers—total of 12 pieces of ordnance.

37th Division— Général de division Hammerstein
Infantry Brigade:

Westphalian Fusilier Guards, 1st and 2nd battalions	(2)	40 - 1,033
8th Westphalian Regiment of the Line, 1st and 2nd bns	(2)	42 - 1,150
2nd & 4th Westphalian Light Battalions	(2)	56 - 888

Cavalry Brigade:

Westphalian Light Lancers of the Guard, 1st—4th sqdrns	(4)	44 - 650
1st Westphalian Hussars,1st and 2nd squadrons, and		
2nd Westphalian Hussars, 1st and 2nd squadrons, combined	(4)	26 - 454

Divisional artillery:
One company of Westphalian foot artillery—total of 8 pieces of ordnance. 6 - 150

27th Division— Général de division Dombrowski
1st (Infantry) Brigade:

2nd Polish Regiment of the Line, 1st and 2nd battalions	(2)	56 - 658
14th Polish Regiment of the Line, 1st and 2nd battalions	(2)	52 - 443

2nd (Cavalry) Brigade:

2nd Polish Uhlans, 1st, 2nd, 3rd, and 4th squdrons	(4)	49 - 811
4th Polish Uhlans, 1st, 2nd, 3rd, and 4th squadrons	(4)	48 - 835

Divisional artillery and train:
One company of Polish horse artillery, consisting of   6 - 86
4 6-pdr. guns and 2 7-pdr. howitzers—total of 6 pieces of ordnance.

Troops Organizing East of the Rhine River
from VI CORPS
23rd Division— Général de division Baron Teste
Brigade:

36th Regiment of the Line	(1)	20 - 490
51st Regiment of the Line	(1)	13 - 614

Originally part of I CORPS, now assigned to II CORPS

1st Division— Général de division Baron Philippon

1st Brigade: Général de brigade Ponchelon

29th Provisional Light Infantry Regiment, consisting of	(2)	26 - 1,355
2nd battalion, 27th Light Infantry Regiment		
2nd battalion, 13th Light Infantry Regiment		
30th Provisional Light Infantry Regiment, consisting of	(2)	30 - 913
2nd battalion, 15th Light Infantry Regiment		
2nd battalion, 33rd Light Infantry Regiment		
31st Provisional Regiment of the Line, consisting of	(2)	35 - 1,230
2nd battalion, 17th Regiment of the Line		
2nd battalion, 30th Regiment of the Line		
32nd Provisional Regiment of the Line, consisting of	(2)	34 - 1,207
2nd battalion, 33rd Regiment of the Line		
2nd battalion, 48th Regiment of the Line		

2nd Brigade:

33rd Provisional Regiment of the Line, consisting of	(2)	38 - 1,211
2nd battalion, 12th Regiment of the Line		
2nd battalion, 21st Regiment of the Line		
34th Provisional Regiment of the Line, consisting of	(2)	39 - 1,423
2nd battalion, 85th Regiment of the Line		
2nd battalion, 108th Regiment of the Line		
35th Provisional Regiment of the Line, consisting of	(2)	37 - 1,384
2nd battalion, 25th Regiment of the Line		
2nd battalion, 57th Regiment of the Line		
36th Provisional Regiment of the Line, consisting of	(2)	43 - 1,318
2nd battalion, 61st Regiment of the Line		
2nd, battalion, 111th Regiment of the Line		

Divisional artillery and train:

One company of foot artillery, consisting of		2 - 100

6 6-pdr. guns and 2 5 1/2-inch howitzers—total of 8 pieces of ordnance.

From the IMPERIAL GUARD

2nd Guard Infantry Division— Général de division Baron Barrois

1st Brigade: Général de brigade Decouz

2nd Old Guard Grenadiers à pied, 2nd battalion	(1)	482
2nd Old Guard Chasseurs à pied, 2nd battalion	(1)	520
Flanker-Chasseurs, 1st battalion	(1)	620

2nd Brigade: Général de brigade Mouton-Duvernet

Flanker-Grenadiers, 1st battalion	(1)	777
Middle Guard Fusiliers, 2nd battalions of each regiment	(2)	18 - 861
3rd Young Guard Voltigeurs, 1st and 2nd battalions	(2)	29 - 1,156

3rd Brigade: Général de brigade Boyeldieu

7th Young Guard Voltiguers, 1st and 2nd battalions	(2)	32 - 1,419
3rd Young Guard Tirailleurs, 1st and 2nd battalions	(2)	32 - 1,425

Divisional artillery and train:

Two Young Guard foot companies, each consisting of		240

6 6-pdr. guns and 2 5 1/2-inch howitzers—total of 16 pieces of ordnance.

Equipage	4 cos.	467

3rd Guard Infantry Division— Général de division Count Delaborde
Forming in Frankfurt, no units yet assigned

4th Guard Infantry Division—
Forming in Paris, no units yet assigned

Guard Cavalry Units Forming—Général de division Count Ornano

Light Lancers of Berg, 3rd and 4th squadrons	(2)
Additional squadrons for the Old Guard Grenadiers à Cheval, Guard Dragoons, 2nd (Red) Guard Light Lancers, and the Gendarmes d'élite	(10)
Young Guard squadrons, Guard Light Lancers	(4)
Young Guard squadrons, Guard Chasseurs à Cheval	(5)
Young Guard squadrons, Guard Dragoons	(2)
Young Guard squadrons, Guard Grenadiers à Cheval	(2)
1st Guards of Honor—organizing at Versailles	(5)
2nd Guards of Honor—organizing at Metz	(5)
3rd Guards of Honor—organizing at Tours	(5)
4th Guards of Honor—organizing at Lyon	(5)

From I RESERVE CAVALRY CORPS: Units de marche

1st Division de Marche— Général de division Milhaud

1st Regiment de Marche	759—forming in Gotha
2nd Regiment de Marche	303—forming in Hanau
3rd Regiment de Marche	650—forming in Gotha
4th Regiment de Marche	482—forming in Gotha

From II RESERVE CAVALRY CORPS: Units de marche

1st Division de Marche— Général de division Saint-Germain

1st Regiment de Marche	746—forming in Gotha
2nd Regiment de Marche	766—forming in Gotha
3rd Regiment de Marche	Not yet formed
4th Regiment de Marche	493—forming in Gotha

III RESERVE CAVALRY CORPS
Général de division Arrighi de Casanova, Duke of Padoua

5th Light Cavalry Division— Général de division de Lorge; plus 5th Heavy Cavalry Division, and the 6th Heavy Cavalry Division

1st Brigade: Général de brigade Lamotte	
1st Regiment de Marche	8 - 335
2nd Regiment de Marche	1 - 118
2nd Brigade: Général de brigade Avice	
1st Regiment de Marche	3 - 237
2nd Regiment de Marche	2 - 288

SITUATION
of the
V Reserve Cavalry Corps
10 May 1813

V RESERVE CAVALRY CORPS
Général de division Count Milhaud

	Number of Squadrons	Present & Under Arms Off.- Others
**9th Light Cavalry Division— **		
3rd Hussars, 1st and 2nd squadrons,	(2)	20 - 210
14th Chasseurs à Chaval, 1st and 2nd squadrons	(2)	31 - 171
6th Chasseurs, à Cheval, 1st and 2nd squadrons	(2)	27 - 189
7th Chasseurs, à Cheval, 1st and 2nd squadrons	(2)	21 - 167
**3rd (*bis*) Heavy Cavalry Division— **		
2nd Dragoons, 1st and 2nd squadrons	(2)	24 - 285
6th Dragoons, 1st and 2nd squadrons	(2)	15 - 196
11th Dragoons, 1st and 2nd squadrons	(2)	25 - 236
13th Dragoons, 1st and 2nd squadrons	(2)	20 - 198
15th Dragoons, 1st and 2nd squadrons	(2)	25 - 239
**4th Heavy Cavalry Division— **		
18th Dragoons, 1st and 2nd squadrons	(2)	24 - 189
19th Dragoons, 1st and 2nd squadrons	(2)	16 - 132
20th Dragoons, 1st and 2nd squadrons	(2)	12 - 124
22nd Dragoons, 1st and 2nd squadrons	(2)	24 - 250
25th Dragoons, 1st and 2nd squadrons	(2)	28 - 216
V Reserve Cavalry Corps Artillery and Train—		
Three companies of horse artillery and three detachments of artillery train.		9 - 242

* No commander yet assigned.

SITUATION
of the
Reorganized
Imperial Guard Corps
15 May 1813

Marshal Mortier, Duke of Treviso
Général de division Count Ornano, commanding the Cavalry of the Guard
Général de division Count Dulauloy, commanding of the Artillery of the Guard
Général de brigade Baron Desvaux de Saint-Maurice, Horse Artillery of the Guard

	Number of Battalions/ Squadrons	Present & Under Arms Off. - Others
1st Guard Infantry Division— Général de division Baron Dumoustier		
1st Brigade: Général de brigade Mouton-Duvernet		
Middle Guard Fusilier Grenadiers, 1st and 2nd battalions	(2)	
Middle Guard Fusilier Chasseurs, 1st and 2nd battalions	(2)	
2nd Brigade: Général de brigade Tindal		
1st Young Guard Voltigeurs, 1st and 2nd battalions	(2)	
6th Young Guard Voltigeurs, 1st and 2nd battalions	(2)	
3rd Brigade: Général de brigade Lanusse		
2nd Young Guard Voltigeurs, 1st and 2nd battalions	(2)	
3rd Young Guard Voltigeurs, 1st and 2nd battalions	(2)	
7th Young Guard Voltigeurs, 1st and 2nd battalions	(2)	
Divisional Artillery and train:		
Two companies of Young Guard foot artillery, each consisting of		
6 6-pdr. guns and 2 51/2-inch howitzers—total of 16 pieces of ordnance.		
Equipage	4 cos.	
1st Guard Infantry Division strength on 15 May 1813:		213 - 7,544
2nd Guard Infantry Division— Général de division Baron Barrois		
1st Brigade: Général de brigade Rottembourg		
1st Young Guard Tirailleurs, 1st and 2nd battalions	(2)	
6th Young Guard Tirailleurs, 1st and 2nd battalions	(2)	
7th Young Guard Tirailleurs, 1st and 2nd battalions	(2)	
2nd Brigade: Général de brigade Berthezène		
3rd Young Guard Tirailleurs, 1st and 2nd battalions	(2)	
Flanker-Grenadiers, 1st battalion	(1)	
Flanker-Chasseurs, 1st battalion	(1)	
Divisional Artillery and train:		
Two companies of Young Guard foot artillery, each consisting of		
6 6-pdr. guns and 2 51/2-inch howitzers—total of 16 pieces of ordnance.		
Equipage	4 cos.	
2nd Guard Infantry Division strength of 15 May 1813:		139 - 4,765

Appendix C
Situation of the Reorganized Imperial Guard Corps—15 May 1813

Old Guard Infantry Division— Général de division Baron Rouget
1st Brigade: Général de brigade Decouz
    1st Old Guard Grenadiers, 1st battalion (1)
    2nd Old Guard Grenadiers, 1st and 2nd battalions (2)
2nd Brigade: Général de brigade Michel
    1st Old Guard Chasseurs, 1st battalion (1)
    2nd Old Guard Chasseurs, 1st and 2nd battalions (2)
3rd Brigade: Général de brigade Boyeldieu
    Vélites of Florence (1)
    Vélites of Turin (1)
Divisional Artillery and train:
    One company of Old Guard foot artillery consisting of
    6 6-pdr. guns and 2 5 1/2-inch howitzers—total of 8 pieces of ordnance.
Old Guard Infantry Division strength as of 15 May 1813:   123 - 3,355

1st Gd Cav Division—Général de division Count Lefebvre-Desnouëttes
Light Lancers of Berg, 1st, 3rd, and 4th squadrons (3)
1st (Polish) Old Guard Light Lancers, 1st, 2nd and 3rd sqdrns (3)
2nd (Red) Guard Light Lancers, 1st—6th squadrons (6)
Young Guard 1st Light Lancers, 1st—4th squadrons (4)
1st Guard Cavalry Division strength as of 15 May 1813:   2,982*

2nd Guard Cavalry Division— Général de division Count Walther
Old Guard Chasseurs à Cheval, 1st, 2nd, 3rd, and 4th sqdrns. (4)
Old Guard Grenadiers à Cheval, 1st, 2nd, 3rd, and 4th sqdrns. (4)
Guard Dragoons, 1st, 2nd, 3rd, and 4th squadrons (4)
Gendarmes d'élite, 1st and 2nd squadrons (2)
Young Guard squadrons, Chasseurs à Cheval (5)
Young Guard squadrons, Grenadiers à Cheval (2)
Young Guard squadrons, Guard Dragoons (2)
2nd Guard Cavalry Division strength as of 15 May 1813:   3,774*

Imperial Guard Artillery Reserve—
Four companies of Old Guard foot artillery, each company consisting of
    6 12-pdr. guns and 2 6-inch howitzers.
One company of Old Guard foot artillery consisting of 6 6-pdr. guns and
    2 5 1/2-inch howitzers.
Three companies of Old Guard horse artillery, each company consisting of
    4 6-pdr. guns and 2 5 1/2-inch howitzers.
Two companies of Young Guard foot artillery, each company consisting of
    6 6-pdr. guns and 2 5 1/2-inch howitzers.
One-half company of Berg horse artillery consisting of 2 6-pdr. guns—total of 76 pieces.
Pontoniers, Ouvriers   2 cos.
Marins of the Guard; Engineers of the Guard   2 cos.
Equipage   6 cos.
Artillery Reserve of the Guard strength as of 15 May 1813:   1,970*
*These totals are officers and other ranks combined.

Total strength of all Imperial Guard officers and other ranks
    present and under arms as of 15 May 1813:   24,865 with 116 guns

SITUATION
of the
GRANDE ARMÉE
15 August 1813

His Majesty
The Emperor Napoleon I, commanding in person

The Emperor's Military Household

Aides-de-Camp to His Majesty
Général de division Count Caffarelli (in Paris)
Général de division Count Lemarois (in Magdébourg)
Général de division Count Rapp (in Danzig)
Général de division Count Lebrun, Duke of Plaisance
Général de division Mouton, Count of Lobau
Général de division Count Durosnel
Général de division Count Hogendorp (in Hamburg)
Général de division Baron Corbineau
Général de division Baron Flahault de la Billarderie
Général de brigade Baron Dejean*
Général de division Baron Drouot
Général de brigade Baron Gueheneue
Colonel of Engineers Bernard
*Nominal Commander of the Guards of Honor Cavalry Division

Ordnance Officers Attending His Majesty
Chef d'escadron Baron Gourgaud, chief ordnance officer
Captain Baron Atthalin
Captain de Caraman
Captain Baron Desaix
Captain d'Hautpoul
Captain Lamezan
Captain Baron Laplace
Captain Baron de Lauriston
Captain Pailhou
Captain Saint-Jacques

* *

The Imperial Staff

Major Général of the Army—Marshal Berthier, Prince de Neuchâtel and of Wagram

Chief of the General Staff

Général de division Count Bailly de Mouthion

Deputy Chiefs of the General Staff

Général de brigade de Lagrange
Général de brigade Durieu
Général de brigade Radet, commanding the Imperial Gendarmes
Colonel Bonne, Chief of the Topographical Service

General Officers attached to the Imperial Staff

Généraux de division—Lefol
Cassagne
Decouz
Gomes-Freyre

Généraux de brigade—Estève
Thomas
Dellard
Latour

Artillery

Général de division Count Sorbier, Commander of the Artillery
Général de division Ruty, Chief of Staff
Général de brigade Neigre, Director of the Artillery Parks
Général de brigade Bouchu, Commander of the Bridge Train

Engineers

Général de brigade Rogniat, Commander of the Engineers
Colonel Montfort, Chief of Staff
Chef de bataillon Finot, General Director of the Park

Equipage

Général de brigade Picard, Inspector General of the Equipage Park

General Administration of the Army

Count Daru, Director of the Administration of the Army
Count Dumas, Intendent General of the Army
Ordonnateurs cu chef Joinville
Marchand
Martelliere
Lambert, Inspector of Reviews
Général de division Sahuc, Inspector of the depots and hospitals

Administrative Service

Inspector general and chief medical officer: Desgenettes
Inspector general and chief surgeon: Larrey
Inspector general and chief pharmacist: Laubert

	Number of Battalions/ Squadrons	Present and Under Arms Off.- Others

IMPERIAL GUARD
Marshal Mortier, Duke of Treviso
Généraux de division Count Nansouty and Walther,
commanding the cavalry of the Guard
Général de division Count Dulauloy, commanding the artillery of the Guard
Général de brigade Baron Desvaux de Saint-Maurice, Horse Artillery of the Guard
Général de division Baron Haxo, commanding the engineers of the Guard
Corps headquarters staff—24 personnel

1st Old Guard Division— Général de division Count Friant
Division headquarters staff—11 personnel
1st Brigade: Général de division Baron Curial

1st Old Guard Chasseurs à pied, 1st battalion	(1)	23 - 648
2nd battalion	(1)	14 - 599
2nd Old Guard Chasseurs à pied, 1st battalion	(1)	26 - 414
2nd battalion	(1)	14 - 195

2nd Brigade: Général de brigade Baron Michel

1st Old Guard Grenadiers à pied, 1st battalion	(1)	25 - 525
2nd battalion	(1)	17 - 587
2nd Old Guard Grenadiers à pied, 1st battalion	(1)	25 - 461
2nd battalion	(1)	8 - 333
Vélites of Florence	(1)	25 - 403
Vélites of Turin	(1)	25 - 438

Divisional artillery and train:

Old Guard Foot Artillery, 1st company, consisting of		4 - 112
6 6-pdr. guns and 2 5 1/2-inch howitzers—total of 8 pieces of ordnance.		
1st Regiment of Artillery Train of the Guard, 6th company		1 - 100

1st Young Guard Division— Général de division Count Dumoustier
Division headquarters staff—11 personnel
1st Brigade: (no commander listed)

Middle Guard Fusilier Chasseurs, 1st battalion	(1)	21 - 607
2nd battalion	(1)	16 - 722
Middle Guard Fusilier Grenadiers, 1st battalion	(1)	23 - 586
2nd battalion	(1)	18 - 604

2nd Brigade: Général de brigade Tindal

1st Young Guard Voltigeurs, 1st battalion	(1)	19 - 527
2nd battalion	(1)	11 - 498
2nd Young Guard Voltigeurs, 1st battalion	(1)	21 - 444
2nd battalion	(1)	12 - 458

3rd Brigade: (no commander listed)

3rd Young Guard Voltigeurs, 1st battalion	(1)	19 - 704
2nd battalion	(1)	13 - 672
6th Young Guard Voltigeurs, 1st battalion	(1)	20 - 665
2nd battalion	(1)	17 - 665

7th Young Guard Voltigeurs, 1st battalion	(1)	19 - 620
2nd battalion	(1)	12 - 577

Divisional artillery and train:

Young Guard Foot Artillery, 1st company	3 - 116
2nd company	3 - 120
8th company	3 - 125

Each company of Young Guard foot artillery consisted of
6 6-pdr. guns and 2 5 1/2-inch howitzers—total of 24 pieces of ordnance.

1st Regiment of Artillery Train of the Guard, 4th company, and	3 - 283
2nd Regiment of Artillery Train of the Guard, 3rd company.	
Equipage Train of the Guard, 1st company	3 - 124

2nd Young Guard Division— Général de division Baron Barrois

Division headquarters staff—10 personnel
1st Brigade: Général de brigade Poret

1st Young Guard Tirailleurs, 1st battalion	(1)	22 - 547
2nd battalion,	(1)	13 - 497
2nd Young Guard Tirailleurs, 1st battalion	(1)	18 - 489
2nd battalion	(1)	11 - 474

2nd Brigade: (no commander listed)

3rd Young Guard Tirailleurs, 1st battalion	(1)	18 - 632
2nd battalion	(1)	12 - 672
6th Young Guard Tirailleurs, 1st battalion	(1)	18 - 492
2nd battalion	(1)	12 - 480
7th Young Guard Tirailleurs, 1st battalion	(1)	19 - 651
2nd battalion	(1)	11 - 512

3rd Brigade: Général de brigade Boyeldieu

Flanker Chasseurs, 1st battalion	(1)	18 - 601
2nd battalion	(1)	12 - 578
Flanker Grenadiers, 1st battalion	(1)	23 - 681
2nd battalion	(1)	12 - 661

Divisional artillery and train:

Young Guard Foot Artillery, 3rd company	3 - 89
4th company	3 - 100
12th company	1 - 108

Each company of Young Guard foot artillery consisted of
6 6-pdr. guns and 2 5 1/2-inch howitzers—total of 24 pieces of ordnance.

1st Regiment of Artillery Train of the Guard, 9th company, and	2 - 288
2nd Regiment of Artillery Train of the Guard, 9th company.	
7th Battalion, Sappers of the Line, 3rd company	3 - 137
Equipage Train of the Guard, 7th company	1 - 115

3rd Young Guard Division— Général de division Count Delaborde

Division headquarters staff—14 personnel
1st Brigade: Général de brigade Gros

4th Young Guard Voltigeurs, 1st battalion	(1)	19 - 649
2nd battalion	(1)	13 - 594
5th Young Guard Voltigeurs, 1st battalion	(1)	23 - 595
2nd battalion	(1)	12 - 694

2nd Brigade: Général de brigade Combelle

8th Young Guard Voltigeurs, 1st battalion	(1)	19 - 703
2nd battalion	(1)	11 - 667
9th Young Guard Voltigeurs, 1st battalion	(1)	21 - 717
2nd battalion	(1)	11 - 685
10th Young Guard Voltigeurs, 1st battalion	(1)	18 - 725
2nd battalion	(1)	12 - 715

3rd Brigade: Général de brigade Dulong

11th Young Guard Voltigeurs, 1st battalion	(1)	19 - 556
2nd battalion	(1)	9 - 550
12th Young Guard Voltigeurs, 1st and 2nd battalions	organizing in Mayence	

Divisional artillery and train:

Young Guard Foot Artillery, 5th company	3 - 96
6th company	2 - 92
7th company	3 - 90

Each company of Young Guard foot artillery consisting of
6 6-pdr. guns and 2 5½-inch howitzers—total of 24 pieces of ordnance.

2nd Regiment of Artillery Train of the Guard, 1st company and 2nd companies	2 - 257

4th Young Guard Division— Général de division Count Roguet
Division headquarters staff—11 personnel

1st Brigade: Général de brigade Boyer de Rébéval

4th Young Guard Tirailleurs, 1st battalion	(1)	21 - 610
2nd battalion	(1)	10 - 599
5th Young Guard Tirailleurs, 1st battalion	(1)	17 - 653
2nd battalion	(1)	11 - 593

2nd Brigade: (no commander listed)

8th Young Guard Tirailleurs, 1st battalion	(1)	19 - 651
2nd battalion	(1)	13 - 624
9th Young Guard Tirailleurs, 1st battalion	(1)	16 - 650
2nd battalion	(1)	12 - 566
10th Young Guard Tirailleurs, 1st and 2nd battalions	(2)	29 - 1,545

3rd Brigade: Général de brigade Pelet

11th Young Guard Tirailleurs, 1st and 2nd battalions	(2)	28 - 1,227
12th Young Guard Tirailleurs, 1st and 2nd battalions	organizing in Paris	

Divisional artillery and train:

Young Guard Foot Artillery, 9th company	2 - 102
10th company	1 - 104
11th company	1 - 103

Each company of Young Guard foot artillery consisted of
6 6-pdr. guns and 2 5½-inch howitzers—total of 24 pieces of ordnance.

2nd Regiment of Artillery Train of the Guard, 4th company and 5th companies	2 - 325

1st Imperial Guard Cavalry Division— Général de division Count

1st Brigade: **Lefebvre-Desnoëttes**

Light Lancers of Berg, 1st, 3rd, and 4th squadrons	(3)	31 - 568
5th squadron—in route	(1)	9 - 226
6th squadron—in route	(1)	9 - 226

The 2nd squadron was not present with the rest of the regiment.

2nd Brigade: Général de brigade Baron de Colbert

2nd (Red) Light Lancers of the Guard, 1st—10th squadrons	(10)	70 - 1,506

3rd Brigade: Général de brigade Count Krasinski

1st (Polish) Old Guard Light Lancers of the Guard	(3)	83 - 1,300
Young Guard squadrons, 1st Light Lancers of the Guard	(4)	incl. above

2nd Imperial Guard Cavalry Division— Général de division Count Ornano

1st Brigade: Général de brigade Guyot

Old Guard Chasseurs à Cheval, 1st—4th squadrons	(4)	90 - 1,747
Young Guard squadrons, Guard Chasseurs à Cheval	(5)	incl. above

2nd Brigade: Général de brigade Baron Letort

Guard Dragoons, 1st, 2nd, 3rd, and 4th squadrons	(4)	64 - 1,301
Young Guard squadrons, Guard Dragoons	(2)	incl. above

3rd Brigade: Général de brigade Castex

Old Guard Grenadiers à Cheval, 1st—4th squadrons	(4)	63 - 1,209
Young Guard squadrons, Grenadiers à Cheval	(2)	incl above

4th Brigade: Général de brigade Durosnel

Gendarmes d'élite, 1st and 2nd squadrons	(2)	17 - 493

Guards of Honor Cavalry Division— Général de brigade Baron Dejean

1st Regiment, Guards of Honor, 1st squadron	(1)	11 - 254
2nd squadron	(1)	3 - 236
3rd squadron	(1)	5 - 240
4th squadron	(1)	5 - 245
5th squadron	(1)	8 - 238
2nd Regiment, Guards of Honor, 1st squadron	(1)	4 - 250
2nd squadron	(1)	4 - 252
3rd squadron	(1)	8 - 247
4th squadron	(1)	4 - 239
5th squadron	(1)	2 - 247
3rd Regiment, Guards of Honor, 1st squadron	(1)	4 - 226
2nd squadron	(1)	6 - 243
3rd squadron	(1)	4 - 236
4th squadron	(1)	4 - 245
5th squadron	(1)	3 - 247
4th Regiment, Guards of Honor, 1st squadron	(1)	2 - 246
2nd squadron	(1)	6 - 285
3rd squadron	(1)	6 - 289
4th squadron	(1)	4 - 238
5th squadron	(1)	2 - 239

Note: The above parade states list all of the 20 squadrons comprising the
Guards of Honor as of 15 August 1813. However, many of these squadrons were
not with their parent regiments, but were in route to join their commands.
All squadrons of the Guards of Honor finally arrived for service during September.

Horse Artillery of the Guard attached to the Guard Cavalry—

Headquarters staff—8 personnel	
Old Guard Horse Artillery, 1st company	3 - 88
2nd company	3 - 84
3rd company	2 - 83
4th company	2 - 87

Each company of Old Guard Horse Artillery consisted of
4 6-pdr. guns and 2 51/2-inch howitzers—total of 24 pieces of ordnance.

Horse Artillery Train, 1st squadron, 1st company	1 - 144
detachment of the 4th company	1 - 13
Horse Artillery Train, 2nd squadron, 12th company	1 - 133
Horse Artillery Train, 3rd squadron, 10th company	1 - 69
11th company	1 - 71
Ouvriers of the Artillery of the Guard	- 7

Artillery Reserve of the Guard—

Old Guard Foot Artillery, 2nd company	3 - 116
3rd company	3 - 115
4th company	4 - 122
5th company	3 - 124

The above Old Guard foot artillery companies each consisted of
6 12-pdr. guns and 2 6-inch howitzers—total of 32 pieces of ordnance.

Old Guard Foot Artillery, 6th company, consisting of	3 - 115
6 6-pdr. guns and 2 51/2-inch howitzers—total of 8 pieces of ordnance.	
Young Guard Foot Artillery, 13th company	2 - 116
14th company	2 - 84
15th company	2 - 115
16th company	2 - 116

The above Young Guard foot artillery companies each consisted of
6 6-pdr. guns and 2 51/2-inch howitzers—total of 32 pieces of ordnance.

Old Guard Horse Artillery, 5th company	3 - 85
6th company	2 - 85

The above Old Guard horse artillery companies each consisted of
4 6-pdr. guns and 2 51/2-inch howitzers—total of 12 pieces of ordnance.

Grand Duchy of Berg Horse Artillery, consisting of 4 6-pdr. guns	4 - 88
and 2 51/2-inch howitzers—total of 6 pieces of ordnance.	

There was a total of 90 pieces of ordnance in the Artillery Reserve of the Guard.

Pontoniers of the Guard	4 - 128
Sappers (Engineers) of the Guard, 1 company	4 - 219
Marins of the Guard, 1 company	3 - 71
Marins of the Italian Royal Guard, 1 company	3 - 103
Marins of the Neapolitan Guard, 1 company	3 - 58
1st Regiment of Artillery Train of the Guard, 2nd company	1 - 139
3rd company	1 - 99
5th company	1 - 127
7th company	1 - 139
8th company	1 - 139
10th company	1 - 69
11th company	1 - 69
2nd Regiment of Artillery Train of the Guard, 6th—8th, 10th—12th cos.	25 - 1,610

Duchy of Berg Artillery Train		3 - 122
Sapper (Engineer) Train of the Guard		1 - 39
Equipage Train of the Guard, 2nd, 3rd, 4th, 5th, 6th, 8th, 9th, 10th, 11th, and 12th companies		20 - 1,246
Ouvriers of administration, 3 companies		17 - 577

I CORPS

Général de division Vandamme, Count of Unsebourg

Général de brigade Revest, Chief of Staff
Général de brigade Baltus, commanding the artillery
Chef de bataillon Moras, commanding the engineers
Corps headquarters staff—11 personnel

1st Division— Général de division Baron Philippon

Division headquarters staff—9 personnel
1st Brigade: Général de brigade Ponchelon

7th Light Infantry Regiment, 1st battalion	(1)	32 - 708
2nd battalion	(1)	17 - 639
3rd battalion	(1)	15 - 682
4th battalion	(1)	19 - 658
12th Regiment of the Line, 1st battalion	(1)	39 - 821
2nd battalion	(1)	18 - 698
3rd battalion,	(1)	17 - 781
4th battalion	(1)	18 - 618

2nd Brigade: Général de brigade Raymond de Montesquiou, Duke of Fezensac

17th Regiment of the Line, 1st battalion	(1)	32 - 775
2nd battalion	(1)	18 - 536
3rd battalion	(1)	17 - 629
4th battalion	(1)	15 - 650
36th Regiment of the Line, 3rd battalion	(1)	21 - 680
4th battalion	(1)	20 - 453

Divisional artillery and train:

2nd Regiment of Foot Artillery, 8th company	2 - 82
9th Regiment of Foot Artillery, 15th company	4 - 59

The above foot artillery companies each consisted of
6 6-pdr. guns and 2 51/2-inch howitzers—total of 16 pieces of ordnance.

4th Principal Artillery Train Battalion, detachment	- 28
9th Principal Artillery Train Battalion, 3rd company	1 - 127

2nd Division— Général de division Dumonceau

Division headquarters staff—9 personnel
1st Brigade: Général de brigade Dunesme

13th Light Infantry Regiment, 1st battalion	(1)	25 - 744
2nd battalion	(1)	22 - 587
3rd battalion	(1)	18 - 740
4th battalion	(1)	17 - 648
25th Regiment of the Line, 1st battalion	(1)	33 - 760
2nd battalion	(1)	17 - 589
3rd battalion	(1)	18 - 730
4th battalion	(1)	17 - 715

2nd Brigade: Général de brigade Doucet
  57th Regiment of the Line, 1st battalion   (1)   36 - 799
    2nd battalion   (1)   30 - 699
    3rd battalion   (1)   16 - 750
    4th battalion   (1)   22 - 725
  51st Regiment of the Line, 3rd battalion   (1)   24 - 705
    4th battalion   (1)   17 - 723
Divisional artillery and train:
  3rd Regiment of Foot Artillery, 23rd company   4 - 63
    24th company   2 - 57
  The above foot artillery companies each consisted of
  6 6-pdr. guns and 2 51/2-inch howitzers—total of 16 pieces of ordnance.
  1st Principal Artillery Train Battalion, 1st company   2 - 153
  8th Principal Artillery Train Battalion, detachment   - 28

23rd Division— Général de division Baron Teste
Division headquarters staff—6 personnel
1st Brigade: Général de brigade O'Meara
  21st Regiment of the Line, 1st battalion   (1)   29 - 617
    2nd battalion   (1)   18 - 599
    3rd battalion   (1)   20 - 820
    4th battalion   (1)   18 - 565
  33rd Regiment of the Line, 1st battalion   (1)   24 - 689
    2nd battalion   (1)   21 - 697
    3rd battalion   (1)   20 - 759
    4th battalion   (1)   19 - 587
2nd Brigade: Général de brigade Quiot du Passage
  85th Regiment of the Line, 1st battalion   (1)   24 - 681
    2nd battalion   (1)   19 - 673
    3rd battalion   (1)   19 - 824
    4th battalion   (1)   25 - 645
  55th Regiment of the Line, 3rd battalion   (1)   19 - 531
    4th battalion   (1)   22 - 741
Divisional artillery and train:
  4th Regiment of Foot Artillery, 5th company,   3 - 53
    21st company   3 - 72
  The 5th company consisted of 4 6-pdr. guns and 2 51/2-inch
  howitzers; the 21st company consisted of 6 6-pdr. guns and
  2 51/2-inch howitzers—total of 14 pieces of ordnance.
  9th Principal Artillery Train Battalion, detachment   1 - 79
  1st *bis* Artillery Train Battalion, detachment   1 - 109

27th Division(-) (attached to I Corps)— Général de division Dombrowski
Division headquarters staff—13 personnel
1st (Infantry) Brigade: Général de brigade Zottowski
  2nd Polish Regiment of the Line, 1st battalion   (1)   31 - 369
    2nd battalion   (1)   21 - 340
  14th Polish Regiment of the Line, 1st battalion   (1)   30 - 383
    2nd battalion   (1)   23 - 245

Cavalry Brigade (attached from IV Reserve Cavalry Corps/7th Lt Cav Div):

2nd Polish Uhlans, 1st squadron	(1)	14 - 170
2nd squadron	(1)	7 - 146
3rd squadron	(1)	5 - 143
4th squadron	(1)	9 - 145
4th Polish Uhlans, 1st squadron	(1)	17 - 158
2nd squadron	(1)	6 - 129
3rd squadron	(1)	7 - 141
4th squadron	(1)	8 - 141

Divisional artillery and train(-):

Polish Horse Artillery company, consisting of 4 6-pdr. guns 8 - 88
and 2 51/2-inch howitzers—total of 6 pieces of ordnance.
Polish Artillery Train   - 70

I Corps Cavalry Brigade— Général de brigade Gobrecht

Corps cavalry brigade staff—1 person

9th (Hamburg) Light Lancers, 1st squadron	(1)	8 - 154
2nd squadron	(1)	9 - 179
Anhalt Chasseurs à Cheval, 1st squadron	(1)	12 - 243
2nd squadron	(1)	7 - 233

I Corps Artillery Reserve—

Corps artillery reserve staff—1 person

7th Regiment of Foot Artillery, 6th company	2 - 88
8th Regiment of Foot Artillery, 9th company	3 - 105
4th Regiment of Horse Artillery, 2nd company	4 - 92
6th Regiment of Horse Artillery, 5th company	3 - 93

Each of the above foot artillery companies consisted of 7 12-pdr. guns
and 1 51/2-inch howitzer; each of the above horse artillery companies
consisted of 4 6-pdr. guns and 2 51/2-inch howitzers—total of 28 pieces
of ordnance in I Corps Artillery Reserve.

7th Principal Artillery Train Battalion, detachment of 4th company	- 15
9th Principal Artillery Train Battalion, detachment of 1st company	1 - 129
13th Principal Artillery Train Battalion, 2nd company	1 - 158
3rd Battalion, Sappers of the Line, 5th company	3 - 126
7th company	3 - 125
13th Battalion of Equipage Train, detachment of 1st company	1 - 51
14th Battalion of Equipage Train, 4th company	2 - 139

I Corps troops in route to join their regiments—

Detachments of the:

7th Regiment of Light Infantry	1 - 111
57th Regiment of the Line	1 - 196
17th Regiment of the Line	1 - 62
33rd Regiment of the Line	2 - 115
36th Regiment of the Line	6 - 319
85th Regiment of the Line	2 - 71
25th Regiment of the Line	1 - 54
55th Regiment of the Line	1 - 237
13th Light Infantry Regiment	2 - 250

II CORPS
Marshal Victor, Duke of Belluno
Général de brigade Baron Montgenet, commanding the artillery
Major Bron, commanding the engineers
Corps headquarters staff—29 personnel

4th Division— Général de division Dubreton
Division headquarters staff—11 personnel
1st Brigade: Général de brigade Ferriere

24th Light Infantry Regiment, 1st battalion	(1)	23 - 775
2nd battalion	(1)	21 - 591
3rd battalion	(1)	21 - 820
4th battalion	(1)	21 - 542
19th Regiment of the Line, 1st battalion	(1)	28 - 746
2nd battalion	(1)	17 - 607
3rd battalion	(1)	22 - 877
4th battalion	(1)	18 - 596

2nd Brigade: Général de brigade Brun

37th Regiment of the Line, 1st battalion	(1)	32 - 576
2nd battalion	(1)	16 - 465
3rd battalion	(1)	15 - 318
56th Regiment of the Line, 1st battalion	(1)	25 - 737
2nd battalion	(1)	21 - 606
3rd battalion	(1)	20 - 805
4th battalion	(1)	21 - 587

Divisional artillery and train:

2nd Regiment of Foot Artillery, 7th company	3 - 92
4th Regiment of Foot Artillery, 11th company	3 - 99

The above foot artillery companies each consisted of
6 6-pdr. guns and 2 51/2-inch howitzers—total of 16 pieces of ordnance.

11th Principal Artillery Train Battalion, detachment of the 1st company	1 - 89
12th Principal Artillery Train Battalion, detachment of the 3rd company	- 21
3rd *bis* Artillery Train Battalion, detachment of the 2nd company	1 - 79

5th Division— Général de division Baron Dufour
Division headquarters staff—7 personnel
1st Brigade: Général de brigade d'Estko

26th Light Infantry Regiment, 1st battalion	(1)	17 - 722
2nd battalion	(1)	16 - 572
3rd battalion	(1)	21 - 820
4th battalion	(1)	18 - 667
93rd Regiment of the Line, 1st battalion	(1)	23 - 648
2nd battalion	(1)	21 - 455
4th battalion	(1)	23 - 491

2nd Brigade: Général de brigade Prince of Reuss

46th Regiment of the Line, 1st battalion	(1)	20 - 693
2nd battalion	(1)	21 - 644
4th battalion	(1)	20 - 572
72nd Regiment of the Line, 1st battalion	(1)	22 - 817

2nd battalion	(1)	20 - 519
3rd battalion	(1)	20 - 804
4th battalion	(1)	21 - 669

Divisional artillery and train:

5th Regiment of Foot Artillery, 13th company		3 - 59
8th Regiment of Foot Artillery, 12th company		4 - 58

The 5/13th company consisted of 6 6-pdr. guns and 2 5 1/2-inch howitzers; the 8/12th company consisted of 4 6-pdr. guns and 2 5 1/2-inch howitzers—total of 14 pieces of ordnance.

Artillery Train, detachments from various battalions and companies	1 - 180

6th Division— Général de division Baron Vial

Division headquarters staff—11 personnel

1st Brigade: Général de brigade Valory

11th Light Infantry Regiment, 1st battalion	(1)	29 - 689
2nd battalion	(1)	18 - 500
4th battalion	(1)	21 - 579
2nd Regiment of the Line, 1st battalion	(1)	31 - 688
2nd battalion	(1)	18 - 533
4th battalion	(1)	17 - 544

2nd Brigade: Général de brigade Bronikowski

4th Regiment of the Line, 1st battalion	(1)	29 - 710
2nd battalion	(1)	16 - 594
4th battalion	(1)	18 - 470
18th Regiment of the Line, 1st battalion	(1)	24 - 777
2nd battalion	(1)	21 - 505
3rd battalion	(1)	18 - 809
4th battalion	(1)	19 - 576

Divisional artillery and train:

3rd Regiment of Foot Artillery, 25th company		3 - 64
26th company		3 - 72

The above foot artillery companies each consisted of 6 6-pdr. guns and 2 5 1/2-inch howitzers—total of 16 pieces of ordnance.

12th Principal Artillery Train Battalion, detachment of 4th company	- 15
14th Principal Artillery Train Battalion, detachment of 3rd company	1 - 107

II Corps Cavalry Brigade— Colonel Hammerstein

Corps cavalry brigade staff—1 person

1st Westphalian Hussars, 1st, 2nd, and 3rd squadrons	(3)	27 - 392
2nd Westphalian Hussars, 1st, 2nd, and 3rd squadrons	(3)	22 - 340

II Corps Artillery Reserve—

Corps artillery reserve staff—1 person

2nd Regiment of Foot Artillery, 9th company	3 - 76
6th Regiment of Foot Artillery, 10th company	3 - 93
2nd Regiment of Horse Artillery, 1st company	3 - 82
3rd Regiment of Horse Artillery, 4th company	2 - 90

The 6/10th foot artillery company consisted of 8 12-pdr. guns;
the 2/9th foot artillery company personnel were in the II Corps
grand park of artillery and had no ordnance attached;
the 2/1st and the 3/4th horse companies each consisted of 4 6-pdr. guns and

2 5$1/2$-inch howitzers—total of 20 pieces of ordnance in II Corps Artillery Reserve.

1st Principal Artillery Train Battalion, detachment of the 3rd company	1 - 25
9th Principal Artillery Train Battalion, detachment of the 2nd company	1 - 58
14th Principal Artillery Train Battalion, detachment of the 2nd company	1 - 114
3rd *bis* Artillery Train Battalion, 3rd company	1 - 59
11th *bis* Artillery Train Battalion, 2nd company	1 - 63
2nd Battalion, Sappers of the Line, 2nd company	3 - 137
3rd Battalion, Sappers of the Line, 3rd company	3 - 118
5th Battalion, Sappers of the Line, 3rd company	3 - 114

II Corps troops in route to join their regiments—
Detachments of the:

18th Regiment of the Line	3 - 173
19th Regiment of the Line	3 - 161
11th Light Infantry Regiment	1 - 50
4th Regiment of the Line	3 - 122
26th Light Infantry Regiment	6 - 260
93rd Regiment of the Line	1 - 131
24th Light Infantry Regiment	4 - 621

III CORPS

Marshal Ney, Prince of the Moscowa

Général de brigade Baron Tarayre, Chief of Staff
Général de division Charbonnel, commanding the artillery
Colonel Valzé, commanding the engineers
Corps headquarters staff—48 personnel

8th Division— Général de division Count Souham
Division headquarters staff—13 personnel
1st Brigade: Général de brigade Brayer
6th Provisional Light Infantry Regiment, consisting of

2nd battalion, 6th Light Infantry Regiment	(1)	24 - 670
3rd battalion, 25th Light Infantry Regiment	(1)	20 - 532

10th Provisional Light Infantry Regiment, consisting of

3rd battalion, 16th Light Infantry Regiment	(1)	21 - 734
1st battalion, 28th Light Infantry Regiment	(1)	21 - 593

14th Provisional Regiment of the Line, consisting of

4th battalion, 34th Regiment of the Line	(1)	24 - 402
1st battalion, 40th Regiment of the Line	(1)	22 - 389

19th Provisional Regiment of the Line, consisting of

6th battalion, 32nd Regiment of the Line	(1)	22 - 464
2nd battalion, 58th Regiment of the Line	(1)	21 - 560

2nd Brigade: Général de brigade Charrière
21st Provisional Regiment of the Line, consisting of

3rd battalion, 59th Regiment of the Line	(1)	19 - 651
4th battalion, 69th Regiment of the Line	(1)	22 - 496

24th Provisional Regiment of the Line, consisting of

3rd battalion, 88th Regiment of the Line	(1)	21 - 354
3rd battalion, 103rd Regiment of the Line	(1)	17 - 433

22nd Regiment of the Line, 1st battalion	(1)	21 - 481
2nd battalion	(1)	17 - 443
3rd battalion	(1)	14 - 492
Divisional artillery and train:		
2nd Regiment of Foot Artillery, 10th company		2 - 70
9th Regiment of Foot Artillery, detachment of 3rd company		1 - 35

The 2/10th foot artillery company consisted of 6 6-pdr. guns and
2 5 1/2-inch howitzers; the 9/3rd detachment fielded 3 6-pdr. guns
and 1 5 1/2-inch howitzer—total of 12 pieces of ordnance.

9th Principal Artillery Train Battalion, detachment of 3rd company		2 - 98
3rd *bis* Artillery Train Battalion, detachment of 4th company		1 - 60

9th Division— Général de division Delmas

Division headquarters staff—9 personnel

1st Brigade: Général de brigade Anthing

2nd Provisional Light Infantry Regiment, consisting of

3rd battalion, 2nd Light Infantry Regiment	(1)	19 - 402
3rd battalion, 4th Light Infantry Regiment	(1)	22 - 393
29th Light Infantry Regiment, 1st battalion	(1)	21 - 369
2nd battalion	(1)	18 - 376
136th Regiment of the Line, 1st battalion	(1)	25 - 523
2nd battalion	(1)	21 - 495
3rd battalion	(1)	30 - 518

2nd Brigade: Général de brigade Vergez

138th Regiment of the Line, 1st battalion	(1)	23 - 519
2nd battalion	(1)	19 - 486
3rd battalion	(1)	21 - 462
145th Regiment of the Line, 1st battalion	(1)	32 - 573
2nd battalion	(1)	18 - 612
3rd battalion	(1)	28 - 591

Divisional artillery and train:

9th Regiment of Foot Artillery, 2nd company		3 - 61
11th company		3 - 50

The above foot artillery companies each consisted of
6 6-pdr. guns and 2 5 1/2-inch howitzers—total of 16 pieces of ordnance.

6th Principal Artillery Train Battalion, detachment of 4th company		2 - 116
10th Principal Artillery Train Battalion, detachment of 7th company		- 12
3rd *bis* Artillery Train Battalion, detachment of 4th company		1 - 41

10th Division— Général de division Baron Albert

Division headquarters staff—14 personnel

1st Brigade: Général de brigade Van Dedem

4th Provisional Light Infantry Regiment, consisting of

4th battalion, 5th Light Infantry Regiment	(1)	24 - 476
4th battalion, 12th Light Infantry Regiment	(1)	23 - 252
139th Regiment of the Line, 1st battalion	(1)	28 - 626
2nd battalion	(1)	25 - 624
3rd battalion	(1)	25 - 653

2nd Brigade: Général de brigade Suden

140th Regiment of the Line, 1st battalion	(1)	28 - 447
2nd battalion	(1)	15 - 461

3rd battalion	(1)	16 - 473
141st Regiment of the Line,1st battalion	(1)	24 - 334
2nd battalion	(1)	21 - 325
3rd battalion	(1)	22 - 308
Divisional artillery and train:		
7th Regiment of Foot Artillery, 3rd company		3 - 81
4th company		2 - 62

The above foot artillery companies each consisted of
6 6-pdr. guns and 2 5$1/2$-inch howitzers—total of 16 pieces of ordnance.

1st Principal Artillery Train Battalion, detachment of the 4th company		1 - 129
10th Principal Artillery Train Battalion, detachment of the 7th company		- 17

11th Division— Général de division Baron Ricard
Division headquarters staff—11 personnel
1st Brigade: Général de brigade Tarayre

9th Light Infantry Regiment, 3rd battalion	(1)	20 - 370
4th battalion	(1)	20 - 304
17th Provisional Regiment of the Line, consisting of		
4th battalion, 43rd Regiment of the Line	(1)	19 - 470
3rd battalion, 75th Regiment of the Line	(1)	21 - 396
50th Regiment of the Line, 3rd battalion	(1)	23 - 509
4th battalion	(1)	21 - 467
65th Regiment of the Line, 4th battalion	(1)	19 - 294

2nd Brigade: Général de brigade Dumoulin

142nd Regiment of the Line, 1st battalion	(1)	35 - 481
2nd battalion	(1)	18 - 478
3rd battalion	(1)	19 - 496
144th Regiment of the Line, 1st battalion	(1)	33 - 556
2nd battalion	(1)	18 - 549
3rd battalion	(1)	27 - 636
Divisional artillery and train:		
7th Regiment of Foot Artillery, 19th company		3 - 82
9th Regiment of Foot Artillery, detachment of the 5th company		2 - 45

The 7/19th foot artillery company consisted of 6 6-pdr. guns
and 2 5$1/2$-inch howitzers; the 9/5th detachment fielded
4 6-pdr. guns—total of 12 pieces of ordnance.

10th Principal Artillery Train Battalion, detachment of the 7th company		- 33
11th Principal Artillery Train Battalion, detachment of the 7th company		1 - 42
13th Principal Artillery Train Battalion, detachment of the 4th company		1 - 105

39th Division— Général de division Count Marchand
Division headquarters staff—12 personnel
1st Brigade: Général de brigade Stockhorn

1st Baden Regiment of the Line, 1st battalion	(1)	15 - 660
2nd battalion	(1)	11 - 593
3rd Baden Regiment of the Line, 1st battalion	(1)	15 - 462
2nd battalion	(1)	13 - 512

2nd Brigade: Général de brigade Prince Emile of Hesse-Darmstadt

Hesse-Darmstadt Leib-Garde Fusilier Regiment, 1st bn	(1)	17 - 502
2nd battalion	(1)	15 - 522
2nd Hesse-Darmstadt Musketeers, 1st battalion	(1)	21 - 503

2nd battalion	(1)	12 - 502
Hesse-Darmstadt Leib-Garde Regiment, 1st battalion	(1)	17 - 518
2nd battalion	(1)	16 - 517
Divisional artillery and train:		
Baden Foot Artillery, 1st company		3 - 120
Hesse-Darmstadt Foot Artillery, 1st company		6 - 226

The above foot artillery companies each consisted of
4 6-pdr. guns and 2 51/2-inch howitzers—total of 12 pieces of ordnance.

III Corps Cavalry Brigade— Général de brigade Beurmann

Corps cavalry brigade staff—2 personnel

10th Hussars, 1st squadron	(1)	15 - 191
2nd squadron	(1)	7 - 184
3rd squadron	(1)	7 - 172
4th squadron	(1)	8 - 178
5th squadron	(1)	7 - 167
6th squadron	(1)	5 - 240
Baden Light Dragoons, 1st squadron	(1)	5 - 81
2nd squadron	(1)	2 - 89
3rd squadron	(1)	2 - 96
4th squadron	(1)	3 - 88
5th squadron	(1)	2 - 110

III Corps Artillery Reserve—

Corps artillery reserve staff—5 personnel

3rd Regiment of Foot Artillery, 6th company	3 - 63
4th Regiment of Foot Artillery, 8th company	3 - 79
15th company	3 - 91
7th Regiment of Foot Artillery, 21st company	2 - 79
1st Regiment of Horse Artillery, 5th company	3 - 102
3rd Regiment of Horse Artillery, 1st company	3 - 72

The 3/6th and the 4/8th foot artillery companies each consisted of
6 12-pdr. guns and 2 6-inch howitzers; the 4/15th foot artillery
company consisted of 8 6-pdr. guns; the 7/21st foot artillery
company consisted of 6 6-pdr. guns; the 1/5th and 3/1st horse
artillery companies each consisted of 4 6-pdr. guns and 2 51/2-inch
howitzers—total of 42 pieces of ordnance in III Corps Artillery Reserve.

1st Principal Artillery Train Battalion, detachment of the 2nd company	2 - 138
detachment of the 3rd company	1 - 102
detachment of the 4th company	- 17
5th Principal Artillery Train Battalion, detachment of the 7th company	2 - 77
6th Principal Artillery Train Battalion, detachment of the 2nd company	1 - 91
8th Principal Artillery Train Battalion, detachment of the 4th company	1 - 16
10th Principal Artillery Train Battalion, detachment of the 3rd company	1 - 102
detachment of the 7th company	1 - 29
3rd *bis* Artillery Train Battalion, detachment of the 3rd company	1 - 54
9th *bis* Artillery Train Battalion, detachment of the 2nd company	1 - 94
Spanish Sappers, 1st company	5 - 152
2nd company	3 - 128
3rd company	3 - 117
4th company	2 - 149

Situation of the Grande Armée—15 August 1813

6th Battalion of Equipage Train, 1st company	4 - 31
2nd company	2 - 120
3rd company	1 - 28
4th company	1 - 37
5th company	1 - 121
6th company	1 - 40
Imperial Gendarmes, detachment	2 - 44

III Corps troops in route to join their regiments—
Detachments of the:

141st Regiment of the Line	6 - 366
140th Regiment of the Line	6 - 540
136th Regiment of the Line	3 - 278
142nd Regiment of the Line	3 - 390
16th Light Infantry Regiment	2 - 95
145th Regiment of the Line	11 - 601
138th Regiment of the Line	3 - 364
139th Regiment of the Line	5 - 215
144th Regiment of the Line	4 - 357
10th Hussars	2 - 104

IV CORPS
Général de division Count Bertrand
Général de brigade Delort, Chief of Staff
Général de division Baron de Taviel, commanding the artillery
Colonel Isoard, commanding the engineers
Corps headquarters staff—34 personnel

12th Division— Général de division Count Morand
Division headquarters staff—18 personnel
1st Brigade: Général de brigade de Belair

8th Light Infantry Regiment, 2nd battalion	(1)	20 - 681
4th battalion	(1)	20 - 677

2nd Brigade: Général de brigade Toussaint

13th Regiment of the Line, 1st battalion	(1)	38 - 693
2nd battalion	(1)	18 - 617
3rd battalion	(1)	16 - 642
4th battalion	(1)	17 - 674
6th battalion	(1)	18 - 606
Regimental artillery company of the 13th Line, consisting of		2 - 46
2 6-pdr. guns—total of 2 pieces of ordnance.		

3rd Brigade: Général de brigade Hulot

23rd Regiment of the Line, 1st battalion	(1)	30 - 589
2nd battalion	(1)	11 - 537
4th battalion	(1)	14 - 587
6th battalion	(1)	14 - 593
Regimental artillery company of the 23rd Line, consisting of		2 - 23
2 6-pdr. guns—total of 2 pieces of ordnance.		

Divisional artillery and train:

2nd Regiment of Foot Artillery, 1st company	3 - 70
3rd company	4 - 67
Each of the above foot artillery companies consisted of	
4 6-pdr. guns and 2 5 1/2-inch howitzers—total of 12 pieces of ordnance.	
7th *bis* Artillery Train Battalion, 1st company	1 - 117
2nd company	1 - 111

15th Division— Général de division Fontanelli

Division headquarters staff—25 personnel
1st Brigade: Général de brigade Martel

1st Italian Regiment of the Line, 3rd battalion	(1)	22 - 531
4th battalion	(1)	19 - 524
4th Italian Regiment of the Line, 2nd battalion	(1)	32 - 459
3rd battalion	(1)	22 - 421
4th battalion	(1)	22 - 435

2nd Brigade: Général de brigade Saint-Andréa

1st Italian Light Infantry Regiment, 2nd battalion	(1)	27 - 755
3rd battalion	(1)	18 - 723
4th battalion	(1)	21 - 700
6th Italian Regiment of the Line, 3rd battalion	(1)	27 - 467
4th battalion	(1)	16 - 460

3rd Brigade: Général de brigade Moroni

Milan Guard Battalion	(1)	23 - 547
7th Italian Regiment of the Line, 2nd battalion	(1)	28 - 434
3rd battalion	(1)	18 - 404
4th battalion	(1)	19 - 414

Divisional artillery and train:

Italian Regiment of Foot Artillery, 1st company	5 - 103
13th company	5 - 103

Each of the above foot artillery companies consisted of
4 6-pdr. guns and 2 51/2-inch howitzers—total of 12 pieces of ordnance.

Italian Artillery Train Battalion, 5th company	3 - 131
6th company	2 - 134
detachment of the 6th *bis* company	- 13

38th Division— Général de division de Franquemont

Division headquarters staff—12 personnel
1st Brigade: Général be brigade de Stockmayer

9th Württemberg Light Infantry Battalion	(1)	13 - 494
10th Württemberg Light Infantry Battalion	(1)	12 - 521
7th Württemberg Regiment of the Line, 1st battalion	(1)	11 - 372
2nd battalion	(1)	10 - 352

2nd Brigade: Général de brigade de Spitzenberg

1st Württemberg Regiment of the Line, 1st battalion	(1)	12 - 460
2nd battalion	(1)	11 - 431
2nd Württemberg Regiment of the Line, 1st battalion	(1)	12 - 484
2nd battalion	(1)	4 - 280

Divisional artillery and train:

Württemberg foot artillery, 1st company, consisting of	3 - 112

4 6-pdr. guns and 2 51/2-inch howitzers—total of 6 pieces of ordnance.

IV Corps Cavalry Brigade— Général de division Briche

Corps cavalry brigade staff—2 persons

1st Württemberg Chevaulegers, 1st, 2nd, 3rd, and 4th sqdrns	(4)	18 - 384
3rd Württemberg Chevaulegers, 1st, 2nd, 3rd, and 4th sqdrns	(4)	14 - 347
Württemberg Horse Artillery, 2nd company, consisting of		3 - 114

4 6-pdr. guns and 2 51/2-inch howitzers—total of 6 pieces of ordnance.

IV Corps Artillery Reserve—

Corps artillery reserve staff—6 personnel

2nd Regiment of Foot Artillery, 24th company	3 - 81
26th company	3 - 62
4th Regiment of Foot Artillery, 25th company	3 - 73
4th Regiment of Horse Artillery, 8th company	3 - 89

The 2/24th and the 2/26th foot artillery companies each consisted of
6 12-pdr. guns; the 4/25th foot artillery company and the 4/8th horse
artillery company each consisted of 4 6-pdr. guns and 2 51/2-inch
howitzers—total of 24 pieces of ordnance in IV Corps Artillery Reserve.

7th *bis* Artillery Train Battalion, 5th company	1 - 109
6th company	1 - 152
7th company	1 - 143
11th *bis* Artillery Train Battalion, 4th company	1 - 134
Ouvriers, detachment of the 13th company	1 - 27
1st Battalion, Sappers of the Line, 2nd company	3 - 133
8th company	4 - 140
Italian Sappers, 8th company	3 - 104
Italian *Marins*, 3rd company	2 - 69
Sapper Train, detachment	- 7
9th Battalion of Equipage Train, 5th company	2 - 79
7th company	2 - 74
Italian Transports, 5th company	2 - 114

IV Corps troops in route to join their regiments—

Detachments of the:

13th Regiment of the Line	2 - 178
1st Italian Regiment of the Line	3 - 148
4th Italian Regiment of the Line	3 - 201
6th Italian Regiment of the Line	1 - 95
7th Italian Regiment of the Line	2 - 201

V CORPS

Général de division Count Lauriston
Général de brigade Baron Baillod, Chief of Staff
Général de brigade Baron Camal, commanding the artillery
Colonel Lamarre, commanding the engineers
Corps headquarters staff—38 personnel

16th Division—Général de division Baron Maison

Division headquarters staff—12 personnel
1st Brigade: Général de brigade Penne

151st Regiment of the Line, 1st—3rd battalions	—in memorial...survivors of the regiment in garrison at Glogau.	
152nd Regiment of the Line, 1st battalion	(1)	30 - 733
2nd battalion	(1)	22 - 765
3rd battalion and regimental artillery company;	(1)	20 - 782

regimental artillery consisted of 2 6-pdr. guns—total of 2 pieces of ordnance.

Situation of the Grande Armée—15 August 1813

2nd Brigade:

153rd Regiment of the Line, 1st battalion	(1)	33 - 771
2nd battalion	(1)	17 - 741
3rd battalion and regimental artillery company;	(1)	16 - 789
regimental artillery consisted of 2 6-pdr. guns—total of 2 pieces of ordnance.		
154th Regiment of the Line, 1st battalion	(1)	20 - 713
2nd battalion	(1)	19 - 659
3rd battalion and regimental artillery company;	(1)	18 - 678
regimental artillery consisted of 2 6-pdr. guns—total of 2 pieces of ordnance.		

Divisional artillery and train:

1st Regiment of Foot Artillery, 1st company	3 - 62
3rd company	2 - 87
6th Regiment of Horse Artillery, 7th company	2 - 53
Each of the above companies consisted of 4 6-pdr. guns and	
2 5 1/2-inch howitzers—total of 18 pieces of ordnance.	
2nd Principal Artillery Train Battalion, 7th company	2 - 96
1st *bis* Artillery Train Battalion, 4th company	1 - 110

17th Division— Général de division Baron Puthod

Division headquarters staff—15 personnel

1st Brigade: Général de brigade Vachot

134th Regiment of the Line, 1st battalion	(1)	28 - 585
2nd battalion and regimental artillery company;	(1)	23 - 527
regimental artillery consisted of 2 6-pdr. guns—total of 2 pieces of ordnance.		
146th Regiment of the Line, 1st battalion	(1)	43 - 718
2nd battalion	(1)	27 - 644
3rd battalion and regimental artillery company;	(1)	27 - 674
regimental artillery consisted of 2 6-pdr. guns—total of 2 pieces of ordnance.		
3rd Foreign Regiment (Irish Legion), 1st battalion	(1)	20 - 218
2nd battalion	(1)	21 - 248

2nd Brigade: Général de brigade Rosserillon

147th Regiment of the Line, 1st battalion	(1)	41 - 662
2nd battalion	(1)	25 - 637
3rd battalion and regimental artillery company;	(1)	25 - 658
regimental artillery consisted of 2 6-pdr. guns—total of 2 pieces of ordnance.		
148th Regiment of the Line, 1st battalion	(1)	42 - 667
2nd battalion	(1)	19 - 647
3rd battalion and regimental artillery company;	(1)	23 - 611
regimental artillery consisted of 2 6-pdr. guns—total of 2 pieces of ordnance.		

Divisional artillery and train:

5th Regiment of Foot Artillery, 1st company	3 - 102
11th company	3 - 92
The above foot artillery companies each consisted of	
4 6-pdr. guns and 2 5 1/2-inch howitzers—total of 12 pieces of ordnance.	
11th Principal Artillery Train Battalion, 1st company	1 - 115
detachment of another (undesignated) company	- 59

19th Division— Général de division Baron Rochambeau
Division headquarters staff—13 personnel
1st Brigade: Général de brigade Harlet
135th Regiment of the Line, 1st battalion	(1)	37 - 726
2nd battalion	(1)	17 - 674
3rd battalion and regimental artillery company;	(1)	17 - 666

regimental artillery consisted of 2 6-pdr. guns—total of 2 pieces of ordnance.
149th Regiment of the Line, 1st battalion	(1)	46 - 777
2nd battalion	(1)	17 - 716
3rd battalion and regimental artillery company;	(1)	15 - 728

regimental artillery consisted of 2 6-pdr. guns—total of 2 pieces of ordnance.
2nd Brigade: Général de brigade Lafitte
150th Regiment of the Line, 1st battalion	(1)	42 - 904
2nd battalion	(1)	18 - 874
3rd battalion and regimental artillery company;	(1)	18 - 949

regimental artillery consisted of 2 6-pdr. guns—total of 2 pieces of ordnance.
155th Regiment of the Line, 1st battalion	(1)	37 - 712
2nd battalion	(1)	19 - 673
3rd battalion and regimental artillery company;	(1)	20 - 667

regimental artillery consisted of 2 6-pdr. guns—total of 2 pieces of ordnance.
Divisional artillery and train:
5th Regiment of Foot Artillery, 12th company	3 - 86
17th company	3 - 53

The 5/12th foot artillery company consisted of 6 6-pdr. guns
and 2 51/2-inch howitzers; the 5/17th foot artillery company
consisted of 4 6-pdr. guns and 2 51/2-inch howitzers—total 14 pieces of ordnance.
4th Principal Artillery Train Battalion, 4th company	1 - 157

V Corps Artillery Reserve—
Corps artillery reserve staff—3 personnel
1st Regiment of Foot Artillery, 15th company	3 - 72
16th company	1 - 73
17th company	2 - 88
5th Regiment of Horse Artillery, 2nd company	3 - 86

The 1/16th and 1/17th foot artillery companies each consisted of
6 12-pdr. guns and 2 6-inch howitzers; the 1/15th foot artillery
company was in the corps park along with 4 51/2-inch howitzers;
the 5/2nd horse artillery company consisted of 4 6-pdr. guns and 2 51/2-inch
howitzers—total of 26 pieces of ordnance in the V Corps Artillery Reserve.
3rd Principal Artillery Train Battalion, 7th company	1 - 137
12th Principal Artillery Train Battalion, detachment	1 - 155
5th *bis* Artillery Train Battalion, 5th company	2 - 143
8th *bis* Artillery Train Battalion, 4th company	1 - 126
9th *bis* Artillery Train Battalion, 4th company	- 60
6th Battalion, Sappers of the Line, 1st company	4 - 57
2nd company	3 - 104
3rd company	3 - 93

V Corps troops in route to join their regiments—

Detachments of the:

149th Regiment of the Line	5 - 441
154th Regiment of the Line	1 - 46
152nd Regiment of the Line	1 - 200
148th Regiment of the Line	1 - 138
153rd Regiment of the Line	1 - 125
147th Regiment of the Line	2 - 310
134th Regiment of the Line	2 - 50
155th Regiment of the Line	- 122

VI CORPS
Marshal Marmont, Duke of Ragusa
Général de brigade Camus, Baron de Richemont, Chief of Staff
Général de division Baron Foucher de Careil, commanding the artillery
Major Constantin, commanding the engineers
Corps headquarters staff—39 personnel

20th Division— Général de division Count Compans

Division headquarters staff—13 personnel
1st Brigade: Général de brigade Pelleport

32nd Light Infantry Regiment, 2nd battalion	(1)	27 - 427
3rd battalion	(1)	19 - 461
1st Regiment de Marine, 1st battalion	(1)	34 - 547
2nd battalion	(1)	18 - 514
3rd battalion	(1)	19 - 517
4th battalion	(1)	18 - 545
5th battalion	(1)	13 - 705

2nd Brigade: Général de brigade Joubert
20th Provisional Regiment of the Line, consisting of

5th battalion, 66th Regiment of the Line	(1)	24 - 451
3rd battalion, 122nd Regiment of the Line	(1)	20 - 443

25th Provisional Regiment of the Line, consisting of

3rd battalion, 47th Regiment of the Line	(1)	24 - 586
3rd battalion, 86th Regiment of the Line	(1)	22 - 563
3rd Regiment de Marine, 1st battalion	(1)	26 - 736
2nd battalion	(1)	17 - 699
3rd battalion	(1)	16 - 703

Divisional artillery and train:

5th Regiment of Foot Artillery, 16th company	3 - 106
8th Regiment of Foot Artillery, 10th company	3 - 91

The above foot artillery companies each consisted of
6 6-pdr. guns and 2 5 1/2-inch howitzers—total of 16 pieces of ordnance.

4th *bis* Artillery Train Battalion, detachment of the 7th company	2 - 123
12th *bis* Artillery Train Battalion, detachment of the 7th company	1 - 121

21st Division— Général de division Count Lagrange

Division headquarters staff—14 personnel
1st Brigade: Général de brigade Jamin

37th Light Infantry Regiment, 1st battalion	(1)	30 - 647
2nd batalion	(1)	20 - 592
3rd battalion	(1)	20 - 567
4th battalion	(1)	20 - 570
Spanish Regiment Joseph Napoleon, 1st battalion	(1)	13 - 470
4th Regiment de Marine, 1st battalion	(1)	29 - 676
2nd battalion	(1)	17 - 679
3rd battalion	(1)	17 - 596

2nd Brigade: Général de brigade Buquet

2nd Regiment de Marine, 1st battalion	(1)	29 - 570
2nd battalion	(1)	16 - 535
3rd battalion	(1)	18 - 543
4th battalion	(1)	19 - 527
5th battalion	(1)	20 - 520
6th battalion	(1)	20 - 555

Divisional artillery and train:

4th Regiment of Foot Artillery, 10th company	2 - 118
9th Regiment of Foot Artillery, 7th company	3 - 78

The above foot artillery companies each consisted of
6 6-pdr. guns and 2 5 1/2-inch howitzers—total of 16 pieces of ordnance.

8th Principal Artillery Train Battalion, detachment of the 1st company	- 30
detachment of the 2nd company	1 - 167
10th *bis* Artillery Train Battalion, detachment of the 1st company	2 - 79

22nd Division— Général de division Baron Friederichs

Division headquarters staff—12 personnel
1st Brigade: Général de brigade Coëhorn
11th Provisional Regiment of the Line, consisting of

4th battalion, 1st Regiment of the Line	(1)	21 - 397
2nd battalion, 62nd Regiment of the Line	(1)	19 - 460

13th Provisional Regiment of the Line, consisting of

3rd battalion, 14th Regiment of the Line	(1)	23 - 721
4th battalion, 16th Regiment of the Line	(1)	21 - 564
23rd Light Infantry Regiment, 3rd battalion	(1)	19 - 307
4th battalion	(1)	18 - 287
15th Regiment of the Line, 3rd battalion	(1)	24 - 460
4th battalion	(1)	17 - 409

2nd Brigade: Général de brigade Bachelet
16th Provisional Regiment of the Line, consisting of

6th battalion, 26th Regiment of the Line	(1)	22 - 428
6th battalion, 82nd Regiment of the Line	(1)	19 - 279
121st Regiment of the Line, 3rd battalion	(1)	20 - 406
4th battalion	(1)	20 - 426
70th Regiment of the Line, 3rd battalion	(1)	22 - 383
4th battalion	(1)	17 - 375

Divisional artillery and train:

4th Regiment of Foot Artillery, 14th company		2 - 119
9th Regiment of Foot Artillery, 22nd company		2 - 100

The above foot artillery companies each consisted of
6 6-pdr. guns and 2 51/2-inch howitzers—total of 16 pieces of ordnance.

8th Principal Artillery Train Battalion, detachment of the 3rd company		2 - 160
10th *bis* Artillery Train Battalion, detachment of the 2nd company		1 - 98

VI Corps Cavalry Brigade— Général de brigade Normann

Corps cavalry brigade staff—3 personnel

2nd Württemberg Chevaulegers, 1st squadron	(1)	6 - 121
2nd squadron	(1)	3 - 109
3rd squadron	(1)	4 - 110
4th squadron	(1)	4 - 109
4th Württemberg Chevaulegers, 1st squadron	(1)	6 - 113
2nd squadron	(1)	3 - 105
3rd squadron	(1)	3 - 107
4th squadron	(1)	4 - 100
Württemberg Horse Artillery, 3rd company, consisting of		3 - 119

4 6-pdr. guns and 2 51/2-inch howitzers—total of 6 pieces of ordnance.

VI Corps Artillery Reserve—

Corps artillery reserve staff—4 personnel

5th Regiment of Foot Artillery, 3rd company	2 - 45
18th company	3 - 102
26th company	3 - 96
1st Regiment of Horse Artillery, 1st company	3 - 101
3rd company	3 - 91

The 5/3rd foot artillery company consisted of 4 12-pdr. guns;
the 5/18th and 5/26th foot artillery companies each consisted of
6 12-pdr. guns and 2 6-inch howitzers; the 1/1st and 1/3rd horse
artillery companies each consisted of 4 6-pdr. guns and 2 51/2-inch
howitzers—total of 32 pieces of ordnance in VI Corps Artillery Reserve.

12th Principal Artillery Train Battalion, detachment of the 4th company	1 - 107
6th *bis* Artillery Train Battalion, detachment of the 4th company	2 - 122
6th company	2 - 126
7th company	1 - 142
10th *bis* Artillery Train Battalion, 7th company	2 - 103
2nd Battalion, Sappers of the Line, 6th company	3 - 125
4th Battalion, Sappers of the Line, 2nd company	3 - 114
9th company	4 - 117
Imperial Gendarmes, detachment	2 - 37

VII CORPS
Général de division Count Reynier
Général de brigade Gressot, Chief of Staff
Colonel Verpeau, commanding the artillery
Corps headquarters staff—15 personnel

24th Division— Général de division de Lecoq
Division headquarters staff—14 personnel
1st Brigade: Colonel de Brause

Saxon Grenadier Guards	(1)	13 - 710
1st Saxon Light Infantry Regiment, 1st battalion	(1)	14 - 617
2nd battalion	(1)	12 - 604
Saxon Regiment Maximilien, 1st battalion	(1)	11 - 568
Saxon Regiment de Rechten, 2nd battalion	(1)	12 - 597
Saxon Chasseurs, 1 company		3 - 133

2nd Brigade: Général de brigade de Mellentin

Saxon Combined Grenadiers, 1st battalion	(1)	10 - 658
Saxon Regiment de Frederic, 1st battalion	(1)	9 - 369
2nd battalion	(1)	11 - 462
Saxon Regiment de Steindel, 1st battalion	(1)	16 - 575
2nd battalion	(1)	15 - 548

Divisional artillery and train:

Saxon Foot Artillery, 1st company	4 - 168
2nd company	4 - 179

Each of the above foot artillery companies consisted of
4 6-pdr. guns and 2 5$1/2$-inch howitzers—total of 12 pieces of ordnance.

Saxon Artillery Train, detachment	2 - 95

25th Division— Général de division de Sahr
Division headquarters staff—12 personnel
1st Brigade: Colonel de Bosch

Saxon Combined Grenadiers, 2nd battalion	(1)	12 - 668
2nd Saxon Light Infantry Regiment, 1st battalion	(1)	14 - 598
2nd battalion	(1)	10 - 545
Saxon Regiment du Roi, 2nd battalion	(1)	12 - 489
Saxon Regiment de Niesmenchel, 1st battalion	(1)	9 - 540

2nd Brigade: Colonel de Rissel

Saxon Regiment de Low, 1st battalion	(1)	12 - 547
2nd battalion	(1)	11 - 519
Saxon Regiment d'Antoine, 1st battalion	(1)	13 - 541
2nd battalion	(1)	12 - 520

Divisional artillery and train:

Saxon Foot Artillery, 3rd company	4 - 104
4th company	3 - 173

The above foot artillery companies each consisted of
4 6-pdr. guns and 2 5$1/2$-inch howitzers—total of 12 pieces of ordnance.

Saxon Artillery Train, detachment	2 - 73

32nd Division— Général de division Baron Durutte

Division headquarters staff—15 personnel

1st Brigade: Général de brigade Devaux

35th Light Infantry Regiment, 1st battalion	(1)	23 - 928
2nd battalion, detachment	(-)	3 - 99
4th battalion	(1)	15 - 650
132nd Regiment of the Line, 1st battalion	(1)	17 - 797
2nd battalion, detachment	(-)	2 - 91
3rd battalion	(1)	21 - 727
4th battalion	(1)	22 - 643

2nd Brigade: Général de brigade Jarry

36th Light Infantry Regiment, 1st battalion	(1)	16 - 560
2nd battalion, detachment	(-)	6 - 76
4th battalion	(1)	21 - 744
131st Regiment of the Line, 1st battalion	(1)	15 - 896
3rd battalion	(1)	20 - 762
4th battalion	(1)	18 - 774

3rd Brigade: Colonel de Lindenau

133rd Regiment of the Line, 2nd battalion detachment	(-)	2 - 53
3rd battalion	(1)	22 - 622
4th battalion	(1)	24 - 689
Würzburg Regiment, 2nd battalion	(1)	25 - 557
3rd battalion	(1)	22 - 542

Divisional artillery and train:

8th Regiment of Foot Artillery, 13th company	3 - 91
1st Regiment of Foot Artillery, 12th company	4 - 87

The above foot artillery companies each consisted of
4 6-pdr. guns and 2 5 1/2-inch howiters—total of 12 pieces of ordnance.

9th Principal Artillery Train Battalion, detachments of 2nd and 4th cos.	2 - 154
9th *bis* Artillery Train Battalion, detachment of the 2nd company	2 - 104

VII Corps Cavalry Brigade— Colonel de Lindenau

Corps cavalry brigade staff—2 personnel

Saxon Hussars, 1st squadron	(1)	5 - 96
2nd squadron	(1)	3 - 89
3rd squadron	(1)	3 - 89
4th squadron	(1)	2 - 85
5th squadron	(1)	2 - 89
6th squadron	(1)	4 - 90
7th squadron	(1)	2 - 86
8th squadron	(1)	3 - 89
Saxon Light Lancers, 1st squadron	(1)	9 - 164
2nd squadron	(1)	4 - 153
3rd squadron	(1)	3 - 152
4th squadron	(1)	5 - 142
5th squadron	(1)	5 - 147
Saxon Horse Artillery, 1st company		4 - 172
Saxon Horse Artillery, 2nd company		4 - 147

Each of the above horse artillery companies consisted of
4 6-pdr. guns and 2 5 1/2-inch howitzers—total of 12 pieces of ordnance.

VII Corps Artillery Reserve—

Corps reserve artillery staff—5 personnel

Saxon Foot Artillery, 5th company, consisting of   4 - 74
4 12-pdr. guns and 2 5 1/2-inch howitzers—total of 6 pieces of ordnance.

Saxon Artillery Train, detachment   5 - 266

Saxon Sappers, 1 company   3 - 206

VII Corps troops in route to join their regiments—

Detachments of the:

131st Regiment of the Line   2 - 226

132nd Regiment of the Line   - 80

133rd Regiment of the Line   1 - 67

VIII CORPS

Général de division Prince Poniatowski

Général de division Rozniecki, Chief of Staff
Colonel Redel, commanding the artillery
Colonel Mallet, commanding the engineers
Corps headquarters staff—32 personnel

26th Division— Général de division Kaminiecki

Division headquarters staff—16 personnel

1st Brigade: Général de brigade Sierawski

1st Polish Regiment of the Line, 1st battalion	(1)	30 - 528
2nd battalion	(1)	24 - 512
16th Polish Regiment of the Line, 1st battalion	(1)	31 - 538
2nd battalion	(1)	24 - 528

2nd Brigade: Général de brigade Matachowski

8th Polish Regiment of the Line, 1st battalion	(1)	29 - 549
2nd battalion	(1)	24 - 530
15th Polish Regiment of the Line, 1st battalion	(1)	30 - 542
2nd battalion	(1)	24 - 523

Divisional artillery and train:

Polish Foot Artillery, 5th company	7 - 132
7th company	6 - 129
18th company	6 - 133

The above foot artillery companies each consisted of
4 6-pdr. guns and 2 5 1/2-inch howitzers—total of 18 pieces of ordnance.

27th Division(-)—

2nd Brigade: Général de brigade Grabowski

4th Polish Regiment of the Line, 1st and 2nd battalions—in garrison at Wittemberg

12th Polish Regiment of the Line, 1st battalion	(1)	32 - 560
2nd battalion	(1)	24 - 549

Divisional artillery and train(-):

Polish Foot Artillery, 10th company	6 - 135
detachment of the 14th company	3 - 61

The 10th company consisted of 4 6-pdr. guns and 2 5 1/2-inch
howitzers; the detachment of the 14th company fielded
2 6-pdr. guns and 1 5 1/2-inch howitzer—total of 9 pieces of ordnance.

VIII Corps Cavalry Brigade—
Corps cavalry brigade staff—1 person
14th (Polish) Cuirassiers, 1st squadron	(1)	17 - 208
2nd squadron	(1)	8 - 195
1st Polish "Avant-Garde", 1st squadron	(1)	17 - 208
2nd squadron	(1)	8 - 195
3rd squadron	(1)	9 - 199
4th squadron	(1)	4 - 114

VIII Corps Artillery Reserve—
Corps artillery reserve staff—1 person
Polish Foot Artillery, 11th company	6 - 129
detachment of the 14th company	3 - 62

The 11th foot artillery company consisted of 4 6-pdr. guns
and 2 5 1/2-inch howitzers; the detachment of the 14th company
fielded 2 6-pdr. guns and 1 5 1/2-inch howitzer—total of 9 pieces of ordnance.
Polish Sappers, 1st company	5 - 135
Polish Equipage, 1st company	9 - 98
Polish Gendarmes, 1st company	4 - 90

IX CORPS
OBSERVATION CORPS OF BAVARIA
Marshal Augereau, Duke of Castiglione
Général de brigade Ménard, Chief of Staff
Général de brigade Pellegrin, commanding the artillery
Général de brigade Dode, commanding the enginers
Corps headquarters staff—22 personnel

51st Division— Général de division Baron Turreau de Garambouville
Division headquarters staff—7 personnel
1st Brigade: Général de brigade Lagarde
  32nd Provisional Demi-Brigade, consisting of
1st battalion, 25th Light Infantry Regiment	(1)	24 - 603
4th battalion, 32nd Light Infantry Regiment	(1)	21 - 688
113th Regiment of the Line, 1st battalion	(1)	24 - 825
2nd battalion	(1)	26 - 678
3rd battalion	(1)	8 - 784
4th battalion	(1)	9 - 796

2nd Brigade: Général de brigade Aymard
  33rd Provisional Demi-Brigade, consisting of
2nd battalion, 27th Regiment of the Line	(1)	17 - 816
2nd battalion, 63rd Regiment of the Line	(1)	14 - 745

  34th Provisional Demi-Brigade, consisting of
3rd battalion, 10th Light Infantry Regiment	(1)	14 - 735
2nd battalion, 21st Light Infantry Regiment	(1)	20 - 749

  35th Provisional Demi-Brigade, consisting of
3rd battalion, 32nd Regiment of the Line	(1)	21 - 758
3rd battalion, 58th Regiment of the Line	(1)	22 - 826

Divisional artillery and train:
2nd Regiment of Foot Artillery, 5th company	3 - 114

1st Regiment of Foot Artillery, 22nd company		3 - 120
1st Principal Artillery Train Battalion, 5th company		1 - 119
5th *bis* Artillery Train Battalion, detachment of the 1st company		1 - 119

52nd Division— Général de division Baron Sémélé

1st Brigade: Général de brigade Bagneris

36th Provisional Demi-Brigade, consisting of

2nd battalion, 24th Regiment of the Line	(1)	10 - 814
2nd battalion, 39th Regiment of the Line	(1)	20 - 563

37th Provisional Demi-Brigade, consisting of

2nd battalion, 17th Light Infantry	(1)	16 - 634
4th battalion, 29th Light Infantry	(1)	21 - 668

38th Provisional Demi-Brigade, consisting of

2nd battalion, 54th Regiment of the Line	(1)	18 - 782
2nd battalion, 95th Regiment of the Line	(1)	19 - 791

2nd Brigade: Général de brigade

39th Provisional Demi-Brigade, consisting of

2nd battalion, 8th Regiment of the Line	(1)	19 - 775
4th battalion, 28th Regiment of the Line	(1)	21 - 820
2nd battalion, 88th Regiment of the Line	(1)	9 - 800

40th Provisional Demi-Brigade, consisting of

6th battalion, 15th Regiment of the Line	(1)	14 - 736
6th battalion, 70th Regiment of the Line	(1)	12 - 780

Divisional artillery and train:

2nd Regiment of Foot Artillery, 21st company		4 - 114
7th Regiment of Foot Artillery, 27th company		2 - 118*
Artillery Train, 2 undesignated companies not yet assigned		4 - 240**

* Establishment strength only—actual strength not reported.

** Establishment strength only—actual units and strength not reported.

53rd Division—forming at Mayence—no general officers yet appointed

Division headquarters staff—1 person

1st Brigade:

121st Regiment of the Line, 6th battalion	(1)	17 - 780
122nd Regiment of the Line, 2nd battalion	(1)	13 - 676
6th battalion	(1)	14 - 740
47th Regiment of the Line, 4th battalion	(1)	15 - 728
6th battalion	(1)	21 - 789

2nd Brigade:

41st Provisional Demi-Brigade, consisting of

6th battalion, 66th Regiment of the Line	(1)	15 - 649
5th battalion, 82nd Regiment of the Line	(1)	17 - 514
86th Regiment of the Line, 2nd battalion	(1)	12 - 640
4th battalion	(1)	4 - 734
6th battalion	(1)	15 - 804

Divisional artillery and train:

7th Regiment of Foot Artillery, 28th company		2 - 118*
1st Regiment of Foot Artillery, 27th company		2 - 118*
Artillery train, 2 undesignated companies not yet assigned.		4 - 240**

* Establishment strength only—actual strength not reported.

** Establishment strength only—actual units and strength not reported.

54th Division—forming at Mayence—no general officers yet appointed

Division headquarters staff—no one yet assigned

1st Brigade:

42nd Provisional Demi-Brigade, consisting of		
2nd battalion, 51st Regiment of the Line	(1)	14 - 555
2nd battalion, 55th Regiment of the Line	(1)	6 - 552
43rd Provisional Demi-Brigade, consisting of		
2nd battalion, 15th Regiment of the Line	(1)	12 - 660
3rd battalion, 62nd Regiment of the Line	(1)	13 - 669
44th Provisional Demi-Brigade, consisting of		
5th battalion, 26th Regiment of the Line	(1)	19 - 621
2nd battalion, 70th Regiment of the Line	(1)	10 - 649

2nd Brigade:

45th Provisional Demi-Brigade, consisting of		
6th battalion, 5th Light Infantry Regiment	(1)	13 - 746
3rd battalion, 17th Light Infantry Regiment	(1)	
46th Provisional Demi-Brigade, consisting of		
7th battalion, 1st Regiment de Marine	(1)	17 - 489
9th battalion, 2nd Regiment de Marine	(1)	9 - 860

Divisional artillery and train:

1st Regiment of Foot Artillery, 28th company	2 - 118*
5th Regiment of Fot Artillery, 27th company	2 - 118*
Artillery Train, 2 undesignated companies	4 - 240**

* Establishment strength only—actual strength not reported.
** Establishment strength only—actual units and strength not reported.

IX Corps Artillery Reserve—

Corps artillery reserve staff—1 person

5th Regiment of Foot Artillery, 28th company	2 - 118*
6th Regiment of Horse Artillery, 3rd company	3 - 90
1st Principal Artillery Train Battalion, various detachments	4 - 200
4th Battalion, Sappers of the Line, 1st company	2 - 159
Ouvriers, detachment of the 16th company	1 - 19

* Establishment strength only—actual strength not reported.

Note: There were no artillery materiel returns for IX Corps. Therefore, no ordnance details have been shown.

X CORPS
(The Garrison of Danzig)
Général de division Count Rapp, Military Governor of Danzig
Général de brigade Lepin, commanding the artillery

7th Division— Général de division Baron Grandjean

There was no formal brigade organization for the 7th Division.

5th Polish Regiment of the Line, 1st , 2nd, and 3rd bns	(3)	63 - 1,731
10th Polish Regiment of the Line, 1st, 2nd, and 3rd bns	(3)	61 - 1,697
11th Polish Regiment of the Line, 1st, 2nd, and 3rd bns	(3)	62 - 1,435
1st Westphalian Regiment of the Line, 1st and 2nd bns	(2)	34 - 1,094
13th Bavarian Regiment of the Line, 1st and 2nd battalions	(2)	41 - 1,032

Situation of the Grande Armée—15 August 1813

33rd Division— Général de division Destrée

There was no formal brigade organization for the 33rd Division.

5th Neapolitan Regiment of the Line, 1st and 2nd bns	(2)	41 - 1,318
6th Neapolitan Regiment of the Line, 1st and 2nd bns	(2)	32 - 1,283
7th Neapolitan Regiment of the Line, 1st and 2nd bns	(2)	27 - 1,345

30th Division— Général de division Count Heudelet de Bierre

1st Brigade: Général de brigade Husson

6th Provisional Demi-Brigade, consisting of

4th battalion, 16th Light Infantry Regiment	(1)	17 - 575
4th battalion, 21st Light Infantry Regiment	(1)	16 - 673
4th battalion, 28th Light Infantry Regiment	(1)	16 - 679

7th Provisional Demi-Brigade, consisting of

4th battalion, 8th Regiment of the Line	(1)	15 - 611
4th battalion, 14th Regiment of the Line	(1)	15 - 642
4th battalion, 94th Regiment of the Line	(1)	12 - 552

2nd Brigade: Général de brigade Breissand

8th Provisional Demi-Brigade, consisting of

4th battalion, 64th Regiment of the Line	(1)	16 - 555
4th battalion, 88th Regiment of the Line	(1)	20 - 418
4th battalion, 95th Regiment of the Line	(1)	20 - 479

9th Provisional Demi-Brigade, consisting of

4th battalion, 24th Regiment of the Line	(1)	22 - 521
4th battalion, 45th Regiment of the Line	(1)	20 - 618
4th battalion, 59th Regiment of the Line	(1)	21 - 555

3rd Brigade: Général de brigade Gault

1st Provisional Demi-Brigade, consisting of

4th battalion, 2nd Light Infantry Regiment	(1)	21 - 791
4th battalion, 4th Light Infantry Regiment	(1)	19 - 632
4th battalion, 17th Light Infantry Regiment	(1)	18 - 649

17th Provisional Demi-Brigade, consisting of

4th battalion, 6th Light Infantry Regiment	(1)	20 - 575
4th battalion, 25th Light Infantry Regiment	(1)	23 - 555
4th battalion, 39th Regiment of the Line	(1)	20 - 782

Attached to 30th Division—

survivors of the former 34th Division: Général de brigade Franceschi

3rd Regiment of the Line, 1 company	(-)	4 - 13
29th Regiment of the Line, 1 battalion	(1)	26 - 214
113th Regiment of the Line, 2 companies	(-)	20 - 210
4th Confederation of the Rhine	(1)	14 - 90
5th Confederation of the Rhine	(1)	22 - 159
6th Confederation of the Rhine	(1)	18 - 281

Divisional artillery and train:

7th Regiment of Foot Artillery, 7th company	3 - 90
17th company	2 - 95
9th Regiment of Foot Artillery, 18th company	2 - 99
8th Principal Artillery Train Battalion, 5th company	1 - 23
12th Principal Artillery Train Battalion, 4th company	1 - 98
7th Battalion, Sappers of the Line, 1st company	2 - 92

Cavalry Division— Général de brigade Cavagnac

There was no formal brigade organization for the cavalry.

9th Polish Uhlans	(2)	8 - 310
17th Polish (Lithuanian) Uhlans, detachment	(1)	1 - 30
19th Polish Uhlans	(1)	3 - 62
1st Provisional (French) Dragoons, consisting of		
the 4th squadrons from the 2nd, 5th, 12th, and 13th regts.	(4)	20 - 485
2nd Provisional (French) Dragoons, consisting of		
the 4th sqdrns from the 14th, 17th, 19th, and 20th regts.	(4)	24 - 443
Regiment under the orders of Colonel Sarne	?	15 - 382

Naval Troops—

4th Flotilla Equipage		10 - 95
17th Flotilla Equipage		12 - 257
Danube Battalion	(1)	7 - 65
Elster Battalion	(1)	15 - 297
Spanish Pontoniers, 1st battalion	(1)	6 - 407
Marins of the (French Imperial) Guard		1 - 1

Depots—

Depot of the French Imperial Guard		19 - 398
Depot of Sappers of the Line		4 - 164

Artillery Reserve of Danzig—

There were 9 companies of French foot artillery, 4 companies of French horse artillery, 1 company of French pontoniers, 3 companies of French ouvriers/armorers, 1 company of Polish foot artillery, detachments of Bavarian and Württemberg foot artillery, plus various detachments of miners, and equipage companies totalling   41 - 2,565

Note: There were no artillery materiel returns for the garrison of Danzig. Therefore, no ordnance details have been shown.

XI CORPS

Marshal Macdonald, Duke of Tarentum

Général de division Grundler, Chief of Staff
Colonel Sautereau, commanding the artillery
Chef de bataillon Marion, commanding the engineers
Corps headquarters staff—34 personnel

31st Division— Général de division Baron Ledru des Essarts

Division headquarters staff—16 personnel
1st Brigade: Général de brigade Fressinet
11th Provisional Demi-Brigade, consisting of

4th battalion, 27th Light Infantry	(1)	21 - 601
6th battalion, 20th Regiment of the Line	(1)	19 - 519
4th battalion, 102nd Regiment of the Line	(1)	19 - 622

13th Provisional Demi-Brigade, consisting of

4th battalion, 5th Regiment of the Line	(1)	20 - 516
4th battalion, 11th Regiment of the Line	(1)	18 - 598
4th battalion, 79th Regiment of the Line	(1)	20 - 613

2nd Brigade: Général de brigade d'Henin

Westphalian Fusilier Guards, 1st battalion	(1)	24 - 448
2nd battalion	(1)	17 - 436
8th Westphalian Regiment of the Line, 1st battalion	(1)	21 - 439
2nd battalion	(1)	19 - 450
4th Westphalian Light Infantry, 1st battalion	(1)	22 - 682

3rd Brigade: Général de brigade Macdonald

Neapolitan Vélites, 1st battalion	(1)	20 - 609
4th Neapolitan Light Infantry Regiment, 1st battalion	(1)	14 - 436
2nd battalion	(1)	12 - 418

Divisional artillery and train:

5th Regiment of Foot Artillery, 20th company	3 - 91
8th Regiment of Foot Artillery, 20th company	3 - 70
Westphalian Foot Artillery, 1st company	4 - 69

The 5/20th and the 8/20th foot artillery companies each consisted of 6 6-pdr. guns and 2 5 1/2-inch howitzers; the Westphalian foot consisted of 4 6-pdr. guns and 2 5 1/2-inch howitzers—total of 20 pieces of ordnance.

8th Principal Artillery Train Battalion, detachments 1st and 4th cos	1 - 177
3rd *bis* Artillery Train Battalion, detachment of the 1st company	1 - 39
Westphalian Artillery Train Battalion, 1st company	2 - 201

35th Division— Général de division Baron Gérard

Division headquarters staff—12 personnel

1st Brigade: Général de brigade Le Sénécal

6th Regiment of the Line, 3rd battalion	(1)	22 - 484
4th battalion	(1)	22 - 502
7th battalion	(1)	20 - 464
Regimental artillery company of the 6th Line,		2 - 45
consisting of 2 6-pdr. guns—total of 2 pieces of ordnance.		
112th Regiment of the Line, 1st battalion	(1)	23 - 487
2nd battalion	(1)	17 - 526
3rd battalion	(1)	18 - 522
4th battalion	(1)	23 - 562
Regimental artillery company of the 112th Line,		2 - 47
consisting of 2 6-pdr. guns—total of 2 pieces of ordnance.		

2nd Brigade: Général de brigade Zucchi

2nd Italian Light Infantry Regiment, 3rd battalion	(1)	20 - 426
4th battalion	(1)	21 - 421
Regimental artillery company of the 2nd Italian Light Infantry,		2 - 36
consisting of 2 6-pdr. guns,—total of 2 pieces of ordnance.		
5th Italian Regiment of the Line, 1st battalion	(1)	23 - 538
2nd battalion	(1)	21 - 521
3rd battalion	(1)	23 - 518
4th battalion	(1)	20 - 483
Regimental artillery company of the 5th Italian Line,		3 - 72
consisting of 2 6-pdr. guns—total of 2 pieces of ordnance.		

Divisional artillery and train:

1st Regiment of Foot Artillery, 6th company	2 - 102
Italian Regiment of Horse Artillery, 3rd company	3 - 92

Appendix D
Situation of the Grande Armée—15 August 1813

The foot artillery company consisted of 6 6-pdr. guns and
2 5½-inch howitzers; the horse artillery company consisted
of 4 6-pdr. guns and 2 5½-inch howitzers—total of 14 pieces of ordnance.

11th *bis* Artillery Train Battalion, detachment of the 1st company		1 - 37
Italian Artillery Train Battalion, 3rd company		1 - 99
4th company		2 - 110

36th Division— Général de division Count Charpentier

Division headquarters staff—13 personnel
1st Brigade: Général de brigade Simmer

22nd Light Infantry Regiment, 1st battalion	(1)	21 - 593
2nd battalion	(1)	18 - 562
3rd battalion	(1)	19 - 557
4th battalion	(1)	21 - 606
Regimental artillery company of the 22nd Light Infantry, consisting of 2 6-pdr. guns—total of 2 pieces of ordnance.		2 - 36
10th Regiment of the Line, 4th battalion	(1)	21 - 429
6th battalion	(1)	18 - 458

2nd Brigade: Général de brigade Meunier

3rd Light Infantry Regiment, 3rd battalion	(1)	19 - 502
4th battalion	(1)	23 - 559
14th Light Infantry Regiment, 3rd battalion	(1)	20 - 548
4th battalion	(1)	23 - 574
7th battalion	(1)	22 - 532
Regimental artillery company of the 14th Light Infantry, consisting of 2 6-pdr. guns—total of 2 pieces of ordnance.		2 - 69

Divisional artillery and train:

1st Regiment of Foot Artillery, 5th company		2 - 80
2nd Regiment of Foot Artillery, 19th company		3 - 82
The above foot artillery companies each consisted of 6 6-pdr. guns and 2 5½-inch howitzers—total of 16 pieces of ordnance.		
7th Principal Artillery Train Battalion, detachment of the 1st company		2 - 60
12th Principal Artillery Train Battalion, 1st company		2 - 172

XI Corps Cavalry Brigade— Général de brigade Montbrun

Corps cavalry brigade staff—3 personnel

4th Italian Chasseurs à Cheval, 1st and 2nd squadrons	(2)	18 - 277
Würzburg Chevaulegers, 1st squadron	(1)	11 - 157
2nd Neapolitan Chasseurs à Cheval, 1st—4th squadrons	(4)	28 - 674

XI Corps Artillery Reserve—

Corps artillery reserve staff—2 personnel

1st Regiment of Foot Artillery, 13th company		3 - 97
5th Regiment of Foot Artillery, 15th company		3 - 87
22nd company		3 - 117
9th Regiment of Foot Artillery, 8th company		3 - 112
6th Regiment of Horse Artillery, 6th company		3 - 78

The 1/13th foot artillery company consisted of 8 12-pdr. guns;
the 5/22 and 9/8th foot artillery companies each consisted of
6 12-pdr. guns and 2 5½-inch howitzers; the 5/15th foot artillery
company consisted of 6 6-pdr. guns and 2 5½-inch howitzers; the

6/6th horse artillery company consisted of 4 6-pdr. guns and
2 51/2-inch howitzers—total of 38 pieces of ordnance.

7th Principal Artillery Train Battalion, detachments of 3rd and 4th companies	3 - 243
8th Principal Artillery Train Battalion, detachment of the 2nd company	- 19
8th *bis* Artillery Train Battalion, detachment of the 2nd company	1 - 30
13th *bis* Artillery Train Battalion, 1st company	1 - 104
5th Battalion, Sappers of the Line, 7th company	3 - 113
7th Battalion, Sappers of the Line, 2nd company	4 - 99
Italian Sappers, 9th company	2 - 33
Ouvriers, detachment of the 14th company	- 9

XII CORPS
Marshal Oudinot, Duke of Reggio
Général de brigade Baron Lejeune, Chief of Staff
Général de brigade Nourry, commanding the artillery
Général de brigade Blein, commanding the engineers
Corps headquarters staff—34 personnel

13th Division— Général de division Count Pacthod
Division headquarters staff—14 personnel
1st Brigade: Général de brigade Bardet

1st Light Infantry Regiment, 4th battalion	(1)	19 - 471
7th Regiment of the Line, 3rd battalion	(1)	21 - 340
4th battalion	(1)	19 - 296
42nd Regiment of the Line, 4th battalion	(1)	21 - 411

2nd Brigade: Général de brigade Cacault

67th Regiment of the Line, 3rd battalion	(1)	21 - 537
4th battalion	(1)	20 - 449
101st Regiment of the Line, 2nd battalion	(1)	20 - 520
3rd battalion	(1)	17 - 538
4th battalion	(1)	18 - 403

Divisional artillery and train:

4th Regiment of Foot Artillery, 4th company	3 - 70
20th company	4 - 77

The above foot artillery companies each consisted of
6 6-pdr. guns and 2 51/2-inch howitzers—total of 16 pieces of ordnance.

4th Principal Artillery Train Battalion, detachment of the 2nd company	1 - 89
7th *bis* Artillery Train Battalion, detachment of the 3rd company	1 - 77

14th Division— Général de division Baron Guilleminot
Division headquarters staff—15 personnel
1st Brigade: Général de brigade Gruyer

18th Light Infantry Regiment, 2nd battalion	(1)	24 - 455
6th battalion	(1)	17 - 382
156th Regiment of the Line, 1st battalion	(1)	22 - 855
2nd battalion	(1)	20 - 893
3rd battalion	(1)	25 - 897

2nd Brigade: Général de brigade Brun de Villeret

Illyrian Regiment, 2nd battalion	(1)	26 - 486
52nd Regiment of the Line, 3rd battalion	(1)	17 - 512

4th battalion	(1)	16 - 544
137th Regiment of the Line, 1st battalion	(1)	27 - 585
2nd battalion	(1)	16 - 586
3rd battalion	(1)	16 - 606

Divisional artillery and train:

4th Regiment of Foot Artillery, 2nd company	3 - 93
8th Regiment of Foot Artillery, 1st company	4 - 71

The above foot artillery companies each consisted of
6 6-pdr. guns and 2 5 1/2-inch howitzers—total of 16 pieces of ordnance.

4th Principal Artillery Train Battalion, detachment of the 1st company	1 - 59
7th Principal Artillery Train Battalion, detachment of the 5th company	3 - 37
3rd *bis* Artillery Train Battalion, detachment of the 4th company	- 19
9th *bis* Artillery Train Battalion, detachment of the 1st company	- 56

29th Division— Général de division de Raglowich

Division headquarters staff—10 personnel

1st Brigade: Général de brigade de Beckers

1st Bavarian Light Battalion	(1)	14 - 452
3rd Bavarian Regiment of the Line, (survivors of) 1st bn	(1)	13 - 36
4th Bavarian Regiment of the Line, 1st battalion	(1)	10 - 387
8th Bavarian Regiment of the Line, 1st battalion	(1)	18 - 432
13th Bavarian Regiment of the Line, 1st battalion	(1)	12 - 364

2nd Brigade: Colonel Maillot de La Traille

2nd Bavarian Light Battalion	(1)	16 - 419
5th Bavarian Regiment of the Line, 1st battalion	(1)	11 - 439
7th BavarianRegiment of the Line, 1st battalion	(1)	18 - 606
9th Bavarian Regiment of the Line, 1st battalion	(1)	17 - 517
10th Bavarian Regiment of the Line, 1st battalion	(1)	20 - 645

Divisional artillery and train:

Bavarian Foot Artillery, 1st company	2 - 60
2nd company	2 - 60
Bavarian Reserve Artillery, 1st company	2 - 280

The 1st and 2nd companies of Bavarian foot artillery
consisted of 4 6-pdr. guns and 2 5 1/2-inch howitzers; on
15 July, the Bavarian reserve artillery company consisted of
only 1 6-pdr. gun and 1 5 1/2-inch howitzer. A later materiel return
for this company not being found, it is assumed that additional ordnance
must have been procured for this company to bring the total ordnance
in the company up to 6 pieces—total of 18 pieces of ordnance.

Bavarian Artillery Train, 1st company	6 - 100

XII Corps Cavalry Division— Général de division Baumont

Corps cavalry brigade staff—7 personnel

1st Brigade: Général de brigade Wolff

Westphalian Chevaulegers, 1st, 2nd, 3rd, and 4th squadrons	(4)	35 - 482
Hesse-Darmstadt Chevaulegers, 1st, 2nd, and 3rd squadrons	(3)	12 - 248

2nd Brigade: Colonel de Saissel

Bavarian Chevaulegers, 1st, 2nd, and 3rd squadrons	(3)	16 - 394

XII Corps Artillery Reserve—

Corps artillery reserve staff—1 person	
4th Regiment of Foot Artillery, 1st company	1 - 73
18th company	4 - 82

The above foot artillery companies each consisted of
6 12-pdr. guns and 2 5 1/2-inch howitzers—total of 16 pieces of ordnance.

4th Principal Artillery Train Battalion, detachment of the 1st company	1 - 102
detachment of the 2nd company	- 89
12th Principal Artillery Train Battalion, detachment of the 4th company	- 6
3rd *bis* Artillery Train Battalion, detachments of the 1st and 3rd companies	- 20
7th *bis* Artillery Train Battalion, detachments of the 3rd, 4th, and 5th cos	2 - 111
2nd Battalion, Sappers of the Line, 4th company	3 - 100
6th Battalion, Sappers of the Line, 4th company	3 - 92
7th Equipage Battalion, 1st, 2nd, and 3rd companies	3 - 271

XII Corps troops in route to join their regiments—
Detachments of the:

137th Regiment of the Line	1 - 90
156th Regiment of the Line	1 - 70

XIII CORPS
Marshal Davout, Prince of Eckmühl
Général de brigade de Laville, Chief of Staff
Général de brigade Jouffroy, commanding the artillery
Chef de bataillon Vinache, commanding the engineers
Corps headquarters staff—33 personnel

3rd Division— Général de division Count Loison

Division headquarters staff—9 personnel
1st Brigade: Général de brigade Mielzinski

15th Light Infantry Regiment, 1st battalion	(1)	16 - 636
2nd battalion	(1)	17 - 599
3rd battalion	(1)	17 - 661
4th battalion	(1)	18 - 521
44th Regiment of the Line, 3rd battalion	(1)	19 - 727
4th battalion	(1)	13 - 649

2nd Brigade: Général de brigade Leclerc

48th Regiment of the Line, 1st—4th battalions	(4)	78 - 2,688
108th Regiment of the Line, 1st—4th battalions	(4)	75 - 2,498

Divisional artillery and train:

8th Regiment of Foot Artillery, 3rd company	3 - 106
17th company	2 - 106

The 8/3rd foot artillery company consisted of 6 12-pdr. guns
and 2 5 1/2-inch howitzers; the 8/17th foot artillery company consisted
of 6 6-pdr. guns and 2 5 1/2-inch howitzers—total of 16 pieces of ordnance.

6th Principal Artillery Train Battalion, detachment of the 1st company	1 - 89
7th Principal Artillery Train Battalion, 5th company	2 - 137

40th Division— Général de division Baron Thiébault

Division headquarters staff—9 personnel
1st Brigade: Général de brigade Delcambre

33rd Light Infantry Regiment, 3rd battalion	(1)	25 - 538
4th battalion	(1)	27 - 643
30th Regiment of the Line, 1st battalion	(1)	29 - 718
2nd battalion	(1)	22 - 755
3rd battalion	(1)	18 - 753
4th battalion	(1)	21 - 678

2nd Brigade: Général de brigade Gengoult

61st Regiment of the Line, 1st battalion	(1)	23 - 765
2nd battalion	(1)	22 - 730
3rd battalion	(1)	22 - 706
4th battalion	(1)	22 - 698
111th Regiment of the Line, 1st battalion	(1)	36 - 748
2nd battalion	(1)	18 - 640
3rd battalion	(1)	16 - 614
4th battalion	(1)	18 - 624

Divisional artillery and train:

2nd Regiment of Foot Artillery, 12th company		3 - 72
8th Regiment of Foot Artillery, 18th company		1 - 45

The 2/12th foot artillery company consisted of 6 6-pdr. guns and
2 51/2-inch howitzers; the 8/18th company consisted of 3 6-pdr. guns
and 1 51/2-inch howitzer—total of 12 pieces of ordnance.

2nd *bis* Artillery Train Battalion, detachment of the 7th company		1 - 78
8th *bis* Artillery Train Battalion, detachment of the 3rd company		- 32

50th Division(-)— Général de division Vichery

Division headquarters staff—4 personnel
1st Brigade: Général de brigade Rome

3rd Regiment of the Line, 2nd battalion	(1)	5 - 429
3rd battalion	(1)	5 - 459
4th battalion	(1)	4 - 509
6th battalion	(1)	8 - 771
105th Regiment of the Line, 3rd battalion	(1)	9 - 710
6th battalion	(1)	11 - 734

Divisional artillery and train:

8th Regiment of Foot Artillery, 11th company		3 - 109
1st Regiment of Horse Artillery, 4th company		2 - 80

The 8/11th foot artillery company consisted of
4 6-pdr. guns and 1 51/2-inch howitzer; the 1/4th
horse artillery company consisted of 3 6-pdr. guns
and 1 51/2-inch howitzer—total of 9 pieces of ordnance.

Danish Auxiliary Division— Prince Frédéric de Hesse

Division headquarters staff—20 personnel
Avant-garde: Colonel de Waldeck

Chasseurs de Sleswig, 1st battalion	(1)	17 - 485
Tirailleurs de Holstein, 1st and 2nd battalions	(2)	33 - 925

Jutland Hussars, 1st and 2nd squadrons	(2)	13 - 216
Brigade artillery: One company of Danish artillery and train		5 - 122

1st Brigade: Général de brigade de Schulembourg

Regiment de la Reine, 1st battalion	(1)	32 - 824
Regiment d'Oldenbourg, 1st—4th battalions	(4)	74 - 2,400
Holstein Cavalry, 1st, 2nd, 3rd, and 4th squadrons	(4)	22 - 467
Brigade artillery: Two companies of Danish artillery and train		5 - 140

2nd Brigade: Général de brigade de Lasson

Regiment de Fionie, 1st battalion	(1)	23 - 774
Regiment de Holstein, 1st and 2nd battalion	(2)	38 - 1,419
Regiment de Sleswig, 1st and 2nd battalion	(2)	29 - 1,042
Jutland Dragoons, 1st, 2nd, 3rd, and 4th squadrons	(4)	24 - 457
Brigade artillery: One company of Danish artillery and train		6 - 84

Note: The Danes had a total of 32 pieces of ordnance in four companies, or 8 pieces per company. According to Napoleon's letter to Davout, *Correspondance*, No. 20287 , 19 July 1813, the Danes actually employed eight 6-pdr. guns, four howitzers, and twenty 3-pdr. guns, for a total of 32 pieces.

XIII Corps Cavalry Brigade— Général de brigade Lallemand
Corps cavalry brigade staff—2 personnel

17th Polish (Lithuanian) Uhlans, 1st, 2nd, and 3rd squadrons	(3)	57* - 428
28th (French) Chasseurs à Cheval, 1st and 2nd squadrons	(2)	14 - 321

*The 17th Polish Uhlans had an extraordinary number of officers present.

XIII Corps Artillery Reserve—
Corps artillery reserve staff—1 person

5th Regiment of Horse Artillery, 4th company, consisting of 4 6-pdr. guns and 2 5½-inch howitzers—total of 6 pieces of ordnance.	2 - 99
6th Principal Artillery Train Battalion, detachment of the 1st company	- 36
5th *bis* Artillery Train Battalion, detachment of the 4th company	- 33
6th *bis* Artillery Train Battalion, detachment of the 3rd company	- 22
4th Battalion, Sappers of the Line, 8th company	1 - 57
Ouvriers, detachment of the 14th company	- 46
12th Equipage Battalion, 3rd, 4th, 5th, and 6th companies	13 - 736

XIII Corps troops in route to join their regiments—
Detachments of the:

48th Regiment of the Line	3 - 77
108th Regiment of the Line	3 - 120
30th Regiment of the Line	2 - 115
111th Regiment of the Line	2 - 239
61st Regiment of the Line	- 53

XIV CORPS
Marshal Count Gouvion Saint-Cyr
Général de brigade Baron Borelli, Chief of Staff
Général de brigade Pernetti, commanding the artillery
Corps headquarters staff—23 personnel

42nd Division— Général de division Baron Mouton-Duvernet
Division headquarters staff—7 personnel
1st Brigade*, also known as 4th Provisional Demi-Brigade, consisting of
  22nd Provisional Light Infantry Regiment, consisting of

2nd battalion, 4th Light Infantry Regiment	(1)	20 - 725
3rd battalion, 12th Light Infantry Regiment	(1)	22 - 790

  4th Provisional Light Infantry Regiment, consisting of

6th battalion, 9th Light Infantry Regiment	(1)	22 - 724
3rd battalion, 28th Light Infantry Regiment	(1)	21 - 678

  3rd Provisional Light Infantry Regiment, consisting of

4th battalion, 10th Light Infantry	(1)	23 - 743
3rd battalion, 21st Light Infantry	(1)	24 - 685

2nd Brigade, also known as 16th Prov. Demi-Brigade: Général de brigade Creutzer
  17th Provisional Regiment of the Line, consisting of

3rd battalion, 27th Regiment of the Line	(1)	24 - 804
3rd battalion, 63rd Regiment of the Line	(1)	24 - 789

  16th Provisional Regiment of the Line, consisting of

4th battalion, 40th Regiment of the Line	(1)	20 - 566
3rd battalion, 43rd Regiment of the Line	(1)	22 - 782
76th Regiment of the Line, 2nd battalion	(1)	21 - 780
3rd battalion	(1)	19 - 819
96th Regiment of the Line, 2nd battalion	(1)	18 - 800
3rd battalion	(1)	18 - 816

Division artillery and train:

7th Regiment of Foot Artillery, 1st company	3 - 108
9th company	2 - 104
11th Principal Artillery Train Battalion, detachment of the 5th company	1 - 136
1st *bis* Artillery Train Battalion, detachments of the 6th and 7th companies	1 - 104

* The parade states of 15 August show that General Mouton-Duvernet was also
acting as the commanding officer for the 1st Brigade.

43rd Division— Général de division Baron Claparède
Division headquarters staff—11 personnel
1st Brigade: Général de brigade Godard

27th Light Infantry Regiment, 2nd battalion	(1)	21 - 738
3rd battalion	(1)	20 - 711
29th Light Infantry Regiment, 3rd battalion	(1)	16 - 726
100th Regiment of the Line, 2nd battalion	(1)	20 - 760
3rd battalion	(1)	22 - 731
4th battalion	(1)	20 - 741

2nd Brigade: Général de brigade Butrand

45th Regiment of the Line, 2nd battalion	(1)	15 - 775
3rd battalion	(1)	21 - 748
103rd Regiment of the Line, 2nd battalion	(1)	21 - 782
4th battalion	(1)	22 - 656
21st Provisional Demi-Brigade, consisting of		
3rd battalion, 65th Regiment of the Line	(1)	19 - 805
2nd battalion, 59th Regiment of the Line	(1)	20 - 705
3rd battalion, 94th Regiment of the Line	(1)	24 - 684

Divisional artillery and train:

7th Regiment of Foot Artillery, 2nd company	3 - 115
6th Regiment of Foot Artillery, 4th company	2 - 107
10th Principal Artillery Train Battalion, detachment of the 4th company	1 - 42
12th Principal Artillery Train Battalion, detachment of the 6th company	1 - 124
1st *bis* Artillery Train Battalion, detachments of the 6th and 7th companies	1 - 25

44th Division— Général de division Baron Berthezène

Division headquarters staff—9 personnel
1st Brigade: Général de brigade Paillard

8th Light Infantry Regiment, 1st battalion	(1)	24 - 787
3rd battalion	(1)	22 - 650
64th Regiment of the Line, 3rd battalion	(1)	22 - 709
4th battalion	(1)	18 - 687
34th Provisional Light Infantry Regiment, consisting of		
2nd battalion, 16th Light Infantry	(1)	21 - 559
1st battalion, 18th Light Infantry	(1)	20 - 725

2nd Brigade: Général de brigade Letellier

19th Provisional Regiment of the Line, consisting of		
2nd battalion, 50th Regiment of the Line	(1)	20 - 607
2nd battalion, 75th Regiment of the Line	(1)	21 - 557
Provisional Regiment of the Line, consisting of		
3rd battalion, 54th Regiment of the Line	(1)	22 - 694
3rd battalion, 95th Regiment of the Line	(1)	17 - 567
Provisional Regiment of the Line, consisting of		
3rd battalion, 24th Regiment of the Line	(1)	20 - 703
3rd battalion, 39th Regiment of the Line	(1)	24 - 500

Divisional artillery and train:

1st Regiment of Foot Artillery, 4th company	2 - 114
7th Regiment of Foot Artillery, 15th company	2 - 106
11th Principal Artillery Train Battalion, detachment of the 3rd company	1 - 131
12th Principal Artillery Train Battalion, detachment of the 3rd company	- 12
1st *bis* Artillery Train Battalion, detachment of the 7th company	2 - 131

45th Division— Général de division Count Razout

Division headquarters staff—9 personnel
1st Brigade: Général de brigade Goguet

6th Light Infantry Regiment, 3rd battalion	(1)	18 - 333
26th Provisional Demi-Brigade, consisting of		
3rd battalion, 5th Regiment of the Line	(1)	19 - 604
3rd battalion, 11th Regiment of the Line	(1)	19 - 634
Provisional Regiment of the Line, consisting of		
3rd battalion, 8th Regiment of the Line	(1)	22 - 754
2nd battalion, 28th Regiment of the Line	(1)	20 - 595

2nd Brigade: Général de brigade d'Esclevin

Provisional Regiment of the Line, consisting of		
4th battalion, 32nd Regiment of the Line	(1)	21 - 698
4th battalion, 58th Regiment of the Line	(1)	22 - 673
18th Provisional Demi-Brigade, consisting of		
3rd battalion, 34th Regiment of the Line	(1)	21 - 738
3rd battalion, 69th Regiment of the Line	(1)	22 - 754
27th Provisional Demi-Brigade, consisting of		
3rd battalion, 79th Regiment of the Line	(1)	22 - 695
6th battalion, 81st Regiment of the Line	(1)	17 - 671
60th Regiment of the Line, 4th battalion	(1)	23 - 692

Divisional artillery and train:

5th Regiment of Foot Artillery, 21st company		2 - 111
1st Regiment of Foot Artillery, 18th company		2 - 96
11th Principal Artillery Train Battalion, detachment of the 4th company		1 - 78
12th Principal Artillery Train Battalion, detachment of the 5th company		1 - 123

10th Light Cavalry Division— Général de division Baron Pajol

Division headquarters staff— 4 personnel
1st Brigade: Général de brigade Jacquet

14th Hussars, 1st, 2nd, 3rd, and 4th squadrons	(4)	29 - 750
2nd Italian Chasseurs à Cheval, 1st—4th squadrons	(4)	35 - 702

2nd Brigade: Général de brigade Stedmann

7th (1st Vistula Legion) Light Lancers, 1st—4th sqdrns	(4)	45 - 670

XIV Corps Artillery Reserve—

XIV Corps artillery reserve staff—1 person

7th Regiment of Foot Artillery, 10th company	2 - 104
6th Regiment of Foot Artillery, 5th company	2 - 110
3rd Regiment of Horse Artillery, 7th company	3 - 96
1st Regiment of Horse Artillery, 6th company	3 - 96
4th Principal Artillery Train Battalion, detachments of the 3rd and 6th cos	2 - 250
1st *bis* Artillery Train Battalion, detachment of the 5th company	2 - 97
10th *bis* Artillery Train Battalion, 4th company	1 - 124
3rd Battalion of Pontoniers, 5th company	3 - 133
2nd Battalion, Sappers of the Line, 8th company	3 - 132
4th Battalion, Sappers of the Line, 5th company	2 - 139
6th company	3 - 137
7th company	3 - 129
Sapper Train, 6th company	3 - 143
2nd Equipage Battalion, 6th company	1 - 95

Note: There were no artillery materiel returns for XIV Corps for this date. However, consult Appendices O and P for artillery materiel returns for the XIV Corps for 1 October and 10 October 1813.

GOVERNMENT OF HAMBURG
Général de division Count Hogendorp
Adjudant commandant Fernif, Chief of Staff
Colonel Castille, commanding the artillery
Colonel de Ponthon, commanding the engineers

50th Division(-)—

2nd Brigade: Général de brigade Avril

33rd Light Infantry Regiment, detachment of 1st battalion	(1)	15 - 33
2nd battalion	(1)	17 - 539
5th (depot) battalion	(1)	2 - 36
Regimental artillery company of the 33rd Light		2 - 107

3rd Regiment of the Line, 2nd battalion	(1)	3 - 210
3rd battalion	(1)	3 - 210
4th battalion	(1)	3 - 208
5th (depot) battalion	(1)	3 - 113
Regimental artillery company of the 3rd Line		2 - 80
29th Regiment of the Line, 2nd battalion	(1)	24 - 555
3rd battalion	(1)	18 - 714
4th battalion	(1)	18 - 635
5th (depot) battalion	(1)	4 - 199
Regimental artillery company of the 29th Line		2 - 87
105th Regiment of the Line, 2nd battalion	(1)	2 - 216
3rd battalion	(1)	2 - 215
4th battalion	(1)	9 - 990
5th (depot) battalion	(1)	5 - 245
Regimental artillery company of the 105th Line		2 - 87

**Provisional Brigade of Cuirassiers of Hamburg—
Général de brigade Duboise**

1st Provisional Regiment of Cuirassiers, consisting of the 4th squadrons from the 1st, 2nd, and 3rd Cuirassier Regiments	(3)	23 - 455
2nd Provisional Regiment of Cuirassiers, consisting of the 4th squadron of the 5th Cuirassiers	(1)	6 - 220
3rd Provisional Regiment of Cuirassiers, consisting of the 4th squadrons of the 9th—12th Cuirassier Regiments	(4)	25 - 622

Cavalry Regiments de Marche of Hamburg—

Detachments of 23 regiments of cavalry		43 - 1,264

Miscelleneous Troops in Hamburg—

28th Chasseurs à Cheval, 3rd—5th squadrons	(3)	36 - 629
17th Polish (Lithuanian) Uhlans, depot squadron	(1)	6 - 66
13th Veterans Battalion	(1)	13 - 450
Various depot troops		14 - 840
Imperial Gendarmes		10 - 245
2nd Battalion, Sappers of the Line, 1st company		4 - 143
5th Regiment of Foot Artilery, 1st company		2 - 109
12th Battalion of Equipage Train, detachment		4 - 62

Note: There were no artillery materiel returns for the Government of Hamburg troops. Therefore, no ordnance details have been shown. However, it is assumed that the regiments with their own artillery company each fielded 2 pieces of ordnance.

CAVALRY RESERVES

Marshal Murat, King of Naples, commanding the cavalry
Général de division Count Belliard, Chief of Staff
Murat's headquarters staff—9 personnel

I RESERVE CAVALRY CORPS

Général de division Baron Latour-Maubourg
Adjudant commandant Mathieu, Chief of Staff
Colonel Lavoy, commanding the artillery
Corps headquarters staff—14 personnel

1st Light Cavalry Division— Général de division Baron Corbineau

Division headquarters staff—10 personnel
1st Brigade: Général de brigade Piré

6th Hussars, 1st and 2nd squadrons	(2)	21 - 377
7th Hussars, 1st squadron	(1)	13 - 186
2nd squadron	(1)	9 - 156
3rd squadron	(1)	5 - 105
8th Hussars, 1st squadron	(1)	13 - 180
2nd squadron	(1)	8 - 159
3rd squadron	(1)	7 - 196

2nd Brigade: Général de brigade Montmarie

16th Chasseurs à Cheval, 1st and 2nd squadrons	(2)	27 - 426
1st Light Lancers, 1st and 2nd squadrons	(2)	24 - 390
3rd Light Lancers, 1st and 2nd squadrons	(2)	16 - 280

3rd Brigade: Général de brigade Piquet

5th Light Lancers, 1st and 2nd squadrons	(2)	24 - 370
8th (2nd Vistula Legion) Light Lancers, 1st and 2nd sqdrns	(2)	30 - 346
1st Italian Chasseurs à Cheval, 1st squadron	(1)	17 - 198
2nd squadron	(1)	7 - 162
3rd squadron	(1)	8 - 166
4th squadron	(1)	8 - 169

3rd Light Cavalry Division— Général de division Baron Chastel

Division headquarters staff—9 personnel
1st Brigade: Général de brigade Vallin

8th Chasseurs à Cheval, 1st and 2nd squadrons	(2)	22 - 393
9th Chasseurs à Cheval, 1st and 2nd squadrons	(2)	17 - 361
25th Chasseurs à Cheval, 1st and 2nd squadrons	(2)	24 - 407

2nd Brigade: Général de brigade Van Merlen

1st Chasseurs à Cheval, 1st squadron	(1)	16 - 149
2nd squadron	(1)	10 - 212
3rd squadron	(1)	4 - 114
19th Chasseurs à Cheval, 1st squadron	(1)	8 - 133
2nd squadron	(1)	8 - 224
3rd squadron	(1)	8 - 252
4th squadron	(1)	7 - 252

3rd Brigade: Général de brigade Dermoncourt

2nd Chasseurs à Cheval, 1st and 2nd squadrons	(2)	26 - 297
3rd Chasseurs à Cheval, 1st and 2nd squadrons	(2)	26 - 419
6th Chasseurs à Cheval, 1st and 2nd squadrons	(2)	23 - 494

1st Heavy Cavalry Division— Général de division Baron Bordesoulle

Division headquarters staff—13 personnel

1st Brigade: Général de brigade Berckeim

2nd Cuirassiers, 1st and 2nd squadrons	(2)	18 - 302
3rd Cuirassiers, 1st and 2nd squadrons	(2)	21 - 265
6th Cuirassiers, 1st and 2nd squadrons	(2)	17 - 222

2nd Brigade: Général de brigade Bessières

9th Cuirassiers, 1st, 2nd, and 3rd squadrons	(3)	28 - 423
11th Cuirassiers, 1st, 2nd, and 3rd squadrons	(3)	26 - 332
12th Cuirassiers, 1st and 2nd squadrons	(2)	22 - 288

3rd Brigade: Général de brigade Lessing

Saxon Garde du corps, 1st squadron	(1)	11 - 175
2nd squadron	(1)	4 - 149
3rd squadron	(1)	6 - 158
4th squadron	(1)	3 - 159
Saxon Zastrow Cuirassiers, 1st squadron	(1)	7 - 148
2nd squadron	(1)	5 - 142
3rd squadron	(1)	4 - 143
4th squadron	(1)	5 - 143

3rd Heavy Cavalry Division— Général de division Baron Doumerc

Division headquarters staff—8 personnel

1st Brigade: Général de brigade Lalaing d'Audenarde

4th Cuirassiers, 1st 2nd, and 3rd squadrons	(3)	28 - 376
7th Cuirassiers, 1st, 2nd, and 3rd squadrons	(3)	20 - 271
14th (Dutch) Cuirassiers, 1st and 2nd squadrons	(2)	12 - 230
Italian Dragoons "Napoleon", 1st squadron	(1)	15 - 176
2nd squadron	(1)	3 - 140
3rd squadron	(1)	5 - 132
4th squadron	(1)	4 - 142

2nd Brigade: Général de brigade Reiset

7th Dragoons, 1st and 2nd squadrons	(2)	24 - 286
23rd Dragoons, 1st, 2nd, and 3rd squadrons	(3)	21 - 341
28th Dragoons, 1st and 2nd squadrons	(2)	25 - 333
30th Dragoons, 1st and 2nd squadrons	(2)	26 - 355

I Reserve Cavalry Corps Artillery Reserve—

1st Regiment of Horse Artillery, 3rd company	4 - 85
3rd Regiment of Horse Artillery, 6th company	3 - 100
4th Regiment of Horse Artillery, 1st company	3 - 100
6th Regiment of Horse Artillery, 1st company	3 - 68
Saxon Horse Artillery, 1st company	3 - 77
Italian Horse Artillery, 4th company	4 - 90

The horse artillery companies each consisted of
4 6-pdr. guns and 2 5 1/2-inch howitzers—total of 36 pieces of ordnance.

1st *bis* Artillery Train Battalion, detachment of the 1st company	1 - 68

detachment of the 2nd company	1 - 86
8th *bis* Artillery Train Battalion, detachment of the 2nd company	1 - 64
detachment of the 5th company	1 - 60
Saxon Artillery Train, 1st company	1 - 72
Italian Artillery Train, 6th company	2 - 71

I Reserve Cavalry Corps troops in route to join their regiments—
Detachments of the:

6th Hussars	6 - 128
7th Hussars	1 - 24
8th Hussars	4 - 63
16th Chasseurs à Cheval	7 - 136
1st Light Lancers	12 - 296
3rd Light Lancers	8 - 195
5th Light Lancers	13 - 317
8th (2nd Vistula) Light Lancers	5 - 99
8th Chasseurs à Cheval	5 - 42
25th Chasseurs à Cheval	6 - 72
1st Chasseurs à Cheval	3 - 94
19th Chasseurs à Cheval	4 - 130
2nd Chasseurs à Cheval	3 - 114
3rd Chasseurs à Cheval	3 - 46
6th Chasseurs à Cheval	6 - 113
2nd Cuirassiers	6 - 109
3rd Cuirassiers	4 - 106
6th Cuirassiers	5 - 111
9th Cuirassiers	2 - 103
11th Cuirassiers	4 - 116
12th Cuirassiers	10 - 222
4th Cuirassiers	8 - 93
7th Cuirassiers	3 - 61
14th (Dutch) Cuirassiers	9 - 176
7th Dragoons	12 - 117
23rd Dragoons	3 - 39
28th Dragoons	- 9

II RESERVE CAVALRY CORPS
Général de division Count Sébastiani de la Porta
Adjudant commandant Lascours, Chief of Staff
Colonel Colin, commanding the artillery
Corps headquarters staff—10 personnel

2nd Light Cav Division— Général de division Baron* Roussel d'Hurbal
Division headquarters staff—9 personnel
1st Brigade: Général de brigade Gérard

11th Chasseurs à Cheval, 1st , 2nd, and 3rd squadrons	(3)	26 - 456
12th Chasseurs à Cheval, 1st, 2nd, and 3rd squadrons	(3)	23 - 416
5th Hussars, 1st squadron	(1)	17 - 153
2nd squadron	(1)	8 - 174
3rd squadron	(1)	5 - 123

2nd Brigade: Général de brigade Domanget

9th Hussars, 1st squadron	(1)	13 - 205
2nd squadron	(1)	8 - 203
3rd squadron	(1)	7 - 202
4th squadron	(1)	8 - 210
2nd Light Lancers, 1st, 2nd, and 3rd squadrons	(3)	21 - 421
4th Light Lancers, 1st squadron	(1)	16 - 163
2nd squadron	(1)	12 - 226
3rd squadron	(1)	4 - 114

*Awarded title "Baron of the Empire" on 28 September 1813.

4th Light Cavalry Division— Général de division Baron Exelmans

Division headquarters staff—9 personnel

1st Brigade: Général de brigade Maurin

6th Light Lancers, 1st and 2nd squadrons	(2)	23 - 351
4th Chasseurs à Cheval, 1st and 2nd squadrons	(2)	18 - 276
7th Chasseurs à Cheval, 1st squadron	(1)	14 - 207
2nd squadron	(1)	7 - 107
3rd squadron	(1)	15 - 199

2nd Brigade: Général de brigade Wathier

20th Chasseurs à Cheval, 1st squadron	(1)	14 - 201
2nd squadron	(1)	9 - 157
3rd squadron	(1)	8 - 170
4th squadron	(1)	4 - 76
23rd Chasseurs à Cheval, 1st squadron	(1)	14 - 182
2nd squadron	(1)	7 - 137
3rd squadron	(1)	6 - 151
4th squadron	(1)	6 - 150
24th Chasseurs à Cheval, 1st squadron	(1)	10 - 110
2nd squadron	(1)	4 - 84
3rd squadron	(1)	7 - 159
11th (Dutch) Hussars, 1st and 2nd squadrons	(2)	19 - 220

2nd Heavy Cavalry Division— Général de division Count* Saint-Germain

Division headquarters staff—3 personnel

1st Brigade: Général de brigade d'Hugérauville

1st Carabiniers, 1st and 2nd squadrons	(2)	21 - 328
2nd Carabiniers, 1st and 2nd squadrons	(2)	24 - 348
1st Cuirassiers, 1st and 2nd squadrons	(2)	22 - 301

2nd Brigade: Général de brigade Thiry

5th Cuirassiers, 1st squadron	(1)	19 - 165
2nd squadron	(1)	7 - 158
3rd squadron	(1)	4 - 82
8th Cuirassiers, 1st and 2nd squadrons	(2)	18 - 221
10th Cuirassiers, 1st and 2nd squadrons	(2)	25 - 339

*Baron Saint-Germain was awarded titled "Count of the Empire" on 28 September 1813.

II Reserve Cavalry Corps Reserve Artillery—

1st Regiment of Horse Artillery, 7th company	4 - 103
4th Regiment of Horse Artillery, 7th company	3 - 94

6th Regiment of Horse Artillery, 8th company   3 - 84
    The above horse artillery companies each consisted of
    4 6-pdr. guns and 2 5½-inch howitzers—total of 18 pieces of ordnance.
11th *bis* Artillery Train Battalion, detachment of the 2nd company   1 - 62
    detachment of the 4th company   - 57
13th *bis* Artillery Train Battalion, 3rd company   1 - 133

II Reserve Cavalry Corps troops in route to join their regiments—

Detachments of the:

11th Chasseurs à Cheval	- 6
12th Chasseurs à Cheval	2 - 18
5th Hussars	15 - 263
9th Hussars	- 51
2nd Light Lancers	5 - 119
4th Light Lancers	3 - 137
6th Light Lancers	8 - 198
4th Chasseurs à Cheval	6 - 130
20th Chasseurs à Cheval	- 14
23rd Chasseurs à Cheval	1 - 40
24th Chasseurs à Cheval	14 - 345
11th (Dutch) Hussars	4 - 120
1st Carabiniers	3 - 127
2nd Carabiniers	4 - 98
1st Cuirassiers	2 - 115
8th Cuirassiers	- 11
10th Cuirassiers	1 - 49
5th Cuirassiers	- 4

III RESERVE CAVALRY CORPS

Général de division Arrighi de Casanova, Duke of Padoua
Adjudant commandant Salel, Chief of Staff
Colonel Chauveau, commanding the artillery
Corps headquarters staff—14 personnel

5th Light Cavalry Division— Général de division Baron Lorge
Division headquarters staff—8 personnel
1st Brigade: Général de brigade Jacquinot

5th Chasseurs à Cheval, 3rd and 4th squadrons	(2)	19 - 451
10th Chasseurs à Cheval, 3rd and 4th squadrons	(2)	12 - 276
13th Chasseurs à Cheval, 5th and 6th squadrons	(2)	17 - 366

2nd Brigade: Général de brigade Merlin

15th Chasseurs à Cheval, 4th squadron	(1)	9 - 218
21st Chasseurs à Cheval, 3rd squadron	(1)	8 - 219
22nd Chasseurs à Cheval, 3rd and 4th squadrons	(2)	13 - 459

6th Light Cavalry Division— Général de division Baron Fournier
Division headquarters staff—6 personnel
1st Brigade: Général de brigade Mouriez

29th Chasseurs à Cheval, 4th squadron	(1)	6 - 222
31st Chasseurs à Cheval, 4th squadron	(1)	9 - 222

1st Hussars, 4th squadron	(1)	5 - 197
2nd Brigade: Général de brigade Amcil		
2nd Hussars, 3rd squadron	(1)	9 - 241
4th Hussars, 5th squadron	(1)	4 - 209
12th Hussars, 4th squadron	(1)	9 - 228

4th Heavy Cavalry Division— Général de division Count Defrance
Division headquarters staff—7 personnel
1st Brigade: Général de brigade Avice

4th Dragoons, 4th squadron	(1)	6 - 111
5th Dragoons, 3rd squadron	(1)	8 - 203
12th Dragoons, 3rd squadron	(1)	9 - 166
14th Dragoons, 3rd squadron	(1)	8 - 155
24th Dragoons, 4th squadron	(1)	1 - 82

2nd Brigade: Général de brigade Quinette

16th Dragoons, 3rd squadron	(1)	4 - 105
17th Dragoons, 3rd squadron	(1)	14 - 208
21st Dragoons, 3rd squadron	(1)	9 - 138
26th Dragoons, 3rd squadron	(1)	1 - 94
27th Dragoons, 5th squadron	(1)	5 - 68
13th Cuirassiers, 5th squadron	(1)	5 - 171

III Reserve Cavalry Corps Reserve Artillery—

5th Regiment of Horse Artillery, 1st company	3 - 93
5th company	2 - 100
1st Regiment of Horse Artillery, 2nd company	3 - 93
6th Regiment of Horse Artillery, 4th company	2 - 89

The above horse artillery companies each consisted of
4 6-pdr. guns and 2 51/2-inch howitzers—total of 24 pieces of ordnance.

4th Principal Artillery Train Battalion, 5th company	2 - 205
1st *bis* Artillery Train Battalion, 5th company	2 - 130

III Reserve Cavalry Corps troops in route to join their regiments—
Detachments of the:

5th Chasseurs à Cheval	7 - 185
10th Chasseurs à Cheval	1 - 129
13th Chasseurs à Cheval	2 - 61
15th Chasseurs à Cheval	2 - 125
21st Chasseurs à Cheval	4 - 126
22nd Chasseurs à Cheval	3 - 125
31st Chasseurs à Cheval	4 - 123
1st Hussars	5 - 125
2nd Hussars	6 - 250
12th Hussars	2 - 201
4th Dragoons	4 - 53
14th Dragoons	5 - 209
24th Dragoons	2 - 105
16th Dragoons	- 66
17th Dragoons	1 - 20
21st Dragoons	- 18
26th Dragoons	2 - 83

27th Dragoons		3 - 150
13th Cuirassiers		2 - 68
5th Dragoons		- 2

IV RESERVE CAVALRY CORPS
Général de division Kellermann, Count of Valmy
Adjudant commandant Tancarsville, Chief of Staff
Corps headquarters staff—2 personnel

7th Light Cavalry Division— Général de division Sokolnicki
Division headquarters staff—14 personnel
1st Brigade: detached to and serving with the 27th Division in I Corps
2nd Brigade: Général de brigade Tolinski

3rd Polish Uhlans, 1st squadron	(1)	19 - 208
2nd squadron	(1)	8 - 195
3rd squadron	(1)	9 - 199
4th squadron	(1)	4 - 144
13th Polish Hussars, 1st squadron	(1)	19 - 164
2nd squadron	(1)	7 - 102
3rd squadron	(1)	8 - 105
4th squadron	(1)	8 - 127

Divisional artillery and train:
Polish Horse Artillery and train, consisting of   6 - 106
   4 6-pdr. guns and 2 51/2-inch howitzers—total of 6 pieces of ordnance.

8th Light Cavalry Division— Général de division Sulkowski
Division headquarters staff—16 personnel
1st Brigade: Général de brigade Ominski

1st Polish Chasseurs à Cheval, 1st squadron	(1)	20 - 181
2nd squadron	(1)	7 - 119
3rd squadron	(1)	8 - 141
4th squadron	(1)	11 - 98
6th Polish Uhlans, 1st squadron	(1)	20 - 182
2nd squadron	(1)	8 - 141
3rd squadron	(1)	9 - 148
4th squadron	(1)	11 - 126

2nd Brigade: Général de brigade Weissenhoff

8th Polish Uhlans, 1st squadron	(1)	20 - 231
2nd squadron	(1)	11 - 167
3rd squadron	(1)	11 - 170
4th squadron	(1)	15 - 164
16th Polish (Lithuanian) Uhlans, 1st squadron	(1)	19 - 193
2nd squadron	(1)	11 - 130
3rd squadron	(1)	11 - 118
4th squadron	(1)	12 - 129

Divisional artillery and train:
Polish Horse Artillery and train, consisting of   8 - 161
   4 6-pdr. guns and 2 51/2-inch howitzers—total of 6 pieces of ordnance.

V RESERVE CAVALRY CORPS
Général de division Baron L'héritier
Adjandant commandant Soubeiran, Chief of Staff
Corps headquarters staff—2 personnel

9th Light Cavalry Division— Général de brigade Baron Klicky
Division headquarters staff—4 personnel
1st Brigade: (no commander yet assigned)

3rd Hussars, 3rd and 4th squadrons	(2)	14 - 374
27th Chasseurs à Cheval, 3rd and 4th squadrons	(2)	10 - 207

2nd Brigade: (no commander yet assigned)

14th Chasseurs à Cheval, 3rd and 4th squadrons	(2)	12 - 337
26th Chasseurs à Cheval, 3rd and 4th squadrons	(2)	14 - 283
13th Hussars, 1st squadron	(1)	7 - 200
3rd squadron	(1)	7 - 145
4th squadron	(1)	7 - 132

5th Heavy Cavalry Division— Général de brigade Baron Collaert
Division headquarters staff—1 person
1st Brigade: (no commander yet assigned)

2nd Dragoons, 3rd squadron	(1)	11 - 157
6th Dragoons, 3rd and 4th squadrons	(2)	14 - 267

2nd Brigade: (no commander yet assigned)

11th Dragoons, 3rd and 4th squadrons	(2)	12 - 209
13th Dragoons, 3rd squadron	(1)	12 - 178
15th Dragoons, 3rd squadron	(1)	8 - 182

6th Heavy Cavalry Division— Général de brigade Baron Lamotte
Division headquarters staff—1 person
1st Brigade: (no commander yet assigned)

18th Dragoons, 3rd squadron	(1)	6 - 89
19th Dragoons, 3rd squadron	(1)	10 - 202
20th Dragoons, 3rd squadron	(1)	9 - 167

2nd Brigade: (no commander yet assigned)

22nd Dragoons, 3rd squadron	(1)	8 - 183
25th Dragoons, 3rd squadron	(1)	9 - 201

V Reserve Cavalry Corps Reserve Artillery—

2nd Regiment of Horse Artillery, 5th company, consisting of	3 - 92
3 6-pdr. guns—total of 3 pieces of ordnance.	

V Reserve Cavalry Corps troops in route to join their regiments—

Detachments of the:

3rd Hussars	3 - 177
27th Chasseurs à Cheval	14 - 375
14th Chasseurs à Cheval	4 - 130
26th Chasseurs à Cheval	5 - 181
2nd Dragoons	7 - 80
6th Dragoons	6 - 158
11th Dragoons	5 - 90
15th Dragoons	3 - 126
18th Dragoons	6 - 91
19th Dragoons	3 - 98
20th Dragoons	- 34
25th Dragoons	3 - 126

V *bis* RESERVE CAVALRY CORPS
Général de division Baron Milhaud

9th *bis* Light Cavalry Division— Général de brigade Baron Vial

1st Brigade: (no commander yet assigned)

3rd Hussars, 1st squadron	(1)	17 - 263
27th Chasseurs à Cheval, 1st and a detachment of the 2nd	(1+)	12 - 305

2nd Brigade: (no commander yet assigned)

14th Chasseurs à Cheval, 1st squadron	(1)	12 - 179
26th Chasseurs à Cheval, 1st squadron	(1)	9 - 239
13th Hussars, 2nd squadron	(1)	8 - 157

5th *bis* Heavy Cavalry Division— Général de brigade Baron Queunot

1st Brigade: (no commander yet assigned)

2nd Dragoons, 1st and a detachment of the 2nd squadrons	(1+)	13 - 325
6th Dragoons, 1st and a detachment of the 2nd squadrons	(1+)	16 - 286

2nd Brigade: (no commander yet assigned)

11th Dragoons, 1st and 2nd squadrons	(2)	20 - 366
13th Dragoons, 1st squadron	(1)	7 - 154
15th Dragoons, 1st and a detachment of the 2nd squadrons	(1+)	19 - 290

6th *bis* Heavy Cavalry Division— Général de brigade Baron Montélégier

1st Brigade: (no commander yet assigned)

18th Dragoons, 1st squadron	(1)	15 - 236
19th Dragoons, 1st squadron	(1)	13 - 205
20th Dragoons, 1st squadron	(1)	3 - 85

2nd Brigade: (no commander yet assigned)

22nd Dragoons, 1st and 2nd squadrons	(2)	15 - 314
25th Dragoons, 1st squadron	(1)	16 - 242

ARMY OF ITALY*

Prince Eugène de Beauharnais, Viceroy of Italy

Général de division Vignolle, Chief of Staff
Général de division Saint-Laurent, commanding the artillery
Colonel Moydier, commanding the enginners
Army headquarters staff—28 personnel
*Officially titled "Corps d'Observation d'Italie"

I CORPS*—ARMY OF ITALY

Général de division Count Grenier

Adjudant commandant Bazin, Chief of Staff
Major Bernard, commanding the artillery
*Officially titled "1ère Lieutenance du Corps d'Observation d'Italie"

1st Infantry Division— Général de division Baron Quesnel du Torpt

Division headquarters staff—10 personnel
1st Brigade: (no commander yet assigned)

84th Regiment of the Line, 1st battalion	(1)	27 - 619
2nd battalion	(1)	22 - 531
3rd battalion	(1)	24 - 604
4th battalion	(1)	22 - 655
Regimental artillery company of the 84th Line, consisting of 2 6-pdr. guns—total of 2 pieces of ordnance.		2 - 48

2nd Brigade: Général de brigade Campy

92nd Regiment of the Line, 1st battalion	(1)	27 - 547
2nd battalion	(1)	20 - 569
3rd battalion	(1)	18 - 469
4th battalion	(1)	20 - 578
Regimental artillery company of the 92nd Line, consisting of 2 6-pdr. guns—total of 2 pieces of ordnance.		2 - 44

30th Provisional Demi-Brigade, consisting of

8th battalion, 6th Regiment of the Line	(1)	21 - 780
3rd battalion, 10th Regiment of the Line	(1)	19 - 472
3rd battalion, 1st Light Infantry Regiment	(1)	22 - 749
8th battalion, 14th Light Infantry Regiment	(1)	13 - 645

Divisional artillery and train:

4th Regiment of Foot Artillery, 9th company	3 - 109
4th Regiment of Horse Artillery, 4th company	2 - 98

The 4/9th foot artillery company consisted of 6 6-pdr. guns
and 2 5 1/2-inch howitzers; the 4/4th horse artillery company
consisted of 4 6-pdr. guns and 2 5 1/2-inch howitzers—total of 14 pieces of ordnance.

1st *bis* Artillery Train Battalion, detachment of the 6th company	2 - 128
detachment of the 7th company	2 - 115
1st Battalion, Sappers of the Line, detachment of the 6th company	2 - 75
9th Battalion of Equipage Train, detachment of the 1st company	1 - 65

4th Infantry Division— Général de division Baron Marcognet

Division headquarters staf—8 personnel
1st Brigade: Général de brigade Ganin

53rd Regiment of the Line, 1st battalion	(1)	32 - 583
2nd battalion	(1)	18 - 471
3rd battalion	(1)	17 - 427
4th battalion	(1)	18 - 537
Regimental artillery company of the 53rd Line,		2 - 45
consisting of 2 6-pdr. guns—total of 2 pieces of ordnance.		

2nd Brigade: Général de brigade Dupeyrower

106th Regiment of the Line, 1st battalion	(1)	35 - 555
2nd battalion	(1)	16 - 585
3rd battalion	(1)	16 - 450
4th battalion	(1)	15 - 489
Regimental artillery company of the 106th Line,		2 - 38
consisting of 2 6-pdr. guns—total of 2 pieces of ordnance.		

20th Provisional Demi-Brigade, consisting of

4th battalion, 20th Regiment of the Line	(1)	21 - 786
6th battalion, 101st Regiment of the Line	(1)	18 - 747
6th battalion, 112th Regiment of the Line	(1)	17 - 573

Divisional artillery and train:

2nd Regiment of Foot Artillery, 6th company	3 - 117
25th company	3 - 111
The foot artillery companies each consisted of	
6 6-pdr. guns and 2 5½-inch howitzers—total of 16 pieces of ordnance.	
10th Principal Artillery Train Battalion, detachment of the 5th company	2 - 97
detachment of the 6th company	1 - 98
1st Battalion, Sappers of the Line, detachment of the 3rd company	1 - 75
9th Battalion of Equipage Train, detachment of the 2nd company	1 - 60

II CORPS*—ARMY OF ITALY
Général de division Count Verdier
Adjudant commandant Hector, Chief of Staff
Major Hottzmann, commanding the artillery
*Officially titled "2ème Lieutenance du Corps d'Observation d'Italie"

2nd Infantry Division— Général de division Baron Rouyier

Division headquarters staff—11 personnel
1st Brigade: Général de brigade Schmitz

9th Regiment of the Line, 1st battalion	(1)	23 - 520
2nd battalion	(1)	21 - 455
3rd battalion	(1)	21 - 514
4th battalion	(1)	23 - 412
Regimental artillery company of the 9th Line,		2 - 41
consisting of 2 6-pdr. guns—total of 2 pieces of ordnance.		

2nd Brigade: (no commander yet assigned)
35th Regiment of the Line, 1st battalion	(1)	24 - 617
2nd battalion	(1)	20 - 577
3rd battalion	(1)	19 - 525
4th battalion	(1)	21 - 512
Regimental artillery company of the 35th Line,		2 - 49

consisting of 2 6-pdr. guns—total of 2 pieces of ordnance.
28th Provisional Demi-Brigade, consisting of
6th battalion, 7th Regiment of the Line	(1)	14 - 793
6th battalion, 52nd Regiment of the Line	(1)	15 - 762
6th battalion, 67th Regiment of the Line	(1)	16 - 802

Divisional artillery and train:
2nd Regiment of Foot Artillery, 4th company	2 - 109
4th Regiment of Horse Artillery, 5th company	2 - 95

The foot artillery company consisted of 6 6-pdr. guns and
2 51/2-inch howitzers; the horse artillery company consisted
of 4 6-pdr. guns and 2 51/2-inch howitzers—total of 14 pieces of ordnance.
10th Principal Artillery Train Battalion, 4th company and a detachment from the 6th company	3 - 132
1st Battalion, Sappers of the Line, detachment of the 3rd company	2 - 62
9th Battalion of Equipage Train, detachment of the 2nd company	1 - 60

3rd Infantry Division— Général de division Baron Gratien

Division headquarters staff—8 personnel
1st Brigade: Général de brigade Piat
35th Light Infantry Regiment, 2nd battalion	(1)	16 - 522
3rd battalion	(1)	18 - 540
36th Light Infantry Regiment, 2nd battalion	(1)	19 - 500
3rd battalion	(1)	13 - 481
102nd Regiment of the Line, 3rd battalion	(1)	18 - 758
6th battalion	(1)	11 - 731

2nd Brigade: Général de brigade de Conchi
42nd Regiment of the Line, 3rd battalion	(1)	16 - 775
6th battalion	(1)	14 - 770

31st Provisional Demi-Brigade, consisting of
2nd battalion, 131st Regiment of the Line	(1)	16 - 497
2nd battalion, 132nd Regiment of the Line	(1)	13 - 476
2nd batalion, 133rd Regiment of the Line	(1)	20 - 534

Divisional artillery and train:
2nd Regiment of Foot Artillery, 17th company	3 - 108
23rd company	3 - 112

The above foot artilery companies each consisted of
6 6-pdr. guns and 2 51/2-inch howitzers—total of 16 pieces of ordnance.
10th Principal Artillery Train Battalion, detachment of the 1st company	1 - 80
detachment of the 2nd company	1 - 75
1st Battalion, Sappers of the Line, detachment of the 6th company	2 - 72
9th Battalion of Equipage Train, detachment of the 1st company	1 - 60

III CORPS*—ARMY OF ITALY
Général de division Count Pino
Adjudant commandant Paolucci, Chief of Staff
Chef de bataillon Vacani, commanding the engineers
*Officially titled "3ème Lieutenance du Corps d'Observation d'Italie"

5th Infantry Division— Général de division Baron Palombini
Division headquarters staff—12 personnel
1st Brigade: Général de brigade Ruggieri

2nd Italian Light Infantry Regiment, 2nd battalion	(1)	11 - 548
1st Italian Regiment of the Line, 1st battalion	(1)	16 - 572
2nd Italian Regiment of the Line, 1st battalion	(1)	36 - 548
2nd battalion	(1)	14 - 545
3rd battalion	(1)	13 - 562
4th battalion	(1)	10 - 577

Regimental artillery company of the 2nd Italian Line (detached—not present)
2nd Brigade: Général de brigade Galimberti

Dalmatian Regiment, 1st battalion	(1)	24 - 510
2nd battalion	(1)	17 - 508

Regimental artillery company of the Dalmatian Regiment (detached—not present)

3rd Italian Regiment of the Line, 1st battalion	(1)	26 - 550
2nd batalion	(1)	15 - 560
3rd battalion	(1)	11 - 481
4th battalion	(1)	13 - 520

Regimental artillery company of the 3rd Italian Line (detached—not present)
Divisional artillery and train:

Italian Foot Artillery, 5th company	4 - 95
11th company	4 - 112

The above foot artillery companies each consisted of
6 6-pdr. guns and 2 5½-inch howitzers—total of 16 pieces of ordnance.

Italian Artillery Train, 1st company	2 - 107
2nd company	2 - 111
1st Battalion, Italian Sappers, 2nd company	3 - 138
Italian Tranports, 3rd company	3 - 102

6th Infantry Division— *
Division headquarters staff—9 personnel
1st Brigade (Italian Royal Guard): Général de brigade Lecchi

Italian Royal Guard Vélites, 1st battalion	(1)	29 - 640
Italian Royal Guards of Honor Cavalry, 1st squadron	(1)	6 - 143
Italian Royal Guard Chasseurs à pied†, 1st battalion	(1)	24 - 488
2nd battalion	(1)	14 - 398
3rd battalion	(1)	14 - 417
4th battalion	(1)	14 - 400
Italian Royal Guard Grenadiers à pied, 1st battalion	(1)	22 - 538

2nd Brigade: Général de brigade Bellotti

3rd Italian Light Infantry Regiment, 1st battalion	(1)	20 - 835
2nd battalion	(1)	19 - 796
3rd battalion	(1)	16 - 640
4th battalion	(1)	18 - 630
Regimental artillery company of the 3rd Italian Light, consisting of 2 6-pdr. guns—total of 2 pieces of ordnance.		3 - 56
4th Italian Light Infantry Regiment, 1st battalion	(1)	15 - 508
2nd battalion	(1)	14 - 500

Divisional artillery and train:

Italian Royal Guard Foot Artillery, 1st company	4 - 68
Italian Royal Guard Horse Artillery, 1st company	2 - 54
Both the foot artillery company and horse artillery company of the Italian Royal Guard consisted of 4 6-pdr. guns and 2 51/2-inch howitzers—total of 12 pieces of ordnance.	
Italian Royal Guard Artillery Train Battalion, 1st and 2nd companies	4 - 274
Marins of the Italian Royal Guard, 1 company	3 - 190
Italian Tranports, 4th company	2 - 115

* There was no commanding officer listed for the 6th Infantry Division.
† This regiment, formerly known as the Conscripts of the Italian Royal Guard, was renamed Chasseurs following their heroic conduct during the 1812 campaign.

RESERVE*—ARMY OF ITALY
*Officially titled "Réserve du Corps d'Observation d'Italie"

7th Infantry Division— Général de division Baron Bonfanti

1st Brigade: Général de brigade Mazzuchelli

25th Provisional Demi-Brigade, consisting of		
2nd battalion, 1st Regiment of the Line	(1)	10 - 654
3rd battalion, 16th Regiment of the Line	(1)	17 - 710
4th battalion, 62nd Regiment of the Line	(1)	19 - 663
1st Italian Foreign Regiment d'élite, 1st battalion	(1)	15 - 589
2nd battalion	(1)	13 - 555
2nd Italian Foreign Regiment d'élite, 1st battalion	(1)	21 - 806

2nd Brigade: (no commander yet assigned)

3rd Provisional Croatian Regiment, 1st battalion	(1)	20 - 820
2nd battalion	(1)	20 - 820
1st Neapolitan Regiment of the Line, 1st—3rd bns	(3)	60 - 2,460
2nd Neapolitan Regiment of the Line, 1st—3rd bns	(3)	60 - 2,460

Divisional artillery and train:

3rd Regiment of Foot Artillery, 3rd company, consisting of 6 6-pdr. guns and 2 51/2-inch howitzers—total of 8 pieces of ordnance.	3 - 105
10th Principal Artillery Train Battalion, detachment of the 5th company	1 - 75

CAVALRY DIVISION—ARMY OF ITALY
Général de division Baron Mermet
Division headquarters staff—4 personnel

1st Brigade: Général de brigade Perfrémond		
3rd Italian Chasseurs à Cheval, 1st squadron	(1)	14 - 221
2nd squadron	(1)	6 - 170
3rd squadron	(1)	7 - 145
4th squadron	(1)	6 - 160
4th Italian Chasseurs à Cheval, 3rd squadron	(1)	10 - 150
4th squadron	(1)	9 - 144
2nd Brigade: Général de brigade Bennemain		
Italian Dragoons "Regina", 1st squadron	(1)	14 - 151
2nd squadron	(1)	5 - 107
3rd squadron	(1)	7 - 118
4th squadron	(1)	7 - 102
Italian Royal Guard Dragoons, 1st squadron	(1)	11 - 140
2nd squadron	(1)	7 - 126
19th Chasseurs à Cheval, 5th squadron	(1)	7 - 233
6th squadron	(1)	8 - 240
3rd Brigade: (no commandwer yet assigned)		
1st Hussars, 1st squadron	(1)	18 - 223
2nd squadron	(1)	4 - 122
3rd squadron	(1)	6 - 252
6th squadron (organizing in Lyon)	(1)	8 - 242
31st Chasseurs à Cheval, 1st squadron	(1)	12 - 217
2nd squadron	(1)	5 - 222
3rd squadron	(1)	4 - 223
6th squadron (organizing in Venice)	(1)	8 - 240
1st Neapolitan Chasseurs à Cheval, 1st squadron	(1)	15 - 200
2nd, 3rd, and 4th squadrons	(3)	24 - 546
Divisional artillery and train:		
4th Regiment of Horse Artillery, 6th company		2 - 95
Italian Horse Artillery, 2nd company		4 - 102
The horse artillery companies each consisted of		
4 6-pdr. guns and 2 5 1/2-inch howitzers—total of 12 pieces of ordnance.		
10th Principal Artillery Train Battalion, detachments from		
the 4th, 5th, and 6th companies		1 - 50
Italian Artillery Train, 3rd company		2 - 112

ARTILLERY RESERVE—ARMY OF ITALY

4th Regiment of Foot Artillery, 19th company	3 - 112
24th company	3 - 114
6th Regiment of Foot Artillery, 19th company	3 - 104
21st company	3 - 108
Neapolitan Horse Artillery, 1st company	3 - 90
Neapolitan Foot Artillery, 1st company	2 - 120

The French foot artillery companies each consisted of 6 12-pdr. guns
and 2 6-inch howitzers; the Neapolitan artillery companies each consisted
of 4 6-pdr. guns and 2 5$_{1/2}$-inch howitzers—total of 44 pieces of ordnance.

6th Principal Artillery Train Battalion, 3rd company	2 - 138
10th Principal Artillery Train Battalion, detachment of the 1st company	- 47
7th bis Artillery Train Battalion, 8th company	- 89
Neapolitan Artillery Train, 1st company	2 - 60
2nd company	2 - 65
Ouvriers, detachment of the 10th company	- 23
3rd Battalion, Sappers of the Line, 8th company	3 - 147
Italian Sappers, 4th company	3 - 145

In addition to the preceding formations, there were numerous French garrisons on the Elbe, Oder, and Vistula Rivers. The strength of these garrisons were as follows:

Danzig (see X Corps)	993 -29,222
Modlin	200 - 3,675
Stettin	272 - 7,960
Custrin	158 - 3,889
Glogau	181 - 5,688
Magdebourg	86 - 3,250
Wittemberg	161 - 2,318
Erfurt	50 - 1,874
Wurzburg	43 - 911

Total manpower in garrisons: 2,144 officers and 58,787 other ranks.

There were also some 140 officers and 6,568 other ranks in the park of artillery and enginners of the army, and 178 officers and 5,975 other ranks (with only a total of 1,206 horses) in the general remount depots of the cavalry located at Magdebourg, Hamburg, and Frankfort. There was also an Observation Corps of Minden under Lemoine which numbered 154 officers and 6,143 other ranks.

Excluding Prince Eugène's Army of Italy, the total strength of all those present and under arms in the *Grande Armée* and in the theater of war amounted to 18,590 officers and 541,622 other ranks, plus 1,941 staff personnel.

Including Eugène's army, the grand total of all those present and under arms amounted to 20,505 officers and 623,666 other ranks, plus 2,033 staff personnel—a combined total of 656,204 people present and under arms.

SITUATION
of the
I RESERVE CAVALRY CORPS
1 September 1813

	Number of Squadrons	Present and Under Arms Off. - Others	Not Present In Hospital Off. - Others

Général de division Baron Latour-Maubourg
Adjudant commandant Mathieu, Chief of Staff
Colonel Lavoy, commanding the artillery
Corps headquarters staff—14 personnel

1st Light Cavalry Division—not present; detached to VI Corps.
3rd Light Cavalry Division— Général de division Baron Chastel
1st Brigade: Général de brigade Vallin

8th Chasseurs à Cheval, 1st squadron	(1)	15 - 157	- 18
2nd squadron	(1)	8 - 163	1 - 18
9th Chasseurs à Cheval, 1st squadron	(1)	not present	
2nd squadron	(1)	18 - 271	- 61
25th Chasseurs à Cheval, 1st squadron	(1)	8 - 159	1 - 44
2nd squadron	(1)	8 - 190	- 26
3rd squadron	(1)	3 - 26	2 - 5

2nd Brigade: Général de brigade Van Merlen

1st Chasseurs à Cheval, 1st squadron	(1)	15 - 183	- 19
2nd squadron	(1)	10 - 183	- 16
3rd squadron	(1)	9 - 181	- 9
4th squadron	(1)	3 - 47	---
19th Chasseurs à Cheval, 1st squadron	(1)	8 - 77	- 20
2nd squadron	(1)	6 - 123	- 22
3rd squadron	(1)	8 - 150	- 5
4th squadron	(1)	8 - 130	- 17

1st Heavy Cavalry Division— Général de division Baron Bordesoulle
1st Brigade: Général de brigade Berckeim

2nd Cuirassiers, 1st and 2nd squadrons	(2)	20 - 298	- 24
3rd Cuirassiers, 1st and 2nd squadrons	(2)	20 - 224	---
6th Cuirassiers, 1st and 2nd squadrons	(2)	17 - 205	---

2nd Brigade: Général de brigade Bessières

9th Cuirassiers, 1st, 2nd, and 3rd squadrons	(3)	27 - 343	2 - 17
11th Cuirassiers, 1st, 2nd, and 3rd squadrons	(3)	26 - 264	- 20
12th Cuirassiers, 1st and 2nd squadrons	(2)	27 - 259	- 33

3rd Brigade: Général de brigade Lessing

Saxon Garde du corps, 1st—4th squadrons	(4)	23 - 521	1 - 13
Saxon Zastrow Cuirassiers, 1st—4th squadrons	(4)	21 - 462	3 - 62

3rd Heavy Cavalry Division— Général de division Baron Doumerc

1st Brigade: Général de brigade Lalaing d'Audenarde

4th Cuirassiers, 1st squadron	(1)	17 - 82	- 24
2nd squadron	(1)	5 - 154	- 26
3rd squadron	(1)	5 - 68	- 2
7th Cuirassiers, 1st squadron	(1)	14 - 98	---
2nd squadron	(1)	4 - 52	- 4
3rd squadron	(1)	4 - 40	- 9
14th (Dutch) Cuirassiers, 1st squadron	(1)	11 - 149	- 14
2nd squadron	(1)	5 - 45	- 1
Italian Dragoons "Napoleon", 1st squadron	(1)	12 - 92	- 3
2nd and 3rd squadrons	(2)	5 - 130	- 4
4th squadron	(1)	9 - 193	- 17

2nd Brigade: Général de brigade Reiset

7th Dragoons, 1st and 2nd squadrons	(2)	14 - 116	- 8
3rd squadron	(1)	9 - 80	- 9
23rd Dragoons, 1st and 2nd squadrons	(2)	20 - 265	1 - 54
28th Dragoons, 1st and 2nd squadrons	(2)	25 - 282	- 12
30th Dragoons, 1st and 2nd squadrons	(2)	25 - 222	- 14

I Reserve Cavalry Corps Artillery Reserve—

1st Regiment of Horse Artillery, 3rd company	3 - 80	- 12
3rd Regiment of Horse Artillery, 6th company	3 - 105	- 8
4th Regiment of Horse Artillery, 1st company	3 - 97	- 10
6th Regiment of Horse Artillery, 1st company	4 - 80	- 10
Westphalian Horse Artillery, 1st company	2 - 64	---
Italian Horse Artillery, 4th company	4 - 65	---

The horse artillery companies each consisted of
4 6-pdr. guns and 2 51/2-inch howitzers—total of 36 pieces of ordnance.

1st *bis* Artillery Train Battalion,		
detachment of the 1st company	1 - 80	---
detachment of the 2nd company	1 - 84	---
8th *bis* Artillery Train Battalion,		
detachments of the 2nd and 5th companies	1 - 151	- 4
Westphalian Artillery Train, 1st company	1 - 65	- 6
Italian Artillery Train, 6th company	3 - 112	---

SITUATION
of the
IMPERIAL GUARD CAVALRY CORPS
15 September 1813

	Number of Squadrons	Present and Under Arms Off. - Others	Not Present In Hospital Off. - Others

Général de division Count Nansouty
Adjudant commandant Leistenschneider, Chief of Staff
Général de brigade Baron Desvaux de Saint-Maurice, Horse Artillery of the Guard

1st Imperial Guard Cavalry Division— Général de division Count Ornano
1st Brigade: Général de brigade Baron de Colbert

Light Lancers of Berg, 1st, 3rd, and 4th sqdrns	(3)	44 - 566	- 46
5th and 6th squadrons	(2)	detached—not present	

The 2nd squadron was not present with the rest of the regiment.

2nd (Red) Light Lancers of the Guard	(10)	76 - 1,101	- 72

2nd Brigade: Général de brigade Linteville

Young Guard squadrons, Guard Dragoons	(2)	19 - 246	---

2nd Imperial Gd Cav Div—Général de division Count Lefebvre-Desnoëttes
1st Brigade: Général de brigade Count Krasinski

Young Guard sqdrns, 1st Light Lancers of the Gd	(4)	47 - 724	---

2nd Brigade: Général de brigade Castex

Young Guard sqdrns, Guard Chasseurs à Cheval	(5)	44 - 1,062	- 36
Young Guard sqdrns, Guard Grenadiers à Cheval	(2)	22 - 402	---

3rd Imperial Guard Cavalry Division— Général de division Count Walther
1st Brigade: Général de brigade Baron Lyon

1st (Polish) Old Guard Lt Lancers of the Guard	(3)	43 - 514	1 - 21
Old Guard Chasseurs à Cheval, 1st—4th sqdrns	(4)	48 - 763	- 9

2nd Brigade: Général de brigade Baron Letort

Guard Dragoons, 1st, 2nd, 3rd, and 4th sqdrns	(4)	48 - 763	- 29

3rd Brigade: Général de brigade Baron de Laferrière-Levêque

Old Guard Grenadiers à Cheval, 1st—4th sqdrns	(4)	58 - 755	- 8
Gendarmes d'élite, 1st and 2nd squadrons	(2)	detached to Imperial HQ	

Guards of Honor Cavalry Division—Attached to the 3rd Division

1st Regiment, Guards of Honor, 1st—5th sqdrns	(5)	13 - 354	- 12
2nd Regiment, Guards of Honor, 1st—5th sqdrns	(5)	16 - 286	- 13
3rd Regiment, Guards of Honor, 1st—5th sqdrns	(5)	7 - 203	- 7
4th Regiment, Guards of Honor, 1st—5th sqdrns	(5)	6 - 202	- 6

Horse Artillery of the Guard attached to the Guard Cavalry—

Headquarters staff—9 personnel

Old Guard Horse Artillery, 1st company	3 - 90	- 10
2nd company	3 - 85	- 7
3rd company	4 - 86	- 6
4th company	2 - 87	- 3
5th company	3 - 90	- 3
6th company	3 - 86	- 9
Grand Duchy of Berg Horse Artillery	2 - 80	1 - 9

Each company of Old Guard Horse Artillery and of Berg consisted of
4 6-pdr. guns and 2 5 1/2-inch howitzers—total of 42 pieces of ordnance.
At this time, all 6 companies of the Old Guard Horse Artillery and the
Grand Duchy of Berg Horse Artillery were attached directly to the Guard Cavalry.

Horse Artillery Train Personnel	8 - 513	1 - 34
Ouvriers of the Artillery of the Guard	- 13	---

Appendix G

SITUATION
of the
II CORPS
15 September 1813

	Number of Battalions/ Squadrons	Present and Under Arms Off. - Others	Not Present In Hospital Off. - Others

Marshal Victor, Duke of Belluno
Colonel Huguet-Châteaux, Chief of Staff
Général de brigade Baron Montgenet, commanding the artillery
Major Bron, commanding the engineers

4th Division— Général de division Dubreton

1st Brigade: Général de brigade Ferriere

24th Light Infantry Regiment, 1st battalion	(1)	20 - 613	1 - 214
2nd battalion	(1)	17 - 444	3 - 175
4th battalion	(1)	18 - 424	3 - 287
19th Regiment of the Line, 1st battalion	(1)	25 - 479	5 - 286
2nd battalion	(1)	13 - 464	2 - 216
4th battalion	(1)	11 - 392	6 - 387

2nd Brigade: Général de brigade Brun

37th Regiment of the Line, 1st battalion	(1)	26 - 392	5 - 366
2nd battalion	(1)	17 - 368	- 228
4th battalion	(1)	16 - 370	1 - 323
56th Regiment of the Line, 1st battalion	(1)	26 - 553	- 213
2nd battalion	(1)	17 - 510	2 - 185
4th battalion	(1)	21 - 421	2 - 238

Divisional artillery and train:

2nd Regiment of Foot Artillery, 7th company		3 - 91	- 18
4th Regiment of Foot Artillery, 11th company		2 - 95	1 - 12

The above foot artillery companies each consisted of
6 6-pdr. guns and 2 5 1/2-inch howitzers—total of 16 pieces of ordnance.

14th Principal Artillery Train Battalion, detachment of the 2nd company		- 11	----
12th Principal Artillery Train Battalion, detachment of the 3rd company		1 - 118	- 10
3rd *bis* Artillery Train Battalion, detachment of the 2nd company		1 - 107	- 4

5th Division— Général de division Baron Dufour

1st Brigade: Général de brigade d'Estko

26th Light Infantry Regiment, 1st battalion	(1)	20 - 548	3 - 186
2nd battalion	(1)	15 - 548	3 - 186
4th battalion	(1)	19 - 547	3 - 186
93rd Regiment of the Line, 1st battalion	(1)	29 - 437	- 215
2nd battalion	(1)	17 - 419	- 189
4th battalion	(1)	24 - 430	1 - 273

2nd Brigade: Général de brigade Prince of Reuss

46th Regiment of the Line, 1st battalion	(1)	30 - 601	incomplete
72nd Regiment of the Line, 1st battalion	(1)	28 - 686	incomplete

Divisional artillery and train:

5th Regiment of Foot Artillery, 13th company	3 - 83	- 12

The 5/13th company consisted of 6 6-pdr. guns and 2 51/2-inch howitzers—total of 8 pieces of ordnance.

11th *bis* Artillery Train Battalion, detachment of the 3rd company — 1 - 95 — - 2

6th Division— Général de division Baron Vial

1st Brigade: Général de brigade Valory

11th Light Infantry Regiment, 1st battalion	(1)	29 - 545	3 - 121
2nd battalion	(1)	19 - 452	- 93
4th battalion	(1)	18 - 430	3 - 230
4th Regiment of the Line, 1st battalion	(1)	31 - 540	1 - 153
2nd battalion	(1)	15 - 552	- 122
4th battalion	(1)	18 - 399	- 186

2nd Brigade: Général de brigade Bronikowski

2nd Regiment of the Line, 1st battalion	(1)	33 - 533	- 190
2nd battalion	(1)	18 - 496	- 58
4th battalion	(1)	17 - 448	1 - 282
18th Regiment of the Line, 1st battalion	(1)	29 - 646	1 - 169
2nd battalion	(1)	17 - 588	- 98
4th battalion	(1)	25 - 544	- 262

Divisional artillery and train:

3rd Regiment of Foot Artillery, 25th and 26th company	6 - 137	- 23

The above foot artillery companies each consisted of 6 6-pdr. guns and 2 51/2-inch howitzers—total of 16 pieces of ordnance.

3rd Principal Artillery Train Battalion, detachment of 3rd company	1 - 75	- 6
14th Principal Artillery Train Battalion, detachment of 3rd company	1 - 93	- 15
Ambulance	- 12	---

II Corps Cavalry Brigade— Général de brigade Baron Bruno

1st Westphalian Hussars, 1st, 2nd, and 3rd sqdrns (3)	8 - 120	- 2
2nd Westphalian Hussars, 1st, 2nd, and 3rd sqdrns (3)	8 - 110	- 11

II Corps Artillery Reserve—

2nd Regiment of Foot Artillery, 9th company	3 - 54	- 13
6th Regiment of Foot Artillery, 10th company	3 - 96	- 10
2nd Regiment of Horse Artillery, 1st company	3 - 95	- 10

The 6/10thth foot artillery company consisted of
8 12-pdr. guns; the 2/9th foot artillery company personnel
were moved to the II Corps grand park of artillery and had no ordnance
attached; the 2/1st horse company consisted of 4 6-pdr. guns and
2 51/2-inch howitzers—total of 14 pieces of ordnance in II Corps Artillery Reserve.

11th Principal Artillery Train Battalion,		
detachments of the 4th and 7th companies	- 28	---
14th Principal Artillery Train Battalion,		
detachment of the 2nd company	1 - 112	- 5
3rd *bis* Artillery Train Battalion, 3rd company	- 23	---
Various other detachments of Artillery Train Personnel	6 - 216	---
Ouvriers, detachment of the 15th company	1 - 18	---
2nd Battalion, Sappers of the Line, 2nd company	3 - 137	- 9
3rd Battalion, Sappers of the Line, 3rd company	3 - 113	- 18
5th Battalion, Sappers of the Line, 3rd company	3 - 120	- 22

SITUATION
of the
III RESERVE CAVALRY CORPS
15 September 1813

	Number of Squadrons	Present and Under Arms Off. - Others	Not Present In Hospital Off. - Others

Général de division Arrighi de Casanova, Duke of Padoua
Adjudant commandant Salel, Chief of Staff
Colonel Chauveau, commanding the artillery

5th Light Cavalry Division— Général de division Baron Lorge
Division headquarters staff—9 personnel
1st Brigade: Général de brigade Jacquinot

5th Chasseurs à Cheval, 1st, 3rd, and 4th sqdrns (3)		20 - 424	1 - 27
10th Chasseurs à Cheval, 1st, 3rd, and 4th sqdrns (3)		11 - 215	1 - 22
13th Chasseurs à Cheval, 5th and 6th squadrons (2)		17 - 253	1 - 26

2nd Brigade: Général de brigade Merlin

15th Chasseurs à Cheval, 4th squadron	(1)	7 - 130	2 - 22
21st Chasseurs à Cheval, 3rd squadron	(1)	7 - 112	- 8
22nd Chasseurs à Cheval, 3rd and 4th squadrons	(2)	8 - 212	- 121

6th Light Cavalry Division— Général de division Baron Fournier
Division headquarters staff—6 personnel
1st Brigade: Général de brigade Ameil

29th Chasseurs à Cheval, 4th squadron	(1)	7 - 110	2 - 23
31st Chasseurs à Cheval, 4th squadron	(1)	9 - 171	- 20
1st Hussars, 3rd and 4th squadrons	(2)	7 - 237	2 - 17

2nd Brigade: Général de brigade Mouriez

2nd Hussars, 3rd and 4th squadrons	(2)	15 - 339	- 9
4th Hussars, 5th squadron	(1)	4 - 39	1 - 13
12th Hussars, 4th squadron	(1)	8 - 250	- 15

4th Heavy Cavalry Division— Général de division Count Defrance
Division headquarters staff—6 personnel
1st Brigade: Général de brigade Axamitowsky

4th Dragoons, 4th squadron	(1)	8 - 113	- 6
5th Dragoons, 3rd squadron	(1)	12 - 209	- 27
12th Dragoons, 3rd squadron	(1)	8 - 121	- 22
14th Dragoons, 3rd and 4th squadrons	(2)	10 - 129	- 14
24th Dragoons, 4th squadron	(1)	- 61	2 - 8

2nd Brigade: Général de brigade Quinette

16th Dragoons, 3rd squadron	(1)	4 - 117	- 2
17th Dragoons, 3rd squadron	(1)	13 - 211	- 19
21st Dragoons, 3rd squadron	(1)	8 - 119	- 8
26th Dragoons, 3rd squadron	(1)	3 - 78	- 7
27th Dragoons, 4th and 5th squadrons	(2)	7 - 120	- 7

Situation of the III Reserve Cavalry Corps—15 September 1813

13th Cuirassiers, 5th squadron	(1)	5 - 148	- 12

III Reserve Cavalry Corps Reserve Artillery—

5th Regiment of Horse Artillery, 1st company	3 - 91	- 6
5th company	3 - 92	- 5
6th Regiment of Horse Artillery, 4th company	1 - 85	- 11

The above horse artillery companies consisted of a total of
6 6-pdr. guns and 3 5 1/2-inch howitzers—total of 9 pieces of ordnance.

4th Principal Artillery Train Battalion, 5th company	1 - 73	- 4
1st *bis* Artillery Train Battalion, 5th company	2 - 142	- 3

-SITUATION
of the
II CORPS
25 September 1813

	Number of Battalions/ Squadrons	Present and Under Arms Off. - Others	Not Present In Hospital Off. - Others

Marshal Victor, Duke of Belluno
Colonel Huguet-Châteaux, Chief of Staff
Général de brigade Baron Montgenet, commanding the artillery
Major Bron, commanding the engineers

4th Division— Général de division Dubreton

1st Brigade: Général de brigade Ferriere

24th Light Infantry Regiment

1st, 2nd, and 4th battalions	(3)	55 - 1,454	8 - 599

19th Regiment of the Line

1st, 2nd, and 4th battalions	(3)	49 - 1,276	14 - 992

2nd Brigade: Général de brigade Brun

37th Regiment of the Line

1st, 2nd, and 4th battalions	(3)	59 - 1,103	5 - 950

56th Regiment of the Line

1st, 2nd, and 4th battalions	(3)	64 - 1,377	4 - 712

Divisional artillery and train:

2nd Regiment of Foot Artillery, 7th company		3 - 91	- 18
4th Regiment of Foot Artillery, 11th company		2 - 94	1 - 13

The above foot artillery companies each consisted of
6 6-pdr. guns and 2 5 1/2-inch howitzers—total of 16 pieces of ordnance.

14th Principal Artillery Train Battalion, detachment of the 2nd company		- 11	----
12th Principal Artillery Train Battalion, detachment of the 3rd company		1 - 100	- 10
3rd *bis* Artillery Train Battalion, detachment of the 2nd company		1 - 92	- 4

5th Division— Général de division Baron Dufour

1st Brigade: Général de brigade d'Estko

26th Light Infantry Regiment

1st, 2nd, and 4th battalions	(3)	53 - 1,587	10 - 590

93rd Regiment of the Line

1st, 2nd, and 4th battalions	(3)	70 - 1,249	1 - 433

2nd Brigade: Général de brigade Prince of Reuss

46th Regiment of the Line, 1st battalion	(1)	29 - 541	14 - 473
72nd Regiment of the Line, 1st battalion	(1)	28 - 618	6 - 473

Divisional artillery and train:

5th Regiment of Foot Artillery, 13th company   2 -   86   1 -   16

    The 5/13th company consisted of 6 6-pdr. guns and 2 5 1/2-inch howitzers—total of 8 pieces of ordnance.

11th *bis* Artillery Train Battalion,
    detachment of the 3rd company   1 - 85   -   4

6th Division— Général de division Baron Vial

1st Brigade: Général de brigade Valory

11th Light Infantry Regiment

    1st, 2nd, and 4th battalions   (3)   68 - 1,353   6 - 500

4th Regiment of the Line

    1st, 2nd, and 4th battalions   (3)   64 - 1,346   1 - 562

2nd Brigade: Général de brigade Bronikowski

2nd Regiment of the Line

    1st, 2nd, and 4th battalions   (3)   66 - 1,406   3 - 593

18th Regiment of the Line

    1st, 2nd, and 4th battalions   (3)   71 - 1,723   3 - 574

Divisional artillery and train:

3rd Regiment of Foot Artillery, 25th and 26th companies   6 - 181   -   26

    The above foot artillery companies each consisted of

6 6-pdr. guns and 2 5 1/2-inch howitzers—total of 16 pieces of ordnance.

3rd Principal Artillery Train Battalion,
    detachment of 3rd company   1 -   80   -   7

14th Principal Artillery Train Battalion,
    detachment of 3rd company   1 -   93   -   14

Ambulance   -   14   ---

II Corps Artillery Reserve—

2nd Regiment of Foot Artillery, 9th company   3 - 84   -   12

6th Regiment of Foot Artillery, 10th company   3 - 97   -   10

2nd Regiment of Horse Artillery, 1st company   3 - 99   -   10

    The 6/10th foot artillery company consisted of 8 12-pdr. guns;
the 2/9th foot artillery company personnel where in II Corps
grand park of artillery and had no ordnance; the 2/1st horse
company consisted of 4 6-pdr. guns and 2 5 1/2-inch howitzers—
total of 14 pieces of ordnance in II Corps Artillery Reserve.

All artillery train personnel   6 - 466   -   11

3 companies of Engineers (Sappers)*   9 - 370   -   44

Imperial Gendarmes   2 - 38   ---

The 29th Light Cavalry Brigade which had previously been attached as II Corps' Cavalry Brigade was no longer present on 25 September.

*See Appendices D and E for these company designations.

SITUATION
of the
V RESERVE CAVALRY CORPS
28 September 1813

	Number of Squadrons	Present and Under Arms Off. - Others	Not Present In Hospital Off. - Others*

Général de division Baron L'héritier
Adjundant commandant Soubeiran, Chief of Staff

9th Light Cavalry Division— Général de brigade Baron Klicky
1st Brigade: (no commander yet assigned)

3rd Hussars, 3rd and 4th squadrons	(2)	11 - 197	
27th Chasseurs à Cheval, 3rd and 4th squadrons	(2)	10 - 180	

2nd Brigade: (no commander yet assigned)

14th Chasseurs à Cheval, 3rd and 4th squadrons	(2)	13 - 190	
26th Chasseurs à Cheval, 3rd and 4th squadrons	(2)	10 - 167	
13th Hussars	(3)	detached—at Magdebourg	

5th Heavy Cavalry Division— Général de brigade Baron Collaert
1st Brigade: (no commander yet assigned)

2nd Dragoons, 3rd squadron	(1)	12 - 144	
6th Dragoons, 3rd and 4th squadrons	(2)	12 - 192	

2nd Brigade: (no commander yet assigned)

11th Dragoons, 3rd and 4th squadrons	(2)	10 - 157	
13th Dragoons, 3rd squadron	(1)	10 - 142	
15th Dragoons, 3rd squadron	(1)	11 - 137	

6th Heavy Cavalry Division— Général de brigade Baron Lamotte
1st Brigade: (no commander yet assigned)

18th Dragoons, 3rd squadron	(1)	3 - 41	
19th Dragoons, 3rd squadron	(1)	5 - 48	
20th Dragoons, 3rd squadron	(1)	6 - 132	

2nd Brigade: (no commander yet assigned)

22nd Dragoons, 3rd squadron	(1)	7 - 65	
25th Dragoons, 3rd squadron	(1)	6 - 92	

V Reserve Cavalry Corps Reserve Artillery—
2nd Regiment of Horse Artillery, 5th company, consisting of 3 6-pdr. guns—total of 3 pieces of ordnance.   2 - 91

4th Principal Artillery Train Battalion, detachments of the 1st and 4th companies   1 - 70

*Parade states for this date listed only those present and under arms. Therefore, no returns are shown for those in hospital(s).

Note: On October 12, this cavalry corps was combined with the V *bis* Reserve Cavalry Corps to form the V Reserve Cavalry Corps under General Pajol which participated at the Battle of Leipzig.

SITUATION
of the
II RESERVE CAVALRY CORPS
30 September 1813

	Number of Squadrons	Present and Under Arms Off. - Others	Not Present In Hospital Off. - Others

Général de division Count Sébastiani de la Porta
Adjudant commandant Lascours, Chief of Staff
Colonel Colin, commanding the artillery

2nd Light Cavalry Division— Général de division Baron Roussel d'Hurbal
1st Brigade: Général de brigade Domanget

11th Chasseurs à Cheval, 1st—3rd squadrons	(3)	26 - 238	- 17
12th Chasseurs à Cheval, 1st—3rd squadrons	(3)	24 - 290	- 40
5th Hussars, 1st—3rd squadrons	(3)	29 - 259	- 65

2nd Brigade: no commanding officer listed

9th Hussars, 1st—4th squadrons	(4)	32 - 441	1 - 74
2nd Light Lancers, 1st—3rd squadrons	(3)	23 - 284	- 40
4th Light Lancers, 1st—3rd squadrons	(3)	29 - 399	- 28

4th Light Cavalry Division— Général de division Baron Exelmans
1st Brigade: Général de brigade Maurin

6th Light Lancers, 1st—3rd squadrons	(3)	27 - 305	- 23
4th Chasseurs à Cheval, 1st—3rd squadrons	(3)	23 - 265	- 29
7th Chasseurs à Cheval, 1st—4th squadrons	(4)	35 - 379	1 - 36

2nd Brigade: Général de brigade Wathier

20th Chasseurs à Cheval, 1st—4th squadrons	(4)	35 - 354	- 24
23rd Chasseurs à Cheval, 1st—4th squadrons	(4)	31 - 441	- 46
24th Chasseurs à Cheval, 1st—3rd squadrons	(3)	21 - 263	- 20
11th (Dutch) Hussars, 1st—3rd squadrons	(3)	24 - 144	- 28

2nd Heavy Cavalry Division— Général de division Count Saint-Germain
1st Brigade: Général de brigade d'Hugérauville

1st Carabiniers, 1st—3rd squadrons	(3)	27 - 301	- 23
2nd Carabiniers, 1st—3rd squadrons	(3)	28 - 297	- 25
1st Cuirassiers, 1st—3rd squadrons	(3)	24 - 235	- 23

2nd Brigade: Général de brigade Thiry

5th Cuirassiers, 1st—3rd squadrons	(3)	28 - 331	- 29
8th Cuirassiers, 1st and 2nd squadrons	(2)	17 - 188	- 33
10th Cuirassiers, 1st and 2nd squadrons	(2)	23 - 283	- 16

II Reserve Cavalry Corps Reserve Artillery—

1st Regiment of Horse Artillery, 7th company	3 - 76	- 18
4th Regiment of Horse Artillery, 7th company	3 - 60	- 8
6th Regiment of Horse Artillery, 8th company	3 - 71	- 2

The above horse artillery companies consisted of a total of
9 6-pdr. guns and 3 5½-inch howitzers—total of 12 pieces of ordnance.

8th *bis* Artillery Train Battalion, detachment of the 2nd co.	- 28	- 4
13th *bis* Artillery Train Battalion, 3rd company	2 - 156	- 11

SITUATION
of the
III CORPS, XI CORPS, and the
II RESERVE CAVALRY CORPS
1 October 1813

Present and
Under Arms
Officers - Others

III CORPS
Général de division Count Souham
All headquarters' personnel   137 - 239

8th Division— Général de division Baron Brayer   287 - 4,155

9th Division— Général de division Delmas   258 - 3,977

11th Division— Général de division Baron Ricard   241 - 4,116

Corps Cavalry— Général de brigade Beurmann   58 - 1,007

III Corps Artillerists, etc.—

Foot Artillerists	29 - 687
Horse Artillerists	8 - 166
Artillery Train personnel	23 - 1,233
Equipage personnel	14 - 569
Engineers (Sappers)	10 - 284
Imperial Gendarmes	2 - 44

Total for the III Corps   1,067 - 16,477

XI CORPS
Marshal Macdonald, Duke of Tarentum
All headquarters' personnel   53 - 317

31st Division— Général de division Baron Ledru   237 - 5,336

35th Division— Général de division Baron Gérard   194 - 3,747

36th Division— Général de div Count Charpentier   189 - 4,590

39th Division— Général de division Count Marchand 184 - 4,928

Corps Cavalry— Général de brigade Montbrun   47 - 449

XI Corps Artillerists, etc.—

Foot Artillerists	31 - 881
Horse Artillerists	6 - 132
Artillery Train personnel	13 - 1,091
Equipage personnel	8 - 376
Engineers (Sappers)	19 - 281
Imperial Gendarmes	2 - 63

Total for the XI Corps 983 - 22,191

II RESERVE CAVALRY CORPS
Général de division Count Sébastiani de la Porta
All headquarters' personnel 35 - 38

2nd Light Cavalry Division— Roussel d'Hurbal 172 - 1,949

4th Light Cavalry Division— Exelmans 189 - 2,188

2nd Heavy Cavalry Division— Saint–Germain 152 - 1,668

II Reserve Cavalry Corps Artillerists, etc.—
Horse Artillerists 9 - 208
Artillery Train personnel 1 - 184

Total for the II Reserve Cavalry Corps 557 - 6,235

SITUATION
of the
V CORPS
1 October 1813

	Number of Battalions/ Squadrons	Present and Under Arms Off. - Others	Not Present In Hospital Off. - Others

Général de division Count Lauriston
Général de brigade Baron Baillod, Chief of Staff
Général de brigade Baron Camal, commanding the artillery
Colonel Lamarre, commanding the engineers
Corps headquarters staff—38 personnel

10th Division— Général de division Baron Albert
Division headquarters staff—11 personnel
1st Brigade: Général de brigade Bachelu
    4th Provisional Light Infantry Regiment, consisting of

4th battalion, 5th Light Infantry Regiment	(1)	17 - 320	10 - 376
4th battalion, 12th Light Infantry Regiment	(1)	22 - 175	2 - 222
139th Regiment of the Line, 1st battalion	(1)	23 - 463	5 - 614
2nd battalion	(1)	19 - 430	6 - 608
3rd battalion	(1)	21 - 483	5 - 503

2nd Brigade: Général de brigade Bertrand

140th Regiment of the Line, 1st battalion	(1)	26 - 216	6 - 959
2nd battalion	(1)	14 - 214	6 - 824
3rd battalion	(1)	14 - 201	5 - 835
141st Regiment of the Line,1st battalion	(1)	23 - 309	7 - 506
2nd battalion	(1)	16 - 297	6 - 491
3rd battalion	(1)	18 - 314	12 - 484

Divisional artillery and train:

7th Regiment of Foot Artillery, 3rd company		4 - 63	- 34
4th company		3 - 59	- 33

    The above foot artillery companies had a total of
    8 6-pdr. guns and 2 5 1/2-inch howitzers—total of 10 pieces of ordnance.
1st Principal Artillery Train Battalion,

detachment of the 4th company		2 - 177	- 17

16th Division—Général de division Baron Maison
Division headquarters staff—9 personnel
1st Brigade: Général de brigade Mandeville
    151st Regiment of the Line, 1st—3rd battalions—in memorial...survivors of the
        regiment in garrison at Glogau.

152nd Regiment of the Line, 1st battalion	(1)	19 - 410	9 - 388
2nd battalion	(1)	8 - 459	10 - 392
3rd battalion	(1)	7 - 393	10 - 444

2nd Brigade:

153rd Regiment of the Line, 1st battalion	(1)	23 - 428	17 - 513
2nd battalion	(1)	11 - 431	5 - 409
3rd battalion	(1)	11 - 429	7 - 469
154th Regiment of the Line, 1st battalion	(1)	23 - 340	4 - 376
2nd battalion	(1)	5 - 365	6 - 269
3rd battalion	(1)	9 - 376	3 - 352

Divisional artillery and train:

1st Regiment of Foot Artillery, 1st company	3 - 68	- 30
3rd company	3 - 88	- 16

    The above foot artillery companies had a total of
    8 6-pdr. guns and 2 5 1/2-inch howitzers—total of 10 pieces of ordnance.

8th *bis* Artillery Train Battalion, 4th company	1 - 141	- 5

19th Division— Général de division Baron Rochambeau
Division headquarters staff—12 personnel
1st Brigade: Général de brigade Lafitte

135th Regiment of the Line, 1st battalion	(1)	26 - 250	8 - 601
2nd battalion	(1)	9 - 245	7 - 543
3rd battalion	(1)	12 - 252	6 - 550
149th Regiment of the Line, 1st battalion	(1)	27 - 270	11 - 507
2nd battalion	(1)	9 - 210	4 - 325
3rd battalion	(1)	10 - 236	3 - 370

2nd Brigade: Général de brigade Harlet

150th Regiment of the Line, 1st battalion	(1)	13 - 160	4 - 290
2nd battalion	(1)	10 - 311	- 309
3rd battalion	(1)	10 - 407	- 233
155th Regiment of the Line, 1st battalion	(1)	35 - 418	7 - 469
2nd battalion	(1)	12 - 384	7 - 460
3rd battalion	(1)	16 - 364	2 - 450

Divisional artillery and train:

5th Regiment of Foot Artillery, 12th company	2 - 82	1 - 24
17th company	3 - 78	- 28

    The above foot artillery companies had a total of
    8 6-pdr. guns and 2 5 1/2-inch howitzers—total of 10 pieces of ordnance.

4th Principal Artillery Train Battalion, 4th company	1 - 134	- 10

V Corps Artillery Reserve—

Corps artillery reserve staff—3 personnel

1st Regiment of Foot Artillery, 15th company	3 - 66	- 41
16th company	2 - 78	- 21
17th company	3 - 56	- 24
5th Regiment of Horse Artillery, 2nd company	3 - 87	- 9
6th Regiment of Horse Artillery, 7th company	2 - 68	- 4

The 1/16th and the 1/17th had a total of 10 12-pdr. guns and 2 6-inch howitzers. Both the horse artillery companies had a total of 6 6-pdr. guns and 2 51/2-inch howitzers. The 1/15th company personnel were in the corps artillery park along with 1 12-pdr. gun and 2 howitzers—total of 23 pieces of ordnance.

3rd Principal Artillery Train Battalion, 7th company	1 - 116	- 23
12th Principal Artillery Train Battalion, detachment	1 - 187	- 10
9th *bis* Artillery Train Battalion, 4th company	1 - 173	- 18
Ouvriers, detachment of the 15th company	1 - 18	---
6th Battalion, Sappers of the Line, 1st company	5 - 45	- 45
2nd company	2 - 84	- 16
3rd company	3 - 81	- 10

Attached to V Corps—from the 3rd Light Cavalry Division—

3rd Brigade: Général de brigade Dermoncourt

2nd Chasseurs à Cheval, 1st—3rd squadrons	(3)	25 - 184	1 - 59
3rd Chasseurs à Cheval, 1st and 2nd squadrons	(2)	17 - 207	- 18
6th Chasseurs à Cheval, 1st—3rd squadrons	(3)	22 - 309	1 - 28

SITUATION
of the
VI CORPS
1 October 1813

	Number of Battalions/ Squadrons	Present and Under Arms Off. - Others	Not Present In Hospital Off. - Others

Marshal Marmont, Duke of Ragusa
Général de brigade Camus, Baron de Richemont, Chief of Staff
Général de division Baron Foucher de Careil, commanding the artillery
Major Constantin, commanding the engineers
Corps headquarters staff—39 personnel

20th Division— Général de division Count Compans
Division headquarters staff—14 personnel
1st Brigade: Général de brigade Pelleport

32nd Light Infantry Regiment, 2nd battalion	(1)	19 - 231	5 - 382
3rd battalion	(1)	15 - 313	5 - 312
1st Regiment de Marine, 1st battalion	(1)	24 - 347	5 - 398
2nd battalion	(1)	16 - 335	3 - 398
3rd battalion	(1)	14 - 358	4 - 369
4th battalion	(1)	16 - 344	3 - 313
5th battalion	(1)	15 - 364	2 - 211

2nd Brigade: Général de brigade Joubert
20th Provisional Regiment of the Line, consisting of

5th battalion, 66th Regiment of the Line	(1)	21 - 319	4 - 496
3rd battalion, 122nd Regiment of the Line	(1)	19 - 300	3 - 310

25th Provisional Regiment of the Line, consisting of

3rd battalion, 47th Regiment of the Line	(1)	20 - 445	3 - 280
3rd battalion, 86th Regiment of the Line	(1)	21 - 357	3 - 362
3rd Regiment de Marine, 1st battalion	(1)	19 - 500	3 - 341
2nd battalion[†]	(1)	1 - 186[†]	- 199
3rd battalion	(1)	13 - 447	3 - 340

Divisional artillery and train:

5th Regiment of Foot Artillery, 16th company	2 - 112	- 30
8th Regiment of Foot Artillery, 10th company	3 - 102	- 14

The above foot artillery companies each consisted of
6 6-pdr. guns and 2 5$1/2$-inch howitzers—total of 16 pieces of ordnance.
12th *bis* Artillery Train Battalion,

detachment of the 7th company	1 - 110	- 10

[†]The 2nd battalion of the 3rd Regiment de Marine had 16 officers and 504 other ranks temporarily detached as a mobile column on this date. Mobile columns were periodically created in order to sweep the nearby countryside to bring in stragglers and deserters.

21st Division— Général de division Count Lagrange

Division headquarters staff—14 personnel
1st Brigade: Général de brigade Jamin

37th Light Infantry Regiment, 1st battalion	(1)	24 - 360	13 - 501
2nd batalion	(1)	18 - 382	2 - 477
3rd battalion	(1)	detached[†]	1 - 251
4th battalion	(1)	16 - 322	4 - 378
Spanish Regiment Joseph Napoleon, 1st battalion	(1)	14 - 316	- 143
4th Regiment de Marine, 1st battalion	(1)	26 - 441	7 - 477
2nd battalion	(1)	12 - 456	8 - 396
3rd battalion	(1)	17 - 431	- 357

2nd Brigade: Général de brigade Buquet

2nd Regiment de Marine, 1st battalion	(1)	39 - 470	1 - 297
2nd battalion	(1)	10 - 426	8 - 205
3rd battalion	(1)	14 - 397	3 - 231
4th battalion	(1)	17 - 446	1 - 234
5th battalion	(1)	14 - 404	4 - 189
6th battalion	(1)	18 - 453	1 - 184

Divisional artillery and train:

4th Regiment of Foot Artillery, 10th company	2 - 117	1 - 33
9th Regiment of Foot Artillery, 7th company	3 - 100	- 15

The above foot artillery companies each consisted of
6 6-pdr. guns and 2 5 1/2-inch howitzers—total of 16 pieces of ordnance.

8th Principal Artillery Train Battalion, 2nd company	2 - 167	- 12
10th *bis* Artillery Train Battalion, detachment of the 1st company	1 - 77	- 6

[†]The 3rd battalion of the 37th Light Infantry Regiment was temporarily detached and serving as a mobile column on this date. Mobile columns were periodically created in order to sweep the nearby countryside to bring in stragglers and deserters.

22nd Division— Général de division Baron Friederichs

Division headquarters staff—14 personnel
1st Brigade: Général de brigade Coëhorn
11th Provisional Regiment of the Line, consisting of

4th battalion, 1st Regiment of the Line	(1)	21 - 276	3 - 230
2nd battalion, 62nd Regiment of the Line	(1)	17 - 335	3 - 238

13th Provisional Regiment of the Line, consisting of

3rd battalion, 14th Regiment of the Line	(1)	24 - 668	- 337
4th battalion, 16th Regiment of the Line	(1)	19 - 416	1 - 255
23rd Light Infantry Regiment, 3rd battalion	(1)	22 - 228	1 - 396
4th battalion	(1)	17 - 280	1 - 241
15th Regiment of the Line, 3rd battalion	(1)	21 - 319	2 - 286
4th battalion	(1)	20 - 291	- 250

2nd Brigade: Général de brigade Dechoisy
16th Provisional Regiment of the Line, consisting of

6th battalion, 26th Regiment of the Line	(1)	18 - 308	5 - 301
6th battalion, 82nd Regiment of the Line	(1)	19 - 221	3 - 291
121st Regiment of the Line, 3rd battalion	(1)	21 - 285	2 - 301
4th battalion	(1)	19 - 266	1 - 306

70th Regiment of the Line, 3rd battalion	(1)	20 - 308	2 - 278
4th battalion	(1)	18 - 293	- 286
Divisional artillery and train:			
4th Regiment of Foot Artillery, 14th company		2 - 107	- 26
9th Regiment of Foot Artillery, 22nd company		3 - 87	- 45
The above foot artillery companies each consisted of			
6 6-pdr. guns and 2 51/2-inch howitzers—total of 16 pieces of ordnance.			
8th Principal Artillery Train Battalion, 3rd company		1 - 168	1 - 14
10th *bis* Artillery Train Battalion,			
detachment of the 2nd company		1 - 96	- 15

VI Corps Cavalry Brigade— Général de brigade Normann

Corps cavalry brigade staff—3 personnel			
2nd Württemberg Chevaulegers, 1st squadron	(1)	8 - 112	- 13
2nd squadron	(1)	4 - 117	---
3rd squadron	(1)	3 - 105	----
4th squadron	(1)	4 - 116	----
4th Württemberg Chevaulegers, 1st squadron	(1)	7 - 112	- 15
2nd squadron	(1)	4 - 113	- 3
3rd squadron	(1)	3 - 115	- 5
4th squadron	(1)	4 - 108	- 6
Württemberg Horse Artillery, 3rd company, consisting of		3 - 121	- 10
4 6-pdr. guns and 2 51/2-inch howitzers—total of 6 pieces of ordnance.			

VI Corps Artillery Reserve—

Corps artillery reserve staff—4 personnel			
5th Regiment of Foot Artillery, 3rd company		3 - 92	- 23
18th company		3 - 108	- 9
26th company		3 - 127	- 10
1st Regiment of Horse Artillery, 1st company		3 - 93	- 21
4th Regiment of Horse Artillery, 3rd company		2 - 77	- 13
The 5/3rd foot artillery company was now in the corps artillery park;			
the 5/18th and 5/26th foot artillery companies each consisted of			
6 12-pdr. guns and 2 6-inch howitzers; the 1/1st and 4/3rd horse			
artillery companies each consisted of 4 6-pdr. guns and 2 51/2-inch			
howitzers—total of 28 pieces of ordnance in VI Corps Artillery Reserve.			
12th Principal Artillery Train Battalion,			
detachment of the 4th company		2 - 108	- 5
6th *bis* Artillery Train Battalion,			
detachment of the 4th company		2 - 93	- 40
6th company		2 - 119	- 11
7th company		1 - 114	- 38
10th *bis* Artillery Train Battalion, 7th company		2 - 94	- 17
2nd Battalion, Sappers of the Line, 6th company		3 - 107	- 40
4th Battalion, Sappers of the Line, 2nd company		3 - 102	4 - 45
9th company		3 - 110	- 37
7th Battalion, Sappers of the Line, 4th company		4 - 104	- 80
Imperial Gendarmes, detachment		2 - 36	---

SITUATION
of the
XIV CORPS
1 October 1813

Marshal Count Gouvion Saint-Cyr
Général de brigade Baron Borelli, Chief of Staff
Colonel Zevort, commanding the artillery
Major Thiébaut, commanding the engineers

	Number of Battalions/ Squadrons	Present & Under Arms Officers - Others
42nd Division— Général de division Baron Mouton-Duvernet		
1st Brigade: Général de brigade Creutzer		
22nd Provisional Light Infantry Regiment, consisting of		
2nd battalion, 4th Light Infantry Regiment	(1)	no report
3rd batalion, 12th Light Infantry Regiment	(1)	17 - 318
4th Provisional Light Infantry Regiment, consisting of		
6th battalion, 9th Light Infantry Regiment	(1)	11 - 355
3rd battalion, 28th Light Infantry Regiment	(1)	16 - 349
3rd Provisional Light Infantry Regiment, consisting of		
4th battalion, 10th Light Infantry Regiment	(1)	23 - 567
3rd battalion, 21st Light Infantry Regiment	(1)	19 - 411
2nd Brigade: Général de brigade Paroletti		
17th Provisional Regiment of the Line, consisting of		
3rd battalion, 27th Regiment of the Line	(1)	20 - 340
3rd battalion, 63rd Regiment of the Line	(1)	21 - 465
16th Provisional Regiment of the Line, consisting of		
4th battalion, 40th Regiment of the Line	(1)	16 - 442
3rd battalion, 43rd Regiment of the Line	(1)	21 - 452
76th Regiment of the Line, 2nd battalion	(1)	19 - 526
3rd battalion	(1)	18 - 513
96th Regiment of the Line, 2nd battalion	(1)—in Leipzig garrison	
3rd battalion	(1)	21 - 349
Division artillery and train:		
7th Regiment of Foot Artillery, 9th company, consisting of		2 - 88
4 6-pdr. guns and 1 51/2-inch howitzer—total of 5 pieces of ordnance.		
11th Principal Artillery Train Battalion, detachment of the 6th company		2 - 118
4th *bis* Artillery Train Battalion, detachment of the 6th company		3 - 122

43rd Division— Général de division Baron Claparède

1st Brigade: Général de brigade Godard

27th Light Infantry Regiment, 2nd battalion	(1)	no report
3rd battalion	(1)	no report
45th Regiment of the Line, 2nd battalion	(1)	20 - 419
3rd battalion	(1)	19 - 424

2nd Brigade: Général de brigade Butrand

65th Regiment of the Line, 3rd battalion	(1)	26 - 548
103rd Regiment of the Line, 3rd battalion	(1)—in Leipzig garrison	
4th battalion	(1)	15 - 313

3rd Brigade: Général de brigade Couture

29th Light Infantry Regiment, 3rd battalion	(1)	12 - 276
100th Regiment of the Line, 2nd battalion	(1)	20 - 497
3rd battalion	(1)	16 - 435
4th battalion	(1)	17 - 571

27th Provisional Demi-Brigade, consisting of

2nd battalion, 59th Regiment of the Line	(1)	22 - 190
3rd battalion, 94th Regiment of the Line	(1)	25 - 504

Divisional artillery and train:

7th Regiment of Foot Artillery, 2nd company, consisting of	6 - 123

5 6-pdr. guns and 2 5 1/2-inch howitzers—total of 7 pieces of ordnance.

10th Principal Artillery Train Battalion, detachment of the 4th company	1 - 34
11th Principal Artillery Train Battalion, detachment	1 - 41
8th Principal Artillery Train Battalion, detachment	- 7
12th Principal Artillery Train Battalion, detachment	- 73

44th Division— Général de division Baron Berthezène

1st Brigade: Général de brigade Goguet

64th Regiment of the Line, 3rd battalion	(1)	26 - 714
4th battalion	(1)	no report

34th Provisional Light Infantry Regiment, consisting of

2nd battalion, 16th Light Infantry Regiment	(1)	18 - 343
1st battalion, 18th Light Infantry Regiment	(1)	11 - 231

2nd Brigade: Général de brigade Letellier

19th Provisional Regiment of the Line, consisting of

2nd battalion, 50th Regiment of the Line	(1)	15 - 456
2nd battalion, 75th Regiment of the Line	(1)	19 - 365

Provisional Regiment of the Line, consisting of

3rd battalion, 24th Regiment of the Line	(1)	19 - 578
3rd battalion, 39th Regiment of the Line	(1)	12 - 329

Provisional Regiment of the Line, consisting of

3rd battalion, 54th Regiment of the Line	(1)	18 - 644
3rd battalion, 95th Regiment of the Line	(1)	16 - 517

Divisional artillery and train:

6th Regiment of Foot Artillery, 4th company, consisting of	2 - 86

4 6-pdr. guns and 1 5 1/2-inch howitzer—total of 5 pieces of ordnance.

12th Principal Artillery Train Battalion	1 - 113
1st *bis* Artillery Train Battalion, detachment of the 7th company	- 19
1st *bis* Artillery Train, detachment	- 14

45th Division— Général de division Count Razout

1st Brigade: Général de brigade d'Esclevin

6th Light Infantry Regiment, 3rd battalion	(1)	23 - 473
26th Provisional Demi-Brigade, consisting of		
3rd battalion, 5th Regiment of the Line	(1)	19 - 596
3rd battalion, 11th Regiment of the Line	(1)	16 - 344
Provisional Regiment of the Line, consisting of		
3rd battalion, 8th Regiment of the Line	(1)	22 - 614
2nd battalion, 28th Regiment of the Line	(1)	20 - 450

2nd Brigade:

Provisional Regiment of the Line		
4th battalion, 32nd Regiment of the Line	(1)	22 - 559
4th battalion, 58th Regiment of the Line	(1)	20 - 506
18th Provisional Demi-Brigade, consisting of		
6th battalion, 34th Regiment of the Line	(1)	21 - 517
3rd battalion, 69th Regiment of the Line	(1)	23 - 492
27th Provisional Demi-Brigade, consisting of		
3rd battalion, 79th Regiment of the Line	(1)	24 - 695
6th battalion, 81st Regiment of the Line	(1)	20 - 650
60th Regiment of the Line, 4th battalion	(1)	22 - 617

Divisional artillery and train:

5th Regiment of Foot Artillery, 21st company, consisting of		3 - 105
5 6-pdr. guns and 2 51/2-inch howitzers—total of 7 pieces of ordnance.		
11th Principal Artillery Train Battalion, detachment of the 4th company		- 15
12th Principal Artillery Train Battalion, 5th company		2 - 123
1st *bis* Artillery Train Battalion, detachment of the 5th company		- 15

10th Light Cavalry Division— Général de division Baron Pajol

1st Brigade: Général de brigade Jacquet

2nd Italian Chasseurs à Cheval, regimental staff		7 - 1
1st squadron	(1)	6 - 136
2nd squadron	(1)	6 - 86
3rd squadron	(1)	4 - 68
4th squadron	(1)	7 - 93
7th (1st Vistula Legion) Light Lancers, regimental staff		6 - 4
1st squadron	(1)	8 - 142
2nd squadron	(1)	8 - 90
3rd squadron	(1)	6 - 54
4th squadron	(1)	5 - 42

2nd Brigade: Général de brigade Stedmann

14th Hussars, regimental staff		3 - 8
1st squadron	(1)	7 - 105
2nd squadron	(1)	6 - 105

XIV Corps Artillery Reserve—

1st Regiment of Foot Artillery, 4th company	(1)	3 - 88
6th Regiment of Foot Artillery, 5th company	(1)	4 - 112
7th Regiment of Foot Artillery, 15th company	(1)	3 - 95
2nd Regiment of Horse Artillery, 5th company	(1)	3 - 79
6th Regiment of Horse Artillery, 3rd company	(1)	3 - 77

The 1/4th and 7/15th foot artillery companies and
both of the horse artillery companies each consisted of
4 6-pdr. guns and 2 51/2-inch howitzers; the 6/5th foot artillery
company consisted of 6 12-pdr. guns and 2 6-inch howitzers—total of 36 pieces.

1st Principal Artillery Train Battalion, detachment of the 1st company	1 - 44
4th Principal Artillery Train, detachment of the 3rd company	- 68
detachment of the 6th company	- 39
11th Principal Artillery Train Battalion, detachment of the 3rd company	2 - 47
detachment of the 5th company	1 - 69
12th Principal Artillery Train Battalion, detachment of the 2nd company	- 19
detachment of the 5th company	1 - 12
detachment of the 6th company	- 14
1st *bis* Artillery Train Battalion, detachment of the 3rd company	1 - 38
detachment of the 7th company	2 - 111
10th *bis* Artillery Train Battalion, detachment of the 4th company	- 40
Ouvriers, detachment of the 17th company	1 - 15

2nd Battalion, Sappers of the Line, 5th company	(1)	2 - 120
8th company	(1)	3 - 132
4th Battalion, Sappers of the Line, 7th company	(1)	3 - 196

Appendix P

SITUATION
of the
XIV CORPS
10 October 1813

Marshal Count Gouvion Saint-Cyr
Général de brigade Baron Borelli, Chief of Staff
Colonel Zevort, commanding the artillery
Major Thiébaut, commanding the engineers

	Number of Battalions/ Squadrons	Present & Under Arms Officers - Others
42nd Division— Général de division Baron Mouton-Duvernet		
Division headquarters staff—12 personnel		
1st Brigade: Général de brigade Paroletti		
10th Light Infantry Regiment, 4th battalion	(1)	23 - 567
21st Light Infantry Regiment, 3rd battalion	(1)	20 - 397
25th Light Infantry Regiment, 3rd battalion	(1)	17 - 276
63rd Regiment of the Line, 3rd battalion	(1)	20 - 447
76th Regiment of the Line, 2nd and 3rd battalions	(2)	40 - 1,004
2nd Brigade: Général de brigade Schramm		
12th Light Infantry Regiment, 3rd battalion	(1)	17 - 315
4th battalion	(1)	21 - 166
27th Regiment of the Line, 3rd battalion	(1)	20 - 240
88th Regiment of the Line, 3rd battalion	(1)	16 - 154
96th Regiment of the Line, 2nd battalion	(1)	22 - 325
3rd battalion	(1)—in Leipzig garrison	
Divisional artillery and train:		
4th Battalion, Sappers of the Line, 6th company		3 - 119
7th Regiment of Foot Artillery, 9th company		2 - 87
11th Principal Artillery Train Battalion, detachment		2 - 120
43rd Division— Général de division Baron Claparède		
Division headquarters staff—13 personnel		
1st Brigade: Général de brigade Godard		
27th Light Infantry Regiment, 2nd battalion	(1)	17 - 149
3rd battalion	(1)	15 - 379
4th battalion	(1)	13 - 412
103rd Regiment of the Line, 2nd battalion	(1)—in Leipzig garrison	
3rd battalion	(1)	12 - 235
4th battalion	(1)	15 - 399
2nd Brigade: Général de brigade Butrand		
29th Light Infantry Regiment, 1st battalion	(1)	20 - 191
2nd battalion	(1)	17 - 130
3rd battalion	(1)	12 - 265

3rd Brigade: Général de brigade Couture

100th Regiment of the Line, 2nd battalion	(1)	20 - 492
3rd battalion	(1)	16 - 428
4th battalion	(1)	17 - 566
94th Regiment of the Line, 3rd battalion	(1)	23 - 483

Divisional artillery and train:

7th Regiment of Foot Artillery, 2nd company		6 - 120
Artillery Train, detachements from various battalions		2 - 154

44th Division— Général de division Baron Berthezène

Division headquarters staff—10 personnel

1st Brigade: Général de brigade Goguet

45th Regiment of the Line, 2nd and 3rd battalions	(2)	33 - 582
64th Regiment of the Line, 3rd battalion	(1)	21 - 406
4th battalion	(1)	15 - 255
75th Regiment of the Line, 2nd battalion	(1)	19 - 357
3rd battalion	(1)	16 - 188

2nd Brigade: Général de brigade Letellier

24th Regiment of the Line, 3rd battalion	(1)	19 - 556
39th Regiment of the Line, 3rd battalion	(1)	12 - 310
54th Regiment of the Line, 3rd battalion	(1)	19 - 608
95th Regiment of the Line, 3rd batalion	(1)	17 - 456

Artillery: Girud

1st Regiment of Foot Artillery, 4th company		2 - 85
Artillery Train, detachments from various battalions		1 - 145

45th Division— Général de division Count Razout

Division headquarters staff—12 personnel

1st Brigade*: Général de brigade d'Esclevin

(*The division had only one brigade at this time.)

8th Regiment of the Line, 3rd battalion	(1)	23 - 608
28th Regiment of the Line, 2nd battalion	(1)	21 - 436
32nd Regiment of the Line, 4th battalion	(1)	23 - 540
6th battalion	(1)	20 - 155
58th Regiment of the Line, 2nd battalion	(1)	17 - 204
4th battalion	(1)	21 - 508
34th Regiment of the Line, 3rd battalion	(1)	21 - 513
4th battalion	(1)	21 - 246
79th Regiment of the Line, 3rd battalion	(1)	24 - 655
4th battalion	(1)	20 - 524
81st Regiment of the Line, 6th battalion	(1)	20 - 650
60th Regiment of the Line, 4th battalion	(1)	23 - 614

Divisional artillery and train:

5th Regiment of Foot Artillery, 21st company		3 - 240**
Artillery Train, detachments of various battalions		

**Combined strength of the artillery company and the artillery train detachments.

10th Light Cavalry Division— Général de division Baron Pajol

1st Brigade: Général de brigade Jacquet

2nd Italian Chasseurs à Cheval, 1st—4th squadrons	(4)	28 - 344
7th (1st Vistula Legion) Light Lancers, 1st—4th squadrons	(4)	38 - 386

2nd Brigade: Général de brigade Stedmann

14th Hussars, 1st and 2nd squadrons	(2)	16 - 116

XIV Corps Artillery Reserve—

6th Regiment of Foot Artillery, 4th company		3 - 86
6th Regiment of Foot Artillery, 5th company		4 - 109
7th Regiment of Foot Artillery, 15th company		3 - 92
2nd Regiment of Horse Artillery, 5th company		3 - 79
6th Regiment of Horse Artillery, 3rd company		3 - 74
1st Principal Artillery Train Battalion, detachment of the 3rd company		1 - 45
4th Principal Artillery Train Battalion, detachment of the 3rd company		1 - 67
detachment of the 6th company		- 44
11th Principal Artillery Train Battalion, 3rd company		2 - 118
detachment of the 5th company		1 - 70
12th Principal Artillery Train Battalion, detachment of the 2nd company		- 13
detachment of the 5th company		- 9
detachment of the 6th company		1 - 114
1st *bis* Artillery Train Battalion, detachment of the 3rd company		- 14
detachment of the 7th company		- 36
10th *bis* Artillery Train Battalion, detachment of the 4th company		- 40
Ouvriers, detachment of the 17th company		1 - 15
2nd Battalion, Sappers of the Line, 5th company	(1)	3 - 120
8th company	(1)	3 - 131
4th Battalion, Sappers of the Line, 7th company	(1)	3 - 130

Ordnance details—

While specifics concerning the composition of the individual artillery companies are not shown on the 10 October parade states, the totals for the corps are given. They are:

12-pounder guns—6
6-inch howitzers—2
6-pounder guns—32
51/2-inch howitzers—12
Total pieces in XIV Corps—52

It is probably safe to assume that the 6th Regiment/5th company of foot artillery still retained its same composition of 6 12-pdr. guns and 2 6-inch howitzers. Therefore, the remaining 6-pounder guns and 51/2-inch howitzers were in the other companies.

SITUATION
of the
IMPERIAL GUARD CAVALRY CORPS
15 October 1813

	Number of Squadrons	Present and Under Arms Off. - Others	Not Present In Hospital Off. - Others

Général de division Count Nansouty
Adjudant commandant Leistenschneider, Chief of Staff
Général de brigade Baron Desvaux de Saint-Maurice, Horse Artillery of the Guard

1st Imperial Guard Cavalry Division— Général de division Count Ornano
1st Brigade: Général de brigade Baron de Colbert

Light Lancers of Berg, 1st, 3rd, and 4th sqdrns	(3)	39 - 409	- 71
5th and 6th squadrons	(2)	detached—not present	

The 2nd squadron was not present with the rest of the regiment.

2nd (Red) Light Lancers of the Guard	(10)	63 - 731	2 - 84

2nd Brigade: Général de brigade Linteville

Young Guard squadrons, Guard Dragoons	(2)	18 - 223	1 - 3

2nd Imperial Gd Cav Div—Général de division Count Lefebvre-Desnoëttes
1st Brigade: Général de brigade Count Krasinski

Young Guard sqdrns, 1st Light Lancers of the Gd	(4)	43 - 535	- 8

2nd Brigade: Général de brigade Castex

Young Guard sqdrns, Guard Chasseurs à Cheval	(5)	38 - 628	- 51
Young Guard sqdrns, Guard Grenadiers à Cheval	(2)	17 - 290	- 1

3rd Imperial Guard Cavalry Division— Général de division Count Walther
1st Brigade: Général de brigade Baron Lyon

1st (Polish) Old Guard Lt Lancers of the Guard	(3)	42 - 530	- 27
Old Guard Chasseurs à Cheval, 1st—4th sqdrns	(4)	51 - 871	- 4

2nd Brigade: Général de brigade Baron Letort

Guard Dragoons, 1st, 2nd, 3rd, and 4th sqdrns	(4)	45 - 747	- 35

3rd Brigade: Général de brigade Baron de Laferrière-Levêque

Old Guard Grenadiers à Cheval, 1st—4th sqdrns	(4)	57 - 881	- 12
Gendarmes d'élite, 1st and 2nd squadrons	(2)	detached to Imperial HQ	

Guards of Honor Cavalry Division—Attached to the 3rd Division

1st Regiment, Guards of Honor, 1st—5th sqdrns	(5)	15 - 269	- 21
2nd Regiment, Guards of Honor, 1st—5th sqdrns	(5)	15 - 246	- 16
3rd Regiment, Guards of Honor, 1st—5th sqdrns	(5)	8 - 146	- 10
4th Regiment, Guards of Honor, 1st—5th sqdrns	(5)	10 - 192	---

Each regiment of the Guards of Honor was attached to a regiment of the Old
Guard Cavalry. The 1st Regiment was attached to the Chasseurs; the
2nd Regiment was attached to the Dragoons; the 3rd Regiment was attached
to the Grenadiers; and the 4th Regiment was attached to the Polish Lancers.

Horse Artillery of the Guard attached to the Guard Cavalry—

Headquarters staff—9 personnel

Old Guard Horse Artillery, 3rd company	4 - 85	- 6
4th company	2 - 83	- 3
5th company	3 - 86	- 6
6th company	3 - 84	- 9

Each company of Old Guard Horse Artillery consisted of
4 6-pdr. guns and 2 51/2-inch howitzers—total of 24 pieces of ordnance.
At this time, the 1st and 2nd companies of the Old Guard Horse Artillery
and the Grand Duchy of Berg Horse Artillery were in the Artillery Reserve of the
Guard.

Horse Artillery Train Personnel	4 - 294	- 7
Ouvriers of the Artillery of the Guard	- 13	---

SITUATION
of the
IMPERIAL GUARD CAVALRY CORPS
1 November 1813

	Number of Squadrons	Present and Under Arms Off. - Others	Not Present In Hospital Off. - Others

Général de division Count Nansouty
Adjudant commandant Leistenschneider, Chief of Staff
Général de brigade Baron Desvaux de Saint-Maurice, Horse Artillery of the Guard

1st Imperial Guard Cavalry Division— Général de division Count Ornano
1st Brigade: Général de brigade Baron de Colbert

Light Lancers of Berg, 1st, 3rd, and 4th sqdrns	(3)	10 - 51	- 71
5th and 6th squadrons	(2)	detached	

The 2nd squadron was not present with the rest of the regiment.

2nd (Red) Light Lancers of the Guard	(10)	52 - 462	---

2nd Brigade: Général de brigade Linteville

Young Guard squadrons, Guard Dragoons	(2)	23 - 269	1 - 1

2nd Imperial Gd Cav Div—Général de division Count Lefebvre-Desnoëttes
1st Brigade: Général de brigade Castex

Young Guard sqdrns, Guard Chasseurs à Cheval	(5)	28 - 341	- 54
Young Guard sqdrns, Guard Grenadiers à Cheval	(2)	15 - 197	- 2

3rd Imperial Guard Cavalry Division— Général de division Count Walther
1st Brigade: Général de brigade Count Krasinski

1st (Polish) Old Guard Lt Lancers of the Guard	(3)	35 - 376	---
Young Guard sqdrns, 1st Lt Lancers of the Guard	(4)	included above	

2nd Brigade: Général de brigade Baron Lyon

Old Guard Chasseurs à Cheval, 1st—4th sqdrns	(4)	50 - 512	- 11

3rd Brigade: Général de brigade Baron Letort

Guard Dragoons, 1st, 2nd, 3rd, and 4th sqdrns	(4)	43 - 430	- 35

4th Brigade: Général de brigade Baron de Laferrière-Levêque

Old Guard Grenadiers à Cheval, 1st—4th sqdrns	(4)	50 - 543	- 11
Gendarmes d'élite, 1st and 2nd squadrons	(2)	detached to Imperial HQ	

Guards of Honor Cavalry Division—Attached to the 3rd Division
There were no returns for the Guards of Honor for this date.

Horse Artillery of the Guard attached to the Guard Cavalry—

Headquarters staff—9 personnel

Old Guard Horse Artillery, 3rd company	3 - 66	- 6
4th company	2 - 84	- 4
5th company	3 - 84	- 7
6th company	3 - 77	- 9

Each company of Old Guard Horse Artillery consisted of
4 6-pdr. guns and 2 5 1/2-inch howitzers—total of 24 pieces of ordnance.
At this time, the 1st and 2nd companies of the Old Guard Horse Artillery
and the Horse Artillery of Berg were in the Artillery Reserve of the Guard.

Horse Artillery Train Personnel	4 - 179	---
Ouvriers of the Artillery of the Guard	- 9	---

Appendix S

SITUATION
of the
V CORPS
1 November 1813

	Number of Battalions/ Squadrons	Present and Under Arms Off. - Others	Not Present In Hospital Off. - Others

Général de division Baron Albert
Général de brigade Baron Baillod, Chief of Staff
Général de brigade Baron Camal, commanding the artillery
Colonel Lamarre, commanding the engineers

10th Division— Général de division Baron Albert

1st Brigade: Général de brigade Edme-Victor Bertrand			
5th Light Infantry Regiment, 4th battalion	(1)	13 - 185	11 - 455
139th Regiment of the Line, 1st battalion	(1)	15 - 206	11 - 903
2nd battalion	(1)	17 - 210	6 - 872
3rd battalion	(1)	18 - 240	5 - 716
2nd Brigade:			
140th Regiment of the Line, 1st battalion	(1)	19 - 173	11 - 656
2nd battalion	(1)	12 - 135	9 - 557
3rd battalion	(1)	10 - 171	10 - 520
141st Regiment of the Line,1st battalion	(1)	18 - 117	13 - 694
2nd battalion	(1)	11 - 133	15 - 655
3rd battalion	(1)	11 - 131	15 - 659
Divisional artillery and train:†			

16th Division—Général de division Baron Maison

1st Brigade: Général de brigade Obert			
151st Regiment of the Line, 1st—3rd battalions—in memorial...survivors of the regiment in garrison at Glogau.			
152nd Regiment of the Line, 1st battalion	(1)	6 - 88	18 - 485
2nd battalion	(1)	2 - 90	12 - 596
3rd battalion	(1)	2 - 93	11 - 636
2nd Brigade:			
153rd Regiment of the Line, 1st battalion	(1)	14 - 132	6 - 450
2nd battalion	(1)	5 - 141	2 - 337
3rd battalion	(1)	6 - 138	1 - 389
154th Regiment of the Line, 1st battalion	(1)	14 - 59	7 - 496
2nd battalion	(1)	8 - 103	3 - 266
3rd battalion	(1)	7 - 83	4 - 357
Divisional artillery and train:†			

19th Division—

1st Brigade:

135th Regiment of the Line, 1st battalion	(1)	16 - 127	2 - 16
2nd battalion	(1)	4 - 114	2 - 16
3rd battalion	(1)	3 - 116	2 - 17
149th Regiment of the Line, 1st battalion	(1)	27 - 191	9 - 259
2nd battalion	(1)	15 - 162	10 - 330
3rd battalion	(1)	10 - 151	6 - 365

2nd Brigade:

150th Regiment of the Line, 1st battalion	(1)	9 - 63	- 23
2nd battalion	(1)	6 - 93	- 85
3rd battalion	(i)	7 - 98	- 115
155th Regiment of the Line, 1st battalion	(1)	6 - 84	13 - 450
2nd battalion	(1)	10 - 90	18 - 479
3rd battalion	(1)	5 - 81	16 - 432

Divisional artillery and train:[†]

V Corps Artillery Reserve—

All artillery reserve companies and train[†]

6th Battalion, Sappers of the Line, 1st company	5 - 49	- 40
2nd company	2 - 84	- 16
3rd company	3 - 66	- 9

Attached to V Corps—from the 3rd Light Cavalry Division—

3rd Brigade: Colonel Thalouet

2nd Chasseurs à Cheval, 1st—3rd squadrons	(3)	- 6	---
3rd Chasseurs à Cheval, 1st and 2nd squadrons	(2)	1 - 24	----
6th Chasseurs à Cheval, 1st—3rd squadrons	(3)	16 - 119	----

[†]All artillerists and train personnel, along with all ordnance, now in the artillery reserve park in Mayence.

SITUATION
of the
III RESERVE CAVALRY CORPS
1 November 1813

	Number of Squadrons	Present and Under Arms Off. - Others	Not Present In Hospital Off. - Others

Général de division Arrighi de Casanova, Duke of Padoua
Adjudant commandant Salel, Chief of Staff
Colonel Chauveau, commanding the artillery

5th Light Cavalry Division— Général de division Baron Lorge
1st Brigade: Général de brigade Jacquinot

		Present	Not Present
5th Chasseurs à Cheval, 1st, 3rd, and 4th sqdrns	(3)	22 - 166	2 - 68
10th Chasseurs à Cheval, 1st, 3rd, and 4th sqdrns	(3)	19 - 147	1 - 34
13th Chasseurs à Cheval, 5th and 6th squadrons	(2)	19 - 172	1 - 32

2nd Brigade: Général de brigade Merlin

15th Chasseurs à Cheval, 4th squadron	(1)	8 - 97	- 22
21st Chasseurs à Cheval, 3rd squadron	(1)	9 - 63	- 2
22nd Chasseurs à Cheval, 3rd and 4th squadrons	(2)	8 - 131	- 75

6th Light Cavalry Division— Général de division Baron Fournier
1st Brigade: Général de brigade Ameil

29th Chasseurs à Cheval, 4th squadron	(1)	6 - 40	- 3
31st Chasseurs à Cheval, 4th squadron	(1)	9 - 27	- 22
1st Hussars, 3rd and 4th squadrons	(2)	8 - 43	---

2nd Brigade: Général de brigade Mouriez

2nd Hussars, 3rd and 4th squadrons	(2)	11 - 106	- 5
4th Hussars, 5th squadron	(1)	2 - 8	1 - 9
12th Hussars, 4th squadron	(1)	6 - 59	- 18

4th Heavy Cavalry Division— Général de division Count Defrance
1st Brigade: Général de brigade Axamitowski

4th Dragoons, 4th squadron	(1)	7 - 36	- 12
5th Dragoons, 3rd squadron	(1)	11 - 63	- 41
12th Dragoons, 3rd squadron	(1)	6 - 50	- 9
14th Dragoons, 3rd and 4th squadrons	(2)	8 - 42	- 17
24th Dragoons, 4th squadron	(1)	3 - 47	1 - 8

2nd Brigade: Général de brigade Quinette

16th Dragoons, 3rd squadron	(1)	4 - 65	---
17th Dragoons, 3rd squadron	(1)	11 - 85	- 20
21st Dragoons, 3rd squadron	(1)	7 - 57	---
26th Dragoons, 3rd squadron	(1)	4 - 54	- 8
27th Dragoons, 4th and 5th squadrons	(2)	6 - 74	- 9
13th (Dutch) Cuirassiers, 5th squadron	(1)	6 - 91	- 12

III Reserve Cavalry Corps Reserve Artillery—
There were no artillery returns for this date.

SITUATION
of the
Reorganized
IV CORPS
5 November 1813

	Number of Battalions/ Squadrons	Present and Under Arms Off. - Others	Not Present In Hospital Off. - Others*

Général de division Count Bertrand
Général de brigade Delort, Chief of Staff
Général de division Baron de Taviel, commanding the artillery
Colonel Isoard, commanding the engineers

12th Division— Général de division Count Morand
1st Brigade: Général de brigade de Belair

8th Light Infantry Regiment, 1st—4th bns	(4)	53 - 533	
13th Regiment of the Line, 1st—4th and 6th bns	(5)	68 - 1,507	
23rd Regiment of the Line, 1st, 2nd, 4th and 6th bns	(4)	40 - 802	
137th Regiment of the Line, 1st—3rd bns	(3)	detached	

There was no longer any divisional artillery and train.

13th Division— Général de division Baron Guilleminot
1st Brigade:

1st Light Infantry Regiment, 4th battalion	(1)	16 - 180	
18th Light Infantry Regiment, detachment	(-)	2 - 25	
7th Regiment of the Line, 3rd battalion	(1)	15 - 189	
42nd Regiment of the Line, 4th battalion	(1)	3 - 50	

2nd Brigade:

52nd Regiment of the Line	(2)	24 - 341	
67th Regiment of the Line, 3rd and 4th bns	(2)	29 - 554	
101st Regiment of the Line, 2nd—4th bns	(3)	51 - 611	
156th Regiment of the Line, 1st—3rd bns	(3)	25 - 392	
Illyrian Regiment, 2nd battalion	(1)	16 - 85	

Divisional artillery and train:

5th Regiment of Horse Artillery, 3rd company		3 - 90	
3rd *bis* Artillery Train Battalion, detachment of the 1st company		1 - 69	

52nd Division— Général de division Baron Séméllé
1st Brigade: Général de brigade Aymard

10th Light Infantry Regiment	(1)	145[†]	
17th Light Infantry Regiment	(1)	206[†]	
21st Light Infantry Regiment	(1)	146[†]	
25th Light Infantry Regiment	(1)	125[†]	
29th Light Infantry Regiment	(1)	170[†]	
32nd Light Infantry Regiment	(1)	97[†]	

2nd Brigade: Général de brigade Sagarde

32nd Regiment of the Line	(1)	154[†]
39th Regiment of the Line	(1)	100[†]
63rd Regiment of the Line	(1)	244[†]
86th Regiment of the Line	(1)	120[†]
121st Regiment of the Line	(1)	108[†]
122nd Regiment of the Line	(1)	25[†]

There was no longer any divisional artillery and train.

[†]These totals include officers.

Independent Division— Général de division Baron Margaron

1st Brigade:

35th Light Infantry Regiment	(1)	3 - 132
36th Light Infantry Regiment	(1)	13 - 277
54th Regiment of the Line	(1)	16 - 200
96th Regiment of the Line	(1)	15 - 342
103rd Regiment of the Line	(1)	11 - 262
132nd Regiment of the Line	(1)	18 - 315

There was no divisional artillery and train.

IV Corps Artillery Reserve—

2nd Regiment of Foot Artillery, 24th company	1 - 66
26th company	3 - 55
8th Regiment of Foot Artillery, 1st company	3 - 37
1st Principal Artillery Train Battalion, detachment of the 5th company	- 9
7th *bis* Artillery Train Battalion, 5th company	2 - 93
Ouvriers, detachment of the 13th company	1 - 12
1st Battalion, Sappers of the Line, 2nd company	2 - 46
8th company	2 - 90
Sapper Train, detachment	1 - 13

IV Corps troops in route to join their regiments—

5th Light Infantry Regiment	600[†]
15th Regiment of the Line	600[†]
26th Regiment of the Line	600[†]
66th Regiment of the Line	600[†]
82nd Regiment of the Line	600[†]
86th Regiment of the Line	500[†]
95th Regiment of the Line	500[†]
96th Regiment of the Line	600[†]
103rd Regiment of the Line	600[†]

[†]These totals include officers.

*Parade states for this date listed only those present and under arms. Therefore, no returns are shown for those in hospital(s).

Appendix V

SITUATION
of the
Reorganized
VI CORPS
15 November 1813

	Number of Battalions/ Squadrons	Present and Under Arms Off. - Others	Not Present In Hospital Off. - Others
Marshal Marmont, Duke of Ragusa			
Général de brigade Baron Meinadieu, Chief of Staff			
Général de division Count Pernetti, commanding the artillery			
Général de brigade Blein, commanding the engineers			

20th Division— Général de division Count Lagrange
Division headquarters staff—27 personnel
1st Brigade: Général de brigade Pelleport

23rd Light Infantry Regiment, 3rd battalion	(1)	20 - 146	2 - 239
37th Light Infantry Regiment, 1st battalion	(1)	21 - 530	- 41
1st Regiment of the Line, 4th battalion	(1)	17 - 212	4 - 36
16th Regiment of the Line, 4th battalion	(1)	16 - 217	- 48
14th Regiment of the Line, 3rd battalion	(1)	2 - 266	4 - 57
15th Regiment of the Line, 3rd battalion	(1)	21 - 210	- 32
70th Regiment of the Line, 3rd battalion	(1)	20 - 309	1 - 237
121st Regiment of the Line, 3rd battalion	(1)	20 - 257	1 - 68
4th battalion	(1)	17 - 52	3 - 6
6th battalion	(1)	12 - 230	- 73

2nd Brigade: Général de brigade Joubert

32nd Light Infantry Regiment, 3rd battalion	(1)	23 - 272	- 87
4th battalion	(1)	17 - 272	- 143
1st Regiment de Marine, 1st battalion	(1)	13 - 251	2 - 128
2nd battalion	(1)	11 - 282	2 - 74
3rd Regiment de Marine, 1st battalion	(1)	22 - 298	- 40
2nd battalion	(1)	13 - 188	- 33
3rd battalion	(1)	11 - 100	2 - 38
62nd Regiment of the Line, 2nd battalion	(1)	13 - 190	4 - 54
3rd battalion	(1)	12 - 522	1 - 141

3rd Brigade: Général de brigade Buquet

2nd Regiment de Marine, 1st battalion	(1)	42 - 530	5 - 70
2nd battalion	(1)	18 - 430	- 132
3rd battalion	(1)	18 - 402	- 78
4th battalion	(1)	18 - 439	- 95
Spanish Regiment Joseph Napoleon, 1st battalion	(1)	11 - 185	1 - 58
4th Regiment de Marine, 1st battalion	(1)	19 - 165	10 - 62
2nd battalion	(1)	11 - 183	6 - 60
3rd battalion	(1)	11 - 186	7 - 55

Divisional artillery and train:
 5th Regiment of Foot Artillery, 13th company   3 - 73   ---
  16th company   3 - 83   ---
 The above foot artillery companies had a total of
 6 12-pdr. guns, 3 6-pdr. guns, and 3 5 1/2-inch howitzers—
 total of 12 pieces of ordnance.
 4th Principal Artillery Train Battalion, detachment   1 - 83   ---
 8th *bis* Artillery Train Battalion,
  detachment of the 2nd company   2 - 125   ---

8th Division— Général de division Baron Ricard
Division headquarters staff—18 personnel
1st Brigade: Général de brigade Fournier
 2nd Light Infantry Regiment, 3rd batttalion   (1)   21 - 119   - 8
 4th Light Infantry Regiment, 3rd battalion   (1)   21 - 121   - 17
 6th Light Infantry Regiment, 2nd battalion   (1)   22 - 64   - 13
 9th Light Infantry Regiment, 3rd battalion   (1)   21 - 329   - 47
 16th Light Infantry Regiment, 2nd battalion   (1)   22 - 381   - 13
 28th Light Infantry Regiment, 1st battalion   (1)   21 - 184   - 3
2nd Brigade:
 22nd Regiment of the Line, 1st battalion   (1)   24 - 484   - 21
 40th Regiment of the Line, 3rd battalion   (1)   21 - 220   - 32
 43rd Regiment of the Line, 3rd battalion   (1)   21 - 291   - 8
 50th Regiment of the Line, 2nd battalion   (1)   20 - 383   - 60
 59th Regiment of the Line, 2nd battalion   (1)   23 - 294   - 12
 65th Regiment of the Line, 3rd battalion   (1)   22 - 233   - 31
 69th Regiment of the Line, 3rd battalion   (1)   21 - 314   - 14
3rd Brigade:
 136th Regiment of the Line, 1st battalion   (1)   25 - 613   - 18
 138th Regiment of the Line, 1st battalion   (1)   25 - 513   - 57
 142nd Regiment of the Line, 1st battalion   (1)   18 - 458   - 57
 144th Regiment of the Line, 1st battalion   (1)   31 - 853   - 36
 145th Regiment of the Line, 1st battalion   (1)   25 - 747   1 - 32
Note: The regiments of the 3rd Brigade were the consolidated survivors of the battalions
of each regiment.
Divisional artillery and train:
 3rd Regiment of Foot Artillery, 6th company   3 - 64   ---
  25th company   2 - 57   ---
  26th company   2 - 58   ---
 The above foot artillery companies had a total of
 6 6-pdr. guns and 2 5 1/2-inch howitzers—total of 8 pieces of ordnance.
 9th *bis* Artillery Train Battalion, 1st company   2 - 107   ---
  detachment of the 5th company   1 - 51   ---

VI Corps Artillery Reserve—
 4th Battalion, Sappers of the Line, 2nd company   3 - 68   - 18
  9th company   2 - 64   - 18
 7th Battalion, Sappers of the Line, 4th company   3 - 46   1 - 7
 Imperial Gendarmes, detachment   2 - 35   ---

SITUATION
of the
I RESERVE CAVALRY CORPS
15 November 1813

	Number of Squadrons	Present and Under Arms Off. - Others	Not Present In Hospital Off. - Others*

Général de division Count Doumerc
Adjudant commandant Mathieu, Chief of Staff
Colonel Lavoy, commanding the artillery

1st Light Cavalry Division— Général de division Berckeim

1st Brigade: Général de brigade Piquet			
6th Hussars, 1st and 2nd squadrons	(2)	4 - 47	
7th Hussars, 1st—3rd squadrons	(3)	2 - 58	
8th Hussars, 1st—3rd squadrons	(3)	5 - 80	
2nd Brigade: Général de brigade Duçoethosquet			
16th Chasseurs à Cheval, 1st and 2nd squadrons	(2)	5 - 111	
1st Light Lancers, 1st and 2nd squadrons	(2)	19 - 207	
3rd Light Lancers, 1st and 2nd squadrons	(2)	14 - 173	
5th Light Lancers, 1st and 2nd squadrons	(2)	10 - 132	
8th (2nd Vistula Legion) Light Lancers, 1st and 2nd squadrons	(2)	3 - 35	
1st Italian Chasseurs à Cheval, 1st—4th sqdrns	(4)	- 4	

3rd Light Cavalry Division— Général de division Baron Chastel

1st Brigade: Général de brigade Vallin			
8th Chasseurs à Cheval, 1st and 2nd squadrons	(2)	14 - 87	
9th Chasseurs à Cheval, 1st and 2nd squadrons	(2)	2 - 46	
25th Chasseurs à Cheval, 1st and 2nd squadrons	(2)	- 5	
2nd Brigade: Général de brigade Van Merlen			
1st Chasseurs à Cheval, 1st—4th squadrons	(4)	12 - 171	
19th Chasseurs à Cheval, 1st—4th squadrons	(4)	none present	

1st Heavy Cavalry Division— Général de division Baron Bordesoulle

1st Brigade: Général de brigade Bonieru			
2nd Cuirassiers, 1st and 2nd squadrons	(2)	13 - 129	
3rd Cuirassiers, 1st and 2nd squadrons	(2)	14 - 120	
6th Cuirassiers, 1st and 2nd squadrons	(2)	14 - 85	
2nd Brigade: Général de brigade Sopranly			
9th Cuirassiers, 1st, 2nd, and 3rd squadrons	(3)	12 - 155	
11th Cuirassiers, 1st, 2nd, and 3rd squadrons	(3)	11 - 46	
12th Cuirassiers, 1st and 2nd squadrons	(2)	8 - 84	
3rd Brigade: Général de brigade Lessing			
Saxon Garde du corps, 1st—4th squadrons	(4)	no return	
Saxon Zastrow Cuirassiers, 1st—4th squadrons	(4)	no return	

3rd Heavy Cavalry Division— Général de division Lalaing d'Audenarde

1st Brigade: Général de brigade Denet

4th Cuirassiers, 1st—3rd squadrons	(3)	19 - 150
7th Cuirassiers, 1st—3rd squadrons	(3)	16 - 143
14th (Dutch) Cuirassiers, 1st and 2nd squadrons	(2)	14 - 70
Italian Dragoons "Napoleon", 1st—4th sqdrns	(4)	4 - 47

2nd Brigade: Général de brigade Reiset

7th Dragoons, 1st—3rd squadrons	(3)	13 - 124
23rd Dragoons, 1st and 2nd squadrons	(2)	4 - 179
28th Dragoons, 1st and 2nd squadrons	(2)	10 - 117
30th Dragoons, 1st and 2nd squadrons	(2)	7 - 19

I Reserve Cavalry Corps Artillery Reserve—

1st Regiment of Horse Artillery, 3rd company;	3 - 60
additional unidentified company of the	
1st Regiment of Horse Artillery	3 - 52

The above horse artillery companies had a total of

4 6-pdr. guns and 2 51/2-inch howitzers—total of 6 pieces of ordnance.

Artillery Train personnel	2 - 104

*Parade states for this date listed only those present and under arms. Therefore, no returns are shown for those in hospital(s).

SITUATION
of the
II RESERVE CAVALRY CORPS
15 November 1813

	Number of Squadrons	Present and Under Arms Off. - Others	Not Present In Hospital Off. - Others

Général de division Count Sébastiani de la Porta
Adjudant commandant Lascours, Chief of Staff
Colonel Colin, commanding the artillery

2nd Light Cavalry Division— Général de division Baron Roussel d'Hurbal

1st Brigade: Général de brigade Domanget			
11th Chasseurs à Cheval, 1st—3rd squadrons	(3)	20 - 107	---
12th Chasseurs à Cheval, 1st—3rd squadrons	(3)	18 - 149	---
2nd Light Lancers, 1st—3rd squadrons	(3)	20 - 118	- 1
2nd Brigade: Général de brigade Lagrange			
5th Hussars, 1st—3rd squadrons	(3)	21 - 101	---
9th Hussars, 1st—4th squadrons	(4)	24 - 98	---
4th Light Lancers, 1st—3rd squadrons	(3)	20 - 141	1 - 13

4th Light Cavalry Division— Général de division Baron Exelmans

1st Brigade: Général de brigade Maurin			
6th Light Lancers, 1st—3rd squadrons	(3)	23 - 156	1 - 43
4th Chasseurs à Cheval, 1st—3rd squadrons	(3)	15 - 99	- 10
7th Chasseurs à Cheval, 1st—4th squadrons	(4)	15 - 106	1 - 3
20th Chasseurs à Cheval, 1st—4th squadrons	(4)	24 - 142	---
2nd Brigade: Général de brigade Wathier			
23rd Chasseurs à Cheval, 1st—4th squadrons	(4)	25 - 243	---
24th Chasseurs à Cheval, 1st—3rd squadrons	(3)	19 - 242	1 - 31
11th (Dutch) Hussars, 1st—3rd squadrons	(3)	19 - 130	---

2nd Heavy Cavalry Division— Général de division Count Saint-Germain

1st Brigade: Général de brigade Leclerc de la Cologne			
1st Carabiniers, 1st—3rd squadrons	(3)	19 - 125	---
2nd Carabiniers, 1st—3rd squadrons	(3)	21 - 204	- 1
1st Cuirassiers, 1st—3rd squadrons	(3)	20 - 148	---
2nd Brigade: Général de brigade Thiry			
5th Cuirassiers, 1st—3rd squadrons	(3)	22 - 103	- 42
8th Cuirassiers, 1st and 2nd squadrons	(2)	12 - 55	- 6
10th Cuirassiers, 1st and 2nd squadrons	(2)	21 - 104	---

II Reserve Cavalry Corps Reserve Artillery—

1st Regiment of Horse Artillery, 7th company		2 - 53	---

The above horse artillery company consisted of
4 6-pdr. guns and 2 5 1/2-inch howitzers—total of 6 pieces of ordnance.

Artillery Train Battalion, detachment		1 - 47	---

SITUATION
of the
V RESERVE CAVALRY CORPS
15 November 1813

	Number of Squadrons	Present and Under Arms Off. - Others	Not Present In Hospital Off. - Others

Général de division Count Milhaud
Adjundant commandant Chafferian, Chief of Staff
Général de brigade Coën, commanding the artillery

9th Light Cavalry Division— Général de division Baron Tyré
1st Brigade: Général de brigade Baron Subervie

3rd Hussars, 1st squadron	(1)	12 - 59	- 4
2nd squadron	(1)	5 - 40	- 5
3rd squadron	(1)	2 - 27	- 11
4th squadron	(1)	4 - 30	- 19
26th Chasseurs à Cheval, 1st squadron	(1)	13 - 97	- 23
3rd squadron	(1)	4 - 20	- 121
4th squadron	(1)	3 - 21	- 8

2nd Brigade: Général de brigade Baron Desmoncourt

14th Chasseurs à Cheval, 1st squadron	(1)	10 - 67	- 25
3rd squadron	(1)	2 - 28	- 8
4th squadron	(1)	5 - 77	- 121
27th Chasseurs à Cheval, 1st squadron	(1)	12 - 142	1 - 17
3rd squadron	(1)	6 - 58	- 15
4th squadron	(1)	5 - 36	1 - 18
5th squadron	(1)	4 - 76	- 9
13th Hussars	(3)	detached—at Magdebourg	

5th Heavy Cavalry Division— Général de brigade Baron Collaert
1st Brigade: Général de Brigade Montelegier

2nd Dragoons,1st, 2nd, and 3rd squadrons	(3)	23 - 326	---
6th Dragoons, 1st, 2nd, and 4th squadrons	(3)	22 - 253	1 - 27
11th Dragoons, 1st, 3rd, and 4th squadrons	(3)	28 - 319	1 - 53

2nd Brigade: Colonel Boudinhoh

13th Dragoons, 1st and 3rd squadrons	(2)	16 - 200	---
15th Dragoons, 1st, 3rd, and 4th squadrons	(3)	27 - 283	- 31

6th Heavy Cavalry Division— Général de division Baron L'héritier

1st Brigade: Général de brigade Baron Lamotte

18th Dragoons, 1st squadron	(1)	11 - 142	- 2
2nd squadron	(1)	1 - 18	---
3rd squadron	(1)	5 - 51	- 2
19th Dragoons, 3rd squadron	(1)	18 - 180	- 17
20th Dragoons, 3rd squadron	(1)	4 - 54	---

2nd Brigade: Colonel Mermet

22nd Dragoons, 3rd squadron	(1)	17 - 196	- 2
25th Dragoons, 1st and 3rd squadrons	(2)	28 - 228	- 6

V Reserve Cavalry Corps Reserve Artillery—

3rd Regiment of Horse Artillery, 2nd company, consisting	2 - 75	- 4

of 4 6-pdr. guns and 2 51/2-inch howitzers—total of 6 pieces of ordnance.

12th Principal Artillery Train Battalion, 1st company	1 - 64	---

APPENDIX Z
Napoleon's Grande Armée of 1813
and Historical Simulation

Napoleon's *Grande Armée* of 1813 offers the historical simulation enthusiast a diverse collection of troops, reflecting wide variations in morale class and combat effectiveness. Equally interesting was the collection of general officers who exhibited differing levels of devotion and skill. This appendix is designed as a "wargamer's guide" to Napoleon's 1813 army and its leaders.

Insofar as the troop ratings are concerned, the branch of service in Napoleon's army which displayed the least amount of variation was the artillery arm. To state it simply, the companies of French Young Guard, line foot, or horse artillerists operated their pieces with a more deadly effect than any Allied crew manning the same number and weight of guns. The French Old Guard foot and horse companies had the highest morale and were the most efficient and effective artillery crews in any army engaged in the 1813 struggle for Germany. Therefore, the Old Guard artillery is clearly better than French Young Guard or line artillery, and vastly superior to any Continental artillery, regardless of nationality.

The infantry of Napoleon's *Grande Armée* of 1813 varied widely in their morale and combat effectiveness. Based upon the author's study of the army, the following table sets forth the morale classes of the various infantry units. These catagories are rated from best (Old Guard) to the worst (Trained Militia). Units with an asterisk (*) should be classified as shock infantry and receive special bonuses relating to close action combat.

While the author has attempted to list the morale ratings for the French artillery, as well as some of the allies, space limitations prevent a comprehensive listing of the morale for all the French–Allied artillery. Generally speaking, French–Allied artillery crews have a morale rating equal to or one step higher than the infantry of their own nationality.

It should be remembered that not all infantry battalions had the same organization. While most French line and light battalions had six companies, four of which were fusiliers (chasseurs in the light infantry), one of which were grenadiers (carabiniers in the light infantry), and one of voltigeurs, some regiments, such as those formed from the cohorts (Line Regiments 135 through 156) had six companies of fusiliers with no elite companies present.

The infantry battalions of the Guard had four companies per battalion, each company stronger than a company of the line or light infantry.

Morale Classifications of the Infantry and Artillery in Napoleon's *Grande Armée* of 1813

Morale Classification	Unit Description
Old Guard—	1st & 2nd Old Grenadiers à pied* 1st & 2nd Old Guard Chasseurs à pied* Old Guard Foot and Horse Artillery
Guards—	Middle Guard Fusilier Grenadiers* Middle Guard Fusilier Chasseurs* Guard Engineers* *Marins* of the Guard*
Grenadiers—	3rd Young Guard Voltigeurs* and 3rd Tirailleurs* Vélites of Florence* Vélites of Turin* 11th Light Infantry Regiment, 1st* & 2nd* Battalions Italian Royal Guard Grenadiers* Italian Royal Guard Artillery Sappers of the Line* Saxon Leib–Garde Grenadiers*
Elites—	37th Light Infantry Regiment* 1st, 2nd, 3rd, & 4th Regiments de Marine* 1st & 2nd Young Guard Voltigeurs* and Tirailleurs* Flanker Grenadiers of the Guard* Line Horse Artillery Young Guard Foot Artillery Vistula Legion* All Polish Infantry Regiments of the 26th and 27th Divisions* Hesse–Darmstadt Leib–Garde Fusiliers* Hesse–Darmstadt Leib–Garde Regiment* Italian Royal Guard Vélites* and Chasseurs* Westphalian Fusilier Gardes* Würzburg Infantry Regiment 84th Regiment of the Line
Crack (or 1st Rate) Line—	32nd Light Infantry Regiment 15th Light Infantry Regiment 8th Light Infantry Regiment 9th Light Infantry Regiment All Light Infantry Regiments of the 32nd Division All other Polish Infantry Regiments Polish Foot Artillery French Line Foot Artillery

Crack Line (continued)—
    Hesse-Darmstadt Musketeer Regiments
    All other Young Guard Infantry Regiments
    Milan Guard Battalion
    Saxon Combined Grenadiers

Veteran Line—
    All Line Infantry Regiments of the 32nd Division
    Württemberg Light and Line Battalions
    All Italian Light and Line Units of the 15th
        and 35th Divisions
    Spanish Regiment Joseph Napoleon
    All French Light Infantry Regiments not
        listed elsewhere
    Dalmatian and Croatian Regiments
    Italian Light Infantry Regiments of the 5th
        and 6th Divisions, Army of Italy
    All Saxon Light Infantry Battalions
    All Westphalian Light Infantry Battalions
    Danish Chasseurs and Tirailleurs
    Baden Light and Line Units
    The following French Line Infantry Regiments:
        2nd, 4th, 6th, 9th, 13th, 15th, 18th, 19th, 22nd,
        23rd, 30th, 35th, 46th, 48th, 53rd, 61st, 70th,
        72nd, 92nd, 93rd, 106th, 111th, 112th, and the
        135th—156th Regiments (the 135th—156th
        Regiments had no elite companies).

Conscript Line—
    All temporary, or provisional, regiments, or
        demi–brigades and the battalions which
        comprise these units, unless specified as
        members of the 51st—54th Divisions.
    All French Line Infantry Regiments or battalions of
        of these regiments not listed elsewhere.
    Westphalian Line
    Danish Line
    Illyrian Regiment
    Bavarian Light and Line Units
    Italian Regiments of the Line in the 5th Division,
        Army of Italy

Landwehr—
    All temporary, or provisional, regiments, or
        demi–brigades and the battalions which
        comprise these units in the 51st—54th Divisions.
    All batallions de marche
    3rd Foreign Regiment (Irish Legion)
    Saxon Line
    Neapolitan Line
    Italian Foreign Regiments

Trained Militia—
    French Line Infantry Regiments 123, 124, and 127

Leaders of the
Grande Armée of 1813

Army or Army Wing Commander	Professional Rating	Inspirational Rating
Napoleon	Superior	Charismatic
Ney	Mediocre	Charismatic
Murat	CR=Various*	Charismatic
Oudinot	Poor	Inspirational
Macdonald	Poor	Inspirational
Prince Eugène	Good	Inspirational

*Marshal Murat's performance in 1813 was erratic. As such, his ratings should vary from hour to hour in a random manner.

CR= Cavalry Reserves.

Corps Commander	Professional Rating	Inspirational Rating
Mortier	Good	Impersonal
Nansouty	CC=Excellent	Inspirational
Vandamme	Good	Inspirational
Lobau	Excellent	Inspirational
Victor	Good	Impersonal
Ney	Good	Charismatic
Souham	Good	Inspirational
Bertrand	Mediocre	Inspirational
Lauriston	Mediocre	Impersonal
Marmont	Excellent	Inspirational
Reynier	Mediocre	Impersonal
Poniatowski	Good	Charismatic
Augereau	Mediocre	Impersonal
Macdonald	Good	Inspirational
Gérard	Good	Inspirational
Oudinot	Good	Inspirational
Davout	Superior	Impersonal
Saint-Cyr	Excellent	Impersonal
Latour–Maubourg	CC=Excellent	Inspirational
Doumerc	CC=Good	Inspirational
Sébastiani	CC=Mediocre	Inspirational
Arrighi de Casanova	CC=Good	Inspirational
Kellermann (the younger)	CC=Excellent	Inspirational
Sokolnicki	CC=Good	Inspirational
L'héritier	CC=Good	Inspirational
Milhaud	CC=Good	Inspirational
Pajol	CC=Good	Inspirational
Grenier	Good	Inspirational
Verdier	Mediocre	Inspirational
Pino	Mediocre	Inspirational

CC= Cavalry Corps.

Superior Division Level Generals

Formation	Commander
Imperial Guard	Friant
	Rouget
	Desvaux de Saint–Maurice (artillery)
III Corps	Souham
	Girard*
IV Corps	Morand
VI Corps	Lagrange
	Foucher de Careil (artillery)
VII Corps	Durutte
XI Corps	Gérard
XIV Corps	Claparède
I Reserve Cavalry Corps	Bordesoulle
	Doumerc

*Served in III Corps during the spring—later transferred and commanded one of the Magdebourg divisions.

NOTES

Chapter I
"Survivors of 1812"

1) Marshal Davout's title was awarded on 15 August 1809 for his victory over the Austrians earlier that year. For a complete biography of Davout, consult John G. Gallaher, *The Iron Marshal* (Carbondale, 1976).

2) The Major General was the official title of the army's chief of staff, which was Marshal Berthier.

3) Berthier, Napoleon's long-time chief of staff, was also known as the Prince of Neuchâtel.

4) Davout to Berthier, 8 January 1813, *Correspondance de la Grande Armée—1813*, Archives du Service historique de l'état-major de l'armée C² 135-166 [all references to the official cartons hereafter cited as Archives du Service historique].

5) C² 525, *Situation of the 1ᵉʳ corps (Davout) 1812*, and C² 701, *Situation de la Grande Armée June 1812*, Archives du Service historique.

6) Ibid.

7) C² 701, Archives du Service historique.

8) Ibid.

9) Ibid.

10) Davout to Berthier, 8 January 1813, Archives du Service historique.

11) Ibid.

12) Comte Paul Philip de Ségur, *History of the Expedition to Russia Undertaken by the Emperor Napoleon in the Year 1812*, 2 volumes (London, 1827), I: 274-276.

13) Gallaher, *Iron Marshal*, pp. 211-216.

14) General Friant to Berthier, C² 134, Archives du Service historique. Friant said: "Except for the infantry of the Middle and Old Guard, our soldiers are the model for the entire army."

15) Henry Lachouque, translated by Anne S. K. Brown, *The Anatomy of Glory* (New York, 1978), p. 265.

16) Napoleon to General Clarke, *La Correspondance de Napoléon Iᵉʳ*, 32 volumes (Paris, 1858-70), No. 19410, 30 December 1812.

17) C² 523-532 and 701, *Situations de la Grande Armée 1812*, Archives du Service historique.

18) Napoleon to Clarke, *Correspondance*, No. 19503, 25 January 1813.

19) Robert Epstein, *Prince Eugène at War: 1809* (Arlington, 1984), p. 16.

20) Lachouque and Brown, *Anatomy of Glory*, p. 275.

21) Napoleon to Eugène, 27 January 1813, Archives du Service historique.

22) Ibid.

23) Eugène to Napoleon, 1 February 1813, Archives du Service historique.

24) Ibid.

25) C² 701, *Situation de la Grande Armée 1812*, Archives du Service historique.

26) Eugène to Napoleon, 1 February 1813, Archives du Service historique.

27) Ibid.

28) Christopher Duffy, *Borodino* (New York, 1973), p.126.

29) C² 701, *Situation de la Grande Armée 1812*, Archives du Service historique.

30) Eugène to Napoleon, 1 February 1813, Archives du Service historique.

31) Ibid.

32) General Bourcier to Clarke, 1 February 1813, Archives du Service historique.

33) C² 701, Archives du Service historique; and Baron de Jean Baptiste Antoine Marcellin Marbot, translated by John Butler, *The Memoirs of Baron de Marbot*, 2 volumes (London, 1892), II:, p. 344.

34) The 23rd Chasseurs à Cheval had a long and distinguished combat record. It was perhaps the best regiment among all the light cavalry formations of the army.

35) Lachouque and Brown, *Anatomy of Glory*, p. 272.

36) Ibid., p.269.

37) Ibid., p.270.

38) Ibid., p. 272.

39) C² 701, Archives du Service historique.

40) Lachouque and Brown, *Anatomy of Glory*, p. 269.

41) Eugène to Napoleon, 1 February 1813, Archives du Service historique.

42) Ibid.

43) Ibid.

44) C² 701, Archives du Service historique.

45) Eugène to Napoleon, 1 February 1813, Archives du Service historique.

46) C² 701, Archives du Service historique.

47) Eugène to Napoleon, 1 February 1813, Archives du Service historique.

48) C² 701, Archives du Service historique; Eugène to Napoleon, 1 February 1813, Archives du Service historique.

49) C² 701, Archives du Service historique.

50) Eugène to Napoleon, 1 February 1813, Archives du Service historique.

51) Ibid.

52) Ibid.

53) Lachouque and Brown, *Anatomy of Glory*, p. 177.

54) C² 531-532, and C² 701, *Situation de corps de réserve de cavalerie 1812*, Archives du Service historique.

55) Eugène to Napoleon, 1 February 1813, Archives du Service historique.

56) Ibid.

57) George Six, *Le Dictionnaire biographique des généraux et amiraux de la Révolution et de l'Empire*, ed. George Saffroy, 2 volumes (Paris, 1934) I: p. 536, II: p. 215.

58) Ibid., II: p. 418.

59) C² 701, Archives du Service historique.

60) Lachouque and Brown, *Anatomy of Glory*, p. 262.

61) Six, *Dictionnaire* , I: p. 532.

62) Ibid., I: p. 313.

63) Ibid., II: pp. 60-61.

64) John R. Elting, *Swords Around A Throne* (New York, 1988), pp. 252-253.

65) These losses, which crippled the officer corps, had enormous repercussions.

66) Brigadier General Vincent J. Esposito, USA (Ret), and Colonel John R. Elting, USA (Ret), *A Military History and Atlas of the Napoleonic Wars* (New York, 1964), text for Map 126 estimates horses lost by Napoleon's 1812 army to be in excess of 175,000. George Nafziger, *Napoleon's Invasion of Russia* (Novato, 1988), p. 333 says that hardly any of the 176,000+ horses in the *Grande Armée* survived the campaign.

67) This is substantiated innumerable times in the official correspondence of the army during 1813-1814, and again in 1815 during the Hundred Days campaign.

68) Nafziger, *Napoleon's Invasion*, p.333-334.

69) Notes on the Council of Ministers held at Fontainebleau, *Correspondance*, No. 19496, 24 January 1813.

Chapter II
"All Resources Will Be Used"

1) "Befreiungskrieg" was the name given the war by the Prussians.
2) I have excluded the survivors of the 1812 army from these broad categories.
3) Napoleon to Clarke, *Correspondance*, No. 19247, 5 October 1812.
4) Clarke to Napoleon, 12 November 1812, Archives du Service historique.
5) *Livret de situation des divisions militaires de l'interieur au 15 janvier 1813*. Archives du Service historique.
6) *Sénatus-consulte*, 13 March 1812, and Napoleon to Clarke, 6 March 1812; both found in *Correspondance*, No. 18549 and 18550.
7) Cdt. E.-L. Bucquoy, "L'Infanterie de Ligne et L'Infanterie Légère," *Les Uniformes du Premier Empire* (Paris, 1986), pp. 80-85.
8) *Sénatus-consulte*, *Correspondance*, No. 18550.
9) Among Napoleon's borrowed ideas from ancient Imperial Rome were the eagles for the regiments and the style of furniture.
10) *Sénatus-consulte*, *Correspondance*, No. 18550.
11) A *sénatus-consulte*, or *sénatus-consultum*, was a formal piece of legislation approved by the French Senate—a body of 80 members.
12) *Sénatus-consulte*, *Correspondance*, No. 18550.
13) This was a common practice among the upper middle class and noble families.
14) *Sénatus-consulte*, 14 March 1812, as described in Camille Rousset, *La Grande Armée de 1813* (Paris, 1871), p 23.
15) Napoleon to Clarke, *Correspondance*, No. 18626, 2 April 1812. Also, see Rousset, *Grande Armée*, pp. 305-309.
16) *Sénatus-consulte*, 14 March 1812, as quoted in Rousset, *Grande Armée*, p.24.
17) Ibid., p.24.
18) Ibid., p.24-25.
19) Ibid., p.24.
20) Bucquoy, , "L'Infanterie de Ligne," *Les Uniformes*, pp. 228-235. Also, see L. Rousselot, *L'Armée Française*, text to plates 28 and 66.
21) *Rapport du ministre de la guerre à l'Empereur*, 15 June 1812, Archives du Service historique; Napoleon to Clarke, *Correspondance*, No. 18723, 26 May 1812.
22) *Rapport du ministre de la guerre à l'Empereur*, 15 June 1812, Archives du Service historique. Also, see Napoleon to Clarke, *Correspondance*, No. 19267, 8 October 1812; and Napoleon to Clarke, *Correspondance*, No. 19272, 14 October 1812.
23) *Situation des divisions militaires de l'intérieur de 1812*, Archives du Service historique, as quoted in Rousset, *Grande Armée*, p. 25.
24) *Sénatus-consulte*, 22 September 1812, as described in Rousset, *Grande Armée*, p. 25.
25) *Livret de situation des divisions militaires de l'interieur au 1er decembre 1812 et au 15 janvier 1813*. Archives du Service historique.
26) *Livret de situation des divisions militaires de l'interieur 15 mars 1813*. Archives du Service historique.
27) Rousset, *Grande Armée*, p. 26.
28) *Sénatus-consulte*, 11 January 1813, as described in Rousset, *Grande Armée*, p. 26.
29) Rousset, *Grande Armée*, p. 26.
30) Ibid., p. 27. I have separated the infantry strengths from that of the artillerists.
31) Ibid, p. 28.
32) Napoleon to Berthier, *Correspondance*, No. 19437, 9 January 1813.
33) Ibid.

34) C^2 536, Archives du Service historique.
35) Ibid.
36) C^2 537, Archives du Service historique.
37) This is based on the assumption that the 66 regular field companies each consisted of 8 pieces of ordnance (528 guns) and that each company serving with their regiment fielded only 2 pieces (44 guns). Consult the OBs in Appendices for artillery materiel details.
38) *Livret de situation des divisions militaires de l'interieur 1er decembre 1812* Archives du Service historique.
39) *Situation des divisions militaires de l'interieur au 15 janvier 1813,* Archives du Service historique; and *Situation de la 26e division militaire du 1er mars 1813*, Archives du Service historique.
40) *Situation de la 26e division militaire du 1er mars 1813*, Archives du Service historique.
41) Ibid.
42) Ibid.
43) Rousset, *Grande Armée*, p. 31.
44) Marmont to General Bonet, 15 April 1813, Archives du Service historique.
45) C^2 705, Archives du Service historique.
46) C^2 540, Archives du Service historique.
47) Auguste F. L. V. Marmont, *Mémoires du Maréchal Marmont, duc de Raguse* (Paris, 1857) 9 volumes, V: p. 12.
48) Napoleon to Clarke, *Correspondance*, No. 19485, 23 January 1813.
49) Rousset, *Grande Armée*, p. 39.
50) Napoleon to Clarke, *Correspondance*, No. 19485, 23 January 1813.
51) Napoleon to Marmont, 1 April 1813, in Marmont, *Memoires*, V: p. 31-41.
52) Ministere de la Marine, *Historique de L'Artillerie de la Marine* (Paris, 1889), pp. 97-98.
53) Ibid., p. 98.
54) Ibid., p. 101.
55) Rousset, *Grande Armée*, pp. 33-34.
56) Clarke to Vice-Admiral Decrès, 20 March 1813, Archives du Service historique.
57) Napoleon to Clarke, *Correspondance*, No. 19808, 5 April 1813.
58) Ministere de la Marine, *L'Artillerie de la Marine* , p. 107 and 117.
59) Napoleon to Marmont, 1 April 1813, in Marmont, *Memoires*, V: p. 31-41.
60) Clarke to Vice-Admiral Decrès, 20 March 1813, Archives du Service historique.
61) Napoleon to Clarke, 1 April 1813, Archives du Service historique.
62) Napoleon to Marmont, *Correspondance*, No. 19822, 7 April 1813.
63) C^2 704—706, Archives du Service historique.
64) Ibid.
65) Ibid.
66) Ibid.
67) Ibid.
68) Ibid.
69) This statement is made in relation to the vast majority of teenage conscripts which comprised most of the 1813 army.
70) Most of the formations in the Peninsula armies were comprised of experienced veterans, although the number of conscripts within these ranks had risen during 1812.
71) Lachouque and Brown, *Anatomy of Glory*, p. 278.
72) Clarke to Mortier, 13 January 1813, Archives du Service historique.
73) Ibid.
74) Lachouque and Brown, *Anatomy of Glory*, p. 278.

75) Napoleon to Clarke, *Correspondance*, No. 19539, 6 February 1813; and Napoleon to Clarke, *Correspondance*, No. 19612, 25 February 1813.

76) Ibid.

77) General Bourcier to Clarke, 27 March 1813, Archives du Service historique.

78) *Situation des divisions militaires de l'interieur au 1er février 1813,* Archives du Service historique.

79) Esposito and Elting, *A Military History and Atlas,* text to maps 122-126.

80) Clarke to the Military Division Commanders, 11 November 1812, Archives du Service historique.

81) Clarke to Napoleon, 12 November 1812, Archives du Service historique.

82) *Situation des divisions militaires de l'interieur au 1er février 1813,* Archives du Service historique.

83) Ibid.

84) Napoleon's decree of 22 September 1812, as cited in Rousset, *Grande Armée,* pp. 17-18.

85) Rousset, *Grande Armée,* p. 40.

86) Ibid., p. 18.

87) Ibid., p. 18.

88) *Situation des divisions militaires de l'interieur au 15 janvier 1813,* Archives du Service historique.

89) *Situation des divisions militaires de l'interieur au 1er mars 1813,* Archives du Service historique.

90) Napoleon to Berthier, *Correspondance,* No. 19437, 9 January 1813. This was formalized in the *sénatus-consulte* of 11 Janaury 1813.

91) Rousset, *Grande Armée,* p. 29.

92) Napoleon to Berthier, *Correspondance,* No. 19437, 9 January 1813. This was formalized in the *sénatus-consulte* of 11 Janaury 1813.

93) Rousset, *Grande Armée,* p. 40.

94) Napoleon to Berthier, *Correspondance,* No. 19437, 9 January 1813. This was formalized in the *sénatus-consulte* of 11 Janaury 1813.

95) Berthier to Clarke, 9 January 1813, Archives du Service historique.

96) Napoleon to Clarke, *Correspondance,* No. 19452, 16 January 1813.

97) *Sénatus-consulte* of 3 April 1813, as described in Rousset, *Grande Armée,* pp. 37-39, and p. 302.

98) *Situation des divisions militaires de l'interieur au 15 janvier 1813,* Archives du Service historique.

99) L. Fallou, *La Garde Impériale* (Krefeld, 1975), pp. 281-287.

100) Napoleon to Berthier, *Correspondance,* No. 19437, 9 January 1813.

101) *Situation des divisions militaires de l'interieur au 15 janvier 1813,* Archives du Service historique.

102) *Sénatus-consulte* of 3 April 1813.

103) *Situation des divisions militaires de l'interieur au 1er février 1813,* Archives du Service historique.

104) General Ornano to Berthier, 25 February 1813, Archives du Service historique.

105) General Dejean to Napoleon, 6 August 1813, Archives du Service historique.

Chapter III
"Being Created From Thin Air"

1) Napoleon to Eugène, *Correspondance*, No. 19522 and 19523, 27 January 1813.
2) Ibid.
3) Ibid.
4) Napoleon to Eugène, *Correspondance*, No. 19523, 27 January 1813.
5) Napoleon to Clarke, *Correspondance*, No. 19568, 11 February 1813.
6) Napoleon to Eugène, *Correspondance*, No. 19522, 27 January 1813.
7) Six, *Dictionnaire* , I: p. 371.
8) The 57th Regiment of the Line had an outstanding combat record from the Revolutionary wars in Italy, through the Russian campaign of 1812, and again in 1815, they greatly distinguished themselves on every battlefield. They were undoubtably one of the best regiments in French service.
9) This was the nickname for the 57th Regiment of the Line.
10) General Doucet to Eugène, 4 February 1813, Archives du Service historique.
11) Ibid.
12) General Doucet to Eugène, 6 February 1813, Archives du Service historique.
13) Ibid.
14) Berthier to Doucet, 11 February 1813, Archives du Service historique.
15) General Doucet to Eugène, 25 February 1813, Archives du Service historique.
16) General Arrighi to Clarke, 23 February 1813, Archives du Service historique.
17) Ibid.
18) General Arrighi to Clarke, 25 February 1813, Archives du Service historique.
19) Establishment of the French line and light infantry is detailed in Scott Bowden and Charles Tarbox, *Armies on the Danube 1809*, revised and expanded edition (Chicago, 1989) pp. 41-42.
20) Napoleon to Clarke, *Correspondance*, No. 19425, 6 January 1813.
21) Rousset, *Grande Armée*, p. 46.
22) Napoleon to Clarke, *Correspondance*, No. 19416, 4 January 1813.
23) This reference is, obviously, to the Duke of Wellington.
24) Rousset, *Grande Armée*, p. 50.
25) *Situation des divisions militaires de l'interieur au 15 janvier 1813*, Archives du Service historique.
26) Ibid.; also see Lachouque and Brown, *Anatomy of Glory*, pp. 276-278.
27) Mortier to Berthier, 17 January 1813, Archives du Service historique.
28) Lachouque and Brown, *Anatomy of Glory*, p. 278.
29) Ibid., p. 278.
30) *Situation des divisions militaires de l'interieur au 15 janvier 1813*, Archives du Service historique.
31) Lachouque and Brown, *Anatomy of Glory*, p. 278.
32) Rousset, *Grande Armée*, p. 80.
33) Ibid., p. 62.
34) Ibid., p. 80.
35) The general commanding the 16th Military Division to Clarke, 27 March 1813, Archives du Service historique.
36) Napoleon to Clarke, *Correspondance*, No. 19689, 10 March 1813.
37) Napoleon to Clarke, *Correspondance*, No. 19708, 13 March 1813.
38) *Livret de situation des divisions militaires de l'interieur 15 mars 1813*. Archives du Service historique.

39) *Rapport du ministre de la guerre à l'Empereur*, 15 March 1813, Archives du Service historique.

40) Ibid.

41) Clarke to Berthier, 14 April 1813, Archives du Service historique.

42) The general commanding the 3rd Military Division to Clarke, 6 April 1813, Archives du Service historique.

43) This unfortunate fact delayed the training and deployment of thousands of sorely needed cavalrymen for the spring campaign.

44) Notes on the Council of Ministers held at Fontainebleau, *Correspondance*, No. 19496, 24 January 1813.

45) Clarke to Berthier, 23 March 1813, Archives du Service historique.

46) Lachouque and Brown, *Anatomy of Glory*, p. 278.

47) Napoleon to General Duroc, *Correspondance*, No. 19454, 16 January 1813. Napoleon to Duroc, *Correspondance*, No. 19629, 1 March 1813. Napoleon to Clarke, *Correspondance*, No. 19794, 2 April 1813.

48) Napoleon to Clarke, *Correspondance*, No. 19458, 18 January 1813.

49) *Situation des divisions militaires de l'interieur au 15 janvier 1813*, Archives du Service historique.

50) Clarke to Berthier, 13 March 1813, Archives du Service historique.

51) *Situation des divisions militaires de l'interieur au 15 janvier 1813*, Archives du Service historique.

52) Six, *Dictionnaire* , II: p. 3.

53) Marshal Kellermann to Clarke, 20 January 1813, Archives du Service historique.

54) Kellermann to Clarke, 12 February 1813, Archives du Service historique.

55) General Lauriston to Clarke, 20 February 1813, Archives du Service historique.

56) Ministry of War Circular, 10 March 1813, Archives du Service historique.

57) Clarke to Napoleon, 21 Feburary 1813, Archives du Service historique.

58) Ibid.

59) Ibid.

60) Rousset, *Grande Armée*, p. 82.

61) General de Laubardière to Clarke, 15 April 1813, Archives du Service historique.

62) Clarke to the Generals Commanding the Military Divisions, 20 March 1813, Archives du Service historique.

63) Circular from Clarke to the Generals Commanding the Military Divisions, 21 April 1813, Archives du Service historique.

64) Ibid.

65) General Commanding the 4th Military Division to Clarke, 24 April 1813, Archives du Service historique.

66) Clarke to the General Commanding the 4th Military Division, 29 April 1813, Archives du Service historique.

67) Napoleon to Clarke, *Correspondance*, No. 19425, 6 January 1813.

68) C^2 538-541, Situations of the army corps in 1813, Archives du Service historique.

69) C^2 704, Archives du Service historique. Also, see Napoleon to Clarke, *Correspondance*, No. 19539, P. S., 6 February 1813.

70) Elting, *Swords* , pp. 166-173.

71) Napoleon to Clarke, *Correspondance*, No. 19416, 4 January 1813.

72) French military academy.

73) *Situation des divisions militaires de l'interieur au 1ᵉʳ février 1813*, Archives du Service historique.

74) Napoleon to Clarke, *Correspondance*, No. 19593, 18 February 1813.

75) Napoleon to General Lacuée,*Correspondance*, No. 18451, 24 January 1812.
76) Marshal Lefebvre to Clarke, 1 February 1813, Archives du Service historique.
77) General Despeaux to Clarke, 1 February 1813, Archives du Service historique.
78) Clarke to Napoleon, 17 February 1813, Archives du Service historique.
79) Rousset, *Grande Armée*, p. 55.
80) Lauriston to Clarke, 3 February 1813, Archives du Service historique. Lauriston to Berthier 3 February 1813, Archives du Service historique. Lauriston made it known in no uncertain terms that, in his opinion, the officers of the cohorts were next to worthless.
81) Napoleon to Lauriston, *Correspondance*, No. 19553, 8 February 1813.
82) Lauriston to Clarke, 13 February 1813, Archives du Service historique.
83) Lauriston to Clarke, 26 March 1813, Archives du Service historique.
84) Napoleon to Clarke, *Correspondance*, No. 19915, 27 April 1813.
85) Napoleon to Clarke, *Correspondance*, No. 19969, 5 May 1813.
86) Lauriston to Clarke, 13 April 1813, Archives du Service historique.
87) Rousset, *Grande Armée*, p. 54.
88) Lauriston to Clarke, 3 February 1813, Archives du Service historique. Lauriston to Berthier 3 February 1813, Archives du Service historique.
89) There were so many men pouring into the training centers that those in charge could not keep them for more than this period of time.
90) War Ministry Circular to Depot Commanders, 10 February 1813, Archives du Service historique.
91) For example, one reprimand was given the general commanding the 4th Military Division for not dispatching troops fast enough from the training centers. When the general informed the Ministry of War by telegraphic dispatch on March 18th, that he could not yet send out the 4th battalion of the 4th Regiment of the Line, because the men had until April 10th to complete their one month training period, the officials in Paris replied immediately. On March 20th, the Ministry of War telegraphed that, upon receipt of the dispatch, the men of this battalion were to be dispatched to the army. Thus, these recruits were in the depot for only 10 days.
92) War Ministry Circular to Depot Commanders, 15 February 1813, Archives du Service historique.
93) General Doucet's note on his inspection of the 2nd battalion, 103rd Regiment of the Line, 27 January 1813, Archives du Service historique.
94) Doucet's comments on 2 March 1813, Archives du Service historique.
95) Arrighi to Clarke, 16 March 1813, Archives du Service historique.
96) Doucet to Clarke, 1 April 1813, Archives du Service historique.
97) Clarke to Eugène, 27 January 1813, Archives du Service historique.
98) Doucet to Clarke, 1 April 1813, Archives du Service historique.
99) Napoleon to Davout, *Correspondance*, No. 19638, 2 March 1813.
100) Ibid.
101) Kellermann to Clarke, 14 February 1813, Archives du Service historique.
102) Colonel Cavalier to General Henry, 14 February 1813, Archives du Service historique.
103) Colonel Cavalier to General Henry, 16 February 1813, Archives du Service historique.
104) Marmont to Berthier, 1 March 1813, Archives du Service historique.
105) Ibid.
106) These were the observations of Generals Compans and Lagrange.
107) These were created in March of 1812 and the men had been together since June, 1812.
108) Lauriston to Berthier, 1 April 1813, Archives du Service historique.
109) Lauriston to Eugène, 15 April 1813, Archives du Service historique.

110) Savory to Berthier, 30 April 1813, Archives du Service historique.
111) Savory to Clarke, 13 May 1813, Archives du Service historique.
112) Like men, it took time to train horses.
113) When the Dutch army was incorporated into French service, the Dutch cuirassiers were renamed the French 14th Cuirassier Regiment, although they were still a Dutch unit.
114) General Bourcier to Clarke, 8 February 1813, Archives du Service historique.
115) Clarke to Berthier, 16 February 1813, Archives du Service historique.
116) Napoleon to Clarke, *Correspondance*, No. 19458, 18 January 1813.
117) C^2 704, Archives du Service historique.
118) Ibid.
119) Napoleon to Clarke, *Correspondance*, No. 19539, P. S., 6 February 1813.
120) Napoleon to Marshal Ney, *Correspondance*, No. 19714, 13 March 1813.
121) Clarke to Arrighi, 20 April 1813, Archives du Service historique.
122) Arrighi to Clarke, 23 April 1813, Archives du Service historique.
123) Clarke to Arrighi, 28 April 1813, Archives du Service historique.
124) Just in Napoleon's *Correspondance,* see No. 19460 and 19501. There are dozens of letters from Clarke relating to the acquisition of horses.
125) General Sébastiani to Berthier, 15 April 1813, Archives du Service historique.
126) Sébastiani to Berthier, 25 April 1813, Archives du Service historique.
127) Elting, *Swords*, pp. 249-250.
128) John A. Lynn, *Bayonets of the Republic* (Urbana, 1984), p. 208.
129) Elting, *Swords*, pp. 250-253.
130) Ibid., pp. 254-255.
131) Ibid., p. 254.
132) Ibid., p. 254 .
133) Numerous and various situations of the *Grande Armée* 1805-1814, 1815.
134) The best of these were at Châlons, Metz, and La Fère.
135) Elting, *Swords*, p. 249.
136) *Livret de situation des divisions militaires de l'interieur 15 mars 1813.* Archives du Service historique.
137) Napoleon to Clarke, *Correspondance*, No. 19808, 5 April 1813. Ministere de la Marine, *L'Artillerie de la Marine* , p. 117.
138) Elting, *Swords*, p. 255.
139) War Ministry Circular, 8 April 1813, Archives du Service historique.
140) Bulletin of the *Grande Armée*, *Correspondance*, No. 19951, 2 May 1813.
141) Commander of the 6th Military Division to Clarke, 10 January 1813, Archives du Service historique.
142) Commander of the 18th Military Division to Clarke, 22 January 1813, Archives du Service historique.
143) Doucet's notes on the inspection of the regiment.
144) Kellermann to Clarke, 10 February 1813, Archives du Service historique.
145) Lauriston to Clarke, 13 February 1813, Archives du Service historique.
146) Cavalier to Henry, 16 February 1813, Archives du Service historique.
147) Lauriston to Clarke, 26 March 1813, Archives du Service historique.
148) Marmont to Clarke, 27 March 1813, Archives du Service historique.
149) General Laubardière to Clarke, 15 April 1813, Archives du Service historique.
150) Marmont to Clarke, 15 April 1813, Archives du Service historique.
151) Ibid.
152) Napoleon to Clarke, *Correspondance*, No. 19915, 27 April 1813.

Chapter IV
"A Large Gathering of Men"

1) Decree—Formation of the *Grande Armée*, *Correspondance*, No. 19698, 12 March 1813.
2) Napoleon to Eugène, *Correspondance*, No. 19475, 22 January 1813.
3) *Livret de situation des divisions militaires de l'interieur 15 mars 1813*. Archives du Service historique.
4) Ibid.
5) Napoleon was relying on Davout to help organize and train these forces. See Napoleon to Davout, *Correspondance*, No. 19638, 2 March 1813.
6) Gallaher, *Iron Marshal*, pp. 215-216.
7) C^2 704, Archives du Service historique.
8) Ibid.
9) Ibid.
10) Ibid.
11) Decree—Formation of the *Grande Armée*, *Correspondance*, No. 19698, 12 March 1813.
12) Ibid.
13) Six, *Dictionnaire* , I: p. 329.
14) C^2 704, Archives du Service historique.
15) Six, *Dictionnaire* , II: p. 308.
16) C^2 704, Archives du Service historique.
17) C^2 539 and C^2 704, Archives du Service historique.
18) Six, *Dictionnaire* , II: p. 254.
19) Decree—Formation of the *Grande Armée*, *Correspondance*, No. 19698, 12 March 1813.
20) Ibid.
21) Six, *Dictionnaire* , I: p. 157; I: p. 504; and II: p. 469.
22) Ibid., II: p. 367.
23) C^2 539 and C^2 704, Archives du Service historique.
24) C^2 539 and C^2 704, Archives du Service historique.
25) Decree—Formation of the *Grande Armée*, *Correspondance*, No. 19698, 12 March 1813.
26) Six, *Dictionnaire* , I: p. 92.
27) Decree—Formation of the *Grande Armée*, *Correspondance*, No. 19698, 12 March 1813.
28) Napoleon to Berthier, *Correspondance*, No. 19900, 24 April 1813.
29) C^2 541, Archives du Service historique.
30) Six, *Dictionnaire* , II: p. 224.
31) C^2 539 and C^2 704, Archives du Service historique.
32) Six, *Dictionnaire* , II: p. 300.
33) C^2 539 and C^2 704, Archives du Service historique.
34) Ibid.
35) Decree—Formation of the *Grande Armée*, *Correspondance*, No. 19698, 12 March 1813.
36) Bowden and Tarbox, *Armies on the Danube*, pp. 173-178.
37) Decree—Formation of the *Grande Armée*, *Correspondance*, No. 19698, 12 March 1813.
38) Relative term only, since the cohorts training was further along than most.
39) Six, *Dictionnaire* , II: p. 142.
40) Ibid., II: p. 34.
41) Ibid., II: p. 379.
42) Lauriston to Berthier, 22 May 1813, Archives du Service historique.
43) C^2 704, Archives du Service historique.
44) Decree—Formation of the *Grande Armée*, *Correspondance*, No. 19698, 12 March 1813.

45) For a detailed listing of the System Year XI artillery, see Scott Bowden, *Armies at Waterloo* (Arlington, 1983), p.45.

46) Elting, *Swords*, pp. 139-140.

47) Six, *Dictionnaire* , II: p. 158.

48) Sir Charles Oman, *History of the Peninsular War* (Oxford, 1914) 7 volumes, V: pp. 383-474.

49) Six, *Dictionnaire* , II: p. 158.

50) Capt. Charles Parquin, *Napoleon's Victories 1803-1814* (Chicago, 1893), p. 230.

51) Decree—Formation of the *Grande Armée*, *Correspondance*, No. 19698, 12 March 1813.

52) C^2 704, Archives du Service historique.

53) Six, *Dictionnaire* , I: p. 121 and 258.

54) Ibid., I: p. 472.

55) C^2 540 and C^2 704, Archives du Service historique.

56) Six, *Dictionnaire* , II: p. 490.

57) Marmont to Berthier, 15 April 1813, Archives du Service historique.

58) C^2 540 and C^2 704, Archives du Service historique.

59) Elting, *Swords*, pp. 159-160.

60) *Livret de situation des divisions militaires de l'interieur au 1er decembre 1812 et au 15 janvier 1813.* Archives du Service historique.

61) Decree—Formation of the *Grande Armée*, *Correspondance*, No. 19698, 12 March 1813.

62) C^2 542, Archives du Service historique.

63) Ibid.

64) The IX Corps was just in the planning stages during the spring. It was formed during the summer of 1813.

65) C^2 541, Archives du Service historique.

66) C^2 546, Archives du Service historique.

67) Ibid.

68) Decree—Formation of the *Grande Armée*, *Correspondance*, No. 19698, 12 March 1813.

69) Ibid.

70) Six, *Dictionnaire* , I: p. 470.

71) C^2 541, Archives du Service historique.

72) Six, *Dictionnaire* , I: p. 498.

73) C^2 541, Archives du Service historique.

74) Six, *Dictionnaire* , I: p. 225.

75) C^2 541, Archives du Service historique.

76) C^2 704, Archives du Service historique.

77) Six, *Dictionnaire* , II: pp. 275-277.

78) Napoleon to Berthier, *Correspondance*, No. 19900, 24 April 1813.

79) C^2 541, Archives du Service historique.

80) Ibid.

81) Ibid.

82) Ibid.

83) Ibid.

84) Ibid.

85) C^2 539 and C^2 704, Archives du Service historique.

86) Clarke to Napoleon, 10 April 1813, Archives du Service historique.

87) Rousset, *Grande Armée*, p. 105.

88) Ibid., p. 105.

89) Napoleon to Bertrand *Correspondance*, No. 19643, 2 March 1813.

90) Napoleon to Lauriston, *Correspondance*, No. 19553, 8 February 1813; Napoleon to Bertrand, *Correspondance*, No. 19643, 2 March 1813; Napoleon to Ney, *Correspondance*, No. 19714, 13 March 1813; Napoleon to Bertrand, *Correspondance*, No. 19775, 27 March 1813; and Napoleon to Marmont, *Correspondance*, No. 19868, 17 April 1813.

91) Napoleon to Lauriston, *Correspondance*, No. 19553, 8 February 1813.

92) Napoleon to Bertrand *Correspondance*, No. 19643, 2 March 1813; copies of this letter were sent to Lauriston and Kellermann.

93) Napoleon to Bertrand, *Correspondance*, No. 19775, 27 March 1813.

94) Napoleon to Ney, *Correspondance*, No. 19714, 13 March 1813.

95) Napoleon to Marmont, *Correspondance*, No. 19868, 17 April 1813.

96) Marshal Macdonald to General Charpentier, 11 April 1813, Archives du Service historique.

97) General Souham to Ney, 18 April 1813, Archives du Service historique.

98) General Girard to Ney, 24 April 1813, Archives du Service historique.

99) Lauriston to Eugène, 15 April 1813, Archives du Service historique.

100) Clarke to Berthier, 1 March 1813, Archives du Service historique.

101) Observations of the various corps commanders, Archives du Service historique.

102) Marmont to Berthier, 15 April 1813, Archives du Service historique.

103) Ney to Clarke, 15 March 1813, Archives du Service historique.

104) Berthier to Eugène, 17 April 1813, Archives du Service historique.

105) The makeshift organization of the army required much of the Emperor's attention during this time, especially the administration of the temporary regiments.

106) Colonel Lanrezac, *La Maneuvre de Lützen 1813* (Paris, 1904), Appendix I.

107) General Camus, Baron de Richemont, 27 April 1813, Archives du Service historique.

108) Marbot, *Memoirs*, II: pp. 209-210; and *Mémoires Militaires du Général Baron Boulart*, as quoted in Colonel H. C. B. Rogers *Napoleon's Army* (New York, 1974) pp. 82-84.

109) Napoleon to Clarke, *Correspondance*, No. 19915, 27 April 1813.

110) Davout to Clarke, 27 April 1813, Archives du Service historique.

111) C^2 704, Archives du Service historique.

112) Six, *Dictionnaire* , I: p. 171.

113) Ibid., I: p. 231.

114) Ibid., I: p. 130.

115) C^2 704 and C^2 705, Archives du Service historique.

116) Ibid.

117) Berthier to Clarke, 27 April 1813, Archives du Service historique.

118) Six, *Dictionnaire* , I: p. 399.

119) Ibid., I: p. 57.

120) Esposito and Elting, *Military History and Atlas*, text to Map 143.

121) C^2 704, C^2 705, C^2 541, and C^2 544, Archives du Service historique.

122) See Esposito and Elting, *Military History and Atlas*, Map 128.

123) Ibid.

124) C^2 704, C^2 705, C^2 541, and C^2 544, Archives du Service historique.

125) Ibid.

126) Ibid.

127) Various situations of the *Grande Armée* 1805-1812, Archives du Service historique.

128) Daru to Berthier, 20 April 1813, Archives du Service historique.

129) Dumas to Napoleon, 16 April 1813, Archives du Service historique.

130) Berthier to Corps Commanders, 27 April 1813, Archives du Service historique.

131) Letter from Napoleon, 27 August 1808, as quoted in Justin Wintle *The Dictionary of War Quotations* (New York, 1989), p. 69.

Chapter V
"Overpowered by Children"

1) A major French depot and stronghold on the Elbe River.
2) Most Russian infantry and cavalry units began the spring campaign at one-half or two-thirds strength. Their losses during the 1812 campaign had been great. The Russian historian Eugene Tarle states in his *Napoleon's Invasion of Russia 1812* (New York, 1942), p. 377, that the Russian army before Maloyaroslavets (24 October 1812) numbered 97,000 combatants and 622 guns. This number was rapidly reduced to only 27,464 answering roll supported by fewer than 200 guns when the army reached Vilna on December 10th. The survivors of the campaign were reinforced by new conscripts.
3) F. Loraine Petre, *Napoleon's Last Campaign In Germany—1813* (London, 1974) pp. 25-26.
4) C² 704, C² 705, C² 706, C² 541, and C² 544, Archives du Service historique.
5) Davout to Eugène, 1 May 1813, Archives du Service historique.
6) A city on the east bank of the Saale River.
7) Souham to Ney, 29 April 1813, Archives du Service historique.
8) Ibid.
9) Ney to Berthier, 29 April 1813, Archives du Service historique.
10) Rousset, *Grande Armée*, p. 119.
11) Napoleon to Berthier, *Correspondance*, No. 19927, 30 April 1813.
12) Napoleon Bonaparte, *The Military Maxims of Napoleon*, translated by George C. D'Aguilar (London, 1901), LVIII.
13) Napoleon to Ney, *Correspondance*, No. 19929, 30 April 1813.
14) R. Ernest Dupuy, and Trevor N. Dupuy, *The Encyclopedia of Military History* (New York, 1970), pp. 538-539.
15) Petre, *Last Campaign*, p. 75.
16) Napoleon's cavalry was not numerous enough to act as the army's advance guard.
17) Petre, *Last Campaign*, p. 75. Esposito and Elting, *Military History and Atlas*, Map 129.
18) Ibid.
19) Souham to Ney, 2 May 1813, Archives du Service historique.
20) Petre, *Last Campaign*, p. 78.
21) Lachouque and Brown, *Anatomy of Glory*, p. 293.
22) Drouot to Berthier, 3 May 1813, Archives du Service historique.
23) This was a misson which Drouot would perform often before the end of the Napoleonic wars.
24) He was obviously leading by example, as mentioned in the 27 April letter to all corps commanders; see footnote #130 of Chapter IV.
25) Drouot to Berthier, 3 May 1813, Archives du Service historique.
26) Ibid.
27) "The Guard to the Fire!", which carries the meaning "Send in the Guard!"
28) Flahaut to Berthier, 2 May 1813, Archives du Service historique.
29) Ibid.
30) Petre, *Last Campaign*, p. 79.
31) Flahaut to Berthier, 2 May 1813, Archives du Service historique.
32) Ibid.
33) Esposito and Elting, *Military History and Atlas*, text to Map 129.

34) Petre, *Last Campaign*, p. 82-83.
35) Flahaut to Berthier, 2 May 1813, Archives du Service historique.
36) Marmont, *Mémoires*.
37) Petre, *Last Campaign*, p. 83; Esposito and Elting, *Military History and Atlas*, text to Map 129.
38) Marmont, *Mémoires*. V.
39) Ibid.
40) Ibid.
41) Petre, *Last Campaign*, p. 83.
42) Bulletin of the *Grande Armée, Correspondance*, No. 19951, 2 May 1813.
43) Proclamation to the Army, *Correspondance*, No. 19952, 3 May 1813.
44) Eugène to Berthier, 2 May 1813, Archives du Service historique.
45) Ney to Berthier, 3 May 1813, Archives du Service historique.
46) One of Marshal Ney's nicknames; another was "The Redhead."
47) Major Chlapowski as quoted in Lachouque and Brown, *Anatomy of Glory*, p. 293.
48) Archives du Service historique.
49) Marmont to Berthier, 8 May 1813, Archives du Service historique.
50) Bertrand to Berthier, 3 May 1813, Archives du Service historique.
51) Lauriston to Berthier, 5 May 1813, Archives du Service historique.
52) *Discours de M. de Jaucourt à l'Assemblée législative dans la discussions sur l'armée*, 19-24 January 1792, as quoted in Rousset, *Grande Armée*, p. 129.
53) Order of the Day for the *Grande Armée*, 6 May 1813, Archives du Service historique.
54) Order of the Day for VI Corps as quoted in Marmont, *Mémoires*, V: p. 87.
55) Kellermann to Berthier, 17 May 1813, Archives du Service historique.
56) Kellermann to Berthier, 19 May 1813, Archives du Service historique.
57) Ibid.
58) Napoleon, *Maxims*, IX.
59) Wintle, *War Quotations*, p. 256.
60) Napoleon, *Maxims*, X.
61) H. Camon, *La Bataille Napoleonienne* (Paris, 1899), and *La Guerre Napoleonienne* (Paris, 1903).
62) Colonel Cavalier to General Henry, 16 February 1813, Archives du Service historique.
63) Number of killed, wounded, and prisonners suffered by the *Grande Armée* at Lützen, 2 May 1813, Archives du Service historique. Returns are not complete for all corps.
64) Strategic consumption was always greater in the first few days of a campaign as those unable to keep up with their unit quickly dropped out.
65) Rousset, *Grande Armée*, p. 92.
66) Lauriston to Berthier, 8 May 1813, Archives du Service historique.
67) C^2 704 and C^2 705, Archives du Service historique.
68) Number of killed, wounded, and prisonners suffered by the *Grande Armée* at Lützen, 2 May 1813, Archives du Service historique. Returns are not complete for all corps.
69) Ibid.
70) C^2 704, C^2 705, and C^2 706, Archives du Service historique.
71) Ibid.
72) Ibid.; Number of killed, wounded, and prisonners suffered by the *Grande Armée* at Lützen, 2 May 1813, Archives du Service historique. Returns are not complete for all corps.
73) C^2 704, C^2 705, and C^2 706, Archives du Service historique.
74) Ibid.
75) Ibid.

76) Number of killed, wounded, and prisonners suffered by the *Grande Armée* at Lützen, 2 May 1813, Archives du Service historique. Returns are not complete for all corps.
77) Ibid.
78) Esposito and Elting, *Military History and Atlas*, text to Map 129.
79) C² 704, C² 705, and C² 706, Archives du Service historique.
80) Lachouque and Brown, *Anatomy of Glory*, p. 295. Esposito and Elting, *Military History and Atlas*, text to Map 130.
81) Esposito and Elting, *Military History and Atlas*, text to Map 130.
82) General Berthezène to Berthier, 5 May 1813, Archives du Service historique.
83) Ibid.
84) Esposito and Elting, *Military History and Atlas*, text to Map 130.
85) Ibid.
86) This is commented on numerous times in the reports of the various Guard officers.
87) C² 704, C² 705, and C² 706, Archives du Service historique.
88) Berthezène to Berthier, 5 May 1813, Archives du Service historique.
89) Another name for the bearskin headgear worn by members of the Old Guard infantry.
90) Lachouque and Brown, *Anatomy of Glory*, p. 295.
91) Ibid., p. 295.
92) Esposito and Elting, *Military History and Atlas*, text to Map 130.
93) Located approximately 12 miles northeast of Dresden.
94) The city caught on fire during the battle and burned down.
95) Macdonald to Berthier, 13 May 1813, Archives du Service historique.
96) A league of about 85 cities and towns in northern Germany which banded together in the Middle Ages for mutual protection and trade advantages.
97) Bourcier to Clarke, 14 March 1813, Archives du Service historique.
98) Ibid.; also, see Gallaher, *Iron Marshal,* p. 274.
99) Davout's nickname, owing to his iron discipline.
100) For details of how Davout was to deal with the rebellious city of Hamburg, see Gallaher, *Iron Marshal,* p. 276.
101) Napoleon to Eugène, *Correspondance*, No. 19734, 18 March 1813.
102) Gallaher, *Iron Marshal,* p. 275.
103) General Vandamme to Davout, 13 May 1813, Archives du Service historique.
104) Petre, *Last Campaign*, p. 119. Colonel Lanrezac, *La Maneuvre de Lützen 1813* (Paris, 1904), p. 210.
105) Located approximately 35 miles northeast of Dresden.
106) Petre, *Last Campaign*, pp. 122-125.
107) Ibid., pp. 125-127.
108) Numerous cartons detailing the returns of the *Grande Armée*, including C² 541, C² 704-706, Archives du Service historique.
109) Ibid.
110) Ibid.
111) Esposito and Elting, *Military History and Atlas*, text to Map 131.
112) Numerous cartons detailing the returns of the *Grande Armée*, including C² 541, C² 704-706, Archives du Service historique. The often repeated number of 20,000 French casualties at this battle would seem definitely too high.
113) Lauriston to Berthier, 19 May 1813, Archives du Service historique.
114) Ibid.
115) Ministere de la Marine, *L'Artillerie de la Marine* , pp. 105-106.
116) Drouot to Berthier, 22 May 1813, Archives du Service historique.
117) Lachouque and Brown, *Anatomy of Glory*, p. 299.

118) Bulletin of the *Grande Armée, Correspondance*, No. 20042, 24 May 1813.

119) Macdonald to Berthier, 27 May 1813, Archives du Service historique.

120) Ibid.

121) General Bruyères to Latour-Maubourg, 27 May 1813, Archives du Service historique.

122) General Bordesoulle to Latour-Maubourg, 27 May 1813, Archives du Service historiq.

123) Latour-Maubourg to Berthier, 30 May 1813, Archives du Service historique.

124) Bourcier to Clarke, 28 May 1813, Archives du Service historique.

125) Arrighi to Berthier, 7 June 1813, Archives du Service historique.

126) Rousset, *Grande Armée*, p. 152.

127) Arrighi to Berthier, 7 June 1813, Archives du Service historique.

128) A day's march usually began before dawn and ended from noon to mid-afternoon.

129) Bertrand to Berthier, 20 May 1813, Archives du Service historique.

130) Petre, *Last Campaign,* p. 113.

131) Bertrand to Berthier, 20 May 1813, Archives du Service historique.

132) Lauriston to Berthier, 25 May 1813, Archives du Service historique.

133) The infantrymen were able to run into the nearby structures from where they fought back.

134) Lauriston to Berthier, 27 May 1813, Archives du Service historique.

135) Rousset, *Grande Armée*, p. 149.

136) Adjudant commandant Galbois to Berthier, 27 May 1813, Archives du Service historique.

137) Marshal Victor to Berthier, 9 May and 12 May 1813, Archives du Service historique.

138) Marshal Oudinot to Berthier, 4 June 1813, Archives du Service historique.

139) Ibid.

140) Lauriston to Berthier, 27 May 1813, Archives du Service historique.

141) Marmont to Berthier, 29 May 1813, Archives du Service historique.

142) C^2 704, C^2 705, and C^2 706, Archives du Service historique.

143) Ibid.

144) Ibid.

145) Lachouque and Brown, *Anatomy of Glory*, p. 300.

146) Baron Fain as quoted in Lachouque and Brown, *Anatomy of Glory*, p. 300.

147) Bertrand to Napoleon, 4 June 1813, Archives du Service historique.

Chapter VI
"This Armistice Stops the Progress of My Victories"

1) Napoleon to Eugène, *Correspondance*, No. 19998, 12 May 1813. See Appendix D for the order of battle for Eugène's Army of Italy.

2) Maret to Caulaincourt, 29 May 1813, Archives du Service historique.

3) Napoleon to Clarke, 2 June 1813, Archives du Service historique.

4) This is generally agreed among most historians. The reasoning is that the Allies had massive problems of their own, compounded by the fact that the Allied armies—consisting largely of conscripts—were on the run, and the Russians were totally demoralized.

5) The non-stop campaigning from 1812, coupled with a string of defeats in 1813, had eaten away much of the tenacity for which the Russian army was famous.

6) Roger Parkinson, *Clausewitz* (New York, 1979), p.226.

7) Esposito and Elting, *Military History and Atlas*, text to Map 132.

8) Daru to Berthier, 29 May 1813, Archives du Service historique.

9) Daru to Clarke, 30 May 1813, Archives du Service historique.

10) Ney to Berthier, 10 June 1813, Archives du Service historique.
11) C² 704, C² 705, and C² 706, Archives du Service historique.
12) Ibid.
13) C² 541, C² 704, C² 705, and C² 706, Archives du Service historique.
14) Ibid.
15) Bertrand to Napoleon 4 June 1813, Archives du Service historique.
16) Rousset, *Grande Armée*, p. 158.
17) Ibid., p. 158.
18) Reports of the chief surgeons for the corps of the army, Archives du Service historique.
19) Ibid.
20) Ibid.
21) Chief surgeon of XII Corps to Marshal Oudinot, 9 June 1813, Archives du Service historique.
22) Oudinot to Berthier, 9 June 1813, Archives du Service historique.
23) Also see Napoleon to Daru, 11 June 1813, *Correspondance*, No. 20112, 11 June 1813.
24) Daru to Dumas, 13 June 1813, Archives du Service historique.
25) Marmont to Berthier, 2 July 1813, Archives du Service historique.
26) Elting, *Swords*.
27) Rousset, *Grande Armée*, p. 162.
28) Ibid., p. 162.
29) Orders of the Day for the *Grande Armée*, 27 June and 2 July 1813, Archives du Service historique.
30) Napoleon to Berthier, *Correspondance*, No. 20296 , 23 July 1813.
31) Napoleon to Berthier, *Correspondance*, No. 20295 , 23 July 1813.
32) Daru to Berthier, 1 July 1813, Archives du Service historique.
33) Ibid.
34) Ney to Berthier, 25 July 1813, Archives du Service historique.
35) The growing size of the Imperial forces during 1809 contributed to the administrative branch ever-increasing difficulties in feeding the far-flung Napoleonic armies. Thus, the daily bread ration was officially reduced.
36) Marmont to Berthier, 27 July 1813, Archives du Service historique.
37) Bertrand to Berthier, 31 July 1813, Archives du Service historique.
38) Lauriston to Berthier, 1 August 1813, Archives du Service historique.
39) Victor to Berthier, 5 August 1813, Archives du Service historique.
40) Macdonald to Berthier, 1 August 1813, Archives du Service historique.
41) Circular of the Ministry of War to All Generals Commanding Military Divisions, 10 June 1813, Archives du Service historique.
42) Circular of the Ministry of War to All Generals Commanding Military Divisions, 13 June 1813, Archives du Service historique.
43) Souham to Ney, 15 June 1813, Archives du Service historique.
44) Ney to Berthier, 11 July 1813, Archives du Service historique.
45) Marmont to Berthier, 15 April 1813, Archives du Service historique.
46) Marmont to Berthier, 29 June 1813, Archives du Service historique.
47) Clarke to Berthier, 6 June 1813, Archives du Service historique.
48) C² 704—708; C² 538—542, Archives du Service historique.
49) Rousset, *Grande Armée*, p. 174.
50) C² 704 and C² 539, Archives du Service historique.
51) C² 538—544 and C² 708, Archives du Service historique.
52) Napoleon to Berthier, *Correspondance*, No. 20326 , 4 August 1813.
53) C² 542 and C² 708, Archives du Service historique.

54) Napoleon to Berthier, *Correspondance*, No. 20172 , 22 June 1813.

55) C^2 538 and C^2 708, Archives du Service historique.

56) Napoleon to Davout, *Correspondance*, No. 20206 , 1 July 1813.

57) The Inspector General of the Military Academies, 18 June 1813, as quoted in Rousset, *Grande Armée*, p. 177.

58) Rousset, *Grande Armée*, p. 177.

59) The Inspector General of the Military Academies, 18 June 1813, as quoted in Rousset, *Grande Armée*, p. 178.

60) Consult Appendices C and D to compare strengths of the Young Guard between 15 May and 15 August 1813.

61) Clarke to Napoleon, 21 July 1813, Archives du Service historique.

62) Clarke to Napoleon, 23 July 1813, Archives du Service historique.

63) Ibid.

64) Referred to in Clarke to Napoleon, 23 July 1813, Archives du Service historique.

65) General Caffarelli to Clarke, 6 June 1813, Archives du Service historique.

66) Notes of Mortier's 1 August 1813 inspection of the Young Guard, Archives du Service historique.

67) C^2 539, C^2 540, and C^2 708, Archives du Service historique.

68) C^2 540 and C^2 708, Archives du Service historique.

69) Bourcier to Clarke, 10 June 1813, Archives du Service historique.

70) Report of Materiel of Artillery in the *Grande Armée*, 31 July 1813, Archives du Service historique. C^2 536, Archives du Service historique.

71) C^2 701, Archives du Service historique.

72) Ibid.

73) General de Laville to Clarke, 25 July 1813, Archives du Service historique.

74) Report of Materiel of Artillery in the *Grande Armée*, 31 July 1813, Archives du Service historique; and C^2 536, Archives du Service historique

75) Ibid.

76) Ibid.

77) Report of Materiel of Artillery in the *Grande Armée*, 31 July 1813, Archives du Service historique. C^2 536, C^2 537, and C^2 708, Archives du Service historique.

78) Adjudant commandant Meinadier's notes following Mortier's 1 August 1813 inspection of the Young Guard, Archives du Service historique.

79) Ibid.

80) Ibid.

81) Meinadier's notes exclude comments on the cavalry.

82) General Nansouty to Berthier, 1 August 1813, Archives du Service historique.

83) Ornano to Berthier, 5 August 1813, Archives du Service historique.

84) Dejean to Napoleon, 6 August 1813, Archives du Service historique.

85) General Desvaux to Napoleon, 1 August 1813, Archives du Service historique.

86) Drouot to Berthier, 6 August 1813, Archives du Service historique.

87) Marmont to Berthier, 1 August 1813, 6 August 1813, Archives du Service historique.

88) Ibid.

89) C^2 708, Archives du Service historique.

Chapter VII
"Withdraw Me From This Hell"

1) Esposito and Elting, *Military History and Atlas*, text to Map 133.

2) Napoleon to Berthier, *Correspondance*, No. 20380 , 15 August 1813. Also, see Petre, *Last Campaign*, p. 170.

3) Napoleon to Oudinot, *Correspondance*, No. 20381 , 15 August 1813. Napoleon to Macdonald, *Correspondance*, No. 20390 , 16 August 1813. Also, see Petre, *Last Campaign*, pp. 171-180.

4) Esposito and Elting, *Military History and Atlas*, text to Map 133; Petre, *Last Campaign*, pp. 181-184.

5) Esposito and Elting, *Military History and Atlas*, text to Map 133; Petre, *Last Campaign*, pp. 181-184.

6) Lauriston to Berthier, 17 August 1813, Archives du Service historique.

7) Lauriston to Berthier, 23 August 1813, Archives du Service historique.

8) Napoleon to Berthier, *Correspondance*, No. 20415 , 20 August 1813; Napoleon to Ney and Marmont, *Correspondance*, No. 20425 , 20 August 1813; Napoleon to Macdonald *Correspondance*, No. 20426 and No. 20428 , 20 August 1813.

9) Esposito and Elting, *Military History and Atlas*, text to Map 133.

10) This is acknowledged in Napoleon's letter to Gouvion Saint-Cyr, *Correspondance*, No. 20445 , 23 August 1813; and in Napoleon's letter to Count Durosnel, Governor of Dresden, *Correspondance*, No. 20447 , 23 August 1813.

11) Napoleon to Maret, *Correspondance*, No. 20449 , 24 August 1813; Napoleon to Berthier, *Correspondance*, No. 20450 , 24 August 1813.

12) Napoleon to Berthier, *Correspondance*, No. 20441 and No. 20442 , 23 August 1813.

13) Esposito and Elting, *Military History and Atlas*, text to Map 134.

14) Napoleon to Berthier, *Correspondance*, No. 20441, 23 August 1813.

15) Mortier to Berthier, 27 August 1813, Archives du Service historique.

16) Notes relating to the march of the *Grande Armée*, 22-26 August 1813, C^2 708, Archives du Service historique.

17) Ibid.

18) Ibid.

19) Lachouque and Brown, *Anatomy of Glory*, p. 308.

20) C^2 537, C^2 538, C^2 540, C^2 542—544, and C^2 708, Archives du Service historique.

21) Lachouque and Brown, *Anatomy of Glory*, pp. 308-309.

22) Immobilzed by the presence of the French cavalry, the squares of Austrian infantry were easy, compact targets for the French gunners.

23) Esposito and Elting, *Military History and Atlas*, text to Map 136.

24) Marbot, *Memoirs*, II: p. 371.

25) General Belliard to Berthier, 27 August 1813, Archives du Service historique.

26) The King of Naples to Napoleon, 27 August 1813, Archives du Service historique.

27) Esposito and Elting, *Military History and Atlas*, text to Map 136.

28) Napoleon to Berthier, *Correspondance*, No. 20442, 23 August 1813.

29) Petre, *Last Campaign*, pp. 252-253.

30) C^2 539, C^2 540, C^2 541, C^2 544, and C^2 708, Archives du Service historique.

31) Petre, *Last Campaign*, p. 251.

32) Macdonald to Berthier, 27 August 1813, Archives du Service historique.

33) Lauriston to Berthier, 27 August 1813, Archives du Service historique.

34) Rousset, *Grande Armée*, p. 199.

35) Exelmans to Sébastiani, 27 August 1813, Archives du Service historique.

36) Marbot, *Memoirs*, II: p. 380.

37) Ibid., II: p. 381.

38) Ibid., II: p. 382 and 389.

39) Allied reports of French guns and prisoners taken, as cited in Petre, *Last Campaign*, p. 256.
40) Evidentally, there no official casualty returns exist for the Army of Silesia.
41) Macdonald to Berthier, 27 August 1813, Archives du Service historique.
42) Ibid.
43) Lauriston to Berthier, 29 August 1813, Archives du Service historique. This dispatch was written after the fate of Puthod's 17th Division was known.
44) Macdonald to Berthier, 3 A.M. and 6 A.M., 29 August 1813, Archives du Service historique.
45) Macdonald to Berthier, Midnight, 29 August 1813, Archives du Service historique.
46) Marmont, *Mémoires*, V: pp. 207 and 209.
47) Marmont to Berthier, 29 August 1813, Archives du Service historique.
48) Ibid.
49) Journal of the VI Corps, describing the action at Falkenhayn, 29 August 1813, Archives du Service historique.
50) Lagrange to Marmont, 29 August 1813, Archives du Service historique.
51) Vandamme to Berthier, 28 August 1813, Archives du Service historique.
52) C^2 538, C^2 542, C^2 543, and C^2 708, Archives du Service historique.
53) Esposito and Elting, *Military History and Atlas*, text to Map 137.
54) Ibid.
55) C^2 542, Archives du Service historique.
56) General Mouton-Duvernet to Marshal Mortier, 2 September 1813, Archives du Service historique.
57) C^2 538 and C^2 708, Archives du Service historique.
58) Petre, *Last Campaign*, pp. 240-241.
59) Napoleon to Lobau, *Correspondance*, No. 20518, 3 September 1813.
60) C^2 539 and C^2 708, Archives du Service historique.
61) C^2 540 and C^2 708, Archives du Service historique.
62) Lauriston to Berthier, 31 August 1813, Archives du Service historique.
63) Macdonald to Berthier, 31 August 1813, Archives du Service historique.
64) The Poles were already close at hand; see Napoleon to Macdonald, *Correspondance*, No. 20454, 24 August 1813.
65) Macdonald to Berthier, 1 September 1813, Archives du Service historique.
66) Macdonald to Berthier, 2 September 1813, Archives du Service historique.
67) Ibid.
68) Lauriston to Napoleon, 2 September 1813, Archives du Service historique.
69) C^2 536, C^2 537, and C^2 540, Archives du Service historique.
70) Rousset, *Grande Armée*, p. 212.
71) Napoleon to Macdonald, *Correspondance*, No. 20516, 3 September 1813; details of supply convoys, Archives du Service historique.
72) Macdonald to Berthier, 5 September 1813, Archives du Service historique.
73) Orders of the Day for the *Grande Armée*, 1813, Archives du Service historique.
74) Gallaher, *Iron Marshal*, p. 282.
75) Esposito and Elting, *Military History and Atlas*, text to Map 133.
76) Petre, *Last Campaign*, pp. 241-242.
77) Ibid., p. 262.
78) Ibid., p. 262.
79) Oudinot to Berthier, 26 August 1813, Archives du Service historique.
80) Bertrand to Berthier, 31 August 1813, Archives du Service historique.
81) General Lemarois to Berthier, 4 September 1813, Archives du Service historique.

82) Gallaher, *Iron Marshal*, p. 282.
83) Duke of Plaisance to Napoleon, 4 September 1813, Archives du Service historique. General Lebrun was one of Napoleon's Imperial aides de camp; he had been sent to the Army of Berlin to observe and report back to the Emperor.
84) Bertrand to Berthier, 4 September 1813, Archives du Service historique.
85) Petre, *Last Campaign*, pp. 271-276.
86) C² 539, C² 541, C² 544, and C² 708 Archives du Service historique.
87) Petre, *Last Campaign*, pp. 272-273.
88) Petre is incorrect when he states on page 275 that Defrance's command consisted of cuirassiers. Defrance's division consisted entirely of dragoons.
89) Petre, *Last Campaign*, pp. 276.
90) Ibid., p. 277.
91) C² 541 and C² 708, Archives du Service historique.
92) Bertrand to Berthier, 9 September 1813, Archives du Service historique.
93) Ney's nickname.
94) Ney to Berthier, 10 September 1813, Archives du Service historique.
95) Napoleon to Berthier, *Correspondance*, No. 20544, 11 September 1813. Aslo, see Napoleon to Berthier, *Correspondance*, No. 20630, 25 September 1813.
96) Ney to Berthier, 12 September 1813, Archives du Service historique.
97) Ney to Berthier, 13 September 1813, Archives du Service historique.
98) Rousset, *Grande Armée*, pp. 221-222.
99) Ney to Berthier, 15 September 1813, Archives du Service historique.
100) Bertrand to Berthier, 15 September 1813, Archives du Service historique.
101) Reynier to Berthier, 15 September 1813, Archives du Service historique.
102) Ney to Berthier, 12 September 1813, Archives du Service historique.
103) Petre, *Last Campaign*, p. 287.
104) Tranié and Carmigniani, *Napoléon 1813*, p. 179.
105) Napoleon to Berthier, *Correspondance*, No. 20561, 14 September 1813.
106) Maret to Clarke, 8 September 1813, Archives du Service historique.
107) Ney to Berthier, 13 September 1813, Archives du Service historique.
108) Rousset, *Grande Armée*, pp. 234-235.
109) Ibid., pp. 238-239.
110) Ibid., p. 238.
111) Ibid., p. 239.
112) Ibid., p. 239.
113) General Noirot to Berthier, 20 September 1813, Archives du Service historique.
114) Combination of two letters written from General Dalton to Kellermann and Augereau, 23 September 1813, Archives du Service historique.
115) Esposito and Elting, *Military History and Atlas*, text to Map 139.
116) Daru to Clarke, 27 September 1813, Archives du Service historique.
117) For this many men to report as quickly as they did to the depots is but one example of how efficiently Napoleon's government was able to call up men to the army.
118) Commander of the 25th Military Division to Clarke, 5 October 1813, Archives du Service historique.
119) This was the actual name of the depot.
120) Report of the colonel commanding the General Depot of Insubordinates and Deserters, 22 October 1813, Archives du Service historique.
121) General Dalton to Berthier 23 September 1813, Archives du Service historique.
122) Rousset, *Grande Armée*, pp. 244-245.
123) Ibid., pp. 244-245.

124) Ibid., p. 246.

125) Saint-Cyr to Berthier, 3 September 1813, Archives du Service historique.

126) Jean-Baptiste Barrès, *Memoirs of a French Napoleonic Officer* (London, 1925), p. 176.

127) Victor to Berthier, 13 September 1813, Archives du Service historique.

128) The food shortage was critical. See Napoleon to Daru, *Correspondance*, No. 20551, 12 September 1813, and *Correspondance*, No. 20559, 13 September 1813.

129) Bertrand to Berthier, 15 September 1813, Archives du Service historique.

130) Lobau to Berthier, 20 September 1813, Archives du Service historique.

131) M. le Duc de Fezensac, *Souvenirs militaires de 1804 à 1814* (Paris, 1864), pp. 443-444.

132) Napoleon to Daru, *Correspondance*, No. 20619, 23 September 1813.

133) This is evidenced in the letter from Napoleon to Maret, *Correspondance*, No. 20796, 13 October 1813.

134) Returns of the various corps of the *Grande Armée*, C² 537—544, and C² 708, Archives du Service historique.

Chapter VIII
"Malbrouck s'en va-t-en en guerre"

1) Esposito and Elting, *Military History and Atlas*, text to Map 139.

2) Petre, *Last Campaign*, pp. 301-302.

3) C² 538, C² 540, and C² 708, Archives du Service historique.

4) C² 537, C² 539, C² 541, C² 543—544, and C² 708, Archives du Service historique.

5) Technically a French foreign regiment, the Vistula Legion was comprised entirely of fanatical Polish volunteers. It had a superb combat record throughout the Napoleonic period.

6) C² 542, Archives du Service historique.

7) C² 541—542, Archives du Service historique.

8) Napoleon to Berthier, *Correspondance*, No. 20628, 25 September 1813.

9) C² 537, Archives du Service historique. Napoleon to Berthier, No. 20628, 25 September 1813.

10) General Doumerc's notes following the inspection of the I Reserve Cavalry Corps, 15 November 1813, Archives du Service historique.

11) Esposito and Elting, *Military History and Atlas*, text to Map 139.

12) Ibid.

13) Ibid.

14) Esposito and Elting, *Military History and Atlas*, text to Map 140.

15) General Delmas to Souham, 11 October 1813, Archives du Service historique.

16) Esposito and Elting, *Military History and Atlas*, text to Map 140.

17) The refusal of the Prussians to retreat forced Bernadotte to advance in support of the Army of Silesia.

18) Napoleon, as quoted in Esposito and Elting, *Military History and Atlas*, text to Map 140.

19) Marmont, *Mémoires*, V.

20) Returns of the various corps of the *Grande Armée*, C² 537—544, and C² 708, Archives du Service historique. Special note should be given to the number of pieces of ordnance confirmed to have been present with the *Grande Armée* at Leipzig.

21) kriegsgeschichtlichen Abteilung des k. und k. Kriegsarchiv, *Befreiungskrieg 1813 und 1814*, 6 volumes (Vienna, 1913), V: pp. 673-691.

22) Ibid., V: pp. 711-714.

23) Ibid., V: pp. 692-699.

24) Ibid., V: pp. 700-710.

25) M. Adolphe Thiers, *History of the Consulate and the Empire of France Under Napoleon,* translated by D. Forbes Campbell and H. W. Herbert, 5 volumes (Philadelphia, 1875), IV: pp. 527-528.

26) Drouot to Berthier, 1 November 1813, Archives du Service historique. This is related in Thiers, *History of the Consulate and the Empire*, IV: p. 528.

27) Parquin, *Napoleon's Victories* p. 256. Parquin refers to the Austrian regiment as Latour's Dragoons, which was the name of this regiment for many years before becoming the Vincent Chevaulegers. To read about the Vincent Chevaulegers at Wagram in 1809, consult Bowden and Tarbox, *Armies on the Danube*, p. 165.

28) *Befreiungskrieg 1813* , V: p. 676.

29) Esposito and Elting, *Military History and Atlas*, text to Map 142. Lachouque and Brown, *Anatomy of Glory*, p. 317.

30) *Befreiungskrieg 1813* , V: pp. 692-693.

31) Marmont's description of the battle, *Journal of the VI Corps*, Archives du Service historique.

32) *Befreiungskrieg 1813* , V: p. 677.

33) *Befreiungskrieg 1813*, V: p. 725.

34) Esposito and Elting, *Military History and Atlas*, text to Map 142.

35) Petre, *Last Campaign*, pp. 355-362. Esposito and Elting, *Military History and Atlas*, text to Map 143.

36) *Befreiungskrieg 1813*, V: pp. 679-680.

37) Drouot to Berthier, 1 November 1813, Archives du Service historique. This episode is related in Thiers, *History of the Consulate and the Empire*, IV: p. 537.

38) Tranié and Carmigniani, *Napoléon 1813*, pp. 215-217 and 234.

39) Lachouque and Brown, *Anatomy of Glory*, p. 318. Thiers, *History of the Consulate and the Empire*, IV: p. 537.

40) Esposito and Elting, *Military History and Atlas*, text to Map 143.

41) Petre, *Last Campaign*, p. 365.

42) Marmont's description of the battle, Journal of the VI Corps, Archives du Service historique.

43) R. F. Delderfield, *Imperial Sunset* (New York, 1968).

44) Petre, *Last Campaign*, p. 380. Esposito and Elting, *Military History and Atlas*, text to Map 143.

45) Petre, *Last Campaign*, pp. 380-381.

46) Ibid., p. 381.

47) The French casualty figures are often distorted by those who count the wounded prisoners twice—once for being wounded and again for being captured. Nevertheless, despite being outnumbered 3 to 2, and outgunned almost 2 to 1, Napoleon's *Grande Armée* inflicted approximately the same number of casualties which it suffered. The French army would have incurred far fewer casualties if had not been for the premature demolition of the Elster River bridge.

48) Esposito and Elting, *Military History and Atlas*, text to Map 143. Petre, *Last Campaign*, pp. 382-383. Tranié and Carmigniani, *Napoléon 1813*, p. 225.

49) Bulletin of the *Grande Armée, Correspondance*, No. 20830, 24 October 1813.

50) Esposito and Elting, *Military History and Atlas*, text to Map 144.

51) When Napoleon saw his famished soldiers retreat through Erfurt, he is supposed to have observed: "At this rate I shall lose 80,000 men by the time we get to the Rhine."

52) Esposito and Elting, *Military History and Atlas*, text to Map 144.

53) Petre, *Last Campaign*, p. 390.
54) Tranié and Carmigniani, *Napoléon 1813*, p. 250.
55) Parquin, *Napoleon's Victories*, p. 263.
56) Parquin, *Napoleon's Victories*, pp. 266-267. Petre, *Last Campaign*, p. 390.
57) Parquin, *Napoleon's Victories*, p. 269. Petre, *Last Campaign*, pp. 390-391.
58) Petre, *Last Campaign*, pp. 391.

Chapter IX
"I Need Men Not Children"—Historical Analysis

1) C^2 537—544, and C^2 708, Archives du Service historique.
2) C^2 537 and C^2 708, Archives du Service historique.
3) Napoleon was also thinking this when he wrote to Clarke, *Correspondance*, No. 20835, 25 October 1813.
4) Rousset, *Grande Armée*, p. vii.
5) General Decaen to Clarke, 15 December 1813, Archives du Service historique.
6) Napoleon to Joseph, 14 March 1814, *Supplement à la Correspondance de Napoléon, Lettres Curieuses Omises par le Comité de Publication, Rectifications*. Edited by Albert DuCasse, Paris, 1887, p. 207.

SELECT BIBLIOGRAPHY

Archival Sources

The Archives du Service historique de l'état-major de l'armée at the Château de Vincennes proved the principal source of manuscript material for *Napoleon's Grande Armée of 1813*. The cartons containing the general correspondence of the *Grande Armée* of 1813 include C² 135 through 166. Other cartons contained specific correspondence from various Napoleonic military and civil officials during 1813. Among those which were used included the correspondence of Maret (C² 121), Belliard (C² 293—295, and C² 709), Vandamme (C² 296), Victor (C² 297, C² 299—302), Macdonald (C² 305), Meinadier, the adjudant commandant of the Young Guard (C² 310), Prince Eugène (C³ 5—6) and specific instructions to the Viceroy (C² 311), Mathieu-Dumas (C² 414 and C² 710), Berthier (C⁴ 83—84, C⁴ 86 [Army of Italy], C¹⁷ 155, C¹⁷ 178—182, C¹⁷ 187—189), and Kellermann the elder (C² 547). The carton C² 371 relating to the raising and the employment of the 1813 army was often consulted. Also used was carton C¹⁷ 189 containing the *Grande Armée's* "Orders of the Day". The strengths of the 1812 army as cited in Chapter I were found in C² 525 (I Corps) and C² 701. The extensive orders of battle (situations) for 1813 *Grande Armée* were taken from the parade states in cartons C² 536—547, C² 565—566, C² 696, and C² 704—708. The états from carton C² 167 were also valuable.

Official Histories

Journal of the VI Corps—1813. Archives du Service historique.
kriegsgeschichtlichen Abteilung des k. und k. Kriegsarchiv. *Befreiungskrieg 1813 und 1814*. 5 volumes. Vienna, 1913.
Ministere de la Marine. *Historique de L'Artillerie de la Marine*. Paris, 1889.

Memoirs and Correspondence

Lejune, General Baron. *Memoirs of Baron Lejune*. Translated and edited by Mrs. Arthur Bell. 2 volumes. London and New York, 1897.
Napoleon I, Emperor. *Correspondance de Napoléon 1ᵉʳ*. 32 volumes. Paris, 1858-1870.
Napoleon I, Emperor. *Supplement à la Correspondance de Napoléon, Lettres Curieuses Omises par le Comité de Publication, Rectifications*. Edited by Albert DuCasse. Paris, 1887.
Marbot, Baron M. de. *Memoris of Baron de Marbot*. English edition. 2 volumes. Paris, 1893.
Marmont, Auguste F. L. V. *Mémoires du Marechal Marmont, Duc de Raguse*. 9 volumes. Paris, 1857.
Rapp, General Jean. *Mémoires*. 2 volumes. Paris, 1821.
Savary, General A.J.M.R. *Memoirs of the Duke of Rovigo*. English edition, 3 volumes. London, 1828.

Secondary Works

Barrès, Jean-Baptiste. *Memoirs of a French Napoleonic Officer*. London, 1925.
Baudus, Lieutenant Colonel. *Etudes sur Napoléon*. 2 volumes. Paris, 1841.
Bowden, Scott. *Armies at Waterloo*. Arlington, 1983.
Bowden, Scott and Tarbox, Charles. *Armies on the Danube 1809*, revised and expanded edition. Chicago, 1989.

Bucquoy, Cdt. E.-L. "L'Infanterie de Ligne et L'Infanterie Légère." *Les Uniformes du Premier Empire*. 7 volumes. Paris, 1986.

Camon, General H. *La Bataille Napoléonienne*. Paris, 1899.

Camon, General H. *La guerre Napoléonienne–Precis des campagnes*. 2 vols. Paris, 1925.

Charrie, Pierre. *Drapeaux et Étendards de la Révolution et de l'Empire*. Paris, 1982.

Davout, Maréchal Louis Nicholas. *Correspondance du maréchal Davout prince d'Ekmühl; ses commandements, son ministere, 1801-1815*. Edited by Charles de Mazade. 4 volumes. Paris, 1885.

Delderfield, R. F. *Imperial Sunset*. New York, 1968.

Duffy, Christopher. *Borodino*. New York, 1973.

Dupuy, R. Ernest, and Dupuy, Trevor N. *The Encyclopedia of Military History*. New York, 1970.

Elting, John R. *Swords Around A Throne*. New York, 1988.

Epstein, Robert M. *Prince Eugene at War: 1809*. Arlington, 1984.

Esposito, Brig. General Vincent J. and Elting, Golonel John Robert. *A Military History and Atlas of the Napoleonic Wars*. New York, 1968.

Fallou, Louis. *La Garde Impériale*. Paris, 1975 reprint of 1901 original.

Foucart, Lieutenant-Colonel P. *Bautzen*. 2 volumes. (Paris, 1897, 1901).

Gallaher, John G. *The Iron Marshal*. Carbondale, 1976.

Lachouque, Commandant Henry. Translated by Brown, Anne. *The Anatomy of Glory*. New York, 1961.

Lanrezac, Colonel. *La Maneuvre de Lützen 1813,*. Paris, 1904.

Lynn, John A. *Bayonets of the Republic*, Urbana, 1984.

Marbot, Baron de Jean Baptiste Antoine Marcellin. Translated by John Butler. *The Memoirs of Baron de Marbot*, 2 volumes, London, 1892.

Nafziger, George. *Napoleon's Invasion of Russia*. Novato, 1988.

Napoleon Bonaparte. *The Military Maxims of Napoleon*, translated by George C. D'Aguilar. London, 1901.

Oman, Sir Charles. *History of the Peninsular War*. 7 volumes. Oxford, 1914.

Pajol, Général comte de. *Général en Chef Pajol*. By his son. 3 volumes. Paris, 1874.

Paret, Peter. *Yorck and the Era of Prussian Reform*. Princeton, 1966.

Parkinson, Roger. *Clausewitz*. New York, 1979.

Petre, F. Loraine. *Napoleon's Last Campaign In Germany—1813*. Reprint edition, New York, 1974.

Picard, Commandant L. *La Cavalerie dans les guerre de la Révolution et de l'Empire*. 2 volumes., Samur, 1895–1896.

Regnault, General. *Les aigles impériales et la drapeau tricolore 1804–1815*. Paris, 1967.

Rogers, Colonel H. C. B. *Napoleon's Army*. New York, 1974.

Rousset, Camille. *La Grande Armée de 1813*. Paris, 1871.

Richardson, Robert G. *Larrey: Surgeon to Napoleon's Imperial Guard*. London, 1974.

Ségur, Comte Paul Philip de. *History of the Expedition to Russia Undertaken by the Emperor Napoleon in the Year 1812*. 2 volumes, London, 1827.

Six, George. *Le Dictionnaire biographique des généraux et amiraux de la Révolution et de l'Empire*. edited by. George Saffroy. 2 volumes. Paris, 1934

Tarle, Eugene. *Napoleon's Invasion of Russia 1812*. New York, 1942.

Thiers, M. Adolphe. *History of the Consulate and the Empire of France Under Napoleon*. translated by D. Forbes Campbell and H. W. Herbert. 5 volumes. Philadelphia, 1875.

Tranie, J. and Carmigniani. J.S. *Napoléon—1813 La campagne d'Allemagne*. Paris, 1987.

Wintle, Justin. *The Dictionary of War Quotations*. New York, 1989.

NAPOLEON'S GRANDE ARMÉE OF 1813

Book and dust jacket design by Scott Bowden
Diagrams by Dane Ridenour
Composed at The Emperor's Press Production Department in Times Roman
Printed by Print Systems, Inc. of Grand Rapids, Michigan, USA
on 70# Lakewood
Bound by Print Systems, Inc. of Grand Rapids, Michigan, USA
with 80# Lakewood endsheets